LADAK
PHYSICAL, STATISTICAL, AND HISTORICAL
WITH
NOTICES OF THE SURROUNDING COUNTRIES

LADAK
PHYSICAL, STATISTICAL, AND HISTORICAL
WITH
NOTICES OF THE SURROUNDING COUNTRIES.

BY
ALEXANDER CUNNINGHAM,
BREVET MAJOR, BENGAL ENGINEERS.

GYAN

Published by

GYAN

Gyan Publishing House
5, Ansari Road
Daryaganj, New Delhi-110002
Phone: 011-47034999, 9811692060
E-mail: books@gyanbooks.com

Distribution Network
gyanbooks.com
India, USA, Canada, UK, Australia, France

ISBN : 978-81-212-3673-7 (PB)
First Published, 1854

2nd Impression 2020

Printed at: Gyan Press, Delhi.

The book at your disposal is the edition of an old book originally published long back. The Text quality of this book may not be at par as compared to our other books but many readers approached us to reprint this important book so that it could satiate their hunger. We request all the readers of this book to help us to improve its quality by providing the necessary text of those pages which are not properly visible. Your valuable support in this case will be highly appreciated and acknowledged and our future readers will be benefitted immensely.

LADÁK,

PHYSICAL, STATISTICAL, AND HISTORICAL;

WITH

NOTICES OF THE SURROUNDING COUNTRIES.

BY

ALEXANDER CUNNINGHAM,

BREVET MAJOR, BENGAL ENGINEERS.

LONDON:

WM. H. ALLEN AND CO.,

7, LEADENHALL STREET.

1854.

PREFACE.

I HAVE endeavoured in the following pages to give, to the best of my ability, and according to my means of information, a full and accurate account of Ladák. I have twice visited the country, in 1846 and again in 1847, and on each occasion by a different route; I have read every work that I could procure (and I have neither spared pains nor expense) regarding Ladák or Tibet. I therefore am willing to think that the various information which I have collected, may not prove altogether uninteresting, even to the general reader. For the antiquary and scientific enquirer, there are several subjects which I would fain hope may merit attention. The subjects for the antiquary are:—

1. The identification of Ladák, or *Khá-chan*, with the *Akhassa Regio* of Ptolemy, and with the *Kie-chha* of Fa Hian.—Chap. I.

2. The proof that *Graucasus* was a Tibetan word, and the consequent deduction that the Tibetan people and language were once spread over a much greater extent of country than they now occupy.—Chap. XIV.

3. A copious vocabulary of the Tibetan language

compared with the various dialects of the Dards, of the Afghans and Kashmiris, of the Hindu races of the Himálaya, and of the Indo-Tibetans of Kanáwar.—Chap. XV.

4. A concise account of the religious belief and practice of the Tibetan Buddhists, and of the rise of the present grand Lamas; with a description of the different buildings, rites and ceremonies, and ritualic instruments of their religion.—Chap. XIII.

The subjects for the man of science are:—

1. The determination of the snow-line on the several mountain-ranges of the Panjáb.—Chap. II.

2. The length of course, and the minimum discharge of the rivers of the Panjáb, compared with that of the Ganges.—Chap. III.

3. The cataclysms of the Indus and the Sutluj; the former caused by a glacier, the latter by the fall of a mountain.—Chap. III.

4. The determination of the cause of the prevailing day and night wind in Ladák.—Chap. VII.

5. The observations for temperature, Chap. VII.; and the Tables of Magnetical and Meteorological Observations.—Chaps. XVI. and XVII.

6. The discovery of fossil *fresh-water* shells in the sandy-clay formations above the level of the present *salt-water* lakes of Ladák, proving that the lakes were once *fresh*, and of much greater extent.

7. The tables of the stature and longevity of the people of Ladák, and the accurate measurements and

drawings of skulls compared with those of the Kashmiris.

To several kind friends I am indebted for valuable assistance in this work.

To Colonel Bates, for the landscape-views which bear his name, and for many important observations for temperature.

To Dr. Carter, A.B., for the different qualitative analysis of the salts and waters of the lakes and hot springs.

To Lieut. Maclagan, Bengal Engineers, for the survey of the Pin Valley, in Spiti.

ALEX[R]. CUNNINGHAM,
Brevet Major, Engineers.

SIMLA,
30th August, 1853.

CONTENTS.

LIST OF PLATES.

*

RULES FOR PRONUNCIATION.

Throughout this work the vowels and consonants are to be pronounced in the following manner :—

a, as in distance, America.
á, as in father, half.
i, as in din, sin.
í, as *ee* in seen.
u, as *oo* in poor.
ú, as *u* in pure.
é, as in thére, théy.
ai, as *y* in my.
o, as in more.
au, as *ou* in our.
k, as in kick.
kh, the same aspirated.
g, as in giggle.
ng, as in sing.
ch, as in church.
chh, the same aspirated.
j, as in jest.
ny, as *ny* in tanyard.
t, as in tittle.
th, the same aspirated.

d, as in dandy.
n, as in ninny.
p, as in puppy.
ph, the same aspirated.
b, as in baby.
m, as in mummy.
ts, as in catseye.
tsh, the same aspirated.
ds, as *ds* in windsail, groundsel.
w, as in woman, dwarf.
zh, *z* aspirated.
z, as in zigzag.
h, as in hair.
y, as in you.
r, as in roar.
l, as in lull.
sh, as in ship.
s, as in senses.
h, as in heart.

I.—INTRODUCTION.

1. The earliest authentic notices of Ladák scarcely reach so far back as the beginning of the Christian era. In A.D. 399-400, when the Chinese pilgrims, Fa-Hian,* Hoeï-King, and others, reached *Yu-thian* (or Kotan), the former determined to remain behind for some time to witness the procession of images, while Hoeï-King proceeded in advance to *Kie-chha.* After the procession had taken place, Fa-Hian travelled by *Tsu-ho* and *Yu-hoeï,* and over the *Tsung-Ling* mountains southward to *Kie-chha,* where he rejoined Hoeï-King. On those mountains, which were one month's journey in breadth, the snow, it is said, never melted, and the natives of the country were known by the name of "men of the snowy mountains." From *Kie-chha* the pilgrims proceeded westward to *Tho-ly,* which they reached in one month. From this account, it appears to me that there can be no doubt of the identity of the ancient *Kie-chha* with the modern Ladák.

2. To reach Ladák from Kotan there were two roads open to the pilgrims, the western by Kukeyar and the southern by Ruthog (or Rudok). By either route the

* See the *Fo-kue-ki,* by Messrs. Remusat, Klaproth, and Landresse, or the Translation by Laidlay.

B

travellers would have to cross the Kárákoram mountains; but as *Tsu-ho* is stated to have been only 1,000 li (about 166 miles) from *Su-le* (or Kashgar), it is clear that Fa-Hian must have followed the western route. This is more distinctly proved by the Chinese identification of *Tsu-ho* with *Chu-kiu-pho*, which was exactly 1,000 li to the westward of Kotan. *Tsu-ho* was therefore midway between Kotan and Kashgar. Klaproth identified it with Kukeyar, and he is probably correct. From *Tsu-ho* the pilgrims proceeded to the south, and over the *Tsung-Ling*, or "Onion Mountains." From Kukeyar to Ladák the road lies to the south over the Kárákoram mountains, which, even as high as 17,000 feet, are covered with wild leeks, thus justifying the Chinese name of Tsung-Ling, or "Onion Mountains."* To the westward of *Kie-chha*, at one month's journey, was *Tho-ly*, or (as it is written by Hwan-Thsang) *Tha-li-lo*, which is an exact transcript of Darel, one of the Dardu districts on the Indus; and which Hwan-Thsang places to the westward of *Po-lu-lo* or Bolor, that is, the modern district of Balti. As Darel is just one month's journey from Lé, the district of Ladák corresponds exactly in geographical position with the ancient kingdom of *Kie-chha*.

3. But the other details, recorded by Fa-Hian, seem to place this identification beyond all doubt. The country was "mountainous, and so cold that no grain but corn ever ripened," which is exactly the case with Ladák. *Kie-chha*, moreover, possessed a stone vase of the same colour as Buddha's alms-dish, besides a tooth of Buddha.

* I owe this fact to Dr. Thomas Thomson, my brother Commissioner on the Tibetan frontier, whose spirit of enterprise carried him to the top of the Kárákoram pass.

Now, one of these relics (the alms-dish) still exists in a temple to the north of Lé. It is a large earthenware vase, similar in shape to the two largest steatite vases extracted from the Bhilsa Topes.* But Ladák also possessed a tooth of Buddha, which was formerly enshrined at Lé in a *dung-ten*, or solid mound of masonry similar to the Topes of Bhilsa and of Afghanistan. The *dung-ten* still exists, though ruinous : but the holy tooth is said to have been carried away by Ali Sher, of Balti, upwards of 200 years ago, when Ladák was invaded and plundered by the Musalmáns of the west, who, most probably, threw the much-prized relic contemptuously into the Indus. At any rate, it has never since been heard of.

4. Lastly, the name of *Kie-chha*, and the designation of the people as " men of the snowy mountains," both point unmistakably to Ladák, which is still known as *Kha-pa-chan*, or *Kha-chan*, " abounding in snow," or Snow-land, and the people as *Kha-pa-chan-pa*, or *Kha-chan-pa*, " men of the snowy land."†

5. In the *Cesi* of Pliny, and in the *A-khassa regio* of Ptolemy, I believe that we have the earliest mention of Ladák. Of the former Pliny‡ says, " hos includit Indus montium coronâ circumdatos et solitudinibus." This description is literally true of the people of *Kha-pa-chan*, or Snow-land, whose whole country lies along

* By Lieutenant Maisey and myself. See my account of the opening and examination of " The Bhilsa Topes, or Buddhist Monuments of Central India," printed for Smith, Elder, & Co. (1853).

† *Kha*, or *Kha-pa*, is " snow," and *chan* means " full." Perhaps Náser-ud-din *Kabáchah*, who reigned in Multan and Sindh, and afterwards disputed the empire of India with Altanish, was a Ladáki. Ptolemy's *A-khassa regio* is no doubt *Kha-chan-yul*, " Snow-land," or Ladák.

‡ Plin. Nat. Hist. vi. c. 20.

the Indus and its tributaries, whilst at the same time it is completely surrounded by deserts and by mountains. The position of Ptolemy's *A-khassa regio* agrees equally well with that of Ladák; for he places his district between the Chatæ Scythæ on the north, and the Chauranæi Scythæ on the south-east, and to the eastward of the Byltæ. The first must be the people of *Chang-thang** (or the "northern plains") to the north and east of Ladák; and the second are most likely the people of *Khor*, who dwell to the south-east of Ladák; while the Byltæ are certainly the inhabitants of Balti, or Little Tibet.

6. A later mention of Ladák, under a new name, is made by another Chinese pilgrim, Hwan-Thsang, towards the middle of the seventh century. He states, that from *Khiu-lu-to* (or Kullu, a hill district to the north of Simla), at 2,000 *li* (or upwards of 300 miles) across the mountains, is the kingdom of *Mo-lo-pho*, which is also called *San-pho-ho*. The former is an exact transcript of *Mar-po-yul*,† or "low land," to distinguish it from the high lands of Chang-thang and Ngari. The other name of *San-pho-ho* is a literal transcript of *Tsang-po*, or the "river," which is a common designation for the Indus in Ladák, and in fact for any great river in the Tibetan language; *San-pho-ho* is, therefore, the country on the *Tsang-po*, or Indus.

7. These notices of Ladák bring us down to that interesting period when the Devanágari alphabet of India was introduced into Tibet from Kashmir, in the first half of the seventh century of our era. Thumi Sambhota was the first who taught the Tibetans the use

* *Byang-thang*, pronounced *Chang-thang*, the *Chan-than* of our maps.

† *Mar-po-yul*, the "low-country."

of the Kashmirian characters, which remain unchanged to this day.*

8. In the beginning of the eleventh century Palgyigon occupied Ladák, and Tashi-Degon took possession of Purang.† In A.D. 1314, Rinchana Bhoti invaded Kashmir.‡ As he entered the valley by Gagangir, on the Sindh river, he must have advanced through Drás, one of the districts of Ladák. It is probable, therefore, that he was the ruler of Ladák. At that time Kashmir had been invaded by an army of 60,000 horse, under the command of Dallach, the minister of a neighbouring chief, named Karma Sena. The invaders advanced to the capital, which, being deserted by the Raja Sena Deva, was plundered and burned. Dallach continued his devastations to the eastern end of the valley, and retired by the Pass of Tár-bal.§ Numbers of the Kashmiris then waited upon Rinchana, who was emboldened to advance against the troops of the Raja Sena Deva. The raja fled; the Bhotiyan chief was victorious, and assumed the sovereignty of the country. He strengthened himself by marrying the daughter of Rama Chandra, the general of Sena Deva; and reigned for three years, from A.D. 1315 to 1318, the undisputed master of Kashmir.

9. Half a century before this time the celebrated Marco Polo had visited the court of the great Kublai, Emperor of China. He had sojourned in the hills of Badakshán for the sake of his health; and he describes the countries of Wakham, Pamer, Bolor, and Kashmir.

* Csoma de Körös, Tibetan Grammar, p. 178.

† Csoma, in Prinsep's useful tables, p. 131. The names are written *dPal-gyi-mGon* and *bKra-shis-lDe-mGon*.

‡ Raja Tarangini. § That is, the "Tar-hill" in Kashmiri.

By some it has been supposed that he must have entered Tibet; but the wonderful account which he gives of the people proves that his information could only have been obtained by hearsay. Indeed, notwithstanding the early and wide-spread fame of Prester John, there is no authentic record that Tibet had been visited by any European prior to the seventeenth century.

10. During the seventeenth and eighteenth centuries, when the Jesuits and Capuchins possessed several monasteries in Lhasa, a considerable number of missionaries must have resided for many years in Tibet; and yet no more than two of these religious fraternities have left any record of their travels and observations behind them.

11. The first of these is Le Père Hippolyte Desideri,* who travelled for six months, between August 1715 and March 1716, through the greater part of the country, from Ladák through Ruthog to Lhasa. Of his travels, the only account that I have seen is that which was published by Klaproth. It is a concise, but very useful geographical account.

12. The second is Frà Franciso Orazio della Penna di Billi, a Capuchin, who travelled to Lhasa in 1730, and resided for some years in the monastery of his order in that city. His account is exceedingly valuable, notwithstanding his prosy repetitions.† He was a man of observation, and his account of the Buddhist religion, as practised in Tibet, is full and accurate.

13. In A.D. 1774 George Bogle‡ was deputed to

* Nouveau Journal Asiatique, tom. viii. pp. 117—121, by the celebrated Klaproth.

† Nouveau Journal Asiatique, tom. xiv.

‡ See the Preface to Turner's Tibet, pp. xiv—xvi.

Tibet by Warren Hastings. The Dalai Lama,* or Grand Lama of Lhasa, was then in his minority, and the country was ruled by the Tashi Lama of Tashi Lhunpo. No account of this mission has been preserved, which is the more to be regretted as Bogle would seem to have been a man of superior intelligence.

14. In A.D. 1783 a second mission was despatched by Warren Hastings to Tibet. Captain Turner, the head of the mission, succeeded in reaching Tashi Lhunpo, but he was prevented from going to Lhasa "by a consideration of the present state of that government,"† as the *Gyat sub Rinpoche* "had usurped, even from the hands of the Dalai Lama, the greatest portion of his temporal power." The Regent of Tashi Lhunpo also dissuaded‡ the envoy from making the attempt, for fear of offending the Chinese. Captain Turner's account of his embassy is the most curious and interesting work on Tibet that has yet appeared.

A Chinese work, called "Notice of the Provinces of Weï and Tsang," was written by *Ma-shao-yun*, the Commissary-General of the Chinese army, which was sent to expel the Gorkhas from Tibet in 1786.§ His account is short but interesting, especially in the notices of the various religious festivals.

The adventurous Moorcroft lived for two whole years in Ladák, from September 1820 to September 1822. His account of the country is marked by great shrewdness of observation, and by the most scrupulous accuracy. A more truthful chronicler than Moorcroft never lived.

* *Ta-lhi-bLa-ma,* is the Dalai Lama of Europeans.

† Account of an Embassy to the Court of the Teshoo Lama, in Tibet, by Capt. Samuel Turner.

‡ Turner's Tibet, 4to. p. 253.

§ Nouv. Journ. Asiatique, tom. iv. et vi.

The Botis of Ladák, the Kahlon of Lé, the merchants of Kashmir, and the Rajah of Rajaore, all spoke to me of the English traveller with the highest respect.* As there has always been a suspicion of foul play in the manner of his death, the second of the following letters, addressed by Trebeck to Syad Muhammad Shah, is of considerable interest and importance, as it distinctly states that Moorcroft *died* at Andkhuï, *after some days' illness.*

Translation of a *parwánah* addressed by Moorcroft to Syad Muhammud Shah Kashmiri :—

"Your letter has arrived, and your faithful services have become known to us. The paper bearing the seals of the merchants and other friends at that place (Kábul), addressed to Muhammad Murád Beg, the ruler of Kunduz, which you forwarded, has been shown. Our escape has been effected, and we have started for Bokhára. Remain in Kábul until our return, and consider your salary fixed at the same rate as formerly. Take fifty pieces of gold from Khoda Baksh Khán, the merchant, for your expenses, and continue day and night to note whatever takes place. More is superfluous."

Syad Muhammad Shah was a young Kashmiri, who had accompanied Moorcroft from his native country to Kashmir. On the departure of the travellers for Balkh, he was discharged at his own request; but as he remained in Kábul, he was employed by them as a news-writer, and on the occasion of Moorcroft's deten-

* Burnes has recorded the estimation in which Moorcroft's memory was held by the people of Balkh; and I am happy to add here the testimony of Major Edwardes (A Year in the Panjab, i. 52) to the same effect. "I am glad to be able to contribute the smallest white pebble to poor Moorcroft's cairn; and cannot pass on without recording that my friend Swahn Khan spoke of him highly in every way."

tion by Murád Beg, of Kunduz, the Syad was of some service in procuring letters from the authorities and merchants of Kábul to prove that the travellers were merchants,* and that the object of their journey was, as they professed it to be, "the establishment of a commercial intercourse which would be as beneficial to Turkistan as to India."† The published account of Moorcroft's travels states that fifty of the principal merchants and bankers of Kábul, unsolicited, had forwarded a certificate that Moorcroft was, as he pretended to be, a merchant; but the above *parwánah,* addressed by Moorcroft to the Syad, shows that this certificate had been obtained through him.

Translation of a *parwánah,* addressed by Trebeck (after Moorcroft's death) to Syad Muhammad Shah Kashmiri :—

"The affairs of that place (Kábul) have become known from the perusal of your letter. Day and night continue to note whatever may occur. You may have heard that Mr. William Moorcroft, *after a few days' illness,* died at *Andkhuï,* whither he had gone to purchase horses. As he had written to you to remain at Kábul until his return, you had better stay until my arrival, which you may expect shortly. Consider your salary fixed at the same rate as formerly, and set your mind at rest in every respect as far as I am concerned. Continue to write the news," &c.

The Syad's services on these occasions were afterwards attested in a certificate, which was furnished to him

* Moorcroft's Travels, vol. ii. p. 448. "I found on my arrival a *Kásid* from Kabul, who brought me a certificate that I was, as I pretended to be, a merchant."

† Moorcroft's Travels, vol. ii. p. 425.

under the seals of Yár Muhammad Khán and Sultán Muhammad Khán. The original is now in my possession. In this certificate they state that, "when the *Sáhibs* arrived at Kúndúz, they got into trouble, and were relieved from their difficulties by the services of the Syad, who was then at Kábul, and that, in consequence of his zeal and devotion, the *Sáhibs* begged him to remain in Kábul until their return."

I obtained all these documents in original from the Syad himself, who, as a Shiah Musulmán, had sought and obtained service at the Shiah court of Lucknow.

Towards the end of the year 1834, the eccentric Dr. Henderson reached Lé, the capital of Ladák, disguised as a Musulmán, calling himself Ishmaïl Khan. His disguise was soon penetrated, but he was kindly treated by the Gyalpo, who at once saw, in the opportune arrival of a British officer, a possible means of averting the ultimate conquest of his kingdom. In August 1834, Ladák had been invaded by Zoráwar Sing, the local Governor of Káshtwár, under Raja Guláb Sing, of Jammu. At the time of Dr. Henderson's arrival at Lé, the invaders had taken possession of the western provinces of Suru and Drás, and had advanced into the valley of Paskyum. Henderson's presence immediately recalled to the Gyalpo's memory the offer which he had once before made, through Moorcroft, of allegiance to the British Government. The rulers of India had already snatched Sindh from the rough grasp of the Lion of Lahor, and the simple Tibetan vainly thought that they would be equally willing to save Ladák from the arms of his lieutenant. Dr. Henderson was therefore applied to; but as he had crossed the British frontier against the positive prohibition of his

Government, and was now in Ladák when he ought to have been in Calcutta, he was unwilling to make any communication which would at once expose his violation of the orders of his Government. The draft of the original tender of allegiance which was forwarded by Moorcroft was shown to him; but his position prevented him from acting as Moorcroft had done. His refusal irritated the Gyalpo, and he was prevented from leaving Ladák without being actually imprisoned.* Meanwhile the people were informed that a British envoy had arrived, and that the invaders would speedily be obliged to depart. Zoráwar Sing immediately reported the circumstance to his master, Raja Guláb Sing, who applied to the Maharaja. Ranjit Sing at once "addressed the political agent at Ludiána to ascertain the meaning of such proceeding. The agent satisfied Ranjit Sing with an assurance that Dr. Henderson, the traveller, had passed the Sutlej in direct violation of the orders of his Government; and that there was not the slightest idea of interfering with Ranjit's plan of extending his conquests northwards. Zoráwar Sing, after this explanation, was desired to proceed with his operations;"† upon which Henderson was allowed to depart. In fact, he was detained so long as his presence was of service to the Gyalpo in delaying the loss of his kingdom.‡

Dr. Henderson was provided with instruments; and as, according to Baron Hugel, he had some tact for

* My information agrees with Hugel's. The Baron obained his version from Henderson himself. I got mine from the Botis of Ladák, and the officers of Zoráwar Sing's force.

† Quoted from Hugel's Travels, p. 102.

‡ Vigne, vol. ii. p. 337, says that Henderson himself complained to Ranjit of his detention at Lé.

observation, an account of his travels would have been particularly valuable. He was probably the first European who had ever visited *Skardo*, or Little Tibet. He took that route to avoid the invading army of Dogras, and succeeded in reaching Kashmir in November 1835. All his observations were lost, along with his baggage, on the road between Ladák and Kashmir.* In 1847, I made repeated inquiries for English books, or English writing, with the hope of recovering some of Henderson's notes, but all in vain.

Ladák was visited by Mr. Vigne shortly after *Moré-Tátsi* had been placed on the throne by Zoráwar Sing. From Balti he proceeded through Lé to the Nubra valley, and returned by the same route. His short stay in Ladák was unfortunate; for, owing to the mutual jealousy of himself and the Dogra authorities, he was deprived of all means of obtaining information. His notice of Ladák is therefore the least interesting part of his rambles in the Alpine Panjáb. His accounts of Kashmir and Balti are full of valuable information, which is half lost for want of arrangement.

Early in 1846, when the result of the first Sikh war had made Raja Guláb Sing the undisputed master of Ladák and its dependencies, and he had no longer to guard himself against the power of the Sikh chiefs, it seemed not improbable that the hope of plunder and the desire of revenge might tempt him to repeat the expedition of 1841 into the Lhasan territory. Such an occurrence would at once have stopped the importation of shawl wool into our territory, and have closed the

* Baron Hugel's Travels, pp. 129, 151. Henderson's servant reported that his baggage was lost in the snow in the *Naubak* Pass. I presume that the *Namyika* Pass is intended.

whole of the petty commerce of our hill states with Tibet. It was possible also that our peaceful relations with the Chinese emperor might be considerably embarrassed by his Celestial Majesty's ignorance of any distinction between the rulers of India and the rulers of Kashmir. As it seemed desirable to prevent the chance of such an occurrence, the British Government determined to remove the most common cause of all disputes in the East,—an unsettled boundary. For this purpose two officers were deputed, in August 1846, to the Tibetan frontier of Ladák, to ascertain the ancient boundaries between the two countries, and to lay down the boundary between the British territories and those of Mahárája Guláb Sing. The settlement of this boundary was one of some importance to the hill states, and more especially to our new acquisition of Nurpur, which received all its shawl wool from the traders of the eastern hill states, and not from Kashmir. Immediately after the war, I had pointed out that, by giving up to Mahárája Guláb Sing the southern dependencies of Ladák, we had actually interposed a rival territory between our own provinces on the Sutluj and the shawl-wool districts of Cháng-Tháng. The southern boundary of Spiti was, in fact, not more than thirty miles from Rámpur, on the Sutluj. As the annual revenue of the Spiti district, derived from all sources, does not amount to more than seven hundred rupees, no difficulty was experienced in making an exchange of territory with Mahárája Guláb Sing, and Spiti was added to the British dominions.

It then became necessary to define the northern boundary of Spiti, with the other districts of Ladák. The two commissioners deputed for this purpose were the late lamented Vans Agnew and myself. We left Simla on the 2nd August, 1846, and proceeded due north through Mandi, Kullu, and Láhul, to the Bara Lácha Pass, just beyond which stands the well-known *phálang-danda*, or boundary-stone, between the British province of Láhul and the Ladáki district of Zanskar. From this point we proceeded to the Tshomoriri lake, and I mapped in the British boundary from the *phálang-danda* to the Chinese frontier.

We were accompanied by Anant Rám, the Vazir of Shassa, in Kanáwar, who was deputed to attend us by the Raja of Bisahar, because he knew Hindustani, and could both speak and write Tibetan. To him we intrusted the Governor-General's letter addressed to the Chinese Governor of Lhasa. Anant Rám proceeded by Tashigong and the valley of the Indus to Gáro. On his arrival, the people at first refused to let him see the Governor; but as he persisted (according to his instructions) in declining to make over the letter to any one but the Governor himself, he was at length admitted within the fort, and then presented the letter. The Governor remarked that no letter had ever yet been received from the British authorities, and that his only communications to the westward were with the Raja of Bisahar. Anant Rám replied that he was the servant of the Bisahar Raja, who had directed him to accompany the British officers to the Chinese frontier, for the purpose of delivering the letter in question. On this, the Governor remarked that he would forward the letter to Lhasa, but that an answer could not be received for a whole year. A tent was then provided for Anant Rám, and he remained at Gáro for eight days, and was well treated the whole time.

Early the following year, as soon as the passes were open, the Raja of Bisahar reported that some Chinese authorities had arrived at Gáro, and that they had been despatched by the Governor of Lhasa. It was therefore determined to send a second commission to the Tibetan frontier for the purpose of laying down the ancient boundary between Ladák and Tibet. Three commissioners were appointed,—

Captain (now Major) Alexander Cunningham, of the Engineers.

Lieutenant (now Captain) Henry Strachey.

Dr. Thomas Thomson.

Captain Henry Strachey had already distinguished himself by his bold and successful visit to the holy well of Mánasarovara in the previous year, and Dr. Thomas Thomson was well known as one of the first botanists in India. The mission was supplied with portable magnetic and meteorological instruments; but as only one barometer was procurable, the observations for atmospheric pressure were confined to the parts of the country which Captain Strachey visited. My observations for temperature and moisture were continued from the south-eastern boundary of Spiti, throughout Ladák and Kashmir, to Shamsábád on the western frontier of the Panjáb. I observed the magnetic dip, declination, and intensity at Puga, Lé, and Molbil in Ladák, at Trinagar, the capital of Kashmir, and at Shamsábád. All these observations, with the exception of those at Ladák, were taken on the regular term-days laid down for monthly magnetic observation.

II.—GEOGRAPHY.

1.—GENERAL DESCRIPTION.

The most striking feature in the physical aspect of Ladák is the parallelism of its mountain-ranges, which stretch through the country from south-east to north-west. This general direction of the mountain-chains determines the courses of the rivers as well as the boundaries of the natural divisions of the country. The general aspect of Ladák is extreme barrenness. Seen from above, the country would appear a mere succession of yellow plains and barren mountains capped with snow, and the lakes of Pangkong and Tshomo Riri would seem like bright oases amidst a vast desert of rock and sand. No trace of man nor of human habitations would meet the eye: and even the large spots of cultivated land would be but small specks on the mighty waste of a deserted world. But a closer view would show many fertile tracts along the rivers, covered with luxuriant crops, and many picturesque monasteries, from which the chant of human voices ascends on high in daily prayer and praise. The yellow plains along the Indus would then be seen covered with flocks of the shawl-wool goat, and all the principal thoroughfares of the country dotted with numerous flocks of sheep laden with the merchandise of China and of India.

The territory of Ladák is one of the most elevated regions of the earth. Its different valleys lie along the head-waters of the Indus, the Sutluj, and the Chenáb; and the joint effects of elevation and of isolation amidst snowy mountains produce perhaps the most singular climate in the known world. Burning heat by day is succeeded by piercing cold at night, and everything is parched by the extreme dryness of the air. The rarefied atmosphere offers but little impediment to the sun's rays, which during a short summer are sufficiently powerful to ripen barley at an elevation of 15,000 feet, although the temperature falls below the freezing point every night. This climate is equally favourable to animal life. The plains between 16,000 and 17,000 feet are covered with wild horses and hares and immense flocks of domestic goats and sheep; and the slopes of the hills up to 19,000 feet abound with marmots and Alpine hares. Such is the extreme dryness of the atmosphere, that no rain falls and but little snow, and both meats and fruits are cured by mere exposure to the air.

2.—BOUNDARIES AND EXTENT.

Ladák is the most westerly country occupied by the Tibetan race who profess the Buddhist faith. On the north it is divided by the Kárákoram mountains from the Chinese district of Kotan. To the east and south-east are the Chinese districts of Rudok and Chumurti; and to the south are the districts of Lahul and Spiti, now attached to British India, but formerly belonging to Ladák. To the west lie Kashmir and Balti, the former separated by the western Himalaya, and the latter by an imaginary line drawn from the mouth of the Dras river to the sources of the Nubra river.

Its greatest extent is from north-west to south-east, from the head of the Dras river, in longitude 75° 30′, to Chibra, on the Indus, in longitude 79° 10′, a distance of 240 miles. Its greatest breadth is 290 miles, from the Kárákoram Pass, in north latitude 35° 10′, to the Rotang Pass in Lahul, in latitude 32° 25′. Its mean length is 200 miles, and its mean breadth 150 miles. Its whole extent is therefore only 30,000 square miles.

The natural divisions of the country are: 1st, Nubra on the Shayok: 2nd, Ladák Proper, on the Indus: 3rd, Zanskar, on the Zanskar river: 4th, Rukchu, around the lakes of Tshomo Riri and Tsho-Kar: 5th, Purik, Suru, and Dras, on the different branches of the Dras river: 6th, Spiti, on the Spiti river: and 7th, Lahul, on the Chandra and Bhaga, or head-waters of the Chenáb. These also are the actual divisions of the country, for the natural boundaries of a mountainous district generally remain unaltered, in spite of the changes wrought by war and religion.

Ladák is divided politically between Maharaja Guláb Sing and the East-India Company. To the former belong all the northern districts, to the latter only the two southern districts of Lahul and Spiti.

3.—DIFFERENT NAMES OF LADÁK.

Ladák, in Tibetan *La-tags*, is the most common name of the country; but it is also called *Mar-yul*,* or

* *dMar-yul* or d*Mar-po-yul*, "Red-land." Csoma de Körös spells the name *Mar-yul*, the "low-country;" but as Hwan Thsang, in A.D.

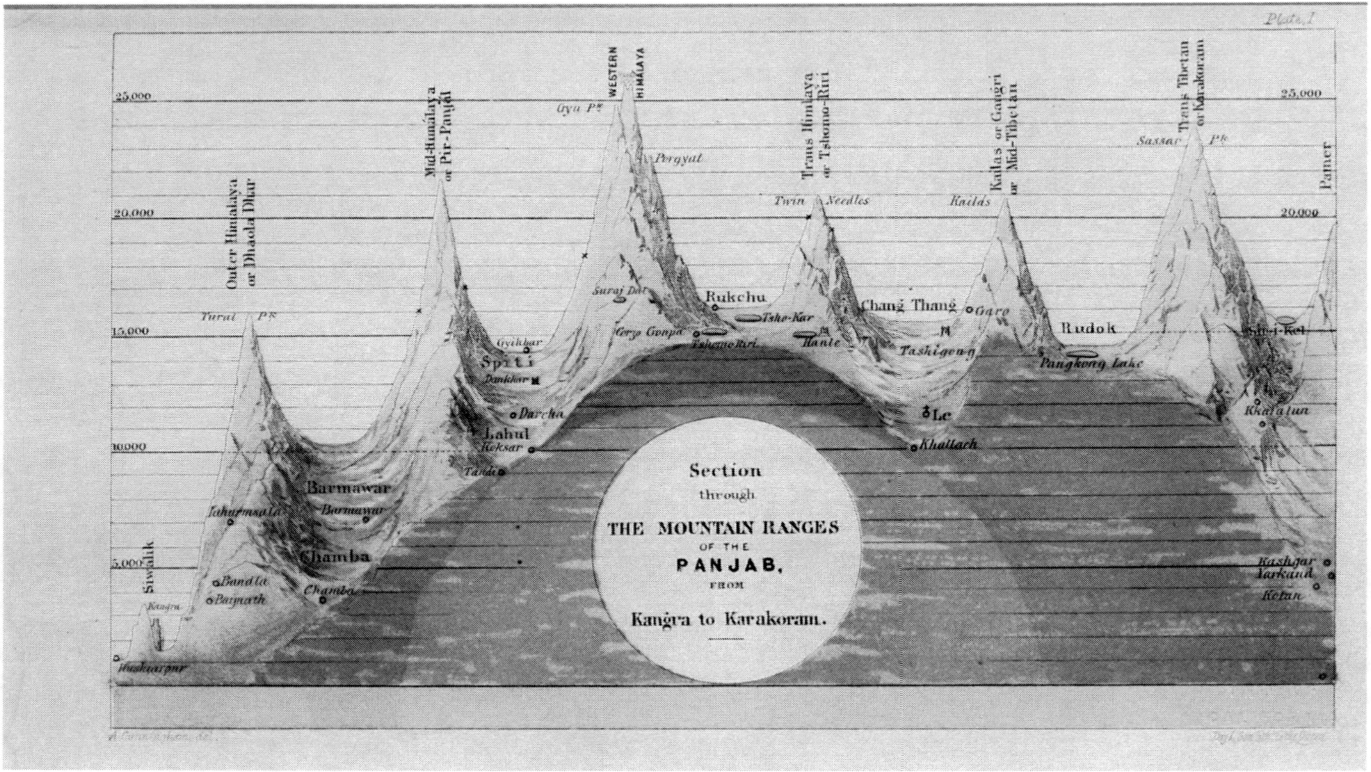
Plate, I
Section
through
THE MOUNTAIN RANGES
OF THE
PANJAB,
FROM
Kangra to Karakoram.
25,000
20,000
15,000
10000
5,000
Siwalik
Outer Himalaya
or Dhaola Dhar
Turai Pk
Mid-Himalaya
or Pir-Panjal
WESTERN
HIMALAYA
Gya Pk
Pergyat
Trans Himlaya
or Tshomo-Riri
Twin Needles
Kailas or Gangri
or Mid-Tibetan
Kailds
Trans Tibetan
or Karakoram
Sassar Pk
Pamer
Kangra
Hushiarpur
Bandla
Baijnath
Jahurmsala
Barmawar
Chamba
Gyldhar
Spiti
Dankhar
Darcha
Lahul
Koksar
Tandi
Suraj Dal
Gergo Gonpa
Tshomo Riri
Rukchu
Tsho-Kar
Hanle
Chang Thang
Garo
Tashigong
Le
Khallach
Rudok
Pangkong Lake
Khalalun
Kashgar
Yarkand
Kotan

Low-land or Red-land, and *Kha-chan-pa*, or Snow-land, both of which names are used by the old Chinese travellers; by Fa-Hian, A.D. 400, who calls the kingdom *Kie-chha;* and by Hwan Thsang, A.D. 640, who calls it *Ma-lo-pho.* The name of *Kha-chan-pa*, or Snow-land, is also applied to the Lhasan kingdom of Great Tibet. The two central districts of Great Tibet are *dBus*, and *gTsang*, usually pronounced *U* and *Tsang*, or jointly *U-Tsang.* But the uncorrupted pronunciation is preserved by Ptolemy in *Dabasæ*, who must be the people of dBus; and in Turner's *Pue-koa-chin*, which is most probably *dBus-Kha-pa-chan*, or the "snowy land of *dBus.*" Ladák was formerly subject to Lhasa, to which it paid a small tribute until A.D. 1834, when it was seized by Zoráwar Sing, the enterprising general of Mahárája Guláb Sing, of Jammu; and it now forms a part of his new kingdom of Kashmir.

Ladák is inhabited by a peculiar race of people, who call themselves *Bot-pa*,* who speak a peculiar language called Tibetan, and who profess the religion of Buddha, under a peculiar hierarchy of monks called Lamas. The name of Tibet is entirely unknown to the people as well as to the Indians, who call them Bhotiyas, and their country Bhutan. The use of the names of Bot and Bhutan is probably not older than the tenth or twelfth century, when the Buddhists, having been expelled from India, the hill country in which they settled naturally acquired the name of Bauddha-sthan or Bauddh-than, and Bod-tan or Bot.

According to Klaproth, Tibet is a Mogul word, which

640, calls it *Ma-lo-pho* or *Mar-po*, that is "red," there is still some doubt about the true meaning of the name.

* The name is spelt *Bod*, but pronounced *Bot.*

should more properly be written Tubet. But the name of Ti-bat (تبت) is mentioned by Abu Zaid Al Hasan, in A.D. 915, by Ibn Haukal in about A.D. 950, by Abu Rihán in 1030, and afterwards by Edrisi in A.D. 1154, all long prior to the Mogul conquests of Changez Khan in the 13th century, before whose time it is highly improbable that any Mogul names could have been in use in Persia. Mir Izzet Ullah says that Tibet is a Turki word signifying shawl-wool: but I should think the shawl-wool was called Tibeti because it came from Tibet. One might as well derive the name of India from indigo. There is no trace of the name of Tibet nor even of Bot in any of the classical authors: but the people are most probably described under the name of Seres, the inhabitants of Chinese Tartary, from whom the western merchants obtained their silks. According to Pausanias,* "the Greeks called the silkworm *Ser*, but the people of Serika probably gave it another name." Now the Tibetans call a worm *Srin*, or *Srin-bu*, and the silkworm *Dar-kyi-Srin;* and Pausanias says that the silkworm was twice the size of a beetle, Σειρην. As the Greeks had not seen the silkworm when they first used the name of Ser, it seems to me more than probable that they would have adopted the native name rather than have invented one of their own.

4.—DISTRICTS OF LADÁK.

The different districts of Ladák have been partially named according to their relative geographical positions; as *Nub-ra*, the western district (or Wessex), and *Lho-yul*, the southern country (or Suffolk). To the south-east

* VI. p. 26.

of Ladák, but to the north of *Ngari*, lies the extensive province of *Chang Thang*, or the "northern plains." Ladák itself is called Mar-yul or Low-land, perhaps from its inferior elevation to all the surrounding districts.

Nubra,* or the north-western district of Ladák, includes all the country drained by the Nubra and Shayok rivers. It is by far the largest district in the country, being about 128 miles in length by 72 miles in breadth, with an area of 9,200 square miles. It is bounded on the north by the Kárákoram mountains, and on the south by the Kailas range, which divides the Indus from the Shayok; and it extends from the frontier of Balti, in east longitude 77°, to the Pangkong lake on the borders of Rudok. The mean elevation of the inhabited parts of the country, from an average of fourteen observations at different places, is 12,763 feet.

Ladák is the central and most populous district of the country, from which it is sometimes called *Mang-yul*, or the "district of many people." It stretches along the Indus in a north-westerly direction from Rukchu to the frontier of Balti, a length of 120 miles, with an average breadth of 33 miles. Its area is about 4,000 square miles, and the mean elevation of the inhabited portions, as deduced from observations along the Indus, is 11,500 feet.

Zanskar includes all the country lying along the two great branches of the Zanskar river, in a general direction from south-east to north-west. It is bounded by Ladák on the north, by Rukchu on the east, by Lahul on the south, and by the small districts of Purik and Wanla on the west. The southern boundary is formed by the

* *Nub-ra*, western.

great Himálaya itself, the western boundary by the transverse range of Singgé Lá, and the northern boundary by the Trans-Himálayan chain. Its greatest length is 72 miles, but its mean length is not more than 56 miles, and its mean breadth is about the same, or 55 miles. It has an area of 3,000 square miles, and a mean elevation of 13,154 feet, as deduced from seven different observations along the course of the valley. The name of *Zangs-kar** means "white copper" or brass; but I have no idea why it is so named.

Rukchu is the most elevated district in Ladák, and one of the loftiest inhabited regions in the known world. The mean height of the plains, as determined from twenty-one different spots where I encamped in 1846 and 1847, is 15,634 feet. This is the mean height of the great plain of Kyang, which extends from the foot of the Thung-lung Pass to the fords of the Sum-Gal, a length of 35 miles. It is also the height of the plains around the *Tsho-kar*, or White Lake, and of the long sloping plains from the Lanák ridge to the Para river. Rukchu is bounded on the north by Ladák Proper, on the east by the Chinese district of Chumurti, on the south by Lahul and Spiti, and on the west by Zanskar. Its length from the Thung-lung Pass to the head of the Hanlé river is 90 miles, and its mean breadth about 62 miles, which give an area of 5,500 square miles.

Purik, *Suru*, and *Dras*† are three small districts to

* *Zangs-dKar*, "copper-white."

† These names are not all Tibetan, as Dras is the Kashmiri name for the district of *Hem-babs*. In Tibetan they are written *Pu-rig*; *Su-ru*; and *Hem-babs*. The last name means "snow-fed or snow-descended,"

the west of Zanskar, on the high road between Kashmir and Lé. To *Purik* belong the villages of the Waka and Phugal rivers, from their sources in the transverse range of Singgé Lá to Kargyil, below their junction. The principal places in Purik are Mulbil, Paskyum, and Sod, each of which once had a petty chief of its own. *Suru* also owned a petty chief who lived at Lung Kartse, the principal place in the valley. The river is sometimes called by this name, but more generally by that of Suru. The Suru river joins the Waka-chu immediately below Kargyil. *Dras* is the most westerly of these small districts. Its Tibetan name of Hem-babs (snow-fed or snow descended) is descriptive of its most striking peculiarity, as the most snowy district of Ladák. It owes this peculiarity to the great depression in the Himálaya, at the head of the Dras river, which allows the constantly humid vapours of Kashmir to pass to the north of the mountains, where they become condensed by the cold, and are precipitated in rain or snow, according to the season of the year. These small districts extend in length from the frontier of Balti to Zanskar, a distance of 84 miles, and in breadth from the head of the Suru valley to the Photo-la, a distance of 50 miles. The area is 4,200 square miles, and the mean height of the inhabited parts, as determined by the elevation of thirteen camps, is 11,196 feet.

*Spiti** is bounded on the north by Rukchu, on the

Hem being the Sanscrit *Hima*, which has long been naturalized in Tibet. See Csoma's Tibetan Dictionary, *in voce*.

* *Spi-ti*. In Kullu and Kanáwar this district is generally called Piti, but the proper name is Spiti.

west by Lahul and Kullu, on the south by Kanáwar, and on the east by the Chinese district of Chumurti. It comprises the whole valley of the Spiti river, from its source to the junction of the Para, a length of about 64 miles. Its mean length is not more than 52 miles, and its mean breadth only 36 miles, which give an area of about 1,900 square miles. The mean elevation of the inhabited parts, as determined by the heights of eight camps, is 12,986 feet.

Lahul (or Lho-yul, the "southern district") is bounded on the north by Zanskar and Rukchu, on the west by Káshtwár, on the south by Chamba and Kullu, and on the east by Spiti. It comprises the valleys of the Chandra and Bhaga rivers, as well as that of the Chandra-Bhaga or united stream as far as Treloknáth, below which the people are of Hindu race and religion, with but little admixture of Tibetan blood. With the single exception of the valley of the Indus, Lahul possesses more cultivable land, and a less rigorous climate than any of the other districts of Ladák. There the currant and the gooseberry are both found wild, and in the lower parts of the valley towards Treloknáth the mountain slopes are covered with fir trees. Like Kanáwar, Lahul partakes somewhat of the climate and productions of India as well as of those of Tibet. The people, their language, and their dwellings are mostly Tibetan, but with a strong mixture of Indian origin. Lahul is 68 miles in length by 34 in breadth, which give an area of 2,312 square miles. The mean elevation of its inhabited parts, as determined by the heights of nine camps, is 11,063 feet.

The following table of the extent and mean elevation

of the different districts of Ladák is added for the sake of comparison.

	District	Extent in sq. miles.		Mean height.
M. Guláb Sing.	Nubra	9,216		12,763
	Ladák	3,960		11,500
	Zanskar	3,080		13,154
	Rukchu	5,580		15,634
	Purik-Suru-Dras	4,200		11,196
			26,036	
British.	Spiti	2,312		12,986
	Láhul	1,872		11,063
			4,184	
	Total sq. miles		30,220	Mean height 12,613

5.—NEIGHBOURING COUNTRIES.

The countries to the north, the west, and the south of Ladák are inhabited by people who speak at least four languages quite distinct from Tibetan. To the north the people of Yarkand and Kotan speak Turki; to the west, beyond Balti, the people of Astor, Gilget, and Hunza Nager speak different dialects of Dardu, while the Kashmiris have a language peculiar to themselves; and to the south the people of Chamba, Kullu, and Bisahar speak a dialect of Hindi, which is chiefly derived from Sanskrit. To the east and south-east the people of Rudok, Chang-Thang, and Ngari speak Tibetan only.

To the north of the Kárákoram range, lie the Chinese districts of Yarkand, Kotan, and Káshgár, which, with the exception of the Chinese functionaries, and Tartar soldiers, are wholly peopled by Musulmáns. As I found it difficult to obtain any truth-like information regarding the statistics of these countries, I confined my inquiries to their natural productions, in the hope of meeting with something that would tend to determine their approximate height above the sea. All my informants agreed in stating that the people of these countries usually drove two and three horses abreast in their carriages or wagons, and that even four horses were occasionally harnessed abreast. On hearing this, I asked the width of the streets, but I obtained no satisfactory reply. Some said ten yards, some twenty yards: but when asked to mark out the width on the ground, not one of them showed more than twenty-five feet.

Yarkand. Moorcroft was informed that the population of Yarkand was between 50,000 and 60,000, a number which would require about 10,000 houses. Of these I was told that 500 houses belonged to Kashmiris alone, and thirty or thirty-two to Argons, or half-bloods. The productions were stated as follows.

Crops.	Vegetables.	Fruits.	Trees.
Rice	Cucumber	Grapes	Deodar
Jawár	Kadu	Apricots	Plane
Wheat	Tarohi	Peaches	Elæagnus M.
Barley	Onions	Apples	
Pease	Radishes	Pears	
Alsi	Turnips	Plums	
Mung*	Carrots	Mulberries	
Urd†	Spinach	Melons	
Masur‡			

In the hill provinces of India we know that the deodar does not flourish under 5,000 feet, and that rice is seldom seen above 6,000 feet. We know, also, that both are found in Kashmir, which has a mean elevation of 5,300 feet. But as Yarkand lies at least four degrees to the

* Phaseolus Mungo. † Dolichos pilosus. ‡ Cicer lens.

northward of Kashmir, the limits of the growth of deodars and of rice will of course be reduced. I do not, therefore, estimate the height of Yarkand at more than 4,000 feet above the sea.

At *Kotan* and *Aksu* the produce was said to be the same, with the sole addition of *gram* or pulse (Cicer arietinum); I should therefore estimate the height of these places at somewhat less, or between 3,500 and 4,000 feet.

The produce of *Kashgar* was said to be much the same as at Yarkand, with the single exception of rice, of which but very little is grown. As this indicates a somewhat higher elevation than Yarkand, I estimate the height of Kashgar at about 4,500 feet above the sea.

The districts lying along the Indus, to the westward of Ladák, are inhabited by two distinct races, the Tibetans, who have become Musulmáns, and the Dards. They speak wholly different languages, and even the Dards themselves speak three distinct dialects, which have but few words common to all. The Tibetan districts are Khapolor, Chhorbad, and Keris, on the Shayok; Khartakshe, Totte, and Parguta, on the Singgé-chu; Shigar, on the Shigar river; and Balti and Rongdo, on the Indus. The district of Astor, also, must once have belonged to the Tibetan race, as the chief even now bears the title of *Makpon*, and traces his descent from the same common ancestor as the Gyalpos of Balti, and several of the other states.*

Chhorbad extends along the Shayok river, from Chulung, on the frontier of Ladák, to Daho, on the boundary of Khapolor, a distance of forty-two miles. Beyond this,

* See also Vigne, Travels, vol. ii. p. 251.

Khapolor stretches twenty-five miles further down the Shayok, the whole length of the chiefship being sixty-seven miles. As the mean breadth is about thirty miles, the area will be 2,010 square miles. The mean height of the villages is about 9,000 feet. The chiefs of Khapolor have for several generations acknowledged the supremacy of the Gyalpos of Balti, but their ancestors most probably had possession of the country for several centuries before the rise of the Balti dynasty, whose very title of *Makpon*, or "General," betrays that they are the descendants of some military chief. The chiefs of Khapolor and Keris, who both trace their families up from Bewán-cho, declare that all the chiefs of these countries are descended from Bikam, the tenth generation from Bewán-cho. But Ahmed Shah of Balti, and the other chiefs of his family, traced their origin to a Fakir, who had married the daughter and only child of the reigning Gyalpo. The probability is, that the Makpons are descended from an adventurer named Bokha, who about A.D. 1500, established himself in the valley of the Indus, and obtained the title of *Makpon*, or General.

The following is the genealogy of the Gyalpos of Khapolor. It opens with Sultan Sikander, or Alexander the Great, whose successors were Abraham and Isaac. This part is evidently fabulous; but from Sultan Yagu, the 39th name, the list is perhaps tolerably correct, for the name of Yagu has descended to the present day as a title in the family, the present chief being styled Sultan Yagu Daolat Ali Khan. As there are sixty-seven princes in all, down to this time, the approximate date of Sultan Yagu's accession to power may be found by allowing a period of fifteen years for each reign. This estimate fixes the rise of Sultan Yagu in A.D. 1410, the very year in which Sikander Butshikan, the Idol-breaker of Kashmir, died. The coincidence of time is curious, and it is not improbable that Sultan Yagu may have been despatched by the bigoted Sikander to propagate the religion of Muhammed amongst the Tibetans on the Indus.

GYALPOS OF KHAPOLOR.

	Names.	Probable Date.	
1	Sultan Sikandar		
2	„ Ibrahim		
3	„ Ishák		
4	Abdul Ralimad		
5	Mir Barâhir		
6	Arman Samáhir		
7	Beshrab Nam		
8	Tinlu Tung		
9	Sultan Mahmud		
10	Mehndi Ghazáli		
11	„ Ibrahim		
12	„ Malik Haider Shah		
13	Sultan Malik Ghazáli		
14	„ Malik Shah		
15	„ Juned Shah		
16	„ Haider Shah		
17	„ Haider Karár		
18	„ Shah Ibrahim		
19	„ Johar Fani		
20	„ Najm Malik		
21	„ Malik Rustam		
22	„ Mehndi Mir		
23	„ Malik Mir		
24	„ Malik Jahar		
25	Sáad Ulla Khan		
26	„ Karun Beg		
27	„ Jalil Khan		
28	„ Rustam Beg		
29	„ Atta Ulla Khan		
30	„ Khalil Khan		

	Names.	Probable Date.	
31	Saád Yakub Khan		
32	„ Mir Ghazi		
33	„ Malik Purnur		
34	„ Babúr Malik		
35	„ Mokhim Khan		
36	„ Shah Azim Beg		
37	„ Gohar Beg		
38	„ Malik Shah Shujá	A.D.	
39	Sultan YAGU	1410	
40	„ Yagu Latif Beg	1425	
41	„ Yagu Sher Ghazi ...	1440	
42	„ Yagu Ahmed Ghazi ...	1455	
43	„ Nur Ghazi	1470	
44	„ Alemgir Ghazi	1485	
45	„ BIWÂN-CHO	1500	
46	„ Hil Ghazi	1515	
47	„ Sher Ghazi	1530	
48	„ Beg Mantar	1545	
49	„ Torab Khan	1560	
50	„ Sălmundé	1575	
51	„ Brol Dé	1590	
52	„ Malik Baz	1605	
53	„ Arzona	1620	
54	„ Tikam	1635	
55	„ Bikam	1650	
56	„ Kurkor	1665	
57	„ Bairam	1680	
58	„ Mir Khan	1695	
59	„ Ibrahim	1710	
60	„ Ghazi Mir Cho	1725	
61	„ Husen Khan	1740	
62	„ Rahim Khan	1755	
63	„ Hatim Khan	1770	
64	„ Daolut Khan	1785	
65	„ Mahmud Ali Khan ...	1800	
66	„ Yahia Khan	1815	
67	„ Daolut Ali Khan ...	1830	now reigning.
	has a son, Md. Ali Khan.		

Keris. The small district of Keris is situated along the lower course of the Shayok, just above its junction with the Indus. It is about sixteen miles in length, and ten miles in mean breadth. Its area is not more than 160 square miles, and the mean height of its villages above the sea is about 8,000 feet. The present chief, Kuram Ali Khan, claims descent from Biwan-cho, one of the Gyalpos of Khapolor, and he gives the following genealogy of that family.

	Names.	Probable Date.	
1	Biwan-cho	1500	
2	Lëo	1540	
3	Raja Ali Mir Sher	1575	
4	Ahmed Mir	1610	
5	Amir	1645	
6	Ali Khan...	1680	{ reigning in A.D. 1685.
7	Mir-Beg	1715	
8	Mirza-Beg	1750	
9	Zulfikar Khan	1785	
10	Kuram Ali Khan	1820	

Parguta. The present chiefship of Parguta extends from Sarmik, ten miles above the confluence of the Shayok and Indus, to Goltari, near the junction of the Drás river, thus including both Khartakshe (or Khar-Mang) and Tolti. Its length is about forty-three miles; its mean breadth thirty-two miles; and its area 1,548 square miles. The mean height of its villages above the sea is about 7,800 feet.

The Gyalpo of Parguta claims to be the eleventh in descent from the Makpon Bokka, who is perhaps the same as the fakir whom Vigne mentions as the progenitor of all the Makpon families. The following is the genealogy, with the probable dates of accession.

	Names.	Probable Date.	
1	Makpon Bokha	1500	
2	„ Sher	1530	
3	„ Ghazi	1560	
4	„ ALI SHER KHAN ...	1590	
5	„ Ahmed Khan	1620	
6	„ Sher Shah	1650	
7	„ Azizcho	1680	
8	„ Azim Khan	1710	
9	„ Sahadat Khan	1740	
10	„ Abdul Rahim	1770	
11	Mahomed Ali	1800	
12	Ali Sher Khan	1830	
	Son, Jafar Ali Khan.		

Ali Sher Khan, the fourth in descent from Bokha, conquered Ladák and Khapolor, and bequeathed them to his son, Ahmed Khan, who was the last of the supreme Makpons. On his death the country was divided amongst his sons: but the former chief of Khapolor soon declared his independence, and ejected the new ruler, Sultan Khan. The Gyalpos of Balti always selected their wives from this family, as the most exalted of their neighbours

Shigar. The little chiefship of Shigar is confined entirely to the valley of the Shigar river, a large feeder of the Indus, to the north of Balti. Its length, from south-east to north-west, is seventy-two miles, and its breadth thirty-six miles. Its area is 2,592 square miles; and the probable mean height of its villages above the sea is not less than 8,000 feet. Shigar possesses a Gyalpo of its own, but he has generally been subject to the chiefs of Balti. The following genealogy was obtained from Sulimán Khan, the present chief of Shigar. It is curious, for two reasons—first, because the title of *Tham*, or King, borne by the earlier princes, proves that the family must be connected with the Dards of Hunza-Nager, whose chiefs bear the same title at present; and second, because the approximate date obtained for the first chief's accession, agrees very nearly with that of Sultan Yagu, of Khapolor. It is probable, therefore, that the Khapolor and Shigar families both owe their rise to some common cause, perhaps connected with the extension of the Muhammedan religion.

	Name.	Probable Date.	
1	Ámáchah	1440	
2	Châh-tham	1455	
3	Chama-tham	1470	
4	Yaksir Gao-tham	1485	
5	Khomulgo-tham	1500	
6	Gobúlgo-tham	1515	
7	Khân	1530	
8	Makhân	1545	
9	Ram	1560	
10	Rahmûm	1575	
11	Daolat Shah	1590	
12	Haripal Marchak	1605	
13	Ambarot	1620	
14	Ghazi Mir	1635	
15	Ali Mir	1650	
16	Ama Chan Dé	1665	
17	Ghir-ze	1680	
18	Haidar Khan	1695	
19	Hasan Khan	1710	
20	Imâm Kuli Khan	1725	
21	Kuli Khan	1740	
22	Azem Khan	1755	
23	Ali Khan...	1770	
24	Husen Khan	1785	

	Name.	Probable Date.	
25	Mohammed Khan	1800	
26	Kuli Khan	1815	
27	Sulimân Khan	1830	

Balti, or *Balti-yul*, is called Palolo, or Balor, by the Dards, and *Nang-kod* by the Tibetans. Balti is the most common name, and perhaps the oldest, as it is preserved by Ptolemy in Byltæ. The country is also frequently called Skardo, from the name of its well-known fort and capital. This name means either the "inclosed place," or more probably the "starry place," as the Lamas of Ladak write the name, *Skar-ma-mDo.** Vigne states that the Botis of Ladak call it Sagar-khoad,† which is only a variety of the same; for Skar-kod means simply the "starry building." The Dogra soldiers always call the place Kardo; but the true name, as written by the Tibetans, is Skardo.

Balti proper is a small district bounded by Shigar on the north, by Keris and Parguta on the east, by Gures on the south, and by Astor and Rongdo on the west. Including the table-land of Deotsu, it is about

* The name is written *Skár-mDo*, or *Skar-ma-mDo*, and is so pronounced by the people. *I*skardo is a cockneyism of the Kashmiris, for no Musulmán can pronounce the double consonants in *s*, without putting an *i* before them, as in the common name of *iSmith*. A remarkable instance of this peculiarity is found in the name of a place in Wákhán, which Marco Polo calls *Scassem*, and Wood, *Ishkashm*. As Wákhán was still a Kafir country when Taimur invaded India, the initial *i* must have been added by the Musulmáns. The double consonants in *s*, and the letter *v* are the Shibboleth of the Musulmáns.

† Travels, vol. ii. p. 249. *Skar-hGod*, is the proper name. Vigne's derivation of Skar-kod (Sagar-khoad) from words in two different languages, from *Sagara*, the ocean, in Sanskrit, and *do*, two, in Persian, is quite inadmissible. *Sagar* is only another attempt to pronounce the double consonant *Sk* in *Skar*.

sixty miles long and thirty-six miles broad. Its area is about 2,160 square miles, and the mean height of its villages above the sea is about 7,000 feet.

The Gyalpos of Balti trace their descent from a Fakir who married the daughter and only child of the ruling sovereign. As the chiefs of Parguta, who are of the same family, trace their descent from Makpon Bokha, it is probable that the Fakir and Bokha are the same person. The story, as related to Vigne by Ahmed Shah himself, is as follows:—The last Gyalpo had an only daughter, whose hand was sought by twelve petty chiefs. Before any choice was made, a fakir was found sitting on a large stone in the village of Shikari. He remained seated day and night, and in a short time acquired a reputation for sanctity; after which the young lady was given to him by the consent of all parties. In proof of this story, the people still show the holy stone called *Burdonas*,* or the "smooth stone cushion," on which the holy man was wont to rest, and on which the heir apparent was always inaugurated on his reaching manhood.

The following is the genealogy of the Gyalpos of Balti, with the probable dates of their accession.

	Name.	Probable Date.	
1	ALI SHER	1590	conquered Ladák.
2	Ahmed	1620	
3	Shah Murad	1650	
4	Rafi Khân	1680	
5	Sultân Murâd Khân ...	1710	
6	Zafar Khan	1740	
7	Ali Sher Khan	1770	
8	Ahmed Shah	1800	deposed by Zoráwar Sing.
9	Mahomed Shah ...	1840	

* Vigne, Travels, vol. ii. p. 251, calls the stone Burdo Nest, but the true name is *dBur-rDo-rNgas*, or *Burdoñas*.

Ali Sher, a descendant of the Fakir, is the first chief of whom anything is mentioned. He built the fort of Skardo, and conquered Ladák in the reign of Jehangir, or about A.D. 1610.* His son Ahmed Shah lost Ladák. Shah Murad, the third prince, is said to have taken possession of Gilgit, Hunza-Nager, and Chitral, and to have reconquered Ladák. His reign extended from about 1720 to 1750 A.D., and his conquest of Ladák was probably only a plundering excursion into the western districts, which the plunderers dignified with the name of a conquest. The last independent chief was Ahmed Shah. In 1840 his country was invaded by Zoráwar Sing, and after a short siege, the fort of Skardo surrendered for want of water. In the winter of 1841, Ahmed Shah accompanied the unfortunate expedition against Lhasa; and on Zoráwar Sing's death, was taken prisoner and confined in Balwáltè near Lhasa, where he soon after died. Balti is now held in jaghir by Muhammad Shah, the disinherited son of Ahmed Shah, who pays an annual tribute of Rs. 7,000 to Maharaja Guláb Sing, of Kashmir.

Rongdo is the last Tibetan district on the Indus to the westward of Balti. On the north lie Shigar and Hunza-Nager, and to the west and south are Gilgit and Astor. The name† means the "district of defiles," and is descriptive of the bed of the Indus, which throughout Rongdo is a deep rocky gorge. The district extends from Gurbidas to a tree at Makpon-i-Shang-Rong, a distance of forty-five miles, with a mean breadth of thirty-two miles. Its area is about 1,440 square miles, and the mean height of its villages about 6,200 feet.

* See also Vigne, vol. ii. p. 253.

† *Rong-mDo,* "Defile-district."

The chief of Rongdo claims descent from the Makpons of Balti, to whom the district has always been subject.

The following list gives the genealogy of the chiefs, with the probable dates of accession.

	Name.	Probable Date.	
1	ALI SHER	1590	
2	Ahmed Khan	1620	
3	Ali Shah	1650	
4	Daolat Sher	1680	
5	Assad Ulla Khan	1710	
6	Mahomed Ali Khan	1740	
7	Murad Khan	1770	
8	Abbas Beg	1800	
9	Ali Khan...	1830	now reigning.
	Husen Khan (son)		
	Abdullah Khan (grandson)		

DARDU DISTRICTS ON THE INDUS.

Of the country inhabited by the Dards, my information is scanty but interesting. When I was in Kashmir I found the Vazirs of Gilgit and Nager in attendance upon the Maharaja Guláb Sing, by whose permission they came twice to visit me. As they both spoke Persian and a little Hindustani, I obtained from them tolerably complete vocabularies of the dialects of their own districts, and a less perfect vocabulary of the dialect of Chitrál. The words in these vocabularies are correctly written according to the spelling in the Persian character, which all the Dards make use of in writing their own language, of which there are three distinct dialects,—the Shiná, the Khajunah, and the Arniya.

The *Shiná* dialect is spoken by the people of Astor, Gilgit, Chelas, Darél, Kohli, and Pálas.

The *Khajunah* dialect is spoken by the people of Hunza and Nager.

The *Arniya* is spoken in Yasan and Chitrál.

These dialects have little in common with each other, and are widely different from those of the surrounding people.

Astor is situated on the left bank of the Indus, below Makpon-i-Shang-Rong. It has an area of about 1,600 square miles. Its chief claims descent from Ali Sher of Balti, and takes the title of Makpon.

*Gilgit** is situated on the right bank of the Indus, along the lower course of the Gilgit river. It is about 100 miles long from north to south, with a mean breadth of twenty-six miles. Its area is therefore about 2,500 square miles. The chief takes the title of Trakhna, from an ancestor.

The districts of Chélas, Darél, Kohli, and Pálas, lie along both banks of the Indus below Gilgit and Astor.

Hunza-Nager is a small tract of country on the upper course of a large feeder of the Gilgit river. It is named from two towns situated close to each other, on opposite banks of the river. The two districts have an area of 1,672 square miles. The chief of Hunza is called Girkhis, and the chief of Nager is called Mágalato. The former name is no doubt the same as the Kirghis, who inhabit the steppes of Pamer to the north of Hunza-Nager beyond the Kárákoram. I presume that this district was formerly inhabited by the Dards, and that they were displaced by the Kirghis nomads. The chiefs of Shigar who take the Khajunak title of Tham, must also be Kirghis.

Yasan is a large district on the upper course of the

* In Tibetan *Gyil-gyid*.

Gilgit river. It is seventy miles long from south-east to north-west, with a mean breadth of sixty miles. Its area is therefore about 4,200 square miles. The chief places are Yasan and Chatorkun. The chief takes the title of Bakhto, which is the name of his tribe.

When Mahmud Ghaznavi invaded India in A.D. 1030, the people of Gilgit, Astor, and Chélas were Turks, who spoke the Turki language.* These Turks were of the *Bhatâwari* tribe, and their king took the title of *Bhata Shah*, or king of the *Bhata* tribe. I presume that these are the same as the Bakhto of the present day; but their language has become mixed with that of all the surrounding people, and no longer bears any affinity to Turki.

Chitrál is a large district on the upper course of the Kunar river. The king takes the title of Shah Kator, which has been held for nearly 2,000 years, and the story of their descent from Alexander may be traced to the fact that they were the successors of the Indo-Grecian kings in the Kabul valley.

The large and interesting country of Kashmir, and the small principalities of the Alpine Panjáb to the south of Ladák, are too numerous to be treated of in this place.

To the east and south-east of Ladák lie the Chinese districts of Rudok, Chang-Thang, and Ngari.

Rudok lies immediately to the east of Ladák and Rukchu, but its climate is like that of the latter district. The principal feature of Rudok is the great Pang-kong lake, which stretches through the whole length of the country from east to west, a distance of about eighty miles. As the mean breadth is about sixty miles, the

* Reinaud's Fragmens Arabes, &c. p. 117.

area of this district will be 4,800 square miles. The mean height is probably not under 14,500 feet, as the lake has an elevation of 14,200 feet above the sea.

Chang-Thang comprises the two districts of Chumurti and Garo on the Indus, but its extent to the eastward is unknown. The monastery of Tashigong is the chief place in those districts; but the government of the country is in the hands of the Gar-pon or Deputy Governor of Garo.

*Ngari** embraces the whole of the upper valley of the Sutluj, from the Manasarovara lake to the crest of the Porgyal mountain. It is subdivided into three smaller districts, Gugé, Gangri, and Purang. Gugé is the largest of the three, and contains the well-known towns of Tholing and Tsaprang. Gangri is the country around the holy lakes, and Purang is the upper valley of the Gogra or Karnali river.

* *mNgah-ris.* This district is called *Hyun-des* (Sanskrit, *Hima-des*) by the Hindus of the Cis-Himalayas; *hyun* being their term for snow. *Hyun-des* has been supposed to mean the Huns; but the name is not *Huna-des*, but *Hyun-des*, "Snow-country," which is a literal translation of the Tibetan name of *Kha-pa-chan*, or "Snow-land." The hill word *hyun* reminds one of the Greek *χιων*.

III.—MOUNTAINS.

I.—GENERAL REMARKS.

The great Himálaya, which bounds India to the north, in one continuous chain of gigantic peaks, from the southward bend of the Brahmaputra to the holy lake of Manasoravara, is extended to the westward from the sources of the Sutluj to the magnificent peaks of Dayamur; and from thence to the sources of the Gilgit and Kunar rivers, where it joins the mountains of Pamer and Hindu Kush. Though less lofty than the eastern Himálaya, the western half of the chain is second to none else; and it is probable that some of its peaks may yet be found superior even to the most elevated of the Andes.* A single glance at the map of India will show the reasons that have induced me to consider the Bara-Lacha range as the continuation of the true Himálaya. It will be seen that the Eastern Himálaya divides the waters of the Tsang-po from those of the Ganges and its tributaries, while the Bara-Lacha forms the water-shed between the Indus and its five affluents. It

* The highest peaks of the Andes are *Sorata*, 25,267 feet; Illimani, 23,952 feet; and Chimborazo, 21,440 feet. The mean of the *three* is 23,553 feet. The highest peaks in the Western Himalaya are, Nanda Devi (or Jawáhir), 25,749 feet; Gyu Peak, 24,764 feet; Monomangli, 23,900 feet; and Porgyal, 22,700 feet. The mean of these *four* peaks is 24,278 feet.

will also be seen that the western, as well as the eastern chain, separates the great Hindu family of India from the Botis of Tibet. Some mixed races are found to the south of each chain: the Láhulis and Kanáwaris to the west, and the Gorkhas and Bhutánis to the east. Lastly, it will be seen that both ranges form the lines of demarcation between the cold and dry climate of Tibet, with its dearth of trees, and the warm and humid climate of India, with its luxuriance of vegetable productions. These facts, joined to the great elevation of the range, are, I think, sufficient to warrant the selection of the Bara-Lacha chain as the continuation of the true Himálaya. But there is one marked difference between the eastern and western ranges which can scarcely fail in striking the most casual observer. The inferior mountains of the eastern chain generally run at right angles to its axis, whereas those of the western chain are mostly disposed in subordinate parallel ranges. The general parallelism of the principal mountain-ranges of the world,—of the Himálayas and the Altai, in Asia,—of the Atlas, in Africa,—and of the Alps and Apennines, the Pyrenees and Carpathians, in Europe,—has already been noticed by Humboldt and others. But this parallelism also exists in the subordinate ranges of the western Himálaya. Thus we find no less than two distinct and independent ranges to the south of the western Himálaya, both stretching in the same general direction from south-east to north-west. These ranges I propose to call the *Mid-Himálaya*, and the *Outer*, or *Sub-Himálaya*, leaving the name of Sewálik unchanged for the lowermost sandstone ranges.

Beyond the Himálaya the same system of parallel chains will be observed in at least three distinct ranges of mountains, which I propose to call the *Trans-Himálaya*, the *Chushal*, and the *Kárákoram*, or *Trans-Tibetan* chains. These names are by no means intended to supersede any that may now exist, but only as descriptive appellations of extensive mountain-ranges which at present have no general names.

1st. The *Trans-Tibetan* range is that which we call the Bolor and Kárákoram, on the west; and which probably merges into the Kuen-lun, on the east.* It is in fact the northern limit of the Tibetan people, and of their peculiar language. To the north are the people of Balti, Ladák, and Chang-Thang, who were known to Ptolemy as the Byltæ and *Chatæ Scythæ*.

2nd. The *Kailás*, or *Gangri* range, runs through the midst of western Tibet, along the right bank of the Indus, to the junction of the Shayok. Neither Moorcroft nor Vigne has given any name to this range, though both of them crossed it several times, and in different places. I have ventured to call it the *Kailás*, or *Gangri* range, because those names are equally celebrated by the Hindus and Tibetans. *Kailás*, or "Ice-mountain," is the Indian Olympus, the abode of Siva and the celestials. *Gang-ri*, or "Ice-mountain," is called *Ri-gyal*, or King of Mountains, by the Tibetans, who look upon Ti-se, or the Kailás Peak, as the highest mountain in the world.†

* Humboldt's Cosmos, vol. ii. p. 154. "The Hindu Kush, or Indian Caucasus, is a continuation of the Kuen-lun of North Tibet."

† *Kailás* means "crystalline, or icy," and is derived from *Kelás*, crystal, which is itself a compound of *ke*, water, and *las*, to shine. The Tibetan name of Gangri (*Gangs-Ri*) means "ice-mountain," and *Rigyal* (*Ri-rGyal*) means "mountain king." This is the origin of the name of Mount *Argillos*, which Plutarch (De Fluviis) gives to the mountain on which Bacchus was born. Mount *Righi*, in Switzerland, is the same as the Tibetan *Ri-ga*, the mountain.

3rd. The *Trans-Himálayan* range divides the head-waters of the Sutluj from those of the Indus, and extends to the western limits of Rongdo and Astor.

4th. The *Bara-Lacha* (or Western Himálaya) has already been noticed. It is the main chain of this vast maze of mountains, and even on the banks of the Indus, where all the other ranges dwindle, the true Himálaya maintains its lofty supremacy in the magnificent peaks of Dayamur.*

5th. The *Mid-Himálaya,* or *Pir-Panjál* range, divides the valleys of Spiti, Lahul, Kashtwar, and Kashmir, on the north, from those of Kullu, Punach, and Chamba on the south, and terminates on the western bank of the Indus, in the celebrated peak of Mahában.

6th. The *Outer*, or *Sub-Himálaya,* stretches through Sukhet and Mandi, to the westward, between Kangra and Chamba, where it is called the *Dhaola Dhár*, or White Mountain. Still further west it forms the Ratan Panjál, and terminates in the well-known peak of *Gandgarh.*

These different ranges form the principal features, and consequently the natural boundaries of the hill states of the Panjáb. The whole mass of mountains, from the crest of the Kárákoram range to the plains of the Panjáb, has an average breadth of 250 miles. The breadth of the Himálaya, from the crest of the Bara-Lacha range to the plains, is about one-half of the whole breadth; for though not more than ninety miles broad from Lahul to Hushiarpoor, it is nearly 150 miles broad through Kashmir to Jammu, on the south. Its length, from the source of the Indus to the source of the Gilgit river, is 600 miles.

* See Plates II. and III. for views of this splendid mountain, which I have seen from Ramnagur in the Panjáb.

A. Cunningham, Delt from a sketch by Dr. Bates. Day & Son Lithrs to the Queen.

View of DAYAMUR

from the Bed of the Astor River

II.—1st. TRANS-TIBETAN RANGE.

The *Kárákoram*, or *Trans-Tibetan* chain, forms the natural boundary of Ladák, and the small Musulmán districts of Balti, Hunza-Nager, and Gilgit on the north. Nothing whatever is known of this range to the eastward of the upper Shayok river, and of the northern portion we know but little. At the head of the Shayok river, it is called Kárá Koram, which is a Turki word, signifying the "Black Mountains." To the north of Balti it is known as the Bolor range: but this name is only the common appellation of Balti, amongst all the races of Dardu origin. It is, however, of some value, as it enables us to state precisely that the Bolor mountains, which have hitherto occupied an uncertain position in our maps, are no other than the mountains of Balti. As this district formerly included Hunza-Nager and Gilgit, the Bolor mountains may now be defined as extending for 300 miles from the source of the Gilgit and Yasan rivers, in east longitude 73°, to the source of the Nubra river, in east longitude 77°. From the latter point eastward, as far as the most remote sources of the Shayok river, the continuation of the chain, about 150 miles in length, is best known as the Kárákoram range. The whole length of the chain, from the eastern sources of the Shayok to the head of the Gilgit river, is 450 miles, the general direction being from east to west.

The learned Humboldt supposes the Bolor mountains to be the transverse chain, running from north to south across the Indian Caucasus, and dividing the sources of the Oxus from those of the Yarkand and Kashgar rivers. But that chain is universally called Pamer, a name which it has borne for many centuries. In A.D. 632-40, the Chinese pilgrim Hwan-Thsang mentions the district of *Pho-mi-lo*, or Pamer, which he makes 167 miles in length from west to east. To the south of Pamer he places *Po-lu-lo*, or Bolor, of which he says that the south-eastern part of the district is inhabited, and that the country produces much gold. Both these facts are true of the present Bolor or Balti; the higher mountains, moreover, abound in rock-crystal, which is consequently called the Belor-stone, or simply Belor. The transverse north and south range of mountains is called *Belut-Tágh*, or the "Cloudy Mountains;" and this name has, I believe, been confounded with Bolor.* Marco Polo is the next who mentions Pamer and the neighbouring districts: I have two copies of his works before me, but they differ so much that I feel quite puzzled which to follow. After the mention of Pamer, the earlier copy has the following—"From hence, the way to Kathay leads for forty days' journey between the *east* and the north-east, through mountains, hills, and valleys, in which there are many rivers, but no villages, except that some huts and cottages are to be seen amongst the mountains. * * * * The country is called *Palow*." The other copy thus renders the above—"Leaving this place, he (the traveller) has to go on forty days between *north* and north-east, and passes many rivers and deserts; and in all this journey finds neither verdure nor habitation. This country is called Belor. The people live in very lofty mountains." In the later copy, the editor

* In speaking, the two T's in Belut-Tágh would coalesce, and the traveller, who knew that *Tágh* meant a mountain, would conclude that *Belu-Tagh* was the true name, which would at once be confounded with Belur-Tágh.

(Hugh Murray) has apparently corrected the Palow of the older copy to agree with his own identification, and has moreover changed the direction from north-east by *east*, to north-east by *north*, perhaps with a view of bringing it nearer to the true bearing of Kashgár, which is the next place mentioned. Now it is evident from Hwan-Thsang's* statement, that the district of *Pa-lo-lo*, or Bolor, must, in his day, have extended to the north of the Kárákoram range, and that the northern portion from Sir-i-kol to Khafalun, was then, as now, almost uninhabited. This, therefore, in my opinion, is the country which Marco Polo describes.

The Kárákoram Pass was traversed by the Chinese pilgrim Fa-Hian, in A.D. 399.† He calls the range *Tsung-Ling*, or "Onion Mountains," a name which they must have received from the number of wild leeks that grow upon them, and scent the air in all directions. They were found by Dr. Thomson on the elevated plateaux to the south of the pass. Mir Izzet Ullah no doubt alludes to the strong and unpleasant smell of these wild leeks, when he ascribes the headache and difficulty of breathing that are usually attendant on ascending great heights, to the *Esh*, which is a Turki word, signifying "smell."‡

The actual height of only one point in this range has

* Fo-kwe-ki. Appendix. The situation of Belor to the *South* of the Kárákoram is also distinctly proved by the testimony of Abu Rihán, who accompanied Mahmud Ghaznavi to India. Speaking of Kashmir he says, " La partie située au midi et à l'orient appartient aux Indiens, et la partie qui se trouve à l'occident dépend de plusieurs rois, dont *le plus proche* est Belor Shah," that is, the king of Balti.

† Fo-kwe-ki, c. iv.

‡ Quarterly Oriental Magazine, March, 1825, p. 113. The Gerards attributed their headaches to the same cause.

yet been ascertained, namely, the Kárákoram Pass, which Dr. Thomson found to be 18,660 feet above the sea. Vigne was of opinion that the height of this pass would be found "somewhat under 15,000 feet," and Mr. Thornton argues, in favour of this opinion, that it was sufficiently depressed to permit Mir Izzet Ullah's passage in the end of October. But though this argument will hold good for the southern Himálayas, it will only mislead when applied to the northern ranges of Tibet, on which the snow falls so scantily that many of them may be crossed even in December.* A single peak to the northward of Sassar was estimated by Dr. Thomson at 24,000 feet. The estimate may perhaps be a little too high, but I have great confidence in the accuracy with which a practised eye may measure heights.

To the eastward, this range maintains its superior elevation, as Captain H. Strachey found several of the passes, on one of its ramifications to the northward of Ruthog, to be between 18,000 and 19,000 feet in height. To the westward, the same general loftiness may be inferred, from the known heights of some peaks in the neighbouring ranges† of Hindu Kush and Pamer (or Belut-Tágh). The average height of the peaks may be estimated at 21,000 feet, and that of the passes at upwards of 18,000 feet. To the eastward of the Shigar valley, Dr. Falconer crossed a pass 16,200 feet, on a spur of the Kárákoram.

* On the 1st of December, Trebeck crossed the Manbár Pass, 16,500 feet high; and on the 9th of the same month he crossed the Chang-lá, which is not under 17,000 feet. Zoráwar Sing crossed the Umási-lá, between 18,000 and 19,000 feet, in October, and the Thung-lung, 17,500 feet, in the end of November or beginning of December.

† Hindu Kush, according to Macartney, 20,493; and by Wood, 20,248; and the Pamer Peaks, 19,000.

Vigne* was informed by the Yarkandi merchants that "the snow does not remain upon Kárákoram for the greater part of the year." But my informants, who were also Yarkandi merchants, stated exactly the reverse; and we know that Izzet Ullah, in the beginning of November, found snow and ice the whole way over the pass. It is always difficult to ascertain the snow limit from the information of travellers and merchants, who, though they generally discriminate sporadic falls of snow, yet very rarely make any distinction between beds of snow sheltered in ravines, and the mass of exposed snow on the mountains that braves the noon-day heat of a whole summer. I believe that the Kárákoram Pass is rarely, if ever, entirely free from snow, although at no period of the year does the snow accumulate upon it in any great mass. There was of course much snow on the pass when Dr. Thomson ascended it in July 1848, and it was lying much lower on the northern than on the southern face. The probability is that the Kárákoram Pass has about the same elevation as the snow-line of the range, and this would at once account for the discrepancies of the different authorities. I would therefore fix a height of 18,500 feet as the snow limit on the southern face, and of 18,000 feet or even less, for the northern face.† For the snow-line, which in Rukchu is about 20,000 feet, has already begun to descend, and in the Pamer range to the north of the Kárákoram has been estimated by Wood at rather more than 17,000 feet.‡

In the Shayok and Nubra valleys, the prevailing rock is limestone.§ Granite occurs in the ridge between the

* Kashmir, II. p. 364.

† See Plate I.

‡ Wood's Oxus, p. 364.

§ Izzet Ullah, Dr. Thomson.

rivers, and clay-slate towards the source of the Shayok. The limestone continues towards Ruthog, and the waters of the Pangkong lake hold a sufficient quantity of lime to form a calcareous deposit, which cements the pebbles together in patches of concrete at the bottom of the lake. But the mass of mountain is composed of granite and gneiss, which in this, as well as in the other lofty ranges of India and Tibet, form the highest peaks and crests of the ridges.

III.—2nd. KAILÁS RANGE.

The *Kailás* or *Gangri* range runs through the midst of Western Tibet along the right bank of the Indus, from its source to the junction of the Shayok. At this point it is cut both by the Indus and by the Shigar river; beyond which it stretches to the north-west, dividing the two valleys, and is terminated at the junction of the Hunza and Nager rivers. The general direction is from south-east to north-west, and the whole length of the range from the celebrated peak of Kailás to Hunza-Nager is not less than 550 miles. In many of our maps the main stream of the Indus or Singgé-chu, is laid down to the northward of the Kailás mountains, and the Garo river or Higong-chu is degraded to a mere tributary, which falls into the great river at Tashigong. But all my informants agreed in stating that the Garo river was the *Singgé-chu* or Indus, and that the stream which joined it at Tashigong was not larger than the Hanlé river. The Kailás or Gangri range therefore extends in one unbroken chain from the source of the Indus to the junction of the Shayok. It forms the natural boundary between Ladák, Balti, and

Rongdo on the south, and Ruthog, Nubra, Shigar, and Hunza-Nager on the north.

This range has been often crossed by Europeans, but always on the same high roads, which generally lead over the lowest and easiest passes. We have the heights of six of these passes in different parts of the range.

	Passes.	Feet.	Authority.
1	Tsaka-la	15,000	Trebeck.
2	Kongta-la	15,495	Moorcroft, MS.
3	Chang-la	18,105	Ditto do.
4	Lazgung or Sabu-lá ...	17,666	Dr. Thomson.
5	Lé Pass	17,600	Ditto.
6	Hanu Pass	16,890	Col. Bates.
	Mean height	16,792 or 16,800 feet.	

As the average height of these passes approaches 17,000 feet, the general elevation of the range may be estimated at not less than 20,000 feet. The height of the celebrated Kailás peak has been determined by Lieut. R. Strachey at 20,700 feet. A peak which I measured on one of the spurs of the range to the north of Mahé was 18,500 feet. In this part, as we may see from the heights of the Kongta-la and Tsakala Passes, the range is much depressed, but in the neighbourhood of Lé, wherever I could see the ridge, it was entirely covered with snow in the beginning of October. As the lofty passes to the northward of Lé are said to be always clear of snow at the end of summer, the snow-line on the Kailás or Mid-Tibetan range may be estimated at 19,000 feet,* or more, on the southern face;

* In the Journal As. Soc. Bengal, vol. xviii. p. 302, Lieut. R. Strachey estimates the snow-line on the southern face of Kailás at not less than 19,500 feet, which agrees with my observations. See Plate I.

and at 18,500 feet on the northern face. In the south-eastern portion of the range, between the elevated table-lands of Chang-Thang, Rukchu, and Ngári, the snow-limit will of course be higher than in the north-western portion, which divides the valley of the Indus from the Shayok. In the neighbourhood of Lé, therefore, we cannot estimate the height of this range at less than 20,000 feet; and although it may be somewhat depressed between the Pangkong and Tshomoriri lakes, yet it rises again towards the south-eastern extremity, where the lofty peak of Kailás towers over the holy lakes of Manasarovara and Ráw-an Hrad. On this part of the range the snow never disappears, and this fact has originated the name of the mountain both in Sanskrit and in Tibetan, in which languages Kailás and Gangri respectively mean the "Ice Mountain."

The geological structure of this range is chiefly clay-slate, gneiss, and granite. In the neighbourhood of Lé it is wholly of granite of a very coarse texture.

IV.—3rd. TRANS-HIMÁLAYAN RANGE.

This range is a branch of the lofty *Ri-Gyal*, or King of Mountains, which it certainly equals, and perhaps surpasses in height. It branches off from the Gangri mountain to the south of Garo, and extends in one unbroken chain through the districts of Chumurti, Rukchu, and Zanskar, to the junction of the Zanskar river, which rushes dark and turbulent through a vast chasm in the mountain, where human foot has never trod. From this it extends to the junction of the Drás river with the Indus, where it is again cut through by the Drás river at a narrow gorge called the Wolf's Leap;* but beyond this point it stretches in one unbroken chain to the great southward sweep of the Indus at the junction of the Gilgit river. Its general direction is from south-east to north-west, and its extreme length is upwards of 350 miles. It forms the natural boundary between Ladák, Balti, and Rongdo on the north, and Rukchu, Zanskar, Purik, Drás, and Astor, on the south.

This range is much better known than either of the preceding chains. I have the measurement of four peaks determined by myself in 1847, and of no less than eleven passes, of which I have myself crossed five. The following are the heights of peaks in the neighbourhood of Hanlé, and in other parts of the range.

	Peaks.	Feet.	Authority.
1	Rongo Peak	20,786	A. Cunningham.
2	Changlung, N. Pk. ...	20,357	Ditto.
3	Changlung, S. Pk. ...	20,141	Ditto.
4	Hanlé Peak	20,650	Ditto.
5	Lának Peaks	20,000	Ditto.
6	Tshomoriri Peaks ...	21,000	Ditto.
7	Gya Peak, W. of Gya ...	21,000	Ditto.
8	Tok Peak (S. of Lé) ...	21,000	Ditto.
	Mean height	20,616 feet.	

The mean height of the peaks in the eastern part of the range, is therefore not less than 20,500 feet.

The following table shows the height of different passes in the eastern half of the range.

* Vigne, Map and Travels in Kashmir, vol. ii.

	Passes.		Feet.	Authority.
1	Pass above Chumur	...	18,500	Capt. H. Strachey.
2	Lának ...	... ...	18,746	A. Cunningham.
3	Nakpo-Gonding	...	18,000	Ditto.
4	Polokonka	... ...	16,500	Ditto.
5	Thunglung	... ...	17,500	Ditto.
6	Kandu Lá	... ...	16,600	Moorcroft.
7	Pangache Lá	... ...	16,495	Dr. Thomson.
8	Singgé Lá	... ...	16,952	Ditto.
		Mean height	17,911 feet.	

The Western half of the range beyond the valley of Zanskar becomes gradually lower and lower until it sinks suddenly into the Indus at the precipitous defile of Makpon-i-Shang-Rong. The following are the heights of some of the western passes.

	Passes.		Feet.	Authority.
1	Namyika	... ...	13,000	A. Cunningham.
2	Burgi Pass on Deotsu	...	15,600	Dr. Falconer.
3	Alampi Lá	... ...	15,500	Vigne corrected.
4	Sir-i-Kotul	... ...	16,000	Ditto.
5	Harpo-Lá	... ...	12,100	Col. Bates.
		Mean height	14,440 feet.	

On this half of the range the snow annually disappears, excepting on some of the loftier peaks which have not yet been measured. To the northward of Paskyum, I saw snow still lying in October 1847, but it was probably only new snow, which had been falling for some days before. I estimate the highest peak of this portion of the range at 17,000 feet. On the eastern half of the range in Rukchu and Ngári, the mean height of the snow-line is about 20,000 feet. Dr. Gerard* indeed asserts that on the southward aspect the snow "has no well-defined boundary at 21,000 feet;" and further that some of the points which he measured had "an absolute height of 22,000 feet free of snow." But a very slight examination of his own data will show that his most elevated snow-line was under 21,000 feet. In the month of September for two successive years, 1846 and 1847, I found snow lying on the ridges to the east and west of the Tshomoriri Lake, which rise to an elevation of 20,000 feet. This agrees with Dr. Gerard's observation, also made in the month of September, that the snow-line on the mountains to the north of the lake rose to a height of "20,000 feet and upwards."† Above this, he says, the snow rested "in vast bodies, having a cliff of several hundred feet." As he afterwards adds, that "it had ceased to melt," 20,000 feet or upwards (or about 20,000 feet) must be taken as the snow limit, as determined by Dr. Gerard's observations for the Tshomoriri mountains. In September 1847, I found the Lának Pass (18,746 feet) perfectly bare, but the peaks to the north and south of the pass (about 19,500 feet)

* Researches, Asiatic Society of Bengal, vol. xviii. pp. 254-56. But when he wrote the first account of his travels, which was read before the Asiatic Society of Bengal, his altitude of the snow line was less lofty. I quote his own words: "The whole circumference of Lake Chimorerel is embayed by mountains, but hillward, on its north-eastern shore, the mass of elevated land rose very abruptly from the water's edge, and entered the regions of snow, which had an *uniform margin* of 19,000 feet." This was the south-western aspect. See Plate I.

† As we have already seen, by the last note, that Dr. Gerard estimated the snow-line on these mountains at only 19,000 feet, the "20,000 feet and upwards," is perhaps intended for the actual height of the mountains themselves. Mr. Agnew and myself estimated them at between 20,000 and 21,000 feet.

had still large patches of snow upon their eastern and northern slopes. In the same month, the four peaks which I measured in the neighbourhood of Hanlé at different heights between 20,000 and 21,000 feet, and averaging 20,483 feet, were all partially covered with snow. The general height of the ridge was about 20,000 feet, and the snow was lying along nearly the whole line of crest to the west. On the eastern face it evidently descended lower, as on the Lának peaks. I estimate the snow-line of Rukchu at not more than 20,000 feet on the western and southern slopes, and at 19,500 feet, or even less, on the eastern and northern slopes.*

The great height of the snow-line on this range is caused chiefly by the radiation of heat from the elevated plains of Rukchu and Gáro, and by the reverberation of heat from the bare sides of the mountains. It is in part also due to its situation in the midst of lofty snowy mountains, which intercept the ascending vapours on all sides, and prevent the precipitation of moisture within this ice-bound region. As the mass of land rises, the snow-line recedes higher and higher, notwithstanding the increase of the latitude. This is shown clearly in Plate 1, which exhibits a section of the mountains from the southern base of the Himálaya to the northern foot of the Kárákoram. In this section the snow-line is seen to rise with the mass of land until both attain their greatest elevation in Rukchu. From this tract the snow-line descends as the country falls to the northward towards Yarkand and Kotan. But the fall is less rapid than the rise. From the eastern peaks of Kullu in latitude 31½°

* Plate I.

to the Lának and Hanlé ranges in Rukchu, the rise of the snow-line is fully 4,000 feet, while the increase of latitude is only one degree; but from Rukchu to Pamer the increase of latitude is five degrees, while the fall of the snow-line is only 3,000 feet. We must therefore attribute the greatest part of this difference to the influence of latitude.

Of the geological structure of this range I can only speak generally. The Lának ridge consists of a core of granite nearly overlaid by clay-slate. To the west of the pass, the plain of Dongan is strewn with rolled boulders of granite for several miles. Thence to the Thung Lung Pass the higher ridges are of gneiss, and the slopes of mica and clay-slates. Throughout Zanskar from the Lachalang Pass to the Singgé-lá the chief formation is limestone, and beyond that the ridge consists of mica and clay-slates crested by granite, which is the prevailing rock on the table-land of Deotsu. Trap occurs in the volcanic district between Hanlé and the hot-springs of Puga.

V.—4th. THE WESTERN HIMÁLAYA.

The great Himálaya forms a natural boundary between India and Tibet. On the east it presents the lofty peaks of Kanchinjinga and Dhwalagiri, which rise to the vast height of more than 28,000 feet. To the westward it is less known, but the peaks that have been measured between the sources of the Sutluj and the Chenáb give an average elevation superior to that of the Andes.

The general direction of the western Himálaya is the same as that of the other chains which have just been described, from south-east to north-west. The whole length of the chain from the peak of Monomangli to the sources of the Gilgit and Kunar rivers is not less than 650 miles. It is pierced in three places by rivers, by the Sutluj and Para at the base of Porgyal, and by the Indus at the foot of Dayamur. Its greatest elevation is the lofty peak of Nanda Devi (Jawáhir) 25,749 feet, and its greatest depression, the pass of Seoji-lá, 11,700 feet, between Kashmir and Ladák. Throughout its whole extent it forms the boundary between the races of Hindu origin and the pure Tibetans of Ladák and Balti. To the south-east it divides the Tibetan district of Garo from the Indian province of Kumaon. Midway it separates the Ladáki districts of Rukchu, Zanskar, Purik, and Drás, containing only pure Botis or Tibetans, from the provinces of Spiti, Kullu, Lahul, Kashtwar, and Kashmir, whose inhabitants are chiefly a mixed race of Indo-Tibetans. To the westward it was once the boundary between the Dards of Chelás and the Tibetans of Astor and Gilgit; but the Dards have since penetrated to the northward, and the Gilgitis of the present day are a mixed race of Dardo-Tibetans.

To the south of the Sutluj the heights of many of the loftiest peaks have been determined by Webb, Hodgson, and the Gerards, but to the north of the Sutluj, no heights were ascertained by them, except only that of Porgyal by Alexander Gerard. Beyond this, not more than five peaks have been measured, with more or less precision, but the general accuracy of these measurements is proved by the ascertained elevation of several passes. The following table gives all the heights to the south of the Sutluj.

	Peaks.	Height.	Authority.
1	Monomangli or Gurla ...	23,900	Lieut. R. Strachey.
2	Kunlas Peak	22,513	Trigonometrical Map.
3	Gula Ghal Peak ...	21,258	Ditto.
4	XX.	20,479	Ditto.
5	XIX.	22,707	Ditto.
6	XVIII.	22,511	Ditto.
7	XV.	22,491	Ditto.
8	Nanda Devi	25,749	Ditto.
9	XIII.	22,385	Ditto.
10	XII.	22,385	Ditto.
11	A No. 1	23,531	Ditto.
12	XI.	20,758	Ditto.
13	A No. 3	23,317	Ditto.
14	N	23,482	Ditto.
15	L	22,266	Ditto.
16	K	22,570	Ditto.
17	I	23,300	Ditto.
18	IX.	21,383	Ditto.
19	VIII.	23,236	Ditto.
20	Badrinath Peak ...	22,954	Ditto.
21	VII.	23,441	Ditto.
22	... ...	22,754	Ditto.
23	H	21,894	Ditto.
24	G	22,556	Ditto.
25	U	21,612	Ditto.
26	Kedarnath	23,062	Ditto.
27	M	22,792	Ditto.
28	St. Patrick	22,798	Ditto.
29	St. George	22,654	Ditto.
30	Rudru Himála	22,390	Ditto.
31	Swarga	22,906	Ditto.
32	The Pyramid	21,579	Ditto.
33	Jaonli Peak	21,940	Ditto.
34	E. C.	21,772	Ditto.
35	F.	21,964	Ditto.
36	G. Srikanta	20,296	Ditto.
37	Rock Peak	21,076	Ditto.
38	Windy Peak (Kyobrang)	20,169	Ditto.
39	Glacier Peak	20,544	Ditto.
40	Raldang or W. Kailás ...	21,103	Ditto.
	Mean height	22,274 feet.	

The distance from Monomangli to the Raldang and Kyobrang Peaks, is only 175 miles, and between these points we find no less than forty peaks, whose well ascertained heights exceed 20,000 feet, and which yield an average of more than 22,000 feet. The passes are less known, because only the most frequented have yet been measured. The heights, however, of nine of them, have been ascertained chiefly by the Gerards and Stracheys.

	Passes.	Height.	Authority.
1	Lankpya	17,750	Capt. H. Strachey.
2	Lakhar	18,300	Lieut. R. Strachey.
3	Unta dura	17,700	Ditto.
4	Kyungar Ghat	17,700	Ditto.
5	Balch dhura	17,700	Ditto.
6	Deo Ghat	18,000	Trigonometrical Map.
7	Niti Pass	16,570	
8	Kyobrang	18,331	Capt. A. Gerard.
9	Gangtang	18,295	Ditto.
	Mean height	17,816 feet.	

The average height of this part of the range, by taking the mean of the greatest elevation, and greatest depressions, is not therefore less than 20,000 feet.

To the westward, the heights of the following peaks and passes have been ascertained, with more or less accuracy.

	Peaks.	Height.	Authority.
1	Pyramidal Peak ...	20,106	Capt. A. Gerard.
2	Porgyal	22,700	Ditto.
3	Chang-Razing Peak ...	20,500	Dr. Gerard.

	Peaks.	Height.	Authority.
4	Gyu Peak*	24,764	A. Cunningham.
5	Parang Peaks	19,500	Ditto.
6	Zanskar Ridge	20,000	Dr. Thomson. A.C.
7	Ser and Mer	20,000	Hugel and Vigne.
8	Bal Tal Peak	19,650	Jacquemont.
9	Dayamur	20,000	Vigne. Col. Bates.
10	Peak to N. of Peshawur	20,493	Macartney.
	Mean height	20,771 feet.	

	Passes.	Height.	Authority.
1	Meyung Lá	17,700	Capt. Gerard.
2	Parang Lá	18,500	A. Cunningham.
3	Bara Lácha	16,500	Ditto.
4	Umási Lá	18,123	Dr. Thomson.
5	Seoji Lá	11,634	A. Cunningham.
6	Gutumi Pass	12,000	Vigne corrected.
	Mean height	15,743 feet.	

Taking the means of the greatest heights and greatest depressions, the average elevation of this portion of the range will be upwards of 18,000 feet; and as that of the other half was found to be upwards of 20,000 feet, the

* The height of this peak depends upon the correctness of the horizontal distance. From Chang-Razing it bore 152° 16′ West, with an elevation of 5° 24′ after correction for error of collimation. I estimated the distance at between twenty and thirty miles; and as I afterwards observed the same peak from the foot of the Lának Pass, I got another bearing which made the horizontal distance twenty-four miles. Should the distance be not more than twenty miles, the height will still be 22,659 feet; but the greater height is supported by the authority of Dr. Gerard, who, from his lofty station, 20,400 feet above Chang-Razing, saw *to the North* a detached group of white tops, which he concluded, from the angles they subtended, to be 24,000 feet above the sea. Researches Asiat. Soc. Bengal, vol. xviii. pp. 255, *note*.

mean height of the crest of the western Himálaya, from Monomangli to the source of the Gilgit river, may be assumed at 19,000 feet.

On this range the snow-line can be determined within very narrow limits. On the three passes crossed by Lieut. R. Strachey,* each about 17,700 feet, no snow was found in September. The Lakhar Pass, 18,300 feet, and the Jayanti Pass, 18,500 feet, were also free from snow. "But the line of perpetual snow was evidently near, for though the Jayanti ridge was quite free, and some of the near peaks were clear, to perhaps upwards of 19,000 feet, yet in more sheltered situations, unbroken snow could be seen considerably below the ridge:" and Lieut. Strachey concluded "that 18,500 feet must be nearly the average height of the snow-line at that place."†

Alexander Gerard found no snow on the Kyobrang Pass (18,313 feet), even in July, and it was equally bare when visited by Jacquemont. On Porgyal, in October, the Gerards‡ found no old snow below 19,400 feet, and their station on the Chang-Razing mountain, 20,400 feet, was also clear; but as Dr. Gerard mentions a range due north, and a peak to the westward, while he is perfectly silent regarding the lofty peaks to the south, it seems certain that their station was on the northern exposure of Porgyal. I can myself vouch for its southern faces being covered with masses of snow in the end of August

* Journal Asiat. Soc. Bengal, vol. xviii. pp. 298, 299.

† See Plate I.

‡ Researches Asiat. Soc. Bengal, vol. xviii. p. 254. The name of Por-Gyal is written *Spor-r Gyal*, the "lofty twins," the double Peak of Por-Gyal being compared to the constellation Gemini (*r Gyal*) the *s* is sometimes pronounced, just as in the name of Spiti, which is also called Piti, although it is invariably written Spiti by the Lamas.

and beginning of September 1847, when the northern side seemed generally bare. The absence of snow on the Pyramidal Peak of Porgyal, 20,106 feet, is more to the purpose, as it is certain that the Gerards could only have seen this peak from the south and west. On crossing the Manerang Pass, on the 30th of August, Alexander Gerard found the last half mile was over the perpetual snow, which he distinguishes from the fresh covering of the former night, in which the foot sank from three to twelve inches. On descending the Pass to the north, he "travelled over the snow for a mile." On recrossing the Pass, on the 7th September, he found that "the snow had not descended above 400 feet; but the great field of ages had a new and deep covering."* The snow, therefore, remains for the whole year on the Manerang Pass.

From the Manerang Pass, Alexander Gerard observed "very distinctly the Paralasa (Bara Lácha) range, covered with snow." I estimate the height of this part of the range at 19,500 feet. On the 8th September, 1847, I found no snow on the southern face of the Parang Pass, 18,500 feet, but there was a glacier one mile and a half in length, on the northern face, on which the snow was frozen hard. Snow was lying in patches on many of the peaks, at about 19,000 feet, but chiefly on the western and southern faces. The exposed faces to the north and east were bare. In September 1846, I crossed the Bara Lácha Pass, 16,500 feet, twice; and on both occasions found it entirely free from snow. The Umási-lá, 18,123 feet, was crossed by Dr. Thomson, in June, at which time it was, of course, covered with snow: but it was not clear in October 1846, when traversed by Vazir Gusaun, the minister of the Mandi Raja. In this part

* Alexander Gerard's Tour of 1821, pp. 155-56, Calcutta edition.

of the range, therefore, the snow limit does not exceed 18,000 feet, and is probably not more than 17,500 feet. On the Baltal Peak, 19,000 feet, close to the Seoji-lá, the snow remains throughout the year. Dayamur, or Nanga Parbat (the bare mountain) is, as its name implies, free from snow; but this is owing entirely to its precipitousness, which prevents the snow from finding any resting-place. Snow, however, does lie in the hollow between the peaks.

The following are the different heights of the snow limit on the western Himálaya.

	Snow Limit.	Height.	Authority.
1	On the Kumaun Range	18,500	Lieut. R. Strachey.
2	Pyramidal Pk. of Porgyal	20,106	A. and J. Gerard.
3	Manerang Range ...	18,000	A. Gerard.
4	Parang Range	19,000	A. Cunningham.
5	Bara Lácha to Umasi ...	17,500	Ditto.
	Mean height	18,021 feet.	

This height agrees so closely with the elevation deduced by Lieut. R. Strachey, that we may conclude, with some confidence, that the snow-line, on the southern face of the western Himálaya, is between 18,500 feet and 19,000 feet. On the northern exposure, the snow limit is somewhat higher. The Gerards, as we have seen, found the northern face of Porgyal bare, to a height of 20,400 feet. In September 1847, I observed very little snow on the northern faces of the Parang Peaks, about 19,500 feet, while in September 1846, the crest of this range, as I saw it from the banks of the Tshomoriri lake, was sheeted in snow. To the westward, as the ridge diminishes in height, with the general fall of the country, the snow-line falls somewhat lower, and in the neighbourhood of the Bara-Lacha Pass is not more than 18,000 feet. The mean of these observations is 19,133 feet, or in round numbers, upwards of 19,000 feet.*

The mass of the western Himálaya, from the Sutluj to the Indus, is limestone. The ridges of Kyobrang, Parang, and Umási-Lá, are all limestone, while the sides are chiefly overlaid with clay-slate. At Seoji Lá, the formation is mica-slate, but the mass of the northern mountains of Kashmir, and the peaks of the magnificent Dayamur, are all of limestone.

VI.—5th. THE MID-HIMÁLAYA, or PIR-PANJÁL RANGE.

This chain consists of four distinct masses of mountain, which may be styled the Bisahar, the Láhul, the Pir-Panjál, and the Swát ranges. The Bisahar range is an offshoot of the western Himálaya, extending for about sixty miles, from the lofty cluster of Jamnotri peaks to the Sutluj, below Shatúl. It is continued to the north of the Sutluj by the Láhul range, which stretches to the north-west for 160 miles, to the great southward sweep of the Chenáb, in Káshtwár. Beyond this again, it is continued in the same direction by the well-known Pir-Panjál, to the great southward sweep of the Jehlam, at Mozafarábád, and across the Jehlam to the Indus, at Derband. To the west of the Indus it terminates in the Swát mountains, which extend for about seventy miles to the junction of the Swát and Panjkora rivers. This portion of the chain, though not remarkable for its height, is worthy of most particular examination, for the

* See Plate I.

sake of identifying the celebrated Aornos, which was beyond all doubt situated in this range, and which I believe to have been the well-known mountains of Mahában.

The whole length of the Mid-Himálaya or Pir-Panjál range, from the Jamnotri peaks to the Swát river, is about 470 miles. Between the Jumna and the Indus the direction is from south-east to north-west, as in the other ranges; but beyond the Indus the Swát mountains run almost due east and west.

The general elevation of this range can be determined with tolerable accuracy from the ascertained heights of a considerable number of points. The following tables show the heights of the principal peaks and passes in the different portions of the range.

BISAHAR RANGE—PEAKS.

	Peaks.	Feet.	Authority.
1	Jamnotri, Great E. ...	20,916	Trigonometrical Map.
2	Ditto Black E. ...	21,155	Ditto.
3	Ditto Lower E. ...	20,122	Ditto.
4	H left	20,501	Ditto.
5	H right	20,668	Ditto.
6	H middle	20,668	Ditto.
7	The Cone	21,178	Ditto.
8	a No. 39	19,481	Ditto.
9	L	19,512	Ditto.
10	The Needle	19,044	Ditto.
11	J	17,425	Ditto.
12	l	17,331	Ditto.
13	h	17,337	Ditto.
14	g Shatul Peak	17,035	Ditto.
15	d or Pyramidal	17,174	Ditto.
16	b	16,982	Ditto.
17	a	17,044	Ditto.
	Mean height 19,033 feet.		

BISAHAR RANGE—PASSES.

	Passes.	Feet.	Authority.
1	Nalgun Pass	14,891	A. Gerard.
2	Rupin	15,460	Ditto.
3	Nibrang	16,035	Ditto.
4	Burang or Buranda ...	15,179	Ditto.
5	Yusu	15,877	Ditto.
6	Shatul	15,556	Ditto.
	Mean height	15,499 feet.	

By taking the mean heights of the peaks and passes, or greatest elevations and greatest depressions, we obtain the average height of the Bisahar range at 17,250 feet.

LÁHUL RANGE—PEAKS.

	Peaks.	Feet.	Authority.
1	Western F.	18,798	Trigonometrical Map.
2	Kotgarh Peak	17,353	Ditto.
3	No. 9 Black	16,203	Ditto.
4	k Peak	17,730	A. Cunningham.
5	j Obelisk Peak	18,062	A. Cunningham.
6	f	19,310	A. Cunningham.
7	e	19,366	A. Cunningham.
8	d	19,922	A. Cunningham.
9	c	19,948	A. Cunningham.
10	b	20,064	A. Cunningham.
11	a	21,786	A. Cunningham.
12	Kali Debi Peaks ...	18,500	A. Cunningham.
	Mean height	18,920 feet.	

LÁHUL RANGE—PASSES.

	Passes.	Feet.	Authority.
1	Rotang Pass	13,000	{ Moorcroft, Dr. Gerard, A. C.
2	Kali Debi Pass	16,700	A. Cunningham.
3	Saj Pass	15,500	Dr. Thomson.
	Mean height	15,066 feet.	

The mean height of the Láhul range is therefore close upon 17,000 feet, and that of the united Bisahar and Láhul ranges upwards of 17,000 feet.

PIR-PANJÁL RANGE.

Of the Pir-Panjál itself we know much less than of the other portions of the Mid-Himálaya. The height of the loftiest peak was ascertained by Jacquemont to be 15,000 feet, and that of the lowest pass 9,690 feet. The mean of these two gives 12,345 feet for the average height of the crest, which is certainly not too much, as the heights of two of the most frequented passes approach 12,000 feet. The Pir-Panjál Pass is 11,970 feet, and the Mirbal Pass is 11,400 feet; and the mean height of the three measured passes is 11,020 feet. The following are the heights of different points in the Pir-Panjál.

	Points.	Feet.	Authority.
1	Highest Peak	15,000	Jacquemont.
2	Tata kuti	14,000	A. Cunningham.
3	Dydyum	13,000	Vigne.
4	Kol-Narwah	12,500	Ditto.
	Mean height	13,625 feet.	

The mean of the mean heights of the peaks and passes is 12,322 feet, which agrees with the mean before deduced from the greatest elevation and greatest depression.

Of the height of the Swát range I cannot speak with any certainty. The peak of Mahában, as seen from the Yusufzai plain, at different distances between twenty-five and thirty miles, I estimated at 6,000 feet, or rather more, and the highest point in the range is probably not more than 7,000 feet.

On the Pir-Panjál and Swát ranges, the snow entirely disappears; but it remains throughout the year on the lofty ranges of Bisahar and Láhul. Of the glacial lines of the Bisahar ranges, we know but little, although the Gerards made a special excursion to most of the passes in this range for the purpose of ascertaining the snow-limit. The following passages, however, bear upon the subject and corroborate each other.

In describing the Buranda Pass (15,179 feet), which they visited in October, 1818,* the two brothers, Dr. John Gerard and Captain Alexander Gerard, state that "the eastern wall rises with a considerable inclination for 500 or 600 feet; thence starting backwards, it terminates in a crown of snow, perhaps 1,500 or 2,000 feet higher." * * * "Its western side rises to a towering summit deeply clad in snow, and corresponds with the opposite or eastern one, being about 2,000 feet in height." From these statements, we learn that both flanks of the pass were certainly bare of snow to 15,179 + 600 = 15,799 feet, and most probably much higher; for the eastern peak is said to terminate in a "crown of snow," and the western peak in a "summit

* Tour of 1818, p. 22, Calcutta edition.

deeply clad with snow." Now, as the height of the peaks on both sides is stated at 17,000 feet or somewhat less, we may fairly estimate the snow-line on the southern faces of the Bisahar range at about 16,000 feet.

Another passage* leads to a similar conclusion: "Tufts of moss and grass with a light soil are seen all the way to the top (of the Buranda Pass), and even rise on each side to 200 and 300 feet, while higher up on the rugged cliffs that are doomed to sustain perpetual snow, animated nature finds a habitation." The snow-limit by this account was therefore certainly as high as 15,179 + 300 = 15,479 feet, which was the boundary of vegetable life, and was no doubt somewhat higher.

Again, some days later, on the Rupin Pass, 15,460 feet, at the head of the Pabar river, Alexander Gerard† describes the strata of the range to the south of the Pabar as vertical, and that above the summit of this "mural portion," which "preserves an elevation of between 15,000 and 16,000 feet, to near Jangleg," the "rocks slant towards the summit, and upon the slope lie banks of congealed snow and ice, having a perpendicular brow of packed appearance, so much resembling blocks of marble and quartz, that I doubted for some time of their reality." This account is more explicit than any other that I have seen in Alexander Gerard's travels. From the Rupin Pass to near Jangleg, a distance of about eight miles, banks of snow lay upon the slope of the ridge, while the summit was entirely covered with packed snow. This agrees with the other statements that no exposed snow was seen below 15,500 feet; that above that line it was observed in banks or patches; and

* Tour of 1818, p. 24, Calcutta edition. † Ditto, p. 27.

that everywhere at 17,000 feet the snow was lying in undisturbed masses.

The Rupin Pass, 15,460 feet, was crossed by Captain Herbert and Captain Patrick Gerard, on the 30th September, 1819. In his map, Herbert writes along the upper course of the Rupin river, "all snow in September;" but Patrick Gerard describes the snow which they found on their way to the Rupin Pass in detail.* "Distance from encamping-ground to large snow-bed 2¼ miles, where crossed a dangerous chasm. Steep ascent through patches of snow (half a mile), fresh and melting fast. A quarter of a mile farther on, *no snow.* To pass over snow, *soft*, knee-deep, thigh-deep, and neck-deep, 3½ miles across eternal snow." The soft knee-deep and neck-deep snow was of course freshly fallen. We have thus another independent and distinct proof that the Rupin Pass (15,460 feet) was clear of old snow on the last day of September.

These different observations of the Gerards on the Bisahar range may be taken as sufficient evidence to prove that there is no perpetual snow below 15,500 feet, and that the actual snow-limit is somewhere about 16,000 feet.

On the 17th September, 1849, I took from Simla the bearings and altitudes of several peaks and snow-lines in the Láhul range with a very good theodolite, reading to half-minutes. To test the performance of the instrument, I first took the altitude of the Sháli Peak, which gave an elevation of 9,629 feet above the sea, or six feet in excess of that determined by the trigonometrical survey. I next turned it upon the Tural Peak, which is the highest in the Dhaola Dhar or Kangra range,

* Patrick Gerard's Manuscript Journals. Tour of 1819.

with a result equally satisfactory; the deduced altitude being 16,167 feet, or ten feet less than the mean altitude obtained from my former observations at Kangra and Nurpur. Lastly, I took the altitude of the Kotgarh peak beyond the Sutluj, to the north of Rámpur. The altitude obtained was 17,353 feet, or eighty-one feet less than Captain Herbert's elevation by trigonometrical survey. These altitudes do not of course pretend to any very great accuracy, but they may be depended upon as near approximations to the truth. Their errors will arise chiefly from the difficulty of obtaining the correct distances of points that have not yet been laid down by a regular trigonometrical survey. The following table gives the heights of the snow-lines on the Láhul range as observed from Simla.*

		Height of Pk.	Lower Edge of Snow.	Mean.
1	On c	19,948	17,656	17,297
2	„ e	19,366	16,837	
3	„ f	19,310	17,399	
4	„ g, Kotgrah Peak ...	17,434	15,983	16,034
5	„ j, Obelisk Peak ...	18,062	16,179	
6	„ k	17,730	15,940	
		Mean height	... ...	16,665

The difference between the heights of the snow-line is simply accounted for by the difference of position in the observed points. The first three are situated in the Kullu range, and are fully exposed to the action of the south-west monsoon, which blows direct up the valleys of the Parbati, Gomati, and Sainj rivers. The other points are situated at the intersection of the lofty trans-

* See Plate I.

verse chain which forms the watershed between the valleys of the Byâs and Sutluj rivers, and which runs in the same direction as the monsoon. In its passage along the ridge, the heat of the blast is gradually abstracted, until when it reaches the snow it is reduced to the temperature of the surrounding atmosphere.

We have thus four distinct and independent observations for the height of the southern snow-line in different parts of the Mid-Himálayan range.

		Feet.	Authority.
1	In Kumaun	16,000	Lieut. R. Strachey.
2	In S. Bisahar	16,000	The Gerards.
3	In N. Bisahar	16,034	A. Cunningham.
4	In E. Kullu	17,297	Ditto.
	Mean height	16,333 feet.*	

On the same range, but farther north, I found the Kali Debi Pass, 16,700 feet, covered with snow in July, and I was assured that the snow never disappeared from the crest of the Pass. On the whole, therefore, the mass of observations agree in fixing the snow-limit on the southern exposure of this range, at 16,000 feet and upwards.

On the northern exposure, the snow-line is probably about 17,000 feet. On crossing the Rotang Pass, in the end of August, 1846, I observed that the snow on the northern face of the Láhul range did not generally descend below 17,000 feet, although on particular peaks it was lying in masses as low as 16,500 feet. On the

* Even if we allow only 15,500 feet for the height of the snow-line in the South Bisahar range, as observed by the Gerards, the mean height of the southern exposure of the outer Himálaya will be 16,208 feet.

Bisahar range, as we have already seen from the observations of the Gerards, the snow remains throughout the year; and as the mean height of the peaks which came under their observation, does not exceed 17,200 feet, it is certain that the northern snow-line cannot be higher than 17,000 feet. From the correspondence of these observations with my own, we may conclude that the northern snow-line of the Bisahar and Láhul ranges is somewhat under 17,000 feet.

According to Herbert, the great mass of the Bisahar range is gneiss. The same rock occurs in the Láhul range, on both flanks of the Rotang Pass: but beyond this it is succeeded by limestone, which forms the crest of the Káli Debi ridge, flanked by silicious schist on the north, and by trap on the south. Beyond this, at the Saj Pass, Dr. Thomson found mica and clay slates; and limestone at the Banahál Pass, on the Pir-Panjál. But the mass of the Pir-Panjál, according to Vigne, is basaltic.

VII.—6th. THE DHAOLA DHÁR or OUTER HIMÁLAYA.

The outer, or Sub-Himálaya, stretches from the bend of the Byâs, at Mandi, to the well-known peak of Gandgarh, on the Indus. It attains its greatest height between the Byâs and Rávi, in the precipitous range of hills called the *Dhaola Dhár*,* or White Mountain, to

* This range is called by several names in our maps; as, "*Mony Mas Kidar*," that is, *Mani-Mahes-ki-dhar*, or the mountain of the holy lake of Mani-Mahes, which, however, is not situated in this range, but beyond the Rávi. Hugel calls the range "Pálam Kidar" and "Chamba Kidar," from the names of the districts to the north and south of the range. The true name is *Dhaola*, from the Sanscrit *Dhavala*, white; and this was most probably the original name written by Abu Rih'án,

the north of Kangra. The general direction is from south-east to north-west, as in the other ranges, and the whole length is nearly 300 miles. The Sub-Himálaya is pierced by the Rávi, the Chenáb, the Punach, and the Jehlam rivers, which divide it into several distinct ridges.

The most easterly of these separate ridges is the Dhaola Dhár, which forms the natural boundary between Kullu and Mandi, and between Chamba and Kangra. It is about eighty miles in length, and is of sufficient height to be covered with snow for about eight months of the year. I have observed this range for four successive years, and I can state positively that the snow entirely disappears from it every year, although the crest of the ridge has an average height of 15,000 feet. In the end of November, 1846, I marched from Kangra to Nurpur, and observed these mountains daily, and they were then entirely bare of snow. On the night of the 30th November, snow fell in considerable quantities, and did not disappear until the end of the following rains. In September and October, 1848, when I was at Simla, I observed this range carefully with a telescope, and could not discover a speck of snow on any part of it. Again, on the 16th and 17th of September, 1849, before leaving Simla, and when not a patch of snow was visible with a telescope sufficiently powerful for observing the occultation of Jupiter's satellites, I took the bearing and altitudes of several peaks and passes, for the purpose of verifying the measurements which I had formerly made from Kangra and Nurpur. The following table gives the results of all these measurements.

who calls these mountains بهاتل *Bhátel*, an easy corruption of دهاول *Dhaola*. See Reinaud's "Fragments Arabes et Persans," p. 94.

		Nurpur.	Kangra.	Simla.	Mean Height.
A	Balen Peak ...	13,783 ft.	—	14,138	13,960
B	Cleft Peak ...	14,981	—	—	14,981
C	Andrár Peak ...	15,642	—	—	15,642
D	Tural Pass ...	—	—	14,808	14,808
E	Tural Peak ...	16,145	16,210	16,167	16,174
F	Thálan Peak ...	—	15,220	—	15,220
G	Sangár Peak ...	—	14,529	—	14,529
H	Satmáru Peak	—	13,575	—	13,575
K	Peak	—	14,240	14,701	14,470
L	Peak	—	15,109	14,244	14,676
M	Surai Peak ...	—	15,644	15,207	15,425
N	Peak	—	—	15,975	15,975
P	Thamsar Peak	—	—	15,826	15,826
			Mean height of the range		15,020

The discrepancies which appear in these results are mostly attributable to the difficulty which I experienced in identifying the peaks from the different stations. I had taken the precaution of making outline sketches of the crest, as seen both from Nurpur and from Kangra; but from Simla, at a mean distance of eighty-five miles, and at a much greater elevation, the ridge presented such a different appearance that I could not satisfy myself as to the identity of more than two or three points. The Tural peak, which is the highest in the range, was, of course, readily recognized, as well as the Tural Pass to the westward. Two other peaks, K and M, agreed tolerably well with the outlines, and with the bearings on the map: but the others were all doubtful. One, L, which I thought I had recognized, was most probably not the same peak, but I have retained it in the table because its height, as determined from Simla (although it is so much below the other), does not decrease the average elevation of the range by more than thirty-four feet. By striking out this one observation, the average height will be 15,054 feet.

The elevation of this range is of considerable importance in determining the long-unsettled question of the snow-line, which, on the joint authority of the great Humboldt and the learned Colebrook, had been fixed at 13,000 feet, between 30½ and 32° of latitude. Lieut. Richard Strachey,* of the Engineers, was the first to correct this error, and to determine by observation that "the height of the snow-line on the more prominent points of the southern end of the belt, may be fairly reckoned at 16,000 feet, at the very least." This conclusion is fully borne out by my own observations, one half of which were made before the publication of Lieut. Strachey's paper. The ascertained height of the Dhaola Dhár, which rises abruptly from the low plains of Kangra, 3,000 feet, to a mean elevation of 15,000 feet, and of 16,000 feet in its loftiest peaks, proves most clearly that the snow-line, in the southern Himálaya, cannot be under 16,000 feet.

The geological structure of this range is almost unknown. In 1839, when I descended the valley of the Rávi, along the northern spurs of the Dhaola Dhár, I noted that the whole of the formations, at from 3,000 to 8,000 feet, were of clay and mica slates, and mostly of a very fine description, well adapted for roofing. The crest of the ridge is, however, most probably granite and gneiss, both of which I found on crossing the Chúari

* Journal Asiat. Soc. Bengal, vol. xviii. p. 292. Since the publication of this paper, however, Alex. Keith Johnston, in his beautiful Physical Atlas, p. 16, has stated the height of the southern snow-line on the Himálaya at 15,000 feet.

Pass, to the south of Chamba. Between Chamba and Chúari, the gneiss was overlaid by chlorite and mica slates. On the south of the range, the same fine roofing-slates (both mica and clay) are found to the north of Kangra, and to the north of Mandi. Both on the north and south of the range, the beds of some of the small streams are washed for iron-sand, which, after washing, yields as much as 90 per cent. of pure metal. The same iron ore is worked at Kumán, near Mandi, where it occurs in thin black, sparkling ribands, in a soft grey sandstone. The sandstone is pounded with a hard round boulder, and after washing yields about the same quantity of metal as the other.

The second portion of the Sub-Himálayan range extends from the Rávi to the Chenáb, a distance of fifty-five miles, and forms the natural boundary between Chamba and Bhadrwár, on the north, and the small districts of Chaneni, Bandrálta, and Baláwar, on the south. Between Bhadrwár and Chamba, the passes of Bhadr Dhár and Chatr Dhár are upwards of 10,000 feet in height, and the ridge may therefore have an elevation of 12,000 feet, or even more. To the south of Chaneni it breaks into a remarkable triple-peaked mountain, which is held sacred by the Hindus, under the name of Tré-kuta Devi (the three-peaked or trident goddess).

The central portion of the Sub-Himálaya is the well-known Ratan Panjál, which is crossed by the Bhimbar road to Kashmir. The pass of Ratan Pir, from which the mountain (*Panjál*) derives its name, has an elevation of 7,700 feet, and the highest peaks rise to about 11,000 feet. It is clothed to the very summit with magnificent trees, and its glens are not surpassed in beauty by anything that I have seen in the Himálaya, always excepting the lovely valley of the Byâs. The length of this ridge is eighty miles, from the neighbourhood of Chaneni to the southern bend of the Punach river.

The fourth portion of the Sub-Himálaya is altogether unknown. It extends from Koteli to Dhángali, the Ghakar capital on the Jehlam, a distance of twenty-five miles.

The fifth, and most westerly portion of the Sub-Himálaya, stretches from the Jehlam to the Indus, a distance of nearly seventy miles. It rises to an elevation of more than 7,000 feet, and is well clothed with trees on its northern slopes.

In this general survey of the mountain-ranges that bound the Panjáb to the north, I have purposely omitted all mention of the vegetable products that occur at different heights, as this subject naturally forms a part of Dr. Thomson's botanical labours. I have also omitted all notice of glaciers: not that I am unaware of their existence, but because I have seen so few of them that I have nothing to say of them which is worth recording. In 1839, I traversed a magnificent glacier which spanned the valley of the Cheli rivulet, below the Kali Debi Pass (16,700 feet). It was fissured in all directions, and down the main fissure, which was five feet wide, I saw the stream trickling at a depth of more than 300 feet. The surface was covered with hardened snow and imbedded stones; but the mass, as seen in the fissures, was clear transparent ice, filled with white specks. This glacier was about one mile long, and a quarter of a mile broad, with an average depth of 200 or 300 feet. In the same range, Dr. Thomson saw a similar glacier to the north of the Saj Pass, about thirty miles to the north-west of Kali Debi. In 1847, I crossed a second and larger glacier, to the north of the Parang Pass, 18,500 feet. It extended down the head of the Para river for $2\frac{3}{4}$ miles. At its termination, it was fifty feet high, but a quarter of a mile upward it was fully 150 feet thick. Its upper end was covered with hardened snow, but the lower end was half-hidden in fragments of stone, which were mixed into the ice for several feet in depth. It was fissured in many places. A still larger glacier was observed by Dr. Thomson, on the northern side of the Umási-Lá, on crossing into Zanskar. It extended from the top of the pass, 18,123 feet, down to a level of 14,500 feet, and cannot have been less than three or four miles in length. All these glaciers are mere still masses of ice, that are only dangerous when one has to cross them; but both above and below Sassar there are several gigantic glaciers that span the noble valley of the Khundan river. At different times, the river has been completely dammed for several months by these mighty barriers, until the accumulated waters have burst their icy chains, and swept away all traces of man and his puny labours, for several hundred feet above the river.

The following table gives a summary statement of all the information collected regarding the great mountain-chains in the north of the Panjáb.*

* See Plate I. for a general section through all these mountain-ranges, which exhibits the heights of the loftiest peaks, and the elevations of the different snow-lines and table-lands.

No.	Chains.	Length in Miles.	Elevation highest Peak.	Mean Height of Chain.	Snow-line.	
					South.	North.
1	Kárákoram, or Trans-Tibetan .	450	24,000?	20,000	18,500	18,000
2	Kailás or Gangri, or Mid-Tibetan .	550	20,700	29,000	19,000	18,500
3	Trans-Himálaya, or Tshomoriri...	350	21,000	19,300	20,000	19,500
4	Western Himálaya, or Bára Lácha	650	25,749	20,000	18,500	19,000
5	Mid-Himálaya, or Pir-Panjál ...	470	21,786	17,000	16,000	17,000
6	Outer Himálaya, Dhaola Dhar ...	300	16,174	15,020	the snow disappears annually.	

IV.—RIVERS.

I.—GENERAL REMARKS.

From the lofty mountains around the holy lake of Manasarovara, spring four celebrated rivers, the Indus, the Sutluj, the Gogra, and the Brahmaputra. These four sources are represented in the ancient Chinese maps; and the well-known story regarding them is common both to the Hindus and the Tibetans. The classical Ganges is fabled to flow from a cow's mouth; and to each of these four rivers is assigned an equally wonderful origin. The Indus is said to flow from a lion's mouth, *Singge-kha-bab;* the Sutluj, from an elephant's mouth, *Langchen-kha-bab;* the Gogra, from a peacock's mouth, *Macha-kha-bab;* and the Brahmaputra, from the holy horse's mouth, *Ta-chhog-kha-bab.** The fable is evidently of Indian origin, as elephants and pea-fowl are only known to the Tibetans by pictures, and because the source of the Brahmaputra, or river of Lhasa, is ascribed to *Ta-chhog*, the holy steed of Shakya Thubba, or Buddha.

* *Kha-po*, or in composition simply *Kha*, is a mouth, and *bab* means "descended." The different names are *Seng-ge-kha-bab*, "lion's mouth-descended;" *gLang-chen-kha-bab*, "elephant's mouth-descended;" *rMa-bya* (pronounced *Ma-cha*)*-kha-bab*, "peacock's mouth-descended;" and *rTa-mChhog-kha-bab*, "Ta-chhok's mouth-descended." Ta-chhok is the name of Sakya's steed, and means "the best horse."

The most remarkable feature about the Indus and its tributaries, is the general parallelism of their courses, which has been determined by the directions of the principal mountain-chains. In the "Novum Organum," Bacon has noticed the "similitudines physicæ in configuratione mundi," and the same similarity may be observed in the peculiar knee-bends which are common to all the Panjáb rivers. For the curious southward sweep which occurs in the Sutluj below Bilâspur, is also found in all the other rivers: in the Byás, below Hajipur; in the Ravi, near Bisoli; in the Chenab, below Káshtwár; in the Jehlam, below Mozafarábád; and in the Indus, at the gorge of Makpon-i-Shang-Rong. The same returning bend also occurs in the Kishen Ganga, above Mozafarábád.

The most common name for a river is *chhu;** as, *Singgé-chhu*, the Lion river, or Indus; and *Zanskar-chhu*, the river of Zanskar. When a river is spoken of generally, it is either called *Chhu-chhen*, or *Tsangpo*, or *Tsangchhen*. The first means simply the "great river," but the latter is a genuine name for a river, and is applied to the Indus as well as to the Brahmaputra, although it belongs strictly only to the great river of the Lhasan territory, which flows through the province of Tsang. It is now used to signify any large river, in the same way as *Ganga* is applied in India. Smaller streams are called *Dok-po*, the "narrow water," or brook; and *Drag-po*, the "rapid water," or torrent; or *Tsang-chung*, the "small stream;" but *Dok-po* is the common term.†

The river system of Ladák consists entirely of the three great mountain-feeders of the Indus, the *Singgé-*

* *Chhu*, "water," generally, a river.

† *Grog-po*, pronounced *Dokpo*. It is also spelt *Dog-po*.

chhu, or Indus Proper, the *Shayok*, and the *Zanskar* rivers. But as my account of Ladák embraces the districts of Lahul and Spiti, which once belonged to it, my description of the rivers must necessarily extend to the Chenab and Sutluj: and to complete the subject I will add some short notices of the other three rivers of the Panjáb,—the Jehlam, the Ravi, and the Byás.

II.—THE INDUS.

By some the real source of the Indus is at present considered an unsettled point,* notwithstanding the distinct and explicit statement of Moorcroft,† that "the Sinh-kha-bab rises from the Gangri or Kailás range, a short way to the south-east of Gartop" (Garo). The information collected by Moorcroft agrees exactly with that which I obtained from different people, that the Garo river is the Singgé-chhu or Indus, and that there is no *great* eastern branch. My principal information was derived from Anant Ram, the vazir of Shasso, in the Sungnam valley, who was despatched to Garo by the late Vans Agnew and myself in September 1846, with

* Thornton, Gazetteer, *in voce* Indus, relies upon Gerard, whom he calls "probably the highest authority upon the subject." The two Gerards are certainly the *highest* authorities for mountains, as they discovered some that were not less than 30,000 feet in height, or 2,000 feet higher than the loftiest known peaks. These are stated to be on the left bank of the Indus, in Rupshu; but when Dr. Gerard visited Rupshu he actually passed, unconscious, within eight or ten miles of the position of those stupendous peaks, which, at a distance of eighty-four miles, had thrown both the brothers into raptures! Thornton strangely quotes Vigne as confirming the height of these mountains; but Vigne simply says that he looked for them, but they were "*not in sight.*" Vigne was too honest a traveller to lend his name to such a statement.

† Travels, I. p. 363.

the Governor-General's letter to the Governor of Lhasa. He went from Hanlé *up the valley of the Singgé-chu* to Garo, or rather to Higong, which is the winter residence of the Governor. For the Garo of our maps, which was visited by Moorcroft, is chiefly a summer encampment, as its name implies, on the right bank of the Higong-chu, while the other Garo is situated two marches lower down the river, and on the left bank. The former is called *Gar-Yaru*, or upper encampment, and the latter *Gar-gang*,* or the snowy encampment, because the people retire to it during the winter, or snow season. Anant Ram passed by Tashigong, but he saw nothing of the great eastern branch, which I believe owes its existence entirely to Gerard, who could only account for the two names of Higong-chu and Singgé-chu by supposing them to belong to different streams.

Thornton, who never misses an opportunity of sneering at Arrowsmith, states in a note that "the existence of this river and confluence is alleged on the credit of the map accompanying Moorcroft's Travels, and stated to have been compiled from his notes and field-books." Now the map referred to, which was published in 1841, represents the eastern Sinh-kha-bab by a dotted line, whereas in Arrowsmith's map of Northern Asia, published in 1834, the eastern branch is defined as distinctly as the Garo river. This branch is just as boldly delineated by the "accurate" Walker in Sheet XI. of the map of India, published in 1836, by the Society for the Diffusion of Useful Knowledge. These dates prove that previous to the publication of the map of Moorcroft's and Trebeck's Travels, an eastern branch of the Indus had been inserted in our *best* maps, and that

* *sGar*, a camp; *Yar*, or *Yaru*, up, upwards; and *Gangs*, ice, snow.

Arrowsmith, after he had seen Moorcroft's and Trebeck's notes and field-books, was so doubtful of its existence, that he only represented it by a dotted line in the map illustrating Moorcroft's travels.*

According to my information, the true source of the Indus lies to the north-west of the holy lakes of Manasarovara and Rawan Hrad, in the south-western slopes of the Gangri or Kailás mountain, in north latitude 31° 20′, and east longitude 80° 30′, and at an estimated height of 17,000 feet. From its source to Garo, the Indus was followed by Moorcroft in 1812. Within eight or ten miles of its source it was 240 feet broad and 2½ feet deep in July, and at Garo, about forty miles from its source, it was "a clear, broad, and rapid, but not deep river." On the 19th September, 1847, I measured the Indus at an uninhabited spot named Rânak, a few miles above the junction of the Puga rivulet, and about 260 miles from the source. The stream was there 240 feet broad, with a mean depth of 1·7916 feet, and an extreme depth of only three feet. Its greatest surface velocity was 3·658 feet per second, or 2½ miles per hour, and its mean surface velocity was 2·727 feet per second, or

* Mr. Thornton, Gazetteer, *in voce* Hindu Kush, accuses Arrowsmith of embellishing the Hindu Kush with "a goodly peak." Mr. Arrowsmith might return the compliment by pointing to the "Panda Talao," with which the Walkers have *embellished* the eastern branch of the Indus. Mr. Thornton then contrasts Mr. Walker's "usual admirable accuracy," as displayed in his map of the countries between the Sutluj and the Oxus. But in this "admirably accurate map" I find Baron Hugel's *Muhal*, and Vigne's *Mihil Mori*, inserted as two distinct places ten miles apart! Walker's excellent map of Afghanistan is likewise disfigured by several errors: thus I find Shabkader and Chepkeder, the latter being only the French spelling of the same name; Daneh Chekow is printed instead of Danish-kot; and Antre Roustam instead of Rustam's Cave.

Day & Son Lithrs to the Queen

Wooden Bridge over the Indus, near LE.

nearly one mile and seven furlongs per hour. From these data I found the discharge of the Indus to be only 774 cubic feet per second. The stream was quite clear, but sluggish, running between grassy banks, half sand, half mud, the sand being quick, and the grass coarse, long, and yellow. The banks were flat and low, and the bottom generally muddy. Below this the character of the stream was quite changed, and the waters rushed impetuously down a narrow channel full of huge boulders and enormous rocks.

It will be observed that the Indus at Rânak had the same breadth, and but little more depth than where Moorcroft saw it above Garo; but as the current was "rapid," its velocity cannot be estimated at less than five or six miles an hour. This would give a discharge of about 1,500 cubic feet for July, and of 560 feet for September. If this estimate be correct, it is certain that no large stream can join the Garo river above Rânak.

The course of the Indus from its source to Rânak is to the north-west, and the distance is about 260 miles, and the fall 2,600 feet, or about ten feet per mile.

From Rânak to Pitak, opposite to Lé, the distance is 130 miles, and the direction the same as before, almost due north-west. The fall of the river is 3,200 feet, or 24·6 feet per mile. Above Rânak the Indus is generally fordable, but from thence to Lé it can only be crossed by bridges. From Lé to the junction of the Dras river, a distance of 125 miles, the river changes its course to west-south-west. From this point to the junction of the Shayok river, a distance of seventy-five miles, its course is generally north-north-west, and from thence to Skardo, a distance of thirty miles, it makes a sweep up to the northward, and returning to the south resumes its former course to the north-north-west.

At Nyimo, just twenty-five miles below Lé, the Indus is joined by the Zanskar river, a dark and turbulent torrent of equal, or perhaps of greater size. The junction of the united Waka, Suru, and Dras rivers with the Indus takes place at Moral, and the confluence of the Shayok and Indus just above Keris (7,500 feet).

On the 26th of November, Dr. Thomson found the Indus at Skardo 520 feet broad, with a mean depth of 7·11 feet, and an extreme depth of 9½ feet. The mean surface velocity was 2·128 feet per second, or about 1½ mile per hour. The greatest surface velocity was 2·586 feet per second, or rather more than 1¾ mile per hour.

From these data I calculate the discharge at 4,525 cubic feet per second in the winter. Of this amount about 2,000 cubic feet are probably supplied by the Shayok river, and the remaining 2,500 cubic feet by the Indus Proper. The small rivers of Wanla, Waka, Suru, and Dras probably supply 500 cubic feet, and the Zanskar river about 1,000 cubic feet; thus leaving 1,000 cubic feet for the discharge of the Indus at Lé during the winter season.

From Skardo to Rongdo and from Rongdo to Makpon-i-Shang-Rong, for upwards of 100 miles, the Indus sweeps sullen and dark through a mighty gorge in the mountains, which for wild sublimity is perhaps unequalled.* Rongdo means the "country of defiles," and Makpon-i-Shang-Rong means the "craggy defile of Astor." Between these points the Indus raves from side to side of the gloomy chasm, foaming and chafing with

* See Plate III. for a view of the bed of the Indus at the Rongdo Bridge.

Bed of the **INDUS** at the Rong-do Bridge

ungovernable fury. Yet even in these inaccessible places has daring and ingenious man triumphed over opposing nature. The yawning abyss is spanned by frail rope bridges, and the narrow ledges of rock are connected by ladders to form a giddy pathway overhanging the seething caldron below. At Makpon-i-Shang-Rong, 4,500 feet, the Indus cuts the Trans-Himálayan chain of mountains by a bold and sudden sweep round to the southward, where it receives the waters of the Gilgit river, a mighty stream, perhaps not inferior to any one of the mountain tributaries. From Skardo to Rongdo the distance is 40 miles, and the fall of the river 800 feet, or 20 feet per mile. From Rongdo to the Shang-Rong the distance is 75 miles, and the fall 1,700 feet, or 22·6 feet per mile.

From the junction of the Gilgit river to Attock, 1,000 feet above the sea-level, the course of the Indus is to the south-west. The distance is 300 miles, and the fall of the river 3,500 feet, or 11·6 feet per mile. This part of its course is but little known; but even at Ohind, 15 miles above Attock, I found the current of the Indus much more rapid than that of any other river of the Panjáb.

From its source to Rânak, the Indus is a broad and fordable stream, rolling its sluggish waters through open grassy plains. Its general width is about 250 feet. From Rânak to the junction of the Zanskar river, the stream is a brawling rapid from 100 to 150 feet broad; and thence to the confluence of the Shayok it is a furious torrent, raving from side to side of a narrow ravine. At the Khallach bridge, the channel is only 50 feet wide below and 60 feet above. In the winter the lower part of the Indus is frequently frozen over, and in 1841 Zorawar Sing's troops crossed the Indus on the ice.

The whole length of the mountain course of the Indus from its source to Attock is 1,035 miles,* and the whole fall is 16,000 feet, or 15·4 feet per mile. From Attock to the sea the length is 942 miles, and its whole length from the Kailás mountain to the Indian Ocean is 1,977 miles. The minimum discharge of the Indus between Attock and Mithankot is about 16,000 cubic feet, which I have estimated in the following manner:—

Discharge at Skardo	4,500 cubic feet.
Shigar, Gilgit, and Astor rivers ...	4,000
Small unknown streams	2,500
	11,000
Kabul river	5,500
	16,500
Loss by evaporation between Attock and Mithankot	1,500
Total discharge	15,000

In May, when it has been increased by the melting of the snows, its discharge is six times as great, or 91,791 cubic feet; and in July and August, when swollen by the seasonal rains, it reaches its maximum discharge of 135,000 cubic feet, or nine times that of the winter discharge. These estimates are for the Indus itself above the confluence of the Panjnad. Below the confluence, the minimum discharge of the Indus is about

* My measurements have all been made by adding one half to the measured lengths obtained by the compasses. Thornton reckons the mountain course of the Indus at 700 miles, but the practised Geographer Alex. Keith Johnston estimates it at 1,060 miles, which is within a few miles of my own estimate. *See* Johnston's Physical Atlas, p. 45.

27,000 cubic feet. The discharge in May is 160,674 cubic feet,* and the maximum discharge is 230,000 cubic feet.

The discharge of the Indus at Rânak has already been stated at 774 cubic feet in September; and I estimate its winter discharge below Lé at 1,000 cubic feet. As the Zanskar river is about the same size, the minimum discharge of the Indus Proper may be taken at 2,000 cubic feet; and the maximum discharge, at nine times the minimum, will be 18,000 cubic feet. That this estimate is not too great, can be proved by the known rise of the river (35 feet) at the Khallach bridge, where the stream is confined between almost perpendicular rocks, only 55 feet apart. A discharge of 18,000 cubic feet at this point would require a surface velocity of not more than 8½ miles per hour, or of 12·46 feet per second.

The waters of the Indus are supplied by the rivers of the Panjáb in the following proportion.

		Cubic Feet.	Authority.
1	Sutluj	5,700	Major Baker, Engineers.
2	Byás	3,100	Major Cunningham.
3	Ravi	2,700	Col. Napier, Engineers.
4	Chenab	4,700	Major Cunningham.
5	Jehlam	4,000	Estimated.
		20,200	
	Loss	8,200	by evaporation, permeation, &c.
	Panjnad	12,000	cubic feet, discharge.
	Indus Proper ...	15,000	
	Minimum discharge	27,000	cubic feet.

* Wood, in Burnes's Cabul, p. 374.

The following table exhibits the discharge of the Indus below Mithankot in several months of the year.*

	Dr. Lord corrected.	Wood.	Burnes corrected.
In March	26,357	—	—
„ April	66,660	—	67,837
„ May	160,162	160,674	—
„ June	163,483	—	—
„ July	223,678	—	—
„ August	230,177	—	—
„ September ...	217,110	—	—

In his Memoir on the Indus, Sir A. Burnes has assigned to the Indus a discharge of 80,000 cubic feet in April, and then contrasted this amount with the minimum discharge of the Ganges, as published by George Prinsep. But the comparison is doubly incorrect, for the lowest state of the Indus occurs in March, when, as we have seen, the discharge is not more than 27,000 cubic feet: and the discharge of the Ganges, at Sikrigali, as stated by George Prinsep, is so manifestly wrong that it is quite astonishing how any one could have repeated such an absurd mistake. On turning to George Prinsep's statement, I find that he assigns 21,500 cubic feet

* Dr. Lord, Medical Memoir of the Valley of the Indus, p. 65, states the discharge in May at 310,393 cubic feet; but his calculation must have been made from the *surface* velocity instead of from the mean velocity of the mass. I have therefore reduced all his discharges by multiplying them by the factor ·516. This makes the May discharge agree with that of the accurate Wood. Sir A. Burnes makes the breadth of the Indus, at Tatta, 670 yards or 2,010 feet, the depth 15 feet, and the velocity $2\frac{1}{2}$ miles per hour. From these data I have calculated the discharge according to the formula $v=\frac{(\sqrt{s}-1)^2+s}{2}1$; in which s is the surface velocity, and v the mean velocity of the mass. The result agrees closely with Dr. Lord's corrected discharge.

as the discharge of the Ganges at Sikrigali, and 20,000 at Benares. The latter, as Burnes remarks, "differs in but a trifling degree from that at Sikrigali;" and the near agreement of these two, he conceives to be a proof in favour of the correctness of the estimated discharge.* Had any one told *him* that the discharge of the Indus at Mithankot was the same as at Dera Ghazi Khan, *above the junction of the Panjnad*, he would at once have exposed the absurdity; and yet he takes the Ganges at Sikrigali to be the same stream as the Ganges at Benares, although between these points it receives the tribute waters of the Gumti, the Gogra, the Son, the Gandak, the Baghmati, the Gogari, the Kosi, and the Mahanadi; of which the Gogra alone is fully equal to the Ganges at Benares.

As the comparison of the two rivers is a subject of much interest, I will here state all that I have gathered regarding the discharge of the Ganges. The estimated discharge at Benares was, without doubt, derived from the measurements of James Prinsep, who was for several years Assay Master of the Benares Mint, and whose high attainments in all branches of science are sufficient to guarantee the correctness of his calculations. Indeed the accuracy of James Prinsep's discharge of the Ganges at Benares is most satisfactorily proved by the measured discharge at Ghazipur, which from data published by the Rev. R. Everest,† I have calculated at 21,757 cubic feet. The only other minimum calculation which I possess, is luckily that which is most wanted, the minimum discharge of the Ganges at the head of the Delta. For this I am indebted to the late Colonel Wilcox, who

* Burnes's Travels, I. p. 199.

† Journal Asiat. Soc. Bengal, I. p. 241.

was formerly employed on the Great Trigonometrical Survey, and afterwards in the Observatory of the King of Oude. The measurements were taken above Comercolly and Pubna, and included the streams of the Jalinghi and Bhágirathi, as well as the main river. The discharge of the Ganges at this point was found to be 96,000 cubic feet, or more than three and a half times that of the Indus. The maximum discharge of the Ganges at Ghazipur, calculated from the data furnished by the Rev. R. Everest, I find to be 476,761 cubic feet, or more than double that of the Indus at its greatest height. The maximum discharge of the Ganges, at the head of the Delta, cannot therefore be estimated at less than 1,500,000 cubic feet, or just six times that of the Indus. George Prinsep* states the maximum discharge at Sikrigali, at 1,850,000 cubic feet; but my calculation, from his data, gives only 1,430,800 cubic feet. This result might have been anticipated from the much greater extent of the Himálayan chain, drained by the Ganges, and from the known greater fall of rain in the Gangetic basin. The latter cause is probably the chief one, as it is known that the annual fall of rain increases rapidly from the Jamna, eastward.

III.—THE SHAYOK RIVER.

The principal mountain tributary of the Indus is the Shayok, or Khundan river, which rises in the Kárákoram mountains, to the northward of Lé, in N. latitude 35°, and E. longitude 78°, and to the south-eastward of the Kárákoram Pass. From its source to the neighbourhood of Sassar, it makes a bold sweep of sixty miles

* Gleanings in Science, III. p. 185.

to the west and south. Thence, for fifty miles, to Mandalik, it takes a south-easterly course; and onward, to the town of Shayok, which gives its name to the stream, it flows due south for fifty miles more. From the source to this point, the whole length of the river is 170 miles, and the fall 6,000 feet, or 35·3 feet per mile. A short distance above the great north-western bend, the Shayok receives the waters of the *Chang-chhen-mo*, or Great Chang river, whose course has been explored by Captain H. Strachey; and below the bend it receives the waters of the *Long-Konma*, from the south-east. From Shayok to Hundar, the course is west-north-west, and the distance is about eighty miles. Near this place it receives the Nubra river, a considerable stream, about 100 miles in length, from the north-west. Beyond this point it pursues the same direction to its confluence with the Indus, at Keris, a distance of 150 miles. From Shayok to the junction, the distance is 230 miles, and the fall is 4,500 feet, or 19·6 feet per mile. From its source in the Kárákoram to Keris, where it joins the Indus, the whole length of the Shayok is just 400 miles, and the total fall is 10,500 feet, or 26·4 feet per mile.

The general character of the Shayok is exactly the reverse of that of the Indus. Its upper course is rushing and turbulent, down a narrow glen, but its middle course is either broad and rapid, or divided into numerous channels, in an open valley; and in these places where the waters are much scattered, the river is generally fordable, although not without difficulty.* Between Tertse and Unmâru, there are seven distinct branches, of which three are between 300 and 400 feet in width, and the others much smaller, with an average depth of

* For this information I am indebted to the kindness of Dr. Thomson.

two feet. At Surmu, the Shayok is also forded by two separate channels, each 300 feet broad, with a depth varying from two to three feet. At the Turtuk bridge, the river narrows to seventy feet, and in the lower part of its course, the Shayok is generally a furious rapid, confined between precipitous cliffs. In the height of summer, when the stream is much swollen by the melted snows, the fords are always difficult. In the winter, the passage is easy; and even in the lower part of its course the Shayok is frequently frozen over, and the stream is crossed upon the ice. I estimate the winter discharge of the Shayok at 2,000 cubic feet, the increased discharge in May at 12,000, and the maximum discharge in August at 18,000 cubic feet.

IV.—THE ZANSKAR RIVER.

The *Chiling-chhu*, or Zanskar river, is formed of two principal branches, *Zanskar* proper, and the *Sum-Gal*, or river of the "Three Fords." The head-waters of the Zanskar river are the Yunam, the Serchu (or Yellow River), and the Cherpa, all of which rise to the north of the Himálaya range, near the Bara Lacha Pass. The head of the Cherpa river, which is the most remote source of the Zanskar river, is situated in N. latitude 32° 40′, and E. longitude 78°. The united stream, below the junction of the Cherpa, is not fordable until the end of September; and the Cherpa itself is not fordable after mid-day, even in the beginning of September, as both the rapidity and depth of the stream are much increased by the daily melting of the snow. The united stream, called Lingti, follows a north-westerly course, as far as Phadam, the chief place in the Zanskar district. From its source to Phadam, the distance is 130 miles, and the fall 4,000 feet, or 34·6 feet per mile. At Phadam the Lingti receives a small stream from the west, and then takes a due northerly course for upwards of eighty miles, to its junction with the Indus, opposite Nyimo. In this part of its course the fall is only 1,500 feet, or 18·7 feet per mile. The whole length of the Zanskar river is 210 miles, and the total fall is 6,000 feet, or 28·5 feet per mile.

About twenty-five miles above its junction with the Indus, the Zanskar river receives the waters of the Sum-Gal, or river of the "Three Fords." The head-waters of this tributary rise in the mountains to the westward of the Tshomo-Riri lake, in N. latitude 33°, and E. longitude 78°. Three branches, of about equal size, join their waters to form this river; and as each of these streams is forded separately within the short distance of one mile, the united stream has received the descriptive name of *Sum-Gal*, or the river of the "Three Fords." From its source to its junction with the Zanskar river, the course of the Sum-Gal is north-north-west; its length is 110 miles, and its fall is about 5,000 feet, or 45·4 feet per mile.

I estimate the discharge of the Zanskar river at 1,000 cubic feet in the winter, at 6,000 cubic feet in May, and at 9,000 cubic feet at its maximum, in August.

V.—OTHER TRIBUTARIES.

Of the other mountain tributaries of the Indus, there are only four that are deserving of particular notice: the rivers of Dras, Shigar, Gilgit, and Astor.

The Dras river is formed of the united streams of the Waka, the Suru, the Dras, and the Kuksar rivers. The

Waká-chu is formed of two main branches, the Waka and the Phu-gal, both of which take their rise to the north of the Himálaya, near the Vingge-lá, in N. latitude 33° 40′, and E. longitude 76° 30′. Each stream is fordable above the junction, but the united stream is crossed by bridges. The whole length of the Waká-chu is about 100 miles, the general direction being north-north-west. The Suru river rises to the north of the Himálaya range, in N. latitude 34°, and E. longitude 76°. Its length is about sixty miles, and its direction about north-north-east. The Dras river rises to the north of the Himálayan range, near the Seoji La Pass, in N. latitude 34° 12′, and E. longitude 75° 45′. Its whole length is about eighty-five miles, and its general direction is north-east. The Kuksar river rises to the westward, in about 34° 40′ N. latitude, and 75° E. longitude. The length of its course is unknown; but it is probably not less than 100 miles. Its general direction is easterly. The whole of these streams unite near Kargyil, below which they cut the Trans-Himálayan range, at the narrow gorge called the Wolf's Leap, and join the Indus opposite Mural. I estimate the discharge of the Dras river at not less than 500 cubic feet.

The Shigar river rises in the Kárákoram mountains, in N. latitude 36° 20′, and E. longitude 75°. It takes a south-easterly direction for 100 miles, and then turns to the south-south-west for nearly forty miles, to its junction with the Indus, opposite Skardo. The discharge of this stream is probably about 500 cubic feet.

The Gilgit river is one of the principal mountain-feeders of the Indus. Its upper course is formed of two principal branches, the Yasan and Parasot rivers. The former rises in N. latitude 37°, and E. longitude 73°, at the point where the Kárákoram merges into the Hindu Kush. The source of the Parasot is in 36° 10′ N. latitude, and 72° 40′ E. longitude, on the eastern face of the range which gives rise to the Chitral, or Kunar river. After a separate course of seventy-five miles each, the two streams join above Roshan, in latitude 36° 20′, and longitude 73° 30′, and take an easterly course for twenty-five miles, to Gakuch, where they are joined by the Chator-Kun river, from the nòrth. Thence to the town of Gilgit its course is east-south-east, for fifty miles, below which it receives the joint tribute of the Hunza-Nager rivers. It continues the same course for about thirty miles further, to its junction with the Indus, below the defile of Makpon-i-Shang-Rong. The general direction of the stream is to the east-south-east, and its whole length not less than 180 miles. The minimum discharge is probably 2,000 cubic feet, or even more.

The Astor, or Hasora river, falls into the Indus in latitude 35° 30′, and longitude 74° 35′. It rises to the east of the great mountain of Dayamur, and takes a northerly course of about 100 miles.

VI.—CATACLYSM OF THE INDUS.

Since Moorcroft visited Ladák, there have been no less than three inundations of the Indus, of which the last and greatest occurred in 1841. Vigne was the first to make known the second of these cataclysms, which, from the information of the people, he attributed to its right cause,* the bursting of a glacier in the upper course of the Shayok river. In 1812, when Izzet Ullah went from Lé to Yarkand, he travelled up the Shayok

* Kashmir, II. p. 362.

river, from its great western bend to its source in the Kárákoram mountains; and in 1822, when Moorcroft was at Lé, the road by the Shayok was still clear. The information which I obtained regarding the Shayok or Khundan glacier, dates the first stoppage of the river in the fourth year after Moorcroft left Ladák, and in the same year that Jehangir Khoja came from Yarkand, or in A.D. 1826. The river was dammed only for a short time, but the road was permanently obstructed. The second cataclysm happened in 1833, when, to use Vigne's account, "the protecting glacier gave way, and the mighty flood, no longer confined, rushed down the valley of the Shayok, destroying every village that came within its reach." The third cataclysm occurred in 1841, when the gallant Syâm Sing Atáriwala (who fell at Sobraon) was encamped in the bed of the river. Suddenly down rushed the wave of the inundation, thirty feet in height, and the whole camp took to flight: most of the men were saved, but the baggage, camp equipage, and guns, were swept away.

The cataclysm of the Val de Bagnes, a small feeder of the Rhone, is the only great flood of this kind of which I can find any account; but the Val de Bagnes is scarcely five miles in length, while the glacier of the Khundan river is not less than 800 miles from the fort of Attock, past whose walls the flood rushed in one tremendous wave about 30 feet high, and continued its overwhelming course to the Indian Ocean, a distance of 1,750 miles.

> Who that from Alpine heights his laboring eye
> Shoots round the wide horizon, to survey
> Indus or Ganges rolling their bright floods
> Through mountains, plains, through empires black with shade,
> And continents of sand, will turn his gaze
> To mark the windings of a scanty rill? AKENSIDE.

The Val de Bagnes is a petty brook, while the Khundan is a mighty river, scarcely inferior to the Indus itself at their junction above the fort of Skardo.

As a magnificent natural catastrophe on so grand a scale as that of the cataclysm of the Indus is worthy of the most particular examination, I trust that the following details will prove both interesting and valuable.

When Vigne and Dr. Falconer* were at Skardo in 1837, they heard that the Shayok or Khundan river had been often "blocked up by avalanches and masses of ice," and that a flood had occurred not many years before. Both of these travellers heard of a lake in the upper course of the Shayok river, but as Mir Izzet Ullah does not mention it, I conclude that my information regarding the origin of the lake is correct. In two different parts of the Shayok or Khundan river, above and below Sassar, the bed of the stream is completely spanned by enormous glaciers. The upper glaciers above Sassar were seen by Dr. Thomson in 1848. They had descended from two lateral ravines on the western bank, and had been thrust right across the bed of the river by their own weight. But the lower glaciers on the Khundan are those to which my informants attributed the obstruction of the river, and they were unanimous in ascribing the flood to the long stoppage and sudden escape of the accumulated waters of the Khundan. The exact position of the great glacier is known within a few miles. It is situated somewhere between Sassar and the junction of the Chang-Chhenmo, and as the distance between these points is only 50 miles, we may place the glacier with tolerable certainty at about 30 miles below Sassar, and 20 miles above the junction of

* Journal Asiatic Soc. Bengal, X. p. 617.

the Chang-Chhen-mo. This part of the course is now quite inaccessible, owing to the accumulated mass of ice and snow. The high road from Lé to Yarkand formerly ascended the bed of the Khundan or Shayok river the whole way to its source in the Kárákoram mountains; but since the obstruction of the channel, the road now takes a more westerly direction up the Nubra river, and then crosses a lofty pass to Sassar on the Khundan. At this point it again leaves the Khundan, on account of the upper glaciers seen by Dr. Thomson, and proceeds over a rugged and elevated tract to the head-waters of the river.

In these cold and lofty regions, almost every ravine is filled with a glacier, which, except during a very warm summer, never moves, but is bound to the rocks every night by the icy chains of frost. A glacier is melted on its under surface by the higher temperature of the soil, and on its upper surface by the thawing of the snow under the direct rays of the sun. The heated stones that lie on the top form hollows and clefts that admit the external air, and little rills of water trickle over the sides in all directions. The glacier is thus furrowed by holes, penetrated by cracks, and undermined below, until it becomes narrower than the ravine which contains it. It then descends by its own weight, and is either rent to pieces by unequal pressure, or checked by some opposing obstacle. In a very warm and dry summer the glaciers in the lateral ravines of the Khundan would be so much diminished by melting and evaporation, that they would be impelled onwards by their own gravity right across the channel of the river. This I suppose to have been the case towards the end of September 1826, from which time the channel of the Khundan river has never been clear, and the accumulated waters have formed a lake of considerable size, to which the people have given the name of *Nubra Tsho,* or the Nubra Lake. The accounts which Vigne received were "various and most conflicting, but all agreed that it was very large;" and he concluded that it might be "three or four miles in length and less than a mile in width." My informant, who had seen the lake, said it was four or five kos (eight or ten miles) in length, and less than a quarter of a kos (half a mile) in breadth; and such is the shape, that I should suppose it must take in the confined channel of the Khundan river.

In 1833* this barrier was burst, and the accumulated waters rushed down the valley of the Shayok, destroying every village within their reach; from Nubra to Skardo, a distance of 120 miles, the flood-wave descended in a single day, at the rate of ten miles an hour; and the marks of its fury were still to be seen at Skardo in 1837. So well was the cause of this inundation known to the people, that it was believed "that the same terrific visitation might be expected to occur again at no very distant period."†

The expected cataclysm occurred in June 1841, but it was immensely greater in volume and more devastating in its effects than the previous inundation of 1833.

During December 1840 and January 1841, the Indus was observed to be unusually low between Torbela and Attock.‡ In February and March it became lower, and

* Two different informants fixed the date as follows:—one said fourteen years before 1847, that is in 1833; the other said "just before Zorawár Sing invaded Ladák." As the invasion took place in 1834, the cataclysm may be dated in 1833.

† Vigne's Kashmir, II. p. 362.

‡ Major James Abbott. Journal Asiat. Soc. Bengal, XVII. p. 230.

was even fordable not far above Attock; but in April and May, though still very low, it was no longer fordable, as the depth of the stream had been much increased by the melted snows. Early in June the barrier was burst, and the collected waters of nearly six months rushed with overwhelming violence down the narrow valley of the Shayok, sweeping everything before them. Houses and trees, men and women, horses and oxen, sheep and goats, were carried away at once, and all the alluvial flats in the bed of the river, which had been irrigated with laborious care, were destroyed in a moment. This happened in the middle of the month of Jyeth in the Sambat year 1898, or about the 1st June, A.D. 1841.

According to the testimony of the people of Chulung and Tartuk, on the western boundary of Chhorbad, the wave of inundation passed their villages at two o'clock in the afternoon. As these villages stand on opposite sides of the river, and are ten miles apart, the concurrence of testimony may be taken as a proof of its correctness. Two days afterwards, and exactly at the same hour, the flood passed by Torbela, a distance of 550 miles. The rate is 11·4583 miles per hour, or 16·81 feet per second, being only just half that of the flood-wave of the Val de Bagnes in 1818 at its first burst into the valley of the Rhone. The fall from the Khundan glacier to Torbela is 16,000 feet, or just 20 feet per mile.

The devastating effects of this terrible flood were still quite fresh in 1847. At Tertse, one of the widest parts of the valley, they could be traced to a height of more than 20 feet above the stream, where straws and twigs were massed together in lines two or three feet broad, and upwards of half a mile from the channel of the river in October 1847. But the most striking effect of the flood was the entire absence of trees in the valley of the Shayok, while the lateral valley of Nubra was full of trees upwards of a hundred years old.* There were of course many young trees in the bed of the Shayok, but they were the growth of only a few years. At Surmu and at other places in the Khapolor district, numbers of fruit-trees were observed standing amidst large tracts of sand and gravel.

The following table shows the loss of life and property in most of the villages along the Shayok from the junction of the Nubra river to the fort of Skardo.

Districts.	Houses.	People.	Horses.	Oxen.	Sheep, Goats.	Khals of Land.	Trees.
Nubra	19	83	18	114	1,040	178	—
Chhorbad ...	140	8	—	—	—	364	140
Khapolor ...	163	1	1	4	—	859	—
Keris	20	—	—	—	—	127	4,900
Skardo	9	—	—	—	—	107	1,190
Parguta ...	—	—	—	—	—	10	1,200
Total ...	351	92	19	118	1,040	1,645	7,430

From this list we learn that the principal loss of life occurred in the Nubra district, where the valley of the Shayok expands to about half a mile in breadth. There the shepherds and herdsmen, with their flocks and herds, were overwhelmed in the midst of the open plain, without a chance of escape. In the lower part of the valley, where the channel is confined, and where the villages are generally built high above the stream, there was no loss of life. Even amongst the low-lying hamlets in the bed of the river, the loss of life was trifling, for the distant roar of the rushing waters was a sufficient warning to

* This fact was communicated to me by Dr. Thomson.

the people who had beheld the inundation of 1833, and with a few exceptions they all made their escape up the mountains.

The effect of the inundation at Torbela has been so graphically described by Major James Abbott from the lips of an eye-witness, Ashraf Khan, of Torbela, that I will quote it entire.* "At about 2 P.M. a murmuring sound was heard from the north-east among the mountains, which increased until it attracted universal attention, and we began to exclaim, 'What is this murmur? Is it the sound of cannon in the distance? Is Gandgarh bellowing? Is it thunder?' Suddenly some one cried out, 'The river's come.' And I looked and perceived that all the dry channels were already filled, and that the river was racing down furiously in an absolute wall of mud, for it had not at all the colour or appearance of water. They who saw it in time easily escaped. They who did not, were inevitably lost. It was a horrible mess of foul water, carcases of soldiers, peasants, war-steeds, camels, prostitutes, tents, mules, asses, trees, and household furniture, in short, every item of existence jumbled together in one flood of ruin; for Raja Gulab Sing's army was encamped in the bed of the Indus at Kulai, three kos above Torbela, in check of Painda Khan. Part of the force was at that moment in hot pursuit, or the ruin would have been wider. The rest ran, some to large trees which were all soon uprooted and borne away; others to rocks, which were speedily buried beneath the waters. Only they escaped who took at once to the mountain-side. About five hundred of these troops were at once swept to destruction. The mischief was immense. Hundreds of acres of arable land were licked

* Journal Asiat. Soc. Bengal, XVII. p. 231.

up and carried away by the waters. The whole of the Sisu-trees which adorned the river's banks, the famous bargat-tree of many stems, time out of mind the chosen bivouac of travellers, were all lost in an instant."

Throughout the mountain-course of the Indus the devastation caused by this terrible flood in the low lands along the bank of the river was complete. All the cultivated lands were swept away, and not even a single tree was left standing to mark the spot where careful tillage and laborious irrigation had for hundreds of years wrung luxuriant crops from the thirsty soil. The fields, the houses, and the trees, were all overwhelmed in one common ruin; while man and the animals which he has domesticated, horses and oxen, sheep and goats, generally managed to escape.

The ruin caused by this awful inundation in the bed of the Indus, between Torbela and Attock, was so overwhelming and so vast, that "it will take hundreds, if not thousands of years, to enable time to repair, with its healing hand, the mischief of that terrible hour. The revenue of Torbela has in consequence dwindled from 20,000 to 5,000 rupees. Chach has been sown with barren sand. The timber, for which the Indus has been celebrated from the days of Alexander until this disaster, is now so utterly gone, that I vainly strove throughout Huzara to procure a Sisu-tree for the repair of the field-artillery carriages. To make some poor amends, the river sprinkled gold dust over the barren soil, so that the washings, for several successive years, were farmed at four times their ordinary rent."*

Opposite Attock, the waters of the Kabul river were checked and forced backward for upwards of twenty

* Major James Abbott.

miles, by the mighty wave of inundation. The fort of Akora, and the village of Messabanda, were overthrown; and when I saw them in January 1848, were mere scattered heaps of ruin.

As everything connected with this tremendous inundation must be interesting, I have attempted to ascertain, approximately, the mass of the accumulated waters in the Nubra Tsho, or Lake, formed by the glacier barrier, as well as the mass and height of the cataclysmal wave. In calculating the accumulation of water, I have estimated the usual winter discharge of the Khundan river at 800 cubic feet, or less than one-half of the discharge at its confluence with the Indus. The increased discharges in April and May are based upon the known rates of increase in the discharge of the Indus, which have already been given. The accumulation began in December.

Date.		Velocity.	Accumulation.
December	1840	800 cubic ft. per sec.	1,249,920,000 cubic ft.
January	1841	800 „ „	1,249,920,000 „
February	„	800 „ „	1,128,960,000 „
March	„	800 „ „	1,249,920,000 „
April	„	2,000 „ „	5,064,000,000 „
May	„	4,800 „ „	12,918,320,000 „
			22,861,040,000 „

From this amount a considerable deduction must be made for loss by evaporation and percolation. I do not, therefore, estimate the whole mass of accumulated waters at more than 20,000,000,000 cubic feet. But even this would be sufficient to form a lake twelve miles in length, with an average breadth of 526 yards, or 1,578 feet, and an average depth of 200 feet. The surface of the lake would have been half a mile or more in breadth, and the depth at the lower end, against the glacier, would have been 400 feet. As the fall in this part of the bed of the river is somewhat less than thirty-five feet, a lake of this depth would be exactly twelve miles in length.

The bursting of the barrier was, I have little doubt, caused by the cutting powers of the overflowing waters, which must quickly have worked enormous clefts in the outer face of the glacier. In a few days these clefts would have been worn deeper and deeper, until the icy mass at length gave way under the mighty pressure of the vast liquid body. Then the imprisoned waters burst forth with a roar of exultation, lashing themselves into foam against the rocks, careering madly from side to side, and sweeping all things before them in the wild might of their untamed strength.

According to the information given by the people of Chulung, on the Shayok, the flood was three whole days in passing off; two days in full height, and the third day considerably decreased; on the fourth day the flood had mostly gone by, but the stream was still much swollen. The following calculation shows the daily discharge of water for each of the three days of flood, with a small allowance for the fourth day.

				Daily discharge.	
1st day at	100,000	cubic feet	per second,	8,640,000,000	cubic feet.
2nd „	80,000	„	„	6,998,400,000	„
3rd „	40,000	„	„	3,499,900,000	„
4th „	20,000	„	„	1,728,000,000	„
Total discharge in four days ...				20,866,300,000	„
Total mass of accumulated water,				20,000,000,000	„

By dividing the maximum discharge of 100,000 cubic feet per second by the ascertained velocity of 11·4583 miles per hour, or 16·81 feet per second, we obtain 5,948 square feet as the sectional area of the cataclysmal wave. From this I have deduced the rise of the river in different parts of the channel according to its width. These heights, however, do not give the actual rise of the water, which must always have been greater immediately above every narrow part of the channel.

	Width of River.	Rise.
Above Tertse	250 feet broad	23·79 feet.
Near Turtuk	100 " "	59·48 "

The height of the flood below Tertse was ascertained to have been between twenty and thirty feet, by the broad lines of straw and twigs which marked the extreme limit of the inundation. In the open plain of Unmâru, the waters must have been kept at the same level as at Tertse, by the obstruction offered to their passage in the narrow channel between Chulung and Turtuk. This would account for the lines of straw and twigs being observed about half a mile from the present bed of the river.

The valley of the Indus, below the junction of the Shayok, narrows in some places to 100 feet, and even less. At these points, therefore, the flood must have risen to a height of sixty feet at least, and must have caused a considerable back wave up the confined channel of the Indus proper, or Lé river. And this was actually the case, for the effect of the inundation is said to have been felt for nearly thirty miles up the Indus, while at Sarmik, ten miles above the confluence, the lower cultivated lands were destroyed, and no less than 1,200 fruit-trees were swept away by the back-water flood.

At Skardo, where the river expands to 520 feet in width, and where the sandy flats rise at least thirty feet*

* Vigne, II. p. 260, states that water is found at a depth of ten yards.

above the general level of the stream, it is probable that the flood did not spread much beyond the usual limits. The rise would, therefore, not have been more than ten feet. But below Skardo, in the confined and rocky channel, which is the prevailing character of the bed of the Indus throughout the Rongdo district, the flood-wave would have risen to its full height of sixty feet; and at the "Craggy Defiles" of Makpon-i-Shang-Rong, the curbed waters must have been massed up at least 100 feet in height.

At Ghori Trap, below Attock, where the width of the river is not more than 250 feet,* the wave of inundation must have attained a height of at least 23·79 feet; and this will at once account for the height of the waters at Attock, which are said to have submerged the fort of Khairabad by their sudden rise of nearly thirty feet.

From Attock to the sea the inundation pursued its ruinous course, but I have no information as to the extent of the country flooded, or the numbers of people swept away. According to the papers of the day, the devastation of the three Deras,—Ismail Khan, Ghaze Khan, and Fateh Khan, was very great; and I trust that full particulars of this extraordinary flood may yet be collected by some of the many British officers now stationed along the Indus.

VII.—THE JEHLAM RIVER.

The *Jehlam* river takes its name from the town of Jehlam, beneath which it flows. In Kashmir, it is called *Behat*, a contraction of the Sanskrit *Vitasta*, which the Greeks slightly altered to Hydaspes. The Jehlam drains

* Wood's Oxus, p. 125.

the whole valley of Kashmir: and the reputed sources of its principal feeders are all esteemed holy. The Behat takes its rise in the small pool of Vira Nág, which Jehangir walled round; but its true source is some miles further to the south-west, in N. latitude 33° 30′, and E. longitude 75° 25′. Its most distant source is in the lake of Sesha Nág, at the head of the Lambodari, or Lidar river, which joins the Behat below the town of Islamabad. Between Shahabad and Islamabad, it receives the river of Brang; and a few miles below Bij Bihâra, it receives the united waters of the Veshau and Shupyen rivers. The Veshau, or Veshavi, rises in the holy fount of Kosa Nag; and the Shupyen river in the Lake of Nandan Sar. Below the city of Srinagar, the Behat is joined on the east by the Sindh, which is the largest of all its tributaries. From this junction the river continues its north-westerly course to the Wular lake, which it leaves above the town of Sopur, and then flows on in a south-west direction to Baráhmula, receiving midway the waters of the Loláb river. The whole length of the Behat, from its source to Baráhmula, is 150 miles. From Sháhábád to Baráhmula, the river is navigable. The fall is only 400 feet in 120 miles, or 3·33 feet per mile; and the usual rate of the current is about a mile and a half per hour. Vigne* says that a piece of wood thrown into the stream at Kánibal, will reach the city in 24 hours. As the distance is about 64 miles, the rate will be 2¾ miles per hour: but I was 2¼ hours in descending the stream from the Islamabad bridge to the Bij Bihâra bridge, a distance of little more than six miles, with two men gently paddling the boat. Again, in descending the stream from Bij Bihâra to Wantipur, I went on shore to

* Kashmir, II. p. 22.

warm myself by walking, and I distanced the boat, although it was paddled by two men. I do not therefore estimate the velocity of the current at more than $1\frac{1}{2}$ mile per hour, and I believe that it is considerably less.

At Islamabad, the breadth of the stream is 120 feet, with a maximum depth of 12 feet 3 inches. It is spanned by a log bridge, 118 feet in length, with two openings. At Bij Bihâra, below the junction of the Lidar river, it is spanned by a bridge 250 feet in length, with four openings. Between these points the water is beautifully clear, and the bed of the river is generally sandy, and ripple-marked, and covered with shells and broken pottery. In a few places the bottom is stony, but the stones are all small and rounded. At Pampur the Behat is spanned by another log bridge, 325 feet in length, with five openings; but the water is slightly muddy, and the bed of the river can no longer be seen. Below Pampur, and opposite Panthasok, the abutments and two piers of a stone bridge are just visible above the water. In its course through the city of Srinagar, the channel of the river is narrowed to 250, and even to 200 feet, with a varying depth of from six to twelve feet. The stream is very sluggish, and the surface of the water in many places is covered with the green slime common to stagnant pools. In December, Moorcroft found the river 210 feet broad, with a mean depth of nine feet, and a velocity of 2,400 feet per hour, or of 0·6666 feet per second; which gives a discharge of 1,150 cubic feet per second.

At Sambhal, or Sambhalpur, below the junction of the Sindh river, the Behat is spanned by another bridge, 340 feet long, with five openings. The average depth of the water is about fourteen feet at the same place. On the 16th December, Trebeck* found the depth of water from one to three fathoms. Assuming twelve feet as the average depth in December, and the rate of the current at 2,400 feet per hour (the same as at Srinagar), the winter discharge of the united streams of the Behat and Sindh rivers will be 2,480 cubic feet. At Barâhmula† the discharge is most probably not more, as the waters of the Loláb river may be supposed to supply the great loss by evaporation on the Wular lake.

From Barâhmula to Mozafarabad, the Behat pursues an easterly course for 100 miles. The total fall between these places is 3,800 feet, or thirty feet per mile; and the character of the river entirely changes from a placid and sluggish stream to a raving torrent. Below Tattamula, and about sixteen miles from Barâhmula, the rocky cliffs rise almost perpendicularly from the river to a height of 300 and 400 feet; and in some places that I noticed, the bare steep cliffs were not less than 800 feet above the stream.

As the height of the Behat, near Tattamula, is about 5,000 feet above the sea, the whole of Kashmir must have been submerged by the waters of the river, before the wearing down of these cliffs.‡ The level of the Kashmirian lake would have been about 5,800 feet above the sea, and from 50 to 100 feet above the Karewahs, or isolated alluvial flats now remaining in Kashmir.

* Moorcroft's Travels, II. p. 220.

† This name is properly *Varâha-mula*, the Boar Avatar's spring. The *Varâha Ganga* is now a dry hole, fifty feet long, thirty feet broad, and twenty feet deep. The spring has become dry, but the place is still esteemed holy.

‡ As Tattamula (*Sanskrit*, Tapta-mula), the "hot spring," may indicate volcanic action, the immediate cause of the bursting of the lake may have been the sudden rending of the rock by an earthquake.

The great Karewah of Nonagar, opposite Avantipur, which rises from 200 to 250 feet above the plain, is a mass of lacustrine deposit. I searched in vain for shells as I crossed over the Karewah to Payachh: but I was more fortunate at Wantipur, where I obtained numerous specimens of *Cyclas rivicola* in the horizontal strata of clay and sand at different heights up to nearly 200 feet above the present level of the river, and about eighty feet below the presumed level of the lake. The high level land of Marttand was probably not submerged, but the horizontal beach-marks are still quite distinct on the limestone cliffs above the cave of Bhaumajo and the holy spring of Bhawan. Above Rámuki Serai, on the Shupyen river, the Karewah forms a bank about 100 feet in height, in horizontal strata of different kinds. The uppermost twenty feet are composed of stiff alluvial soil; the next twenty feet of rolled stones and loose earth; and the lowermost sixty of indurated blue clay. The last must have been deposited by the lake in its state of quiescence; but the middle stratum could only have been formed by the first grand rush of waters on some sudden burst of the rocky barrier below Tattamula; and the uppermost would have been deposited by the subsiding waters as they reached the newly-formed level. Then, as the rocky bed was gradually worn down, the different streams worked new channels for themselves in the former bed of the lake, until the present Karewahs of Nonagar, Pampur, and Kánikpur were left first as islands in the decreasing lake, and eventually as long flat-topped hills in the midst of the open plain, just as we now see them. The Karewah of Nonagar is about five miles in length by two and a half miles in extreme breadth.

Above Uri the Behat has once been spanned by a stone bridge thrown across a very narrow part from cliff to cliff; but to judge from the lowness of the remaining portions of the abutments, the bridge must have been swept away by the very first extraordinary rise of the river. High up on the right bank stands a ruined serai of the Mogal emperors. Opposite Uri the river is now crossed by a suspension-bridge of leather ropes. Above Hatiya there is a second suspension-bridge of twisted leather ropes 258½ feet in length.

At Mozafarabad the Behat is joined by the Kishen Ganga, a considerable stream which rises in the mountains to the north of Kashmir, in N. latitude 34° 30′, and E. longitude 75° 20′. It flows first to the westward through the districts of Gures, Suti, and Drawá, then turning to the south-west it pursues its course through Kerigám and Karnâ to Mozafarabad. The late Mr. Vans Agnew ascended this river on his way to Gilgit; but as he was not a surveyor, his travels were confined to a mere descriptive account. The whole length of the Kishen Ganga is not less than 180 miles, and its probable discharge about 1,000 cubic feet. The total discharge of the Behat below Mozafarabad will therefore be 3,500 cubic feet.

Below Mozafarabad the Behat sweeps suddenly round to the southward, and after receiving the Kunihâr river continues the same course to the town of Jehlam, a distance of 150 miles. The fall in this part of the river is 1,200 feet, or only eight feet per mile. The Kunihâr river rises in the Nila mountain, eight days' journey to the north of Mozafarabad. Its whole length is about 100 miles. From the junction of the Kunihâr to Dhangali the Behat has been surveyed by Mr. Ingram, an assistant to Lieut. D. Robinson, of the engineers; and in this part of its course it receives no tributary worth mentioning. Near Mángali, at the foot of the hills, it is joined by the Punach river, a considerable stream, which is said to rise in the lake of Nandan Sar, in N. latitude 33° 35′, and E. longitude 74° 40′. It takes an easterly course between the Pir-Panjál and Ratan-Panjál, ranges past Bahrámgala to Punach, where it turns to the southward, and follows a south-westerly course to its junction with the Behat or Jehlam. Its whole length is 140 miles, and its discharge about 500 cubic feet.

The whole discharge of the Behat or Jehlam as it enters the plains is therefore just 4,000 cubic feet; this estimate is borne out by the statements of Moorcroft, who says that the river at Jehlam in October was 450 feet broad and from twelve to sixteen feet deep, with a current of about a mile an hour. These data give a discharge of 4,800 cubic feet per second for October, which would certainly be reduced to 4,000 cubic feet by February and March. The whole mountain course of the Behat, from beyond Virnag to Mángali, is 380 miles, and its fall is about 8,000 feet, or twenty-one feet per mile. From the hills to its junction with the Chenáb between Jhang and Uch, its general direction is south-south-westerly, and its length about 240 miles. Its whole length from its source to its confluence with the Chenáb is therefore about 620 miles.

VIII.—THE CHENÁB RIVER.

The Chenáb is formed of two principal feeders, the Chandra and the Bhaga, from which it derives its Sanskrit name of Chandra Bhaga. Ptolemy calls it Sandabal; but the Greek historians of Alexander named it the Akesines, because its proper name was one of ill omen.* The Chandra and the Bhaga rise on opposite sides of the Bara Lacha pass, in N. latitude 32° 45′, and E. longitude 77° 22′, at an elevation of 16,500 feet above the sea. The Chandra flows at first to the south for fifty-five miles, and then sweeps suddenly up to the north-west for sixty miles farther, to the junction of the Bhaga river at Tandi. The fall to this point is 7,500 feet, or sixty-five feet per mile, for the Chandra river, and 125 feet per mile for the Bhaga river, which has a course of only sixty miles to the south-west. At Koksar, twenty-five miles above Tandi and 10,000 feet above the sea, the Chandra river averages 200 feet in width, with a mean depth of two and a half feet, and a current of not less than four miles per hour in October, when it is fordable with very great difficulty. The discharge at that time is therefore not less than 2,000 cubic feet per second; and the minimum discharge is probably about 1,500 cubic feet, or of the united stream below Tandi about 2,000 cubic feet. From Tandi the Chandra Bhaga pursues a north-westerly course to Káshtwár, a further distance of 115 miles. The whole length to this point is 330 miles, and the fall is 11,500 feet, or 34·8 feet per mile.

Between Tandi and Káshtwár the Chandra Bhaga receives many snow-fed torrents of considerable size, of which the largest are the Chukam and Chatrgarh rivers. The discharge at Káshtwár cannot therefore be less than

* Bishop Thirlwall says perhaps owing to its similarity in sound to Αλεξανδρου φαγος, " devourer of Alexander." Aka-sin in Pushtu would mean river of the Akas; who probably gave their name to the town of Akanâwar or Aknur.

4,000 cubic feet, or just double that at Tandi, which is half-way between the source and the town of Káshtwár. Below the town it receives from the north the large river of Wardwan, about sixty miles in length, by which the discharge is probably increased to 4,500 cubic feet.

At Koksar, 10,000 feet above the sea, which is the highest inhabited village on the Chandra river, a suspension-bridge of twisted birchen ropes is annually constructed. A second suspension-bridge of the same kind formerly spanned the mouth of the Bhaga river at Tandi, but this was carried away some time after Dr. Gerard's visit in 1830. In 1839 I saw the ropes lying high and dry on the northern bank; but when I visited Tandi again in 1846, there was no trace of them. A small wooden bridge of thirty-eight feet span, and forty feet above the stream, is thrown across the Bhaga river about four miles from Tandi. Fifteen miles below Tandi, and five miles above Treloknáth, the Chandra Bhaga is crossed by a couple of spars covered with loose planks. The bridge is eighty-five feet long and forty-three feet above the water. Two miles above this bridge the river was not less than 300 feet broad. Above Chatrgarh and opposite Káshtwár, the Chandra Bhaga is crossed by suspension-bridges.

From Káshtwár the river sweeps suddenly round to the south-west as far as Doda. It then turns due west towards the fort of Riyâsi, where it resumes its south-westerly course to Aknur, at the foot of the hills, a total distance of 150 miles. In this part of the course the fall is 4,000 feet, or 26·6 feet per mile. It receives the Banahal and the Budhil, above Aknur, and the two Tohis of Rajaori and Chaneni above Vazirabad. By these and some other small streams, its winter discharge is increased to 4,750 cubic feet per second. This discharge has been calculated from my own data obtained at Ramnagar in January 1849. Our military bridge of boats afforded me every facility for obtaining the most accurate measurements, and I have therefore full confidence in the correctness of the result. The river was divided into two streams; that on the left bank having a maximum depth of fifteen feet four inches, and that on the right bank a maximum depth of ten feet six inches. The total breadth, including the sand-bank in the centre, which was barely covered with water, was 646 feet, or, excluding the sand-bank, 533 feet. The greatest surface velocity was 3·6666 feet per second, or just two miles and three-quarters per hour. The mean depth was exactly five feet, and the mean surface velocity 2·3 feet per second, or nearly one mile and five furlongs per hour. I have calculated each portion of the stream separately, and the result gives a discharge of 4551·038 cubic feet per second. A similar result may be obtained from the rough measurements of Sir Alexander Burnes,* made at the same place in the middle of February. His data make the breadth 900 feet, greatest depth nine feet, and current one and a half mile per hour. Taking four and a half as the average depth, the discharge will be 4,860 cubic feet. I only give this to show the correctness of my own measurements.

From the Bara Lacha pass to Aknur, the length of the Chenáb is 380 miles, and the whole fall is 15,500 feet, or 40·8 feet per mile. From Aknur to Mithankot the length is 570 miles in a south-south-west direction, and the whole length from its source to its junction with the Indus is 950 miles.

* Burnes' Travels, Vol. I. p. 46.

During the dry season the Chenáb is fordable in many places between Sodra and Ramnagar. Opposite Sodra in 1848 there was a good ford, crossing no less than seven branches of the stream. The Ramnagar ford was open during the whole of our operations in December 1848, and January and February 1849. The other fords were constantly liable to shift, but three days before the battle of Gujrat I discovered a good ford between Vazirabad and Ramnagar, by which Brigadier Markham's brigade crossed the Chenáb on the 19th February.

I have no means of ascertaining the maximum discharge of the Chenáb during July and August. Macartney measured it in July at Vazirabad, when the stream was 7,590 feet (nearly one mile and a half) broad, with a depth of fourteen feet, and a current of five miles an hour; but these data are too vague for even an approximate result. The depth for one half of this breadth was probably not more than one or two feet.

In July 1839, I found the main channel of the Chenáb above Vazirabad to be 2,760 feet broad, but the depth could not be ascertained with any certainty; in many places it was more than eighteen feet. The mean depth was probably about nine feet, and if we allow two and a half miles as the average rate of the current, the maximum discharge would be 56,000 cubic feet, or with the six small branches to the westward, not less than 60,000 cubic feet. The increase of the Indus is nine-fold, while that of the Ganges is fifteen-fold. The mean between these is twelve-fold, which, if applied to the Chenáb, would give a discharge of 54,600 cubic feet for the maximum. The actual maximum discharge is probably between 50,000 and 60,000 cubic feet.

IX.—THE RÁVI RIVER.

The Rávi is the smallest of the Panjáb rivers. In the hills it is generally called Ráwá or Râwati, which is only a spoken form of the Sanskrit Trâvati, from which the Greeks made Hydraotes. The Rávi is formed of three principal branches,—the Rávi proper, the holy Budhil, and the Nai, which make a triple junction below Wulás, in the district of Chamba. I have seen all these rivers myself, and am indeed the only European who has yet visited the head-waters of this stream.

The Rávi rises in the petty dismembered state of Bangál, in N. latitude 32° 20′, and E. longitude 77° 0′. It takes at first a south-westerly course, and then bending to the north-west receives its principal tributaries at Wulás, a distance of sixty miles from its source. Its highest springs rise at the junction of the Dhaola Dhar and Lahul mountains, at an elevation of not less than 16,000 feet. As the height of the river at Wulás is only 5,000 feet, the fall is 183·3 feet per mile. From Wulás to Bisoli it continues its easterly course for fifty miles, and then turns to the south-west for twenty miles, to the neighbourhood of Tirikot, where it enters the plains. Its whole length is only 130 miles, while its fall is 15,000 feet, or 115·4 feet per mile.

The sacred Budhil rises in the Lahul mountains, to the north of the Rávi. Its whole course is not more than thirty-five miles from east to west, while the fall is 11,000 feet, or 314·3 feet per mile. Below Barmawar, the former capital of Chamba, the Budhil is crossed by a wooden bridge formed of spars covered with loose planks. The width is four and a half feet, the span sixty-eight feet, and the height above the river ninety-eight feet. This bridge has a hand-rail knee high on each side. A petty feeder of the Budhil rises in the small and holy lake of Mani Mahés.

The Nai river rises on the western face of the Kali Debi mountain, in the Lahul range. Its general course is to the south-west, and its whole length is only thirty miles. Its fall is therefore 366·6 feet per mile.

The Ráwá or Râwati, just above the junction of the Budhil and Nai at Wulás, is spanned by a birchen-rope suspension-bridge 116 feet in length. It is therefore about double the size of the Budhil river. Below Wulás the road leaves the river and crosses over the mountains, to avoid the precipitous cliffs which overhang the stream. At Mahila, ten miles above Chamba, the Rávi is crossed by another suspension-bridge of 169 feet span. Between the bridge and Chamba the river takes a sudden sweep to the left, between overhanging rocks not more than fifteen feet apart. A curling wave returns to meet the rushing stream, and a shower of mist is perpetually rising from the shock. Then all is smooth, and the stream pours headlong into a gulf below, and is instantly dashed back by the opposing rocks in a huge curling wave.

Just below Chamba the Rávi receives a considerable feeder from the north. This is the Sáwá, or Sár Nala, which rises in the Saj Joth, in the Lahul range. On entering the plains the Rávi takes a south-westerly course past Lahore for 430 miles to Chichawatni, where it turns to the west, and after seventy miles more falls into the Chenáb below Sirdarpur. The whole length of the Rávi from its source to its confluence with the Chenáb is 630 miles, and its minimum discharge is 2,700 cubic feet. The Rávi is fordable throughout the winter season, but the bed is full of quicksands.

X.—THE BYÁS RIVER.

The Byás is perhaps the best known of all the Panjáb rivers, from its source to the foot of the hills below Mirthal. Its Sanskrit name is *Vipása*, from which the Greeks made Hyphasis and Bibasis. The common name of Byás is derived from the small pool at the source of the river, which is called Vyás Rikhi or Vyása Rishi. This sacred spot is situated in the Rotang pass, at the head of the Kullu valley, in N. latitude 32° 25′, and E. longitude 77° 10′, at an elevation of 13,000 feet above the sea. For seventy-five miles the river flows nearly due south past Sultánpur, the capital of Kullu, to the village of Larji, where it is joined by two large tributaries,—the Sainj and the Tirthan. Above this it receives the Parbati and the Gomati rivers from the east, besides many smaller streams. The Gomati is fordable with difficulty, but the others can only be crossed by bridges. The Sainj has a course of about fifty miles, the Parbati and the Gomati of forty miles, and the Tirthan of thirty miles. From the source to Larji the fall is 9,400 feet, or 125·3 feet per mile. From Larji the Byás sweeps suddenly to the westward through a narrow chasm in the rocks several hundred feet in depth. The stream is deep and rapid, but before the wearing down of this cleft the whole of the lower part of the valley must have been submerged. From Larji to Mandi the distance is not more than twenty-five miles, while the fall is 1,000 feet, or forty feet per mile.

The Byás continues its westerly course through this narrow channel to Mandi, above which it receives the Ul river from the north, and the Sukhet river from the south. The former is upwards of fifty miles in length, and the latter about thirty miles. At Mandi the river is crossed by a boat for the greater part of the year, but during the height of the seasonal floods the current is too strong for a boat, and the passage is then made on inflated skins. Between Sultanpur and Larji the river can only be crossed on skins, but from Sultanpur upwards it is spanned in many places by spar bridges.

From Mandi to Mirthal the general direction of the river is to the west; but the course is very winding, and the length cannot be less than 150 miles. Between these points it receives several large streams from the north, of which the chief are the Binwa, the Nigwal, the Bán-Ganga, the Gaj, and the Chakki.

The *Binwa* rises in the Dhaola Dhar range, and after a southerly course of forty miles past Baijnáth falls into the Byás opposite Kamalagarh. The road from Kangra and Mandi ascends this stream to its source, and crosses over the Surai pass into Chamba on the upper course of the Rávi.

The *Nigwal* rises in the same range, and after a southerly course of forty miles through the beautiful districts of Pálam, falls into the Byás opposite the large town of Shujanpur-Tira.

The *Bán-Ganga* is formed of two principal feeders,—the Bán-Ganga and the Patál-Ganga, which rise in the Dhaola-Dhar, and join immediately below the fort of Kangra. The general direction as far as Kangra is south-west, but below the fort the stream winds very much, and changes its direction first to the south and then to the west as far as Haripur and Guler, from whence it resumes its south-west direction, and falls into the Byás at the village of Nireyána, after a course of about sixty miles through the district of Katoch.

The *Gaj* or *Ghar-Gaj* is one of the largest feeders of the Byás, and was thought worthy of mention by Abu Rihán, who accompanied Mahmud of Ghazni to Kangra. It is formed of the united streams of the Gaj, the Kohli, the Brál, the Dehar, and the Bhet, all of which rise in the Dhaola Dhar range, and flow to the south through the district of Guler. The whole length of the Gaj to its junction with the Byás below Siba is not less than sixty miles.

The *Chakki* rises in the western end of the Dhaola Dhar, and is the smallest and longest of all these northern tributaries of the Byás. Its whole length from its source near the Chuâri pass to its junction with the Byás at Biyánpura below Mirthal is not less than seventy miles.

On the south the Byás receives only one feeder of any consequence,—the Kunihâr, which joins it a few miles above Nadon; but except in the rains, it contains very little water.

From Mandi to Mirthal, a distance of 150 miles, the fall of the river is only 1,600 feet, or 10·6 feet per mile. The whole fall from the source to Mirthal is 12,000 feet, or forty-eight feet per mile. In this part of its course the Byás maintains its supremacy as the most beautiful river in the Panjáb. From Biyánpura, below Mirthal, the Byás flows in a south and south-westerly direction past the towns of Rahila, Bhairowal, and Govindwál, to its junction with the Sutluj at Hariki-patan, a distance of 100 miles. The whole length of the Byás, from its source to its confluence with the Sutluj, is 350 miles, and its minimum discharge is not less than 3,000 cubic feet.

On the 10th November, 1838, I measured the Byás a few miles above its junction with the Sutluj. Its breadth was 450 feet, and its greatest depth seven feet four inches. Its greatest surface velocity was 4·04 feet per second, or a little more than two miles and three-quarters per hour. The discharge was then 3,425 cubic feet, from which we may calculate the minimum discharge at not less than 3,000 cubic feet.

During the melting of the snows the Byás rises every night in the plains from one foot to one foot and a half. It attains its maximum in the morning and subsides during the day. When I was making the bridges at Govindwál for the passage of the army in March, 1846, I pitched my tent on the sand close to the water's edge, and in the morning I was surprised to find one line of tent-pegs completely under water. This rise is caused by the melted snows of the Dhaola Dhar, which are brought down during the day by the Binwa, the Nigwal, the Bán-Ganga, and the Gaj, and which do not reach Bhairowal and Govindwál until past midnight of the second day, after a lapse of 36 hours. The Byás is fordable in many places in the plains.

XI.—THE SUTLUJ RIVER.

The *Sutluj* is the largest and longest of all the Panjáb rivers. Its Sanskrit name is *Satadru*, or the "hundred channelled," from which the Greeks made Hesudros and Zadadros; but the common names throughout the hills are Satludr, or Satrudr, and Sutluj. The Tibetans call it *Lang-chhen-kha-bab*, or "elephant-mouth-fed" river, according to the commonly received notion of the descent of rivers from animals' mouths.

The rise of the Sutluj in the holy lakes of Manasarovara and Ráwan-Hrad has been satisfactorily ascertained by the adventurous journeys of Captain H. Strachey and Lieut. R. Strachey. The most remote sources of the Sutluj are the eastern feeders of the holy lakes, in N. latitude 30° 35′, and E. longitude 81° 35′. Numerous small streams flow from all sides into the great lake of Manasarovara, which overflows at its north-eastern corner into the lake of Ráwan-Hrad. From this point to its junction with the Spiti river, at the base of Porgyal, the Sutluj takes a west-north-westerly direction through a country but little known, but which I believe to be similar to that of the upper valley of the Indus. From its source to the confluence of the Spiti river the length of the Sutluj is 280 miles, and the whole fall is 9,400 feet, or 33·8 feet per mile.

From the base of Porgyal to Biláspur the Sutluj takes a west-south-westerly direction for 180 miles. In this part the fall increases to thirty-nine feet per mile, and the river becomes a furious torrent. Many old channels still exist to show that the Sutluj once flowed at a higher level, and that all the alluvial flats must have been the deposits of a series of lakes. Eddy-worn holes also may be seen high up in the rock, even up to 1,000 feet above the present level of the river. Two of these ancient channels are on the left bank, one just above Rampur, and the other opposite the Wongto bridge. The Rampur channel is 150 feet above the stream, and 100 feet broad, between large dykes of quartz, the intervening mica-slate having been scooped out for some depth. A little higher up, the river has made a perpendicular cut through one of these quartzose dykes about sixty feet deep.

From Bilâspur the Sutluj makes a sudden sweep to the north-west, and then back again to the south-east, round the end of the lowermost range of hills, and finally enters the plains at Ropar. The distance is 100 miles, and the fall about 500 feet, or five feet per mile. The whole length of the Sutluj, from its source beyond Manasoravara to the foot of the hills at Ropar, is 560 miles, and the whole fall about 17,000 feet, or thirty feet per mile. From Ropar, the Sutluj takes an easterly direction for 120 miles past Lodiana, to the confluence of the Byasat Hari-ki-patan, beyond which it flows to the south-west for 400 miles to its junction with the Chenáb opposite Uch. The whole length of its course is, therefore, 1,080 miles, or 130 miles more than the length of the Chenáb.

The minimum discharge of the Sutluj at Ropar is 5,400 feet. As a small addition must be made for the Sirsa Nadi, the Kali Vehi, and the Dhaoli Vehi,* we may reckon the discharge of the Sutluj, above its confluence with the Byás, at 5,500 cubic feet, or just 1,000 cubic feet more than that of the Chenáb. The Sutluj is fordable in many places above the junction of the Byás, below which it becomes deeper, and is usually called the Ghara river.

Like the other Punjáb rivers, the Sutluj has a daily rise and fall, owing to the increase and decrease of the melted snows. On 29th May, at Kepu, below Kotgarh, I measured a rise of ten inches, the higher level being obtained at 3 A.M. In July the Spiti river at Kyi attained its maximum of four inches and a half at

* In November, 1838, I measured the Kali Vehi and Dhaoli Vehi, and found that each of them discharged a little more than 100 cubic feet per second.

3 P.M. This is in fact the hour at which I have found that all these snow-fed streams reach their highest level. If, therefore, we assume that the Sutluj, at the mouth of its last great feeder, the Baspa, reaches its maximum at 3 P.M., we shall obtain a mean velocity of six miles and a quarter per hour as far as Kepu, a distance of seventy-five miles.

XII.—THE SPITI RIVER.

The Spiti river, which is perhaps as large as the Sutluj itself, is formed of two principal branches,—the Spiti and the Párá-ti or Zang-sum river. It takes its rise near the Bara Lacha Pass, in N. latitude 32° 4′, and E. longitude 77° 40′, at an elevation of 16,500 feet (the height of the Bara Lacha Pass). From its source to the village of Mane, it flows in a south-easterly direction for eighty-five miles, and then turns to the eastward for thirty-five miles to its junction with the Párá river. The fall is 6,000 feet, or fifty feet per mile. From Chang-Razing the river turns to the south for twenty-five miles, through a narrow rocky channel to its confluence with the Sutluj. The fall to this point is 2,000 feet, or eighty feet per mile; and the whole fall, throughout its entire course of 145 miles, is 8,000 feet, or fifty-five feet per mile.

In the upper part of its course, the Spiti river partakes of the general character of the Tibetan streams, and spreads its waters over a breadth of nearly half a mile. It thus becomes fordable, during the winter season, as far as Dangkhar, where it receives the Pin river from the south. Below this, it is crossed by several suspension-bridges. Opposite Rangrig, it is spanned by a spar bridge with a hurdle footway. At Shálkar, below the junction of the Párá, it is crossed by another spar bridge ninety-two feet long; and there is a third wooden bridge between Liya and Nako.

The Párá-ti, or Párá river, was considered by Alexander Gerard to be larger than the Spiti; but there is no comparison between the two. The Párá is only a very large rushing torrent, while the Spiti is a very deep rapid river. The Párá rises in the Parang Pass, to the north of the Bara Lacha range, in N. latitude 32° 25′, and E. longitude 77° 50′, at an elevation of 18,000 feet. It first flows for about twenty-five miles to the north-east, and for about twenty-five miles to the east as far as Chumur. From this point it turns to the south-east, and afterwards to the south-west, to its junction with the Spiti at Chang-Razing. Its whole length is 130 miles, and its fall about 7,500 feet, or 57·7 feet per mile.

Just above the confluence of the two rivers, there is a hot spring named Zang-sum, and the lower part of the Párá is sometimes called by this name. Alexander Gerard took the Zang-sum for another river, and has accordingly entered it in his map. But it is quite evident that he mistook the Gyu, a small tributary which joins the Spiti just above the confluence of the Párá, for the Párá itself. I surveyed this locality with some care, and can therefore state positively that Alexander Gerard was mistaken.

Four miles above its confluence with the Spiti, the Párá river is spanned by a single block of granite, which forms a vast natural bridge eighty-five feet in length, and from twenty-five to thirty feet in breadth and depth. The stream below is contracted to a raging torrent, not more than fifteen feet in width.

XIII.—CATACLYSM OF THE SUTLUJ.

About midnight on the 26th day of the month of Kartik, and in the Sambat year 1819 (10th November, A.D. 1762), the shoulder of a vast mountain gave way, and fell from a great height headlong into the Sutluj. The slip took place in the neighbourhood of the hot springs at Seoni, about twenty miles nort h by west fom Simla, where the river is confined between precipitous cliffs that rise several thousand feet above the stream. The narrow channel was instantly choked with a vast mass of rock, earth, and rubbish, to a height of more than four hundred feet, and the stream for the space of forty days was so completely dammed that the water ceased to flow below the barrier. The bed of the Sutluj was reduced to a succession of deep pools, scattered amongst the huge boulders and angular masses of rock, and the people passed over with dry feet. The waters of the river accumulated till they rose nearly four hundred feet in height opposite the Rana's residence at Bhaji, and the effect of the obstruction is said to have been felt as high up the river as Rámpur, a distance of forty kos, or about sixty miles. At Bhaji, a lofty semal, or cotton-tree, which was half-submerged, is still pointed out; and as the height of this cotton-tree above the Sutluj is estimated by the Rana at 120 yards, the rise of the river cannot have been less than 400 feet.

A similar account was obtained by Alexander Gerard* in 1817, when numbers of people who had witnessed the flood were still alive. "About fifty-five years since, forty or fifty miles above this town (Bilâspur), an im-

* Kanawar, p. 55. Gerard says fifty-five years ago; that is, from A.D. 1817; which gives A.D. 1762, agreeing with my date.

mense mountain gave way, filled the bed of the Sutluj, and arrested the stream for six weeks. During this time the inhabitants were anxiously looking out for the bursting of the embankment. When it did give way, the rush of such an overwhelming body of water may be more easily conceived than described. People were stationed on the heights all along from the place where the stream was stopped as far as Bilâspur, and they gave notice of the approach of the flood by firing matchlocks. The news arrived in time to save the inhabitants, but the whole of the town was swept away."

This account is not quite correct, for it was only the lower town that was swept away, as the houses of the upper town, including the Raja's palace, and several old temples, are situated on an elevated flat far above the reach of any inundation. The distance from Seoni to Bilâspur is not more than forty-five miles by the river, and about thirty miles by land. The wave of inundation would therefore have reached Bilâspur in three hours, at the rate of fifteen miles per hour, while the news of the bursting of the barrier could have been signalled by matchlocks in half an hour.

As my information is derived from the Rana of Bhaji, in whose principality Seoni is situated, I have full confidence in the general accuracy of my account, even including the statement that the bed of the Sutluj became quite dry for the space of forty days. At first I was disinclined to believe this startling fact, but a little reflection showed me that it must have been the case; for as the fall of the Sutluj in this part of its course is not more than twenty feet per mile, the accumulated waters must have filled the bed of the river for twenty miles before they attained a height of 400 feet, level with the top of the barrier. To fill this gulf would have required the accumulated discharge of the river for about forty days. The minimum discharge being 5,400 cubic feet at Ropar, the discharge at Seoni in November cannot be less than 5,500 cubic feet. This discharge accumulated for forty days would have amounted to 19,008,000,000 cubic feet, a mass of water which would only just have been sufficient to fill the gulf in the bed of the Sutluj for twenty miles above the barrier to a mean depth of 200 feet, with an average breadth of 900 feet. The flow of the river must therefore have been quite stopped below the barrier for the whole period of forty days.

When the accumulated waters once began to pour over the obstructing barrier, the mass of loose earth and rocks must have been speedily cut up in all directions, until it soon yielded to the pressure of the mighty body of water; and the long-imprisoned river burst its fetters and rushed headlong down its rocky channel in one mighty wave, from fifty to more than one hundred feet in height This occurred on the fifth day of the month of *Paush*, or the 19th of December. Of its progress in the hills I know nothing more than what I have already quoted from Gerard of the destruction of the lower town of Bilâspur. But after reaching the plains, the mighty wave was swept more and more to the northward by its own speed off the Sewalik hills at Ropar, and thus took a new course under Phalor to the north of the old channel until it joined the Byasat Hari-ki-patan, where its further course to the northward was stopped by the stiff high cliffs on the right bank of the Byás. From this time the Sutluj, when swollen by the annual rains, continued to pour its waters down the new channel until about A.D. 1790, when the whole body of water finally deserted the old bed by Lodiana and Dharmkot, and joined the Byás at Hari-ki-patan, some thirty miles above the former point of junction at Firozpur. For six months the Sutluj remained above its usual level until the rise of the river in June, when the last remains of the once mighty barrier were swept away by the swollen river.

The following table embodies all the principal points of information contained in the preceding pages.

	Rivers.	Length.			Fall per mile.		Discharge.	
		In Hills.	In Plains.	Total.	In Hills.	In Plains.	Min.	Max.
1	Indus Proper	1,035	942	1,977	15·4	1·06	16,500	
2	Shayok	400	—	400	26·4	—	2,000	
3	Zanskar	210	—	210	28·5	—	1,000	
4	Jehlam	380	240	620	21·0	—	4,000	
5	Chenab	380	570	950	40·8	—	4,550	54,000
6	Rávi	130	500	630	115·4	—	2,700	
7	Byás	150	100	350	48·0	—	3,000	
8	Sutluj	560	520	1,080	30·0	—	5,500	
9	Panjnad	—	—	—	—	—	12,000	100,000
10	Indus alone........	—	—	—	—	—	15,000	130,177
11	Indus and Panjnad	—	—	—	—	—	27,000	230,177
12	Ganges at Ghazipur	250	1,500	1,750	52·0	0·66	21,757	476,761
	Ganges at Pubna ..	—	—	—	—	—	96,000	1,500,000

V.—LAKES AND SPRINGS.

All sheets of water are known by the general name of *Tsho*, which is applied to the smallest pond as well as to the largest lake: as *Tsho-Máphan*, the Manasarovara Lake, "which is about sixteen miles square," and *Kyang-Tsho*, the "Wild Horses' Pond," which is a mere seasonal puddle of melted snow. The ocean is called *Gya-Tsho*, or the "Vast Lake."* The proper appellation, however, for a small piece of water is *Tshá-hu;* but the pronunciation of the two words is so much alike that the difference is almost imperceptible. In fact none but Lamas ever make the distinction, either in writing or in utterance. With a single exception, all the lakes of Ladák are land-locked, and consequently more or less salt; although the time has been when every one of them poured its tributary waters into the affluents of the Indus.

The *Pangkong*† Lake is a very long, narrow sheet of water, extending from east to west through the whole length of Ruthog, in N. latitude 33° 40′, to the neighbourhood of Chushal, from whence it trends to the north-west for about twenty-five miles, and forms the boundary between Ladák and Ruthog. Its eastern extremity is

* *mTsho*, a lake; *rGya-mTsho*, the great lake.

† *mTsho-dPangs-kong*, "Lake of the great hollow."

Ancient Lake System of Ladak.

Plate V

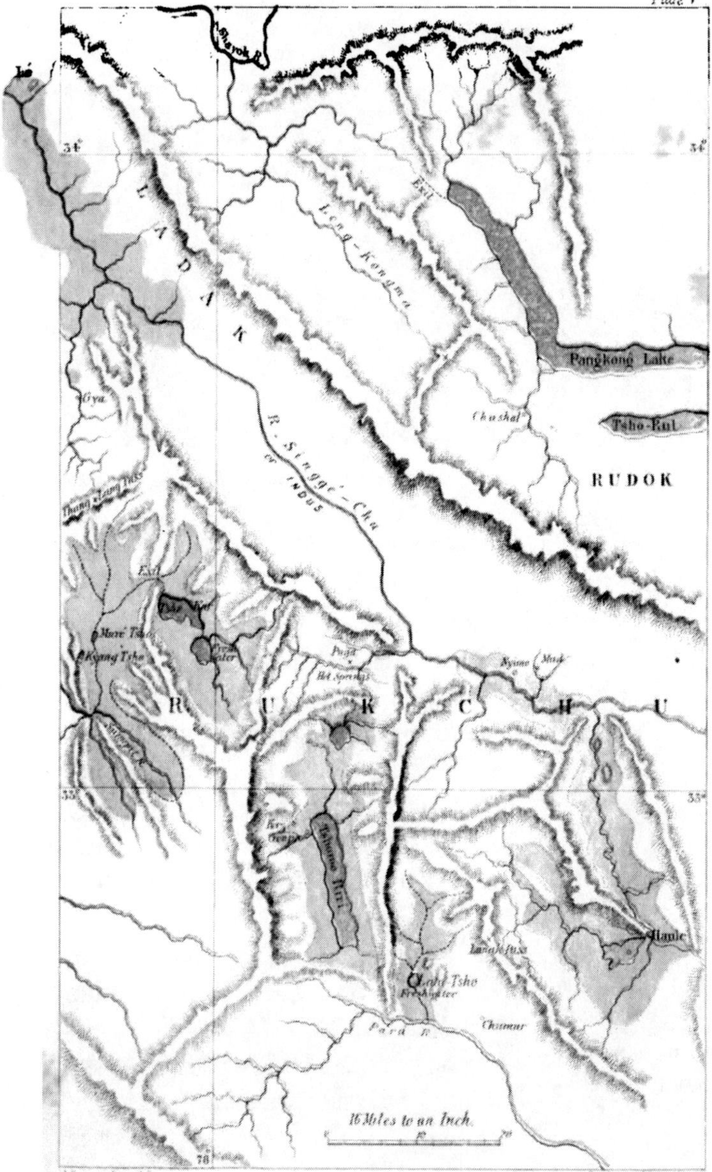

unknown; but from the neighbourhood of Ruthog to its north-western extremity beyond Pangmik, the Pangkong Lake is not less than eighty-five miles in length, with an average breadth of about three miles.* The extent of the known portion is, therefore, upwards of 250 square miles, or about the same size as the holy lake of Manasarovara. The superior size of this lake may be inferred from the probable etymology of its name, *Pang-kong*, which means the "extensive concavity" or hollow; or *Pang-khung*, the "extensive pit." The water is clear and extremely salt.† This lake has been surveyed by Captain H. Strachey, whose observations place it at an elevation of 14,224 feet above the sea. In former ages there can be no doubt that the Pangkong Lake had an outlet at its north-western extremity, through a gorge in the limestone cliffs,‡ into the present scanty stream that passes by Muglib, and joins the Shayok river just above the village, which gives its name to the stream. At some remote period, therefore, the waters of the Pangkong Lake must have been fresh; a fact which has been placed beyond all doubt by Captain H. Strachey's discovery of fossil shells of the *Lymnæa auricularia* in the ancient clay deposits above the present level of the lake. The mountain-ranges at the north-western extremity of the lake are of limestone, which probably affects the waters of the lake, as the small pebbles on its shores are firmly united together by calcareous matter.

The *Tsho-Rul*,§ or "Bitter Lake," is situated about five miles to the south of Pangkong. It is about sixteen miles in length, and somewhat less than two miles in

* Moorcroft, I. p. 435. † Ibid. I. pp. 434-35.

‡ This gorge was traversed by Moorcroft (I. 434.)

§ *Rui-ba* bad, fetid, bitter.

breadth. Its waters are extremely bitter. On its shore Captain H. Strachey likewise found fossil shells of the *Lymnæa auricularia* and of some kind of *Helix*, of which the specimens are perhaps too small to be identified with certainty. The waters of this lake must, therefore, once have been fresh.

The *Tshomoriri*,* or "Mountain Lake," is a very fine sheet of water, about sixteen miles in length from north to south, and from two to three miles in breadth. It is situated in the middle of the elevated district of Rukchu, in N. latitude 32° 50′, and E. longitude 78° 15′, at a height of 15,000 feet above the sea. Its name is characteristic of its situation in the midst of mountains, by which it is completely shut in. The summits of these mountains rise to a height of about 5,000 feet above the lake, and 20,000 above the sea. To account for its name, the Ladakis have invented a story, which though silly enough, is quite as good as many that have been gravely recorded by learned Greeks. The story was probably originated by the inventive Kashmiris. "A woman riding a yák was carried into the lake. At first the yák swam boldly out, and the woman was delighted: but after a time the animal grew tired, and sank deeper in the water. The woman (*chomo*) became frightened, and screamed out *Ri-Ri, Ri-Ri*,† until the yák sank and she

* *Tsho-mo-Rhi-ri*, "Lake Mountainous."—Running water, being active, is considered as a male, as *Tsang-po*, the river of *Tsang*;—and still water, being passive, as a female, as *Tsho-mo*. *Po* and *Mo* are the masculine and feminine affixes, but they are seldom used in composition. *Ri* is a mountain; and *Rhi-ri-yi*, or simply *Rhi-ri*, is the adjective, mountainous.

† *A-ra-ra*, commonly pronounced *Re-re*, or *Ri-ri*, is the Tibetan exclamation of surprise or fear. As the word is written with an initial vowel, it is certainly borrowed from the Indian *Ari-ari*, for there is no word in the Tibetan language beginning with a vowel that is not of foreign origin.

was drowned: since which the people have always called the lake *Chomo-Riri.*"

This lake has no outlet at present, and the waters are consequently brackish, although not very perceptibly so to the taste. But the time has perhaps once been, when the Tshomoriri lake was a noble sheet of fresh water, about thirty miles in length, from the foot of the Nakpo Gonding Pass to the low ridge that now separates the lake from the bed of the Párá river. When encamped at the south end of the lake in September, 1846, both the late Mr. Vans Agnew and myself estimated the height of this ridge at 700 feet; but it must have been somewhat more, as the bed of the Parang river at Norbu Sumdo is 15,700 feet. From this point, however, the apparent height of the ridge is not more than 150 feet. This will make its actual height above the lake between 800 and 900 feet. Such, therefore, must have been the depth of the lake in former days, if, as is supposed, it once had an outlet towards the Párá river. In September, 1846, I was encamped for three days on its banks. The water was beautifully limpid and of a deep blue colour. Here and there I observed white patches of saline matter, but I could not discover any shells. The salts are hydro-chlorate of soda and hydro-chlorate of magnesia. I could not see any fish in the water, but the wild fowl were numerous at the northern end of the lake. On the 18th September I fixed a pole in the water, which I examined twice during that day, and again early the next morning; but I found no perceptible difference between the levels of the day and night. The extra quantity of water that is supplied during the day by the melted snow must, therefore, be compensated by the greater evaporation during the heat of the day. In the same month of the year, Dr. Gerard* could not find any water-mark above five feet, which he consequently fixed as the limit of fluctuation; but I doubt whether the rise and fall of the lake amount to so much as one foot. In the middle of May, Trebeck† says that it is "frozen over sufficiently to be crossed by a man;" and according to the information that I received, it is usually frozen over by the end of October. During the winter there can be no fluctuation of level, as the whole surface of the ice is protected from the sun's rays by a mass of snow about knee deep. Towards the end of May or the beginning of June the ice breaks up and melts, and by the end of July the surface of the lake attains its highest level, which from the water-marks that I saw, cannot be more than one foot above the winter level.

Thogji-Chanmo is the name of the "Salt-covered Plain,"‡ in the midst of which lies the *Tsho-Kar*, or "White Lake," or as it is called by the Hindus of Chamba and Bisahar, *Khaori-Talao*, or the Salt Lake. It is situated about thirty miles to the north-west of the Tshomoriri, in N. latitude 33° 15′, and E. longitude 77° 50′, at an elevation of 15,684 feet§ above the sea. It is extremely irregular in shape; its greatest length from east to west being about five miles, and its extreme breadth about two and a half miles. It is supplied at its south-eastern corner by a small stream ten feet broad and one foot deep, which flows slowly from a small fresh-water lake. In the middle of the south side, where a

* Researches As. Soc. Bengal, vol. xviii. p. 259.

† Moorcroft's Travels, II. p. 52.

‡ The proper name is probably *Thang-Tsha-chan-mo*, "Plain-salt-full-of."

§ Dr. Gerard, As. Res. Bengal, vol. xviii. p. 260, makes the elevation 15,500 feet.

rocky promontory juts out into the lake, the water is very deep. On the north and east sides it is shallow; but on the west, the steep slope of the mountains appears to be continued beneath the surface. The water is exceedingly brackish and bitter, and the whole of the ground on the south-eastern shore glitters with a saline matter, which forms a thick crust of some extent. The southern road passes over this vast cake of salt, which cracks and crunches beneath the feet of the traveller. The salt is natron, or sub-carbonate of soda. On all sides the mountains still retain the ancient beach-marks in distinct lines, at all heights up to about 150 feet above the present level of the lake. In the numerous deposits of fine alluvial clay, both white and yellow, we found myriads of fossil shells of the *Lymnæa auricularia*, and a few specimens of a *Cyclas*, preserved inside the Lymnæa. When these animals existed, the lake must have formed a vast sheet of fresh water with a narrow passage to the westward, which connected it with a second and larger lake, that must have covered the whole of the present plain from Kyang, from the foot of the Thung Lung Pass to the forks of the Sum Gal river, a length of about thirty-five miles. In the clay deposits of this plain, as well as in the connecting gorge, we found myriads of the same fossil shells (*Lymnæa auricularia*) before mentioned. The Tsho-kar lake abounds with many kinds of water-fowl, especially with wild geese and wild ducks. To the south of the Tsho-kar there is a small fresh-water lake of no great depth, that supplies the salt-water lake. It is a very favourite haunt of the *Kyang*, or wild horse.

The *Yunam Tsho* is a small sheet of fresh water in the

bed of the Yunam river, which flows through it. In former times it must have been of some extent, and of considerable depth. When I saw it, in September, 1846, it was only 1,000 yards long and 500 yards broad. Moorcroft was informed "that it had been more extensive, but had been contracted by the falling into it of masses of rock." The gradual decrease in size has, however, been brought about by a very different cause; by the constant wearing away of the rocky barrier, which once dammed the river about one mile below the present end of the lake. Between these points the river has worn a channel through a mass of fine cream-coloured clay,* which once formed the bed of the Yunam lake. I found the lake of a very pale yellowish colour, which it had received from the cream-coloured clay deposits in the bed of a small stream upwards of half a mile above the lake. The extreme length must once have been about three miles, and the breadth varying from a quarter of a mile to more than a mile.

The *Hánlé-Tsho* is the largest sheet of fresh water that to my knowledge exists in Ladák. The extent of open water is not great, but the whole extent of swamp is between three and four miles in length. It is principally supplied by a rivulet called the Kongra-chu, which drains the lofty range of mountains to the westward of the Tshomoriri lake as far south as the Lának Pass. A second feeder flows from a southern range of mountains, that divide Rukchu from the Chinese district of Chumur-ti. A third small stream, which joins it from the north-west, is full of fish, which attain a size of fourteen or fifteen inches. To the east of the lake is situated the

* Moorcroft, I. p. 217, also notices this fine clay.

picturesque monastery of Hanlé, on the end of a rocky spur about 500 feet above the plain. Round the foot of this spur the waters of the lake find an outlet into the long and level plain of Mangkang, through which the Hanlé rivulet winds from side to side for a distance of thirty miles. Towards the northern end of the valley there are several low flat-topped hills, with large masses of alluvial clay deposits still adhering to them in horizontal strata. As the total fall from Hanlé to the northern end of the valley cannot be more than 150 feet, there can be little doubt that the Hanlé Tsho once covered the whole of these level plains, and formed a noble lake fully forty miles in length by fifteen miles in extreme breadth, to the south of Hanlé. The plain is now pretty thickly covered with Dámá or Tibetan furze, which here grows to the unusual height of three and four and even five feet.

Small pieces of water are numerous all over Ladák, but none that I have seen are deserving of notice for any peculiarity, excepting the celebrity of their names. Two of them are mentioned by Abul Fazl in the Ayin Akbari.* "From the top of the mountains of Keetwar (Kashtwar) issue two springs, one called Chandra and the other Bhágá; * * they unite their streams and are then called Chandra Bhágá," which is the well-known Sanscrit name of the Chenáb. The Suraj Dal is a small oblong sheet of clear green water, dammed at the western end by masses of splintered rock that have fallen from above. It is about a quarter of a mile long and only half as broad. A small rill of melted snow flows into it from the east; but the rill is altogether so

* Gladwin's Ayin Akbari, II. p. 108.

insignificant, that the Suraj Dal may fairly be considered, as it is reputed to be, the source of the Bhágá river. But the Chandra Dal, although double the size of the Suraj Dal, is situated at least twenty-five miles below the real source of the Chandra river, in the Bara Lacha Pass. It is, however, always spoken of as the source of the Chandra river. Dal is a Kashmiri term for any sheet of water, whether large or small: but it is also a Tibetan word, signifying "still, quiet."*

Many hot springs exist in different parts of Ladák; but the best known are those of Nubra, Puga, and Chushul. The first two were visited by Moorcroft, who found the waters "quite clear, and of the same temperature of 167°, at mouths distant two hundred yards from each other." Below the springs were beds of soda.

The hot springs of *Puga*,† I have myself examined. The springs occur in the bed of a rivulet called the Rulang-chu, for a length of about two miles. The springs vary in strength, from gentle bubbling to strong ebullition, and in temperature from 80° to 148°, the hottest containing chloride of soda and sulphuretted hydrogen in solution, and those of low temperature containing chloride and borate of soda, both in solution. Sulphur occurs on the northern bank of the rivulet in pure transparent crystals, and in thin laminæ disseminated throughout the gypsum rock. The volcanic neighbourhood of Puga is something like that of the Tuscan lagoons near Monte Cerbole, which now supply Europe with the same minerals: "These lagoons consist of springs in a furious state of ebullition, whose vapours

* *Dal*, "quiet;" compare the English "dull."

† *Bu-ga*, a hole.

contain boracic acid, and the ground is covered with crystallizations of sulphur and other minerals."* The volcanic agency is still active in Tuscany; in Ladák, though not extinct, it is evidently dying.

The hot spring of Chushul was visited by Moorcroft and Trebeck. It is without taste or smell, but is said to have medicinal properties. Its temperature is 96°.

* M'Culloch's Commercial Dictionary—Art. Borax.

VI.—ROADS, PASSES, BRIDGES.

I.—ROADS.

In Tibetan every road is called *Lam;* but the high-roads are distinguished by the name of *Lam-chhen*, or "Great Roads," and *Gya Lam*, or "Passable Roads."* The principal road is that between Kashmir and Yarkand; the next in importance is the road to Lhasa, viâ Garo, and the third is that which leads through Rukchu, Láhul, and Kullu, to the cities of Nurpur, Amritsar, and Ludiana. Some of the other roads, though not much frequented by merchants, are still deserving of notice, as they have on three different occasions been made use of by the conquerors of Ladák. About A.D. 1600, the Musalmans of Balti, under Ali Sher, invaded Ladák on the west by the valley of the Indus. In 1686, the Sokpos or Sacæ invaded it on the east by the Rudok road; and in 1834, the Hindus of Jammu, under Zorawar Sing, invaded it on the south by the route from Kashtwar into Suru. Moorcroft mentions another commercial line between India and Kotan,† "which was frequented in the time of Shah Jehan and closed by the Chinese subsequently to their acquisition of Kashgar."

* *Lam*, a road; *Lam-chhen*, a great road; *b,rGya-lam*, a passable road.

† Transactions Royal Asiat. Soc., I. p. 55.

In another place* he says that this road ran through Garo and Ruthog to Sarikia, half-way between Yarkand and Kotan; and in a third place† he states that from Rudok across the mountains to Kotan is a journey of three or four days only. Now both the Chinese geographers and the Jesuit missionaries agree in placing Kotan in N. latitude 37°, or just three and a half degrees, or about 250 miles, to the north of Rudok. The journey must therefore be one of three or four weeks, instead of three or four days. The only probable explanation of Moorcroft's statement is, that the frontier of Kotan is only three or four days' journey from Rudok. His very mention of Sarikia, a place half-way between Yarkand and Kotan, shows that Moorcroft must have known the true distance of Kotan, as his own munshi, Izzet Ullah, makes Sarighout (or Sarikia) just thirteen marches from Lé. It cannot, therefore, be less than eighteen or twenty days' journey from Rudok. The road from India to the Niti Pass, through Garo and Rudok to Yarkand, is, therefore, the same as that from Lhasa to Yarkand, by the valley of the Indus. The two routes join at Garo, and follow the Indus to Kak-jung, from whence the traveller may proceed either down the Indus to Lé, and across the mountains to the Shayok river, or he may cross the Tsaka Lá and proceed direct to the Shayok by Chushal or Pangkong.

The different roads that lead to Lé, on all sides, are the following:—

1. The western road from Kabul and the Punjab, through Kashmir.

2. The south-western road from the central Punjab, through Jammu, Kashtwar and Zanskar to Lé. A

* Travels, I. p. 373. † Travels, I. p. 361.

branch of this road runs from Zanskar through Rukchu to Lé.

3. The southern road from Lahor and Amritsar, through Kullu, Láhul and Rukchu to Lé. A branch road from Bisahar, viâ Spiti, joins this road in Rukchu.

4. The south-eastern road from Lhasa to Garo and the Indus to Lé. A branch from India, viâ the Niti Pass, joins this road at Garo.

5. The eastern road from Chinese Tartary, through Rudok and the valleys of Chushal and Sakte to Lé.

6. The northern road from Yarkand and Kotan, over the Karakorum mountains and down the Shayok and Nubra rivers to Lé. The old route, which is now closed by glaciers that dam the stream, followed the Shayok from its source to Sassar, and thence either continued down that river, or across the mountains and down the Nubra river to Lé.

7. The north-western road from Balti, viâ the Shayok and Indus rivers, to Lé.

II.—1st. THE WESTERN ROAD.

The road from Kashmir traverses nearly the whole extent of Ladák from west to east, from the Seoji Lá, at the head of the Dras river, to Lé. From the Kashmirian Pass it follows the course of the Dras river to its junction with the Suru river, up which it proceeds as far as Kargyil. From thence it ascends the Purik valley past the fort and town of Paskyum, as far as Waka, where it leaves the Waka river, and crosses the Namyika Pass (13,000 feet) to the bed of the Kanji river. Thence over the Photo Lá, an easy pass (13,240 feet), to the village of Lama Yurru, from which it follows the course of the Wanla-chu to its junction with the Indus, below the bridge of Khallach, where it crosses the river to its right bank. From this point it ascends the Indus, past the villages of Nurla, Saspul, Bazgo, and Nyimo, to Pitak, where it leaves the river and turns to the north-east for a few miles to the city of Lé. The whole distance from Kashmir to Lé is 228 miles.

I have travelled this road myself, and I can vouch for its being one of the most excellent and most easy routes to be found throughout the Alpine Punjab. It is passable from March till November, when it is closed by the vast masses of snow that accumulate on the Kashmir side of the Seoji La, and which render the passage very dangerous, both in March and April as well as in November. The greater portion of this road which lies in Ladák was made by Zorawar Sing after the conquest of the country in 1834. The large bridge over the Indus at Khallach, as well as the smaller bridges on this road over the Wanlá, Kanji, Waká, Suru, and Dras rivers, were all built by the energetic invaders, who, knowing the value of good communications, have since kept them in excellent repair. No road can well be worse than the few marches on the Kashmirian side of the pass, which are still in the same state as described by Izzet Ullah* in 1812: "The road is difficult and rocky, so as to be impassable to a mounted traveller." This is the most frequented of all the roads into Ladák, with perhaps the single exception of the northern line from Yarkand to Lé.

The following table shows the names and distances of the stages.

* Quarterly Oriental Magazine, March 1825, p. 104.

FROM KASHMIR TO LÉ.

		Miles.	
1	Gándar Bal	$9\frac{3}{4}$	left bank of Sindh river.
2	Kangan	$9\frac{5}{8}$	right bank ditto.
3	Surbara	$9\frac{5}{8}$	left ditto ditto.
4	Gagangir	$10\frac{5}{8}$	right ditto ditto.
5	Sonamarg	$7\frac{1}{8}$	ditto ditto ditto.
6	Báltal	$8\frac{3}{8}$	ditto foot of Pass.
7	Maten	$15\frac{7}{8}$	cross the Seoji Lá (Pass).
8	Drás	$11\frac{1}{8}$	left bank of Dras river.
9	Jasgund	$7\frac{5}{8}$	on the left bank (opposite).
10	Kharbu	$12\frac{1}{8}$	right bank ditto.
11	Kargyil	$11\frac{3}{4}$	at junction of Waka and Suru river.
12	Dok	$11\frac{5}{8}$	left bank of Waka river.
13	Molbil	$8\frac{3}{8}$	right bank ditto.
14	Charak	$7\frac{1}{2}$	cross the Namyika Pass.
15	Hesku	$11\frac{1}{8}$	right bank of Kanji river.
16	Lama Yurru	9	cross the Photo Lá (Pass).
17	Khallach	$8\frac{5}{8}$	cross the Indus by bridge.
18	Nurla	$8\frac{1}{8}$	right bank of Indus.
19	Hemis-tokpo	$8\frac{6}{8}$	ditto ditto.
20	Sáspul	$9\frac{5}{8}$	ditto ditto.
21	Bazgo	8	ditto ditto.
22	Tháru	$11\frac{1}{4}$	ditto ditto.
23	Lé	$11\frac{3}{4}$	ditto ditto.
		228 miles.	

III.—2nd. THE SOUTH-WESTERN ROAD.

During the first years of the occupation of Ladák by Zorawar Sing, the different roads from Jammu to Lé were constantly traversed by the Dogra troops, who latterly always took the route through Káshtwár and Zanskar in preference to that of Káshtwár and Suru—which they thought considerably longer. Dr. Thomson travelled from Jammu to Lé, in 1848, but he took the hill route, from Bhadawár to Chatrgarh. In the same year he had also travelled from Kashmir to Jammu. We are therefore able to compare the route from Jammu to Lé, viâ Zanskar, with that by Kashmir. The comparison is altogether in favour of the road by Kashmir, with respect to the facility of crossing the different passes, which are less lofty and much more easy of ascent and descent than those of the other road. With respect to distance, the two roads are much about the same. The road travelled by Dr. Thomson is actually eighteen miles longer than the route by Kashmir; but as the route from Zanskar to Lé, viâ Marka and Kiyo, is two days' journey less than that followed by Dr. Thomson, the two roads by Kashmir and Zanskar may be considered about the same length.

From Jammu the Zanskar road proceeds direct through Ramnagar to Bhadarwár, a distance of seventy-three miles. From thence it crosses the Bhadri-Dhar Pass, 10,165 feet, into the Chamba district, and over the Saj-Joth (14,794 feet) into the valley of the Chandra-bhága near Chatrgarh, a further distance of 116 miles. From the Chenab the road crosses the Bara Lácha range by the Umasi-Lá or Burdar Pass (18,125 feet) to Phadam, the chief town in Zanskar, a distance of fifty-six miles. In this rugged district the road is bad and difficult. At first it follows the course of the Zanskar river as far as Chand-Lá, where it enters the mountains. Beyond Pangache it proceeds over another pass (16,495 feet) and descends rapidly to the river, which it crosses by the Nira bridge. From thence it ascends the lofty mountains that bound Zanskar on the west, and enters the Wanlá district by the Sing-gé-Lá (16,952 feet), from which it follows the Wanlá river to Lama Yurru, and thence to Lé, as in the first route. The lofty passes on this road are seldom open before June, and they are always closed by the end of October.

The following are the marches made by Dr. Thomson from Jammu to Lé.

		Miles.			Miles.
				Brought forward ...	189
1	Tuton-ki-kuï (the mulberry well)	8	23	Chishot	8
2	Sarohi Sar	7	24	Sumcham	8
3	Thalaura	8	25	Camp	6
4	Ramnagar	10	26	Ditto	5
5	Garta	7	27	Ditto	10
6	Pata	9	28	Markim	10
7	Dudu	6	29	Phadam	9
8	Camp	8	30	Tungdé	8
9	Bhadarwar	10	31	Chandla	10
10	Camp	7	32	Sumdo	10
11	Langera	8	33	Pangache	9
12	Dego	11	34	Nira	8
13	Buju	10	35	Yulchung	5
14	Kaltor	11	36	Plutaksa	11
15	Banderi	7	37	Haunpata	8
16	Camp	7	38	Wanla	10
17	Ditto	9	39	Khallach	11
18	Ditto	12	40	Nurla	8
19	Pargwál	8	41	Saspol	10
20	Asdhari	10	42	Nyimo	10
21	Shol	9	43	Lé	11
22	Lyundi	7			
	Carried forward ...	189		Total miles ...	374

From Phadam there are two other routes to Lé, the direct route through Zanskar and the winter route through Rukchu. The latter was taken by the Vazir Zorawar Sing, in the winter of 1835, when all the passes on the more direct road had long been closed.

TWO ROUTES FROM PHADAM IN ZANSKAR TO LÉ.

	Winter Route.		Direct Route.
1	Muni.	1	Tondé.
2	Yang Jhul.	2	Jand-lá.
3	Maleng.	3	Sumdo.
4	Kina Jhula.	4	Dagmoche.
5	Zongmar.	5	Karna Sumdo.
6	Chumik Marpo.	6	Rabrang.
7	Tokpo Soma.	7	Marka.
8	Charáp.	8	Kyo (Skyo or Skio).
9	Dong chéchan.	9	Shingo (Pass).
10	Pachálong.	10	Rumbak.
11	Kyang-cho.	11	Pitak.
12	Rukchin.	12	Lé.
13	Debraug.		
14	Gya.		
15	Miru.		
16	Ugshi.		
17	Hemis.		
18	Thagna Goupa.		
19	Chachot.		
20	Lé.		

IV.—3rd. THE SOUTHERN ROAD.

By this route the shawl wool is brought to the large cities of Nurpur, Amritsar, and Ludiana, all of which make a return in manufactured shawls and coarse brocades. The roads from all these places meet at Mandi (the market) or Maudinagur (market-city) on the Byas river, the capital of the small state of that name. From Nurpur the merchants proceed viâ Kangra and Baijnath; from Amritsar, viâ Hushiyarpoor and Nadon; and from Ludiana, viâ Ropar and Bilaspur; the distances of the first and last being about 120 miles; of the second, about 150 miles.

From Mandi this road proceeds by the iron-mines of Kumán to Sultânpur, the capital of Kullu. From thence it ascends the Byas to its source on the Rotang Pass (13,000 feet), and descends upon the Chandra river at Koksar, the first village in Lahul, at an elevation of 10,000 feet. It then follows the Chandra river to its junction with the Bhaga, opposite Tandi, from whence it ascends the latter to its source in the Bara Lacha Pass (16,500 feet). From this pass it descends the Yunam river into Rukchu, and thence crosses the Lunga-Lacha Pass (17,000 feet) to the triple confluence of the Sumgal river. There it ascends the plain of Kyang to the crest of the Thung-Lung Pass (17,500 feet), from whence it descends the Gya rivulet to the Indus at Ugshi, and thence down that river to Lé. All the passes on this route are easy, especially the Bara Lacha, over which a road might be made passable for carriages, so gradual is the ascent and descent. The Bara Lacha and Rotang Passes are generally closed in the end of October, and are not open again until the end of May or beginning of June. The most difficult part of this route is the crossing of the Chandra river, as the suspension-bridge of birchen-twig ropes is annually overwhelmed beneath a dense mass of drifted snow. In August, 1846, the late Mr. Vans Agnew and myself were detained for two days opposite Koksar until the bridge was partially put up, when with the assistance of plenty of rope, which we had purposely carried with us, we managed to pass over all baggage without any difficulty.

From Mandi the route is as follows :—

			Miles.	
1	Kumân	... ...	11	an iron-mine.
2	Bajaora	... ...	14	right bank of Byas river.
3	Sultanpur	... ...	9	capital of Kullu.
4	Dwára	... ...	10	right bank of Byas river.
	Carried forward	...	44	

		Miles.	
	Brought forward ...	44	
5	Monáli	14	right bank of Byas river.
6	Ralha	10	camp foot of Pass.
7	Koksar	11	cross the Rotang Pass.
8	Sisu	10	right bank of Chandra river.
9	Gundla	9	ditto ditto.
10	Kárdang	10	left bank of Bhaga river.
11	Kolang	13	right bank ditto.
12	Dárcha	10	ditto ditto.
13	Patseo	8	a rude stone bridge.
14	Mongba	10	foot of Pass.
15	Kelang	12	cross the Bara Lacha.
16	Charpa	8	mouth of Cherpa river.
17	Sumdo	14	foot of Pass.
18	Sumgal	12	cross Langa Lácha Pass.
19	Mure-Tsho	10	a small pond of fresh water.
20	Rukchin	7	Boti camp.
21	Larsa	14	foot of Pass.
22	Gya	$14\frac{3}{8}$	cross the Lunga Lácha.
23	Miru	$7\frac{1}{8}$	
24	Ugshi	$7\frac{1}{4}$	left bank of Indus.
25	Marchalang	$8\frac{1}{2}$	ditto ditto.
26	Chachot	11	ditto ditto.
27	Lé	$9\frac{1}{8}$	cross Indus by bridge.
	Total ...	$283\frac{3}{8}$	miles.

The Bisahar road, viâ Kullu, joins this road at Sultânpur, the capital of Kullu, from which Rampur is eight marches distant. Since 1846, this road has been much improved by the British government, and the access to Kullu, both from Simla and from Rampur, is now easy. The road from Bisahar, through Spiti into Rukchu, joins the above road either at the crest of the Bara Lacha Pass or at the foot of the Thung Lung Pass. The former is the more easy route, but the latter is the more frequented. From Rampur the road ascends the Sutluj river to the Wongto bridge, where it passes over and enters the mountains to Babé. From thence it crosses the Tari Pass (15,282 feet) into the Pin valley, which it descends to the junction of the Pin river with the Spiti. The latter is crossed by a jhula to Dangkhar, from whence the road proceeds to the monastery of Kyi and up the left bank of this stream to Losar, where it changes to the right bank. Beyond Losar it leaves the Spiti river and crosses the Kulzum Pass (14,821 feet) into the upper course of the Chandra river, which is quite uninhabited, and ascends the stream to its source in the Bara Lacha Pass. The other road branches off from the monastery of Kyi and crosses the Parang Pass (18,502 feet) into Rukchu at the source of the Para river. It then follows the river to Norbu Sumdo, whence it crosses a low range of hills to the southern end of the Tshomo-Riri lake. From this lake it crosses the Nakpo Gonding Pass (18,000 feet) and the Polokonka Pass (16,500 feet) to the Tsho-kar or White Lake, beyond which it joins the first road at the foot of the Thung-Lung Pass.

The following are the stages on the road by the Bara Lacha Pass.

FROM RAMPUR TO LÉ.

			Miles.	
1	Gaora	... ...	10	left bank of Sutlej.
2	Saráhan	... ...	10	ditto ditto.
3	Tránda	... ...	14	ditto ditto.
4	Nichár	... ...	12	ditto ditto.
5	Yangpa	... ...	11	cross the Sutlej.
6	Larsa ...	... ...	16	cross the Tári Pass.
7	Mud ...	... ...	12	on Pin river in Spiti.
8	Tangti	... ...	12	ditto ditto.
9	Danghkar	... ...	15	cross the Spiti Pass.
10	Lara ...	...	$8\frac{3}{4}$	left bank of Spiti river.
11	Rangrig	... ...	$8\frac{1}{8}$	ditto, halting-ground.
	Carried forward	...	$128\frac{7}{8}$	

		Miles.	
	Brought forward ...	$128\frac{7}{8}$	
12	Chikyam	10	
13	Kirla	12	
14	Losar	12	right bank.
15	Camp	10	foot of Pass.
16	Ditto	9	cross the Kulzum Lá.
17	Ditto	12	left bank of Chandra.
18	Ditto	14	ditto ditto.
19	Ditto	12	ditto ditto.
20	Ditto	12	cross the Bara Lacha Pass.
		$232\frac{7}{8}$	
	Thence 12 to Lé,	$122\frac{3}{8}$ miles.	
	Total ...	$355\frac{1}{4}$ miles.	

The following are the stages on the road by the Tshomo-Riri Lake.

FROM RAMPUR TO LÉ.

		Miles.	
11	Rangrig	$129\frac{1}{8}$	
12	Gyihbar	$6\frac{7}{8}$	
13	Bongrochan	$8\frac{7}{8}$	
14	Tratung Kongma ...	7	cross the Parang Pass.
15	Camp	11	
16	Norbu Sumdo ...	11	
17	Tshomo Riri	10	south end of lake.
18	Korzo Gonpa... ...	13	
19	Ramzung	11	
20	Polokonka Pass ...	15	2 miles to W. of Pass.
21	Tsho-kar	11	
22	Larsa	16	
		$252\frac{5}{8}$	
	Thence 6 to Lé,	$57\frac{3}{8}$	
	Total ...	310 miles.	

V.—4th. THE SOUTH-EASTERN ROAD.

Of the portion of this road that lies between Lhasa and Kailas, very little is known except by report.

From Lhasa, which I do not think can be less than ten or eleven thousand feet above the sea, the road ascends the Sanpu river, past Tashi Lhunpo and Gáldán to its source on the eastern face of the Kailas mountain. It then crosses this mountain to the northern bank of the holy Manasarovara Lake (15,200 feet). The direct distance between these points on the map is upwards of 10° of longitude, which in the 30th degree of latitude are equal to 600 English miles, to which one-half* more must be added for the windings and ascents and descents of a road in a mountainous country. This will give a distance of 900 miles, equal to a journey of three months, which the people always state it to be. From the Manasarovara Lake to Garo the road has been traversed by Moorcroft. The distance is about 110 miles, or ten days' journey—past the Lake of Rawan Hrad, and over several lofty spurs of the Kailas range, which give rise to numerous small feeders of the Sutluj and Indus. Garo itself is situated, according to my information, on the main branch of the Indus, which is there called the Higong-chu or Higong river, simply because it flows past the village of that name. From Garo to Chibra, and thence to Lé, the road lies down the valley of the Indus, and generally along the bank of the river. The distance from Garo to Lé is not less than 350 miles, or

* This is not a mere assumption, but a fact deduced from actual surveys. Thus my survey makes the distance between Lé and Kashmir 228 English miles. The difference of longitude is 2° 40′, which, in the latitude of 34°, is equal to 154 miles; to which by adding one-half more, we obtain 231 miles, which is within three miles of the actual measurement. Again, the difference of latitude between Mandi and Lé is 2° 30′, equal to 174 English miles. By adding one-half more, we obtain 260 miles, the measured distance, according to my survey, being 283 miles.

about thirty-five days' journey. The whole distance from Lhasa to Lé is therefore about 1,350 miles, a journey of four months and a half.

The principal places on this route are the well-known Tashi-Lhunpo, the residence of the Tashi Lama, who was visited by Turner; Gáldán, which was for some time the residence of the Tibetan court; Garo, which is now a great mart for the interchange of the productions of India and China; and Tashi Gong, which is a celebrated monastery. I will say nothing more regarding this road, as all the accessible portions of it have been traversed by Captain H. Strachey.

VI.—5th. THE EASTERN ROAD.

This road leads from the unknown countries inhabited by various Mongol tribes, through Rudok to Lé. Nothing whatever is known of it to the eastward of Rudok, except that by it the Mongol tribe of Sokpo invaded Ladák in 1686 and 1687; and again in the beginning of 1841, immediately after Zorawar Sing's death, about three thousand Changpas* are said to have entered Ladák for the purpose of assisting the young Gyalpo. They advanced to Lé, where they remained about six weeks; but on the approach of Dewán Hari Chand and Vazir Ratanu with troops from Kashmir, they fled hastily back again by the same route. As this road has been surveyed by Captain H. Strachey, from the neighbourhood of Ruthog to Lé, any further remarks from me are quite unnecessary.

* *Byang-pa,* pronounced *Chang-pa,* "northern men," or men of Chang-thang, the northern plains.

VII.—6th. THE NORTHERN ROAD.

This road leads from Yarkand and Kotan, over the Karakoram mountains (18,660 feet) to Lé. The best account of it that we possess is that by Izzet Ullah, who traversed it in 1812. But since that time several glaciers have stretched their mighty masses across the bed of the Shayok, and the old road by the river has been completely closed. The new road from Karakoram leaves the Shayok, or Khundan, river at the foot of the pass, and crosses over an elevated table-land to Sassar, where it again meets the Khundan. A short distance above Sassar Dr. Thomson examined two glaciers that stretched across the river. From this point the road quits the Khundan and crosses a lofty range to the bed of the Nubra river, above Panámik. It then follows the course of the Nubra river to its junction with the Shayok, from which it proceeds direct to Lé.

Izzet Ullah's route was the following :—

FROM YÁRKAND TO LÉ.

		Hours.		Miles.	
1	Chagachag	4	=	6	
2	Tokaji...	9	=	13½	on the Kerghalek river.
3	Langer	10	=	15	
4	Aurtang	2	=	3	
5	Ak Masjid	9	=	13½	
6	Khalastan	7	=	10½	
7	Chakilak	6	=	9	
8	Mizár	6	=	9	
9	Tezak Lak Payin ...	8	=	12	
10	Yagni Dawan ...	9	=	13½	
11	Yartoli	5	=	7½	right bank of river.
12	Bagh Haji Mohammad	2	=	3	
13	Igersal di	9	=	13½	
14	Taghteh	7	=	10½	
	Carried forward ...	93	=	139½	

			Miles.	
	Brought forward ...	93	=139½	
15	Khafalun	9	= 13½	
16	Aktagh	10	= 15	
17	Surighout	9	= 13½	
18	Camp	7	= 10½	foot of Karakoram Pass.
		128	=192 miles.	
1	Camp to S. of Pass ...	10	= 15	
2	Yapchan	10	= 15	
3	Khundan	10	= 15	right bank of Shayok.
4	Chong Tash	9	= 13½	right ditto.
5	Yartobi	7	= 10½	
6	Mandalik	5	= 7½	left ditto.
7	Dong Bailak	10	= 15	left ditto.
8	Chong Aolang ...	9	= 13½	right ditto.
9	Chong Jangal ...	4	= 6	right ditto.
10	Chunchar	9	= 13½	right ditto.
11	Dakchu Dunga ...	4	= 6	right ditto.
12	Adgam	7	= 10½	left ditto.
13	Digar	...	4½	
14	Camp	...	12	
15	Lahu	...	7½	cross a Pass.
16	Lé	...	7½	
	Karakoram to Lé	...	172½ miles.	
18	Yarkand to Karakoram	...	192	
	34 marches. Total	...	364½ miles.	

Dr. Thomson's route from Lé to Karakoram Pass is a more direct one, and consequently a shorter one; the whole distance being only 147½ miles, or twenty-five miles less than Izzet Ullah's route. But the longer route up the Khundan river had the advantage of being tolerably level, whereas the present route crosses no less than three lofty passes, and is besides much more rugged and difficult. The Karakoram Pass is not less than 18,600 feet above the sea, and it is perhaps very nearly

19,000 feet high. Dr. Thomson's route from Lé to the Karakoram Pass is as follows :—

		Miles.			Miles.
1	Camp	6		Brought forward ...	68½
2	Kardong	10	11	Camp	8
3	Kalsar	9	12	Ditto...	4½
4	Diskit	8	13	Ditto...	6
5	Lyakjung	5	14	Sassar	8
6	... ...	} 9	15	Margai	9½
7	Chirasa		16	Camp	9
8	Panámik	10	17	Ditto...	12
9	Takshe	4	18	Ditto...	12
10	Changlung	7½	19	Karakoram Pass ...	10
	Carried forward ...	68½		Total ...	147½

VIII.—7th. THE NORTH-WESTERN ROAD.

This road leads from Balti and the neighbouring Musalman district up the bed of the Indus to Lé. During the summer season, when the waters of the river are much swollen by the melted snow, the Indus route is very difficult, and travellers generally prefer ascending the Shayok river as far as Chhorbad, and thence crossing the mountains by the Hánu Pass, 16,890 feet, to the Indus at the fort of Hánu. From Hánu to Lé the route ascends the Indus. Both of these routes have been travelled by Mr. Vigne. Dr. Thomson's route was by the Shayok alone; and to him we are indebted for the survey of that river between Tirit and Keris, where it joins the Indus. The distance from Skardo to Lé, by this route, is 236 miles, or just eight miles more than the road from Kashmir to Lé. The following are the marches from Lé to Skardo, by the Latsa Pass, 17,666 feet.

		Miles.			Miles.
1	Sabu ...	6		Brought forward	147
2	Foot of Pass	12	17	Turtuk	7
3	Digar	5½	18	Pránu	11
4	Chatti	16	19	Siksa	7
5	Tirit ...	8½	20	Kábás	8
6	Tagar	8½	21	Surma	12
7	Panámik	13	22	Khapolor	7
8	Chirasa	10	23	Karku	10
9	Lyakjung	9	24	Bragar	4
10	Hundar	9½	25	Kunes	6½
11	Tertse	10	26	Kuru	6
12	Unmáru	5½	27	Keris	8
13	Karu	9½	28	Golochu	9
14	Waris	8	29	Camp	9½
15	Bogdan	7	30	Skardo	4
16	Chulungka	9			
	Carried forward	147		Total	236

The above are the principal thoroughfares throughout Ladák. Many other roads might be enumerated in all directions, but they are less frequented and more difficult. These by-paths are called *Lam-than,** and *Lam-dogpo.* They are used chiefly by the people of the country in passing from their own districts into the next; such are,—1st, the road over the Omba Lá, between Suru and Drás; and 2nd, the road over the Vingé Lá, between Zanskar and Purik. Other roads are used only by smugglers; but these are always difficult, although frequently more direct than the high-roads. One of the best known of these smugglers' paths is that which leads from the Chinese district of Chumurti into Láhul and Kullu. From Chumurti the road is followed over the Budhpu Pass to the bed of the Pårá river. From thence a rugged path leads over a lofty mountain to the

* *Lam-phran,* pronounced *Lam-than,* "little road;" and *Lam-Dogpo,* "narrow road."

upper course of the river, which is crossed a second time, and over another range of mountains to the head of the Charpa river. From the bed of the Charpa different routes were followed over the mountains to the upper and uninhabited course of the Chandra river, from whence the northern road leads over the Bara Lacha Pass into Láhul, and the southern road direct into Kullu by the Parbati river.

IX.—PASSES.

A Pass in Tibetan is called *Lá*. The crest of a Pass is named *La-tse*, and the foot of a Pass *La-tsa*.* The last word is variously pronounced: by some it is called Larsa, of which spelling many examples may be found in our maps at the bottom of Passes; by others it is called Lacha, as in Bara Lacha (for Bara Latsa). Others again pronounce the *s* distinctly; which last has given rise to Dr. Gerard's spelling of Para Lassa. *Rong* is a defile, and *chong-rong* is a narrow defile. The principal passes have already been mentioned in my description of the high-roads of Ladák; but a tabular enumeration of them may be useful for comparison.

Names.	Heights.	Authorities.	Positions.
Karakoram ...	18,660	Dr. Thomson ...	Head of Shayok river.
Sassar	17,500	Ditto ...	between Nubra and Shayok river.
Hanu	16,890	Col. Bates ...	between Indus and Shayok river.
Lé Pass ...	17,666	Dr. Thomson ...	between Lé and Nubra.
Lazgung ...	17,500	(estimated) ...	ditto ditto.

* *Lá* is the simple form. *La-r Tse,* is the crest of a Pass.

Names.	Heights.	Authorities.	Positions.
Changlá ...	18,105	Moorcroft, MS.	between Indus and Long Kongma.
Kongta-la ...	15,495	Ditto ...	between Long Kongma and Chushal.
Singgó ...	16,952	Dr. Thomson ...	between Zanskar and Lama Yurru.
Vinggé ...	—		
Pangache ...	16,495	Dr. Thomson ...	in Zanskar.
Photo Lá ...	13,240	A. Cunningham	between Kashmir and Lé.
Namyika ...	13,000	Ditto ...	ditto ditto.
Thung Lung ...	17,500	Ditto ...	South of Lé.
Polokonka ...	16,500	Ditto ...	near the Tsho-kar.
Nakpo Gonding	18,000	Ditto ...	to North of Tshomo Riri lake.
Lanak... ...	18,746	Ditto ...	between Tshomo Riri and Hanle.
Lunga Lácha ...	17,000	Ditto ...	between Zanskar and Rukchu.
Párang Lá ...	18,502	Ditto ...	North of Spiti.
Bára Lacha ...	16,500	Ditto ...	between Lahul and Zanskar.
Umási Lá ...	18,123	Dr. Thomson ...	between Kashtwar and Zanskar.
Seoji Lá ...	11,634	A. Cunningham	between Kashmir and Dras.
Harapo Lá ...	12,104	Col. Bates ...	in Astor.
Kutzum ...	14,851	Capt. Broome ...	between Lahul and Spiti.
Manerang ...	18,612	A. Gerard ...	between Kanawar and Spiti.
Tari Pass ...	15,282	Lieut. Maclagan	ditto ditto.
Rotang Joth ...	13,000	A. Cunningham	between Kullu and Lahul.
Kali Joth ...	16,700	Ditto ...	between Lahul and Chamba.
Saj Joth ...	15,500	Dr. Thomson ...	ditto ditto.
Pir Panjal ...	11,970	A. Cunningham	South of Kashmir.
Tural Pass ...	14,808	Ditto ...	between Kangra and Chamba.

X.—PASSAGE OF RIVERS.

The great rivers of Ladák are crossed by ferries, fords, and bridges. Fording is the most usual means of crossing both the Indus and the Shayok, in the upper parts of their sources, where their waters are widely spread and shallow. In the neighbourhood of Lé, where the Indus becomes deep and rapid, it is spanned by three bridges, and just below Lé, where the current is less rapid, people are ferried across on inflated skins. The Zanskar river is bridged in two places: and is not I believe ever fordable. In Láhul the Chandra and Bhaga rivers are both bridged; but I have seen the Chandra forded at Koksar in October, and I have been ferried across it at the same place in September. In Spiti, the Párá river is crossed by a natural bridge formed of an enormous mass of rock that has fallen across the stream; and the Spiti river itself is bridged in several places. In the winter season it is fordable in many places.

A ford is called *Gal* in Tibetan; and the name is applied to one of the principal branches of the Zanskar river, which is called *Sum-gal*, or the "Three Fords," because it is formed of three streams that are forded one after the other just above their junction. In the summer the fording of many of the streams can only be accomplished in the morning; for after ten and eleven o'clock the waters are so much increased by the melted snows that they become quite unfordable. This I have myself witnessed with the Chandra river in October, and with the Charpa river in September; and I have ascertained that it is also the case with the Spiti river.

A ferry is called *Gru-kha*, and the ferryman *Gru-ba*. In Ladák itself the ferrymen use only rafts made of inflated skins; but on the Sanpu river, even above Lhasa, boats are said to be numerous; and there has always been one on the Indus at Skardo. The name, therefore, is well known in Ladák, more particularly as most of the Lamas have visited Lhasa. The common people are ferried over on a single inflated skin (*phagpa*), but great men usually have a raft formed by placing a bed over two inflated skins. The skin is generally the hide of a buffalo, with the openings carefully sewn up, excepting one of the hind legs, which is kept for inflation. The skin floats with the legs uppermost. The ferryman throws his arm over it, holding the closed leg in his left hand, and a small wooden paddle in his right. The passenger sits down, native fashion, on the skin, and secures himself by holding the ferryman's shoulder as well as the leg of the skin. The ferryman paddles with his right hand, and pushes the skin forward by striking out his legs as in swimming. I have often crossed the Byâs and Chandra rivers in this way. The raft is managed in the same manner; but it cannot be used either in such rough water or in such rapid currents as the single skin.

The bridges of Ladák have different names, according to the materials of which they are constructed. The finest bridges, such as those of Lé and Khallach, are called *Shing-zam*, or "Wooden Bridges," because they span the river with large beams of poplar. A small bridge over the Bhaga river in Láhul is dignified with the name of *Do-zam*, or the "Stone Bridge," because the footway is made of rough stone slabs. *Chag-zam**

* *Zam-pa* is a bridge; and the different terms of *Shing*, wood; *rDo*,

or "Iron Bridges," and *Gru-zam* or "Boat Bridges," are known only in the Lhasan territory; but the *Chug-zam* or suspension-bridge is common in many parts of Ladák.

One of the finest specimens of the *Shing-zam* or wooden bridge that I have seen, is the great bridge over the Indus near Lé. I have given a sketch of it in Plate V. It was built by Zorawar Sing, and is called *Chhog-lam-Sar-Zampa,** or the "New Bridge on the high-road." The Khallach Bridge is similar in construction. They are both railed, and may be ridden over with perfect safety. As the details of construction may be seen quite as clearly in the sketch as in any description, I will only give the dimensions of these two bridges.

The Lé Bridge is a double one, the smaller one having a span of thirty feet, and the larger one of eighty feet. Both are strongly and substantially built of poplar spars, laid touching each other. On each side is a stout railing—the clear breadth between the railings being eight feet. Height above the stream (on 2nd October) fifteen feet.

The Khallach Bridge is seventy-seven feet long and eight feet broad, with a stout railing on each side. Height above the water (on the 15th October) forty-five feet. This bridge is protected by a small square field-work of sun-dried bricks, which covers the northern end on the right bank. It is occupied by twelve men, who are relieved regularly from Lé.

stone; *lChags*, iron; are added to discriminate the material of which the bridge is formed.

* *Chhog-lam-Sar-zam-pa*, "high-road new bridge."—See Plate V. for a view of this bridge.

The *Chug-zam* or suspension-bridges are different from the *jhulas* or swinging-bridges of the Hindu states of Chamba and Bisahar. The passenger walks across the former, but is pulled across the latter. Suspension-bridges are common on the Indus and Shayok above their junction. They are used also in Zanskar, Spiti, and Lahul; and in the Hindu state of Chamba. The Chug-zam is formed of two stout ropes of twisted birch-twigs, about the thickness of a man's arm. The ropes are suspended side by side, about five feet apart at the ends: but they are drawn nearer together in the middle by the weight of the side-ropes and roadway. The side-ropes, about one inch thick, are also made of birchen twigs, and in them is laid the roadway: which, in the bridges that I have seen, always consisted of three ropes (of the same size as the suspension-ropes) laid side by side. In the best bridges of this kind the side-ropes are connected by a close wattling of wicker-work from end to end, to prevent passengers as well as sheep and goats from slipping through. The Chug-zam is a very cheap and a very easy mode of bridging a stream; and when new and well constructed, it is a very safe and not an unpleasant way of crossing. But some old bridges of this kind that I have crossed were both difficult and dangerous. In them the suspension-ropes formed a great curve, the sides were unwattled and completely open; and the roadway in many places was reduced to a single rope. Alexander Gerard* states that he should "think the best *Su-zum* (*Chug-zam*) of 100 feet not altogether safe:" but I have crossed several of greater span, and one of very nearly double that span.

* Kanawar, p. 35.

			Span.
The Koksar Chug-zam over the	Chandra	...	106 feet.
Wulás „ „	Ravi	...	116½ „
Mahila „ „	ditto	...	169 „

The last span was undoubtedly too great for this kind of bridge; for though the points of suspension were six feet apart, yet in the middle the ropes could only be kept asunder by a piece of wood. The perpendicular or versed sine of the arc was thirty feet. I find the following remark recorded in my note-book immediately after crossing this bridge in August, 1839:—"When riding rapidly in a coach, trees, houses, and fields all seem to be moving past, while the coach stands still; but just the reverse happens in crossing one of these bridges; for the bridge seems to be carried along sideways, while the boiling river appears to stand still."

VII.—CLIMATE.

I.—GENERAL REMARKS.

THE various meteorological processes which combine to form a climate, are all generated by the sun. Thunder and lightning, snow and rain, the pleasant breeze and the mighty whirlwind, all alike owe their origin to the sun. Through the changes produced by the varying diffusion of solar heat through the atmosphere, the still air is put in motion, and becomes a gentle breeze, a high wind, or a mighty hurricane. By the sun's beams the multitudinous waters of the ocean and its tributary rivers are vapourized and formed into clouds, which, rising with the ascending and heated air, are borne upon the wings of the wind to loftier or more northerly regions, where, as they become condensed by the cold, they sink with their burthen towards the earth, and fall down in the shape of rain, hail, or snow. The rain washes over the surface, or permeates through the ground, the snow melts as it falls, and percolates through the fissures of the rocks; both to appear again in countless rills, which join and form mighty rivers, that bear back again to the sea all the water formerly abstracted by evaporation.

II.—WINDS.

The constancy of the prevailing winds in different quarters of the globe is one of the most interesting phenomena of nature. In the Trans-Himálayan districts of Ladák, the dry wind is nearly always southerly and westerly, both in summer and in winter. This fact was partially observed by Alexander Gerard,* who remarks, that "on peaks upwards of 20,000 (feet) and at heights of 16,000 (feet) the winds were always W. or S.W." The same fact was also noticed by my brother, Captain Joseph Cunningham, who resided for nearly a whole year, including one entire winter season of 1841-42, in the districts of Upper Kanáwár, Spiti, and Chumurti. He observed that "the winds blew almost constantly from the south or south-west, as noticed by the Gerards. A northerly wind was of rare occurrence."†

When I first observed the steadiness of the day-breeze in these regions, I was under the impression that the wind blew constantly in the same direction from the south-south-west and west, but after a few days' observation I found that the morning wind blew generally from the north-east. It then struck me that the prevailing winds alternated day and night, like the land and sea breezes on the coast of India. I was confirmed in this opinion by finding on one occasion a due northerly wind blowing about midnight, and when I afterwards began to observe the magnetical instruments, I always found a light northerly breeze from two to five in the morning, which, as the day broke, gradually took a north-easterly direction. I then observed the course and strength of the wind at half-hour intervals, and my first day's

* Kanawar, p. 62.

† Moorcroft rarely mentions the winds; but in one place he incidentally alludes to them. Speaking of the sheep-folds of Kakjung on the Indus, he says that they were "screened from the *prevailing* winds by the hills to their *south*."—I. 440.

observations at once convinced me that my opinion was right. I continued my observations at different places during August, September, and October, and always with the same results. Since then my opinion has been most completely substantiated by my brother's observations for one whole year in Spiti.

The generality of travellers get too much fatigued with their exertions by day to be able to make any observations at night; and thus the south-westerly wind, which was found to prevail during the day, was supposed to last through the night, and to be a mere continuation of the south-westerly monsoon, which blows up the valleys of the Chenáb, the Byâs, and the Sutluj. But as the day-and-night wind of Ladák blows throughout the entire year, it is clear that it must be due to some other cause; for in the intertropical regions the course of the wind is dependent upon the sun's declination, which when northerly attracts the ascending current of heated equatorial air in its own direction, thus producing a south wind. But as this stream of air, when it reaches the higher northerly latitudes, where the surface motion of the earth is less rapid, still retains its superior equatorial velocity, it gains daily more and more upon the easterly motion of the earth, until at length, when it descends to the surface, it becomes a south-westerly breeze, which blows steadily during the six months of the sun's northern declination. But when the declination becomes southerly, just the reverse of this process takes place; for the ascending current of heated air follows the sun towards the south, thus producing a northerly breeze, which, owing to the difference of rotatory velocities before mentioned, gradually becomes a north-westerly breeze, which blows steadily during the six months of the sun's southern declination. These are the monsoons or seasonal winds, which depend entirely upon the sun's position in the ecliptic; the south-westerly monsoon being the summer wind, and the north-easterly monsoon the winter wind. But the alternation of the day-and-night wind throughout Ladák is constant throughout the year; and as the subject is one of some interest, I will here attempt to explain what appears to me to be the cause that generates it, and that afterwards carries it round all the points of the compass.

This cause is, I believe, the great mid-day radiation of heat from the bare surface of the vastly elevated plains of Ladák and the neighbouring districts, which have a mean height of 13,000 feet above the sea. The following table shows the extent and mean elevation of these great masses of table-land.

EXTENT AND MEAN HEIGHT OF THE TIBETAN TABLE-LAND.

Districts.	Extent.		Height.	
	Sq. miles.	Total.	Sq. miles.	Mean.
Rukchu	5,580		15,634	
Gáro	6,500		15,500	
Rudok	4,800		14,500	
		16,880		15,211
Zanskár	3,080		13,154	
Spiti	2,312		12,986	
Nubra	9,216		12,763	
Ngári	9,000		12,500	
		23,608		12,851
Ladák	3,960		11,500	
Purik	4,200		11,196	
Láhul	1,872		10,535	
		10,032		11,077
	Sq. miles	50,520	Mn. height	13,026

Now as nearly one-half of our terrestrial atmosphere lies beneath the level of these elevated regions, the highly rarefied air offers but little check to the direct transmission of the solar rays, which are more powerful in Ladák, at a height of 15,000 feet, than in the low-lying plains of India. At Gwalior the greatest heat of the sun's räys in the hot winds of 1850 was 133°; at Simla, 7,500 feet, it was 134°; but in Rukchu, 15,500 feet, Trebeck observed a solar heat of 144°, and in the same district Gerard measured the incredible rise of 158°, which is only 27° below the boiling point of water in that district.

Towards mid-day the lower strata of the atmosphere become rapidly heated, and the rarefied air begins streaming towards the north pole, as a light southerly breeze. As the day advances, the current of air quickly increases in strength until it becomes a high wind, which blows steadily during the afternoon, with occasional gusts of great violence. In the evening it becomes fainter. The progress of this wind is well shown in the following observations made by myself with Lind's wind-gauge.

DIRECTION AND PRESSURE OF THE WIND.

Time.	Direction.	Pressure.
10h. 30m. A.M.	N.E.	faint
11 00 ,,	E.	very faint
11 30 ,,	S.	light puffs
Noon.	S.W.	0·2
12 30 P.M.	W.S.W.	0·4
1 00 ,,	W.S.W.	0·5
1 30 ,,	W.	0·8
2 00 ,,	W.	1·0
2 30 ,,	N.W.	1·2
3 00 ,,	W.N.W.	0·8
3 30 ,,	N.W.	0·8
4 00 ,,	N.N.W.	1·0
4 30 ,,	N.N.W.	0·4

The greatest pressure was at 2h. 30m. P.M., when the wind exerted a force of 6·25 lbs. per square foot. This is a single example of what I observed daily. The day-breeze or southerly wind always began to blow before mid-day, and continued rising and veering towards the west with frequent strong gusts until three or four o'clock in the afternoon, when it reached its greatest force, and remained steady for some time. Towards sunset it changed to the west-north-west, and gradually lessened, until at 9 P.M. it was only a gentle breeze from the north-west. At midnight there was always a light northerly wind, which became fainter towards the morning, when it often freshened into a north-easterly breeze.

The following extracts in support of my opinion are taken from my brother's journal.

1842.

Jan. 3 *from noon to* 4 P.M. a strong *southerly* wind.
5 *southerly wind after* 2 P.M.
10 *afternoon*, wind *southerly*, blowing in violent gusts.
11 after 9 A.M. wind southerly in strong gusts.
18 after 5 P.M. light snow with north wind.
19 *night*, a *light northerly wind*.
20 *morning*, a *light northerly wind*.
afternoon, *south wind* blowing in gusts.
21, 22 } *afternoon*, strong *south* wind chiefly in gusts.
23 strong wind from south and south-west.
24 a light *northerly* wind *until noon*.
28 wind in gusts from *south after* 10 A.M.
30 *northerly* wind *until* 10 A.M.
Feb. 4 *early morning*, *wind northerly*, afterwards, gusts from south.
6 *until* 10 A.M. *northerly wind*.
7, 8 } *ditto* *ditto*.
25 *afternoon*, wind *southerly*.
March 22 afternoon, wind in gusts from south.
29 ditto ditto.

1842.		
April	8	puffs of wind from south.
	12—18	ditto ditto.
		A very cloudy month.
May	14	mid-day, strong south wind.
	16, 17	noon to evening, light south wind.
	18, 19	after 9 A.M. strong southerly wind.
	21	after 10 A.M. strong southerly wind chiefly in gusts.
	24	after 11 A.M. light southerly wind chiefly in prolonged puffs.
	26 to 31	afternoon, moderate south wind.
June	1 to 4	afternoon, ditto.
	5	from 9 A.M. high southerly wind to 7 P.M.
	6 to 9	ditto ditto until dusk.
	10—12	after 10 A.M. strong south wind.
	14	after 2 P.M. light south wind.
	15	after 11 A.M. south wind.
		The same for the rest of the month.
July	1 to 31	south wind for 28 days.
August	1 to 31	south wind every day.
Sept.	1 to 30	south wind ditto.
October		no observations.
November		strong south wind.

In these observations it will be observed that whenever the morning wind is recorded it is always northerly, and that the southerly wind never rises until 9 A.M., and usually later. The constancy of the southerly wind here recorded is simply accounted for by the fact, that the valleys of the Lé and Párá rivers, where my brother's observations were made, run almost due north and south. The course of the wind was therefore influenced by the direction of the valleys. This is proved by the change of the wind at Sumra, on the Spiti river, where the direction of the valley being from east to west, my brother found the afternoon wind blowing from the east. I found the same in the Spiti valley during

August and September, when the wind was always up the valley or easterly during the heat of the day. On the Parang river, on the contrary, the wind was south-westerly during the afternoon, but north-easterly before mid-day, both the up and down currents taking the direction of the valley. At the foot of the Lanak Pass the wind was north-easterly and unsettled until noon, after which it blew steadily from the south-west up the valley.

I have already stated that the cause of the southerly or day breeze is the intense solar heat and greatly increased radiation, which are due to the vast elevation of the mass of the table-land of Ladák and the neighbouring districts. The air, rarefied by the heat radiated from the soil, streams towards the north pole in a southerly current. As it advances, it is gradually deflected to the south-west and west by the greater rotatory velocity which it possesses; and as the evening approaches, it unites with the north wind, and becomes a north-westerly breeze. This northern or night breeze is due to the intense cold generated by the great nocturnal radiation, and which begins in the loftier snowy regions at 3 P.M. The condensed air finds an outlet to the south towards the low plains of India, and becomes a northerly current of air. At first it is deflected into a north-westerly current by its meeting with the westerly breeze of the afternoon, but as the evening grows colder, the nocturnal breeze prevails, and streams gently southward towards the plains. As it advances towards the equator, its inferior rotatory velocity causes it to be deflected gradually towards the north-east and east until the sun has again raised the southern wind, and then the gentle breeze of night becomes fainter and fainter, and dies gradually away.

This explanation seems to me sufficient to account for the constancy of the day and night breezes of the table-land of Ladák; but the violent gusts which my brother mentions, and which I have myself experienced, are due to another cause. The lighter gusts in a single valley are most probably caused by the small eddies of wind meeting the onward current at every turn; but the violent gusts which I have felt at the Thung-Lung Pass, can only be attributed to the meeting of two strong currents of the same southerly breeze, which have been deflected during their courses into almost opposite winds. Thus, the day wind, which blows up the plain of Kyang towards the Thung-Lung Pass, is a south-westerly current, while that which blows up the Puga rivulet and over the plain of Tsho-kar towards the same point, is an easterly current. The meeting of these two strong currents blowing from opposite directions, would produce small whirlwinds and most violent gusts.

III.—RAIN AND SNOW.

The quantity of rain and snow that falls in Ladák is exceedingly small. In the more elevated districts of Rukchu, Nubra, Zanskar, and Ladák Proper, it rains, or rather drizzles, for an hour or two about three times a year.* Snow falls much oftener, but not in any quantity, and in Ladák and Rudok it is never more than six inches deep. In Rukchu, as a Lama of the Korzo Gonpa on the Tshomo-Riri Lake told me, the winter snow is never more than knee-deep, and the people reside at the monastery during the whole year.

* During Moorcroft's residence in Ladák, it rained only *ten* times in two years, and then only in very small quantities.—I. 269.

Light falls of snow occur at night, even in the middle of summer, as the nocturnal temperature is generally below freezing. In the end of September, 1846, I was encamped on the bank of Tshomo-Riri Lake, in a snow-storm which lasted for twenty-two hours, but the snow was not more than six inches deep, and it disappeared during the following day. In Drás the fall of snow is so great, that by the end of November the Seoji-lá Pass into Kashmir is always closed, from which the district takes its Tibetan name of Hem-babs, or "snow-fed." In Láhul and Spiti, the snow falls to a very great depth, and in many places is doubled by accumulations of drift. The suspension-bridge at Koksar, in Láhul, is annually carried away by a mass of drift-snow, which buries it during the winter. In both these districts whole villages are occasionally snowed up for three weeks at a time; but so long as the houses stand, the people suffer but little inconvenience. In 1838, however, the village of Tunda, near Treloknáth, was overwhelmed by a mass of snow, when several houses were thrown down, and sixteen people perished. The temple of Treloknáth was half-buried, and the bed of the river was filled with snow.

Heavy showers of rain fall along the Chandra river in Láhul during July and August; but after the end of September the snow begins to fall, at first in small quantities which soon disappear; but the fall gradually increases until November, when the snow ceases to melt, and the passes are finally closed.

In Spiti the fall of snow is much less than in Láhul, its greatest depth, where not drifted, being only two feet and a half. During my brother's residence* in Spiti

* Journal Asiatic Society Bengal, XIII. p. 238.

the snow "commenced regularly on the 27th November, and from that date until the end of February, 1842, it snowed more or less heavily, and nearly all day and night, for thirty-nine days. It was cloudy or hazy and snowing on the heights for thirty-four days, leaving twenty-one fine clear days out of ninety-four." During July and August, light showers of rain were frequent, but only one heavy fall occurred during the whole year.

IV.—TEMPERATURE.

The climate of Ladák is characterized by great extremes of heat and cold, and by excessive dryness. If the earth did not possess an atmosphere, the extremes of burning heat by day and of freezing cold by night would be unbearable. It follows, therefore, that the rarer the atmosphere becomes as one ascends above the general surface-level of the earth, so much greater will be the extremes of temperature between the day and the night. This is a general rule when the atmospheric changes are not otherwise affected by peculiar circumstances. It is thus in Ladák, and more particularly in Rukchu, where the dry and highly evaporative day breeze exhausts the little moisture held in the atmosphere, and the clear dry air becomes intensely cold by the great terrestrial radiation under a cloudless sky. In the elevated district of Rukchu it freezes almost every night during summer; but the highly rarefied atmosphere offers so slight a check to the transmission of the sun's rays, that the noon-day sun is sometimes 25° hotter than it is in any part of India. In the less lofty districts in Spiti, both the cold and the heat decrease; but in Spiti the noon-day sun is still 15°

hotter than in India, while in Ladák it is about the same. The extremes of cold are equally great, and in the more elevated districts the winters are particularly severe. In Rukchu the thermometer falls as low as +9° of Fahrenheit, even in September, and the minimum temperature of the month is only 23·5°, while the mean temperature is 42° 93′. In Spiti, during the same month, the minimum temperature is only 37° 2′, and I have seen the thermometer as low as 22°, the mean temperature being 55° 5′. Most of the travellers who have visited Rukchu have been there in September. Trebeck, it is true, traversed it alone in June, yet both Moorcroft and Dr. Gerard passed through it in September, and I have twice visited it in that month. We have, therefore, good observations for the temperature of September, while that of the rest of the year is almost unknown. But as the climate of Spiti approaches nearest to that of Rukchu, both in its extremes of temperature and in its excessive dryness, we may obtain a tolerably accurate approximation to the annual mean temperature of the latter district by a comparison with that of the other. The following table gives the result of all my brother's observations for one whole year in Spiti, with the addition of my own for the months of August and September.

TEMPERATURE OF SPITI.

—	Temperature.			Extremes.		Moisture.			Sum.
	–	+	Max.	–	+	Dry Bulb.	Wet.	Diff.	
January ..	11·7	31·0	19·18	–11	35				50
February ..	7·3	35·0	18·68	– 6	40				56
March ..	10·8	40·0	24·46	– 4	45				71
April ..	31·5	50·0	40·89	+26	65				84

—	Temperature.			Extremes.		Moisture.			Sum.
	−	+	Max.	−	+	Dry Bulb.	Wet.	Diff.	
May	38·0	60·0	49·00	34	75				95
June.. ..	45·0	74·0	59·50	44	85				120
July	48·0	80·0	63·60	46	90·0				148
August ..	43·0	74·3	58·60	41	83·5	78·25	53·25	25	98
September ..	37·2	75·3	55·50	22	84·5	70	45	25	97·6
October ..	28·0	56·0	40·12	20	65				80
November ..	17·0	35·0	22·85	+16	50				60·5
December ..	2·5	35·7	14·35	−13	42				50·7
Mean annual temperature 38·89									

By this table it will be seen that the mean annual temperature in Spiti is just one-third less than the mean temperature of September. On applying the same rule to the September mean temperature of Rukchu, 43·08°, we obtain 28·72° for the mean annual temperature. The extreme of cold is probably between twenty and thirty degrees below zero,* and the mean temperature of the winter months cannot be more than a few degrees above zero.

For Ladák Proper, I possess observations for the months of September and October, which, when compared with the Spiti observations, would give a mean annual temperature of 39° for the valley of the Indus. The following are the observations.

—	Min.	Max.	Mean.	Extremes.	
				−	+
September ...	44·93	70·00	57·01	24·0	82·0
October ...	22·22	60·87	38·95	0	66·5

* Dr. Gerard, Asiat. Res. Bengal, vol. xviii. p. 252, supposes −20° to −25°. He observed −2° in November, but this must have been in Spiti.

By deducting one-third from the September mean, we get 38·01° for the annual mean temperature, and by deducting one-twentieth from the October mean, we get 37·00°. The mean of these two gives 37·5° as the mean annual temperature of the valley of the Indus in Ladák.

The climate of Zanskar is like that of Spiti, and that of Nubra like that of the valley of the Indus. The climate of Láhul is similar to that of Kanáwar, but somewhat colder, as Láhul is more elevated. The mean height of Láhul is 10,535 feet, while that of Kánam, in Kanáwar, is only 9,296 feet. The following results are calculated from the observations made for two successive years by the celebrated Tibetan scholar Csoma de Körös, while he was studying with a Lama in the monastery of Kánam.*

TEMPERATURE OF KANÁWAR.

—	Min.	Max.	Mean.	Extremes. —	Extremes. —
January ...	24·87	40·00	34·00	14	
February ...	28·82	46·00	36·00	21	
March	30·04	52·37	40·49	18	
April	4·23	59·23	49·88	26	68
May	50·30	68·80	59·77	40	78
June	57·60	74·94	66·28	48	82
July	61·26	77·59	69·22	56	80
August ...	59·91	75·40	67·65	56	79
September ...	54·78	73·71	63·90	49	78
October ...	47·27	67·82	56·16	40	74
November ...	36·46	55·43	43·68	32	67
December ...	30·71	49·05	37·25	26	
Mean Annual temperature 52·02					

* In *Manuscript*, taken at Dr. Gerard's request; these observations are now in my possession.

Láhul is subject to greater extremes both of heat and cold than Kanáwar. The greatest temperature observed by Csoma de Körös was only 82°, whereas I have seen the thermometer at 84° on the 2nd September in Láhul. The lowest temperature of Kanáwar in August was only 56°, but in Láhul the minimum temperature is always under 50°, and the lowest that I observed was 42°. The temperature of Láhul for several days in August was

Min.	Max.	Mean.	Extremes.	
			−	+
46·00	78·2	62·1	42	84

From the similarity of climate and of geographical position, the mean annual temperature of Láhul may be deduced from its September temperature by taking the same proportion as we find in the Kanáwar observations. This proportion will give a mean annual temperature of 47° 30′ for the inhabited parts of Láhul. The uninhabited portions of the district on the upper courses of the Chandra and Bhaga rivers partake more of the climate of Spiti.

The mean annual temperature for the whole of Ladák may be obtained approximately from the details before given. See also the detailed Meteorological Observations, Chapter XVII.

TABLE OF ANNUAL MEAN TEMPERATURE.

Districts.	Height.	Annual Temperature.
Rukchu	15,634	28°·72
Garo	15,500	28·62
Rudok	14,500	30·00
Zanskar	13,154	39·00
Spiti	12,986	38·89

Districts.	Height.	Annual Temperature.
Nubra	12,763	39°·00
Ngári	12,500	38·00
Ladák	11,500	37·00
Purik	11,196	42·00
Láhul	10,535	47·30
Mean	13,026	36·85

The following table shows the mean daily range of the thermometer; by which it will be seen that the difference between the temperature of day and night increases with the elevation.

DAILY RANGE OF TEMPERATURE.

Districts.	Height.	Daily Range.	Extreme Range.
Rukchu	15,634	40°·28	57°·00
Spiti	12,986	36·00	43·50
Ladák	11,500	33·00	39·75
Purik	11,196	32·50	39·50
Láhul	10,535	31·14	34·00

V.—MOISTURE.

The excessive dryness of the climate of Ladák is due chiefly to elevation, by which the air is so rarefied as to be incapable of holding much moisture in suspension. It is also partly due to the great radiation of heat from the bare soil, by which any moisture is rapidly evaporated. The dryness of the climate increases with the height, and the temperature of the dew-point is so very low, that the deposition of dew is quite unknown in the more elevated districts. The depression of the wet-bulb thermometer in different districts of Ladák is shown in the following table, to which I have added for comparison the mean of one week's observations at Gwalior during the hot winds in the end of May 1850, and the mean of another week in the end of March and beginning of April, which is the more correct time for comparison.

TABLE OF MOISTURE.

Month.	Districts.	Height.	Moisture.			Dew Point.	Greatest Dep^n.
			Dry.	Wet.	Dep^n.		
September	Rukchu	15,634	67°·5	40°·5	27°·0	18°·9	31°·0
September	Spiti	12,986	70·0	45·0	25·0	25·0	30·0
September	Ladák	11,500	65·7	42·9	22·8	24·6	23·5
October	Purik	11,196	55·8	37·2	18·6	20·5	19·7
August	Láhul	10,535	74·3	52·9	21·4	38·0	28·0
May—June	Gwalior		110·12	33·80	33·80	35·32	38·5
Mar.—Apr.	Ditto		91·75	25·83	25·83	42·68	28·75

The hottest time in India is the end of May and the beginning of June, and the hottest month in Ladák is July. The fairest comparison therefore that can be made between the dryness of the two climates is that of September in Ladák, and of the end of March and the beginning of April in India. By this comparison it will be seen, that the plains of India are less arid than the lofty table-land of Rukchu, and that their dryness is about equal to that of the Spiti valley. The most convincing proof which I can give of the excessive dryness of the climate of Rukchu is the fact, that the stock of my gun, which had been exposed to *fourteen* hot seasons in India, shrank at least one-eighth of an inch during a single month's residence in Rukchu.

VI.—RADIATION.

I have already observed that the noon-day radiation of heat from the elevated table-lands of Ladák is one of the principal causes of the great dryness of the climate. The following table exhibits the maximum radiation of solar heat at about 1 P.M. in different districts of Ladák during the months of September and October, and in the plains of India in May and June, and in March and April. The observations were taken with a black-bulb thermometer, by Newman, the instrument being invariably placed at a height of three inches above the ground, and fully exposed to the sun.

TABLE OF SOLAR RADIATION.

Month.	District.	Height.	Air.	Black Bulb.	Diff.	Greatest Diff.
September	Rukchu	15,634	65°·75	86°·75	23°·00	23°·5
September	Spiti	12,986	70·00	91·31	21·31	28·5
October	Ladák	11,500	58·54	85·33	26·79	39·5
October	Purik	11,196	55·83	73·16	17·33	25·5
May—June	Gwalior		109·87	129·66	19·46	23·75
Mar.—April	Ditto		88·37	111·40	23·37	26·25

As the climate of India during March and April is just two months removed from the hottest season of the year, a fair comparison can be made between it and the climate of Ladák during the month of September. The comparison shows that the mean noon-day radiation of solar heat throughout Ladák is about the same as it is in the plains of India.

My observations for the terrestrial radiation of Ladák were all taken during the day, as I was afraid to leave the instrument exposed on a dark night amongst loose cattle. The instrument was one of Newman's register spirit thermometers, with the bulb fixed in the focus of a parabolic metallic mirror exposed to the clear northern sky. Compared with the observations taken on the plains of India for March and April, the terrestrial radiation of Ladák is extremely great. The lowest temperature observed at Gwalior was 10° below the external air, and the mean of the minima was only 6° below it. The minimum generally occurred about sunrise.

TABLE OF TERRESTRIAL RADIATION.

	Hours.	VII.	VIII.	IX.	X.	XI.	Noon.	I.	II.	III.	IV.	V.	Mean daily dep.
Puga	Air	18	25	38·5	45·7	54	56	58	61·75	59·75	56	50·5	
	Rad. Th.	9	18	27·5	35·0	43	45	49	55	52·5	48	44	
	Diff.	9	7	11	10·7	11	11	9	6·75	7·25	8	6·5	8·84
Gya	Air			39	40	40·75	45·5	45·75	45	47			
	Rad.				31	32	36	36·5	36·5	38			
	Diff.				9	8·75	9·5	9·25	8·5	9			9·00
Lé	Air		38	46	48·5	55	56·5	58·5		60·5	57	58	
	Rad.		33	37	42	48	49	49		55	51	47	
	Diff.		5	9	6·5	7	7·5	9·5		5·5	6	11	6·80
Lé	Air		36	39	41·5	45·5	53	52·25					
	Rad.		31	32	36	40	47	47·5					
	Diff.		5	7	5·5	5·5	6	4·75					5·80
Gwalior	Air			78·5			86·25			87·75			
	Rad.			77·0			87·00			87·00			
	Diff.			1·5			0			·75			

In the lofty table-land of Ladák, the greatest depression, which usually took place at 9 A.M., was 11° lower than the temperature of the external air. This was in Rukchu; but even in Ladák Proper the depression was no less than 9°. The mean hourly depression throughout the day was 8° 92′ in Rukchu, but only 6° 30′ in Ladák.

VII.—SUPPOSED MILDNESS OF FORMER CLIMATE.

Various circumstances induce me to believe that the climate of Ladák was formerly much milder and much less dry than it is at present. The occurrence of vast quantities of fossil *fresh-water* shells in the sandy alluvium above the level of the present *salt-water* lakes of Ladák, proves that these lakes must once have been very extensive sheets of fresh water. In the case of the *Tsho-kar* or "White Lake," this is proved beyond all doubt, by the occurrence of fossil shells on the plain of Kyang, and in the deep gorge through which the waters of the lake once had exit into this place. As the plain itself had a gradual slope from the foot of the Thung-Lung Pass to the Sumgal River, the whole extent of this double lake can be seen by a glance at the accompanying sketch-map,* which illustrates the ancient lake system of Ladák in those parts of the country which I have visited.

1. The *Kyang-Tsho* formerly extended from the foot of the Thung-Lung Pass to near the source of the Sumgal River, a length of thirty-five miles. It is difficult to ascertain the mean breadth, but it must have been about five miles. This would give an area of 175 square miles.

2. The *Tsho-kar* formerly flowed into the Kyang-Tsho, and was about twenty-five miles in length by five miles in breadth. The old beach-marks are distinctly visible on the mountain-sides, both to the north and south of the lake. I traversed along the southern end of the Tsho-kar in two different directions in 1846, and in 1847 along the northern end, and through the gorge which

* See Plate VI.

formed its old exit into the Kyang-Tsho. Its principal feeder is a small fresh-water lake to the south, which once formed part of the old lake. The greatest extent of the Tsho-kar must have been about twenty-five miles by five miles, or 125 square miles. The two lakes together covered about 300 square miles.

3. The *Tshomo-Riri* formerly included a small salt-water lake, now lying about eight miles to the northward of it. The greatest extent was about twenty-five miles by five miles, or 125 square miles. It seems highly probable that it once had an exit from its southern end into the Párá River, or perhaps into the Sumgal River.

4. The *Hanlé* Lake is still of considerable size; but the clay deposits, which are found adhering in horizontal strata to the small isolated hills in the middle of the valley, and in sheltered positions at the sides, show that this lake must once have been one of the largest sheets of water in Ladák. Its greatest extent must have been about twenty-five miles by twelve miles, or 300 square miles, with a mean depth of at least 100 feet.

5. *Lam-Tsho* is now only a small piece of fresh water, but it was most probably once a fine sheet of water about fifteen miles long by three miles broad, or forty-five square miles in extent.

6. The bed of the Indus, like that of all the other rivers, has once been crowded with a series of lakes. Two of these which came under my observation are shown in Plate VI. The smaller one must have filled the valley, opposite Nyimo and Mûd, for a length of twenty-five miles by three miles, or for about seventy-five square miles.

7. Above Lé, the vast plain of Chachot must once have

been covered with water for some miles above Marcha-lang down to Lé and Pitak. At Pitak, the lacustrine deposits of fine clay are still adhering to the rocks in horizontal strata, to a height of 750 feet above the level of the river. The whole extent must have been about thirty-five miles by six miles, or 210 square miles. Below Pitak, the former channel of the Indus can be traced for many miles, by Phyang and Tharu, to Nyimo.

It is impossible to say what may have been the whole extent of the former lakes of Ladák, but as the ancient lakes of Rukchu, which I have described, must have covered a space of 840 square miles, or nearly one-sixth of the whole extent of the district, a vague idea may be formed of the general extent of the lake system, which must once have prevailed over Ladák. The vast lake of Pang-kong was probably not less than twenty miles in breadth by 100 miles in length, and must have covered an area of 2,000 square miles. This lake, with the others which I have described, would have occupied about one-tenth of the whole extent of the country.

The former existence of these vast sheets of fresh water rests neither upon general appearances nor upon the vague assertions of tradition, but upon the distinct evidences of vast beds of fine clay, which are found adhering to the rocks in horizontal strata, and which could only have been deposited in comparatively still water. Their existence is further proved by the abundance of fossil *fresh-water* shells that are found in the sandy clay deposits around the present *salt-water* lakes, and on the dry plain of Kyang. These shells are of two kinds,—*Lymnæa auricularia* of all sizes, and

Cyclas rivicola, which is only found of very small size preserved in the interior of the larger shells.* As these mollusca do not now exist in Ladák at a greater elevation than between eleven and twelve thousand feet, it seems a probable conclusion that the country must at some former period have enjoyed a very much milder climate than that of the present day. This conclusion might indeed have been deduced from the former existence of the vast lakes which have been described. For the waters vapourized by the sun must have been condensed by the cold of night, and the plains would then have been fertilized by rain, and the mountains covered by snow. Numerous streams would have flowed down the hill-sides in all directions, and the overflowing lakes would have formed mighty rivers.

Throughout Ladák there are numbers of vast ravines, many of them 500 feet deep, and as many yards broad, which could not possibly have been formed by the scanty brooks that are now nearly lost in their meanderings from side to side of these enormous channels. In one of these vast river-beds the scanty rill of the Sum-gal now purls along at the southern end of the plain of Kyang. The sides of this channel are masses of alluvial boulders and gravel, which once formed the bed of the Kyang-Tsho. The rocky barrier, below the junction of the Sum-gal rivers, was probably worn away, gradually at first, until the plain of Kyang became almost dry: after which, on the occurrence of any sudden disruption, the waters of the Sum-gal would have rushed violently onward, cutting for themselves a deep channel in the soft bed of the lake. The Kyang-Tsho must have been

* See Plate IX. for these shells.

gradually drained; but I have a suspicion that the Tshomo-Riri Lake once had an exit into the Sum-gal, and that its accumulated waters were suddenly drained off by the disruption of the Sum-gal barrier. That the subsidence of the waters of the Kyang-Tsho must have been very gradual is proved by the abundance of shells now lying on the upper part of the plain, all of which would have been swept away by even a moderate current. Is it possible that the whole mass of the country can have been gradually elevated?

Plate VI

The KYANG, or Wild Horse. Equus Kyang.

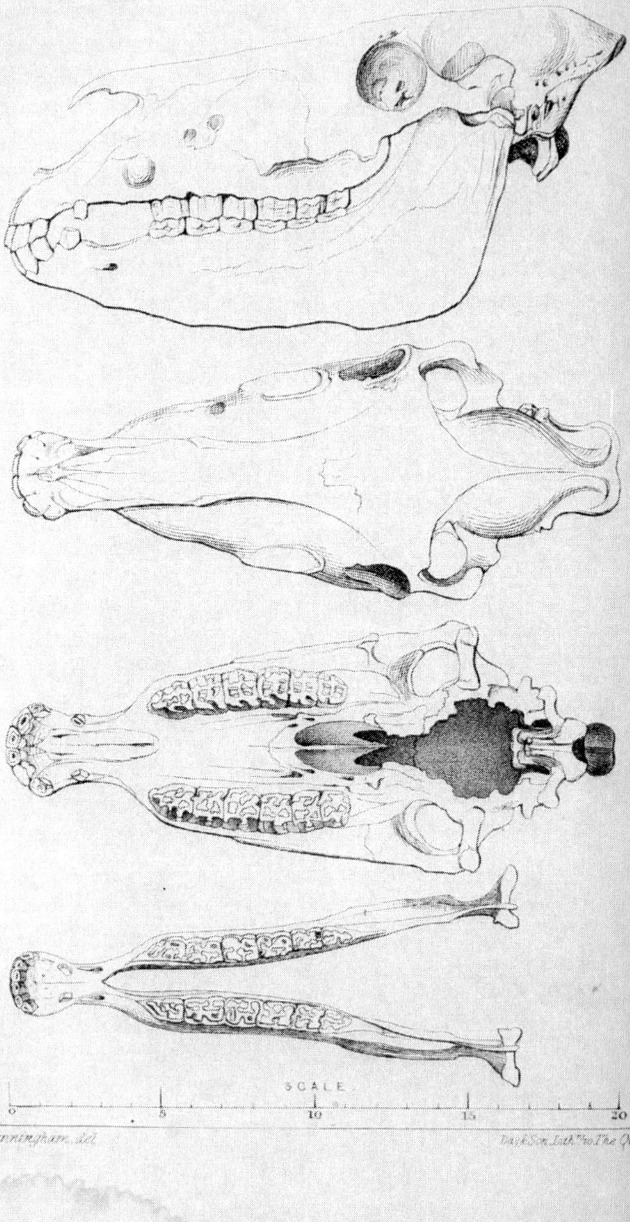

SCALE.

0 5 10 15 20

A. Cunningham, del. Day & Son, Lithrs to The Queen

VIII.—PRODUCTIONS.

I.—ANIMAL.

THE animal productions of Ladák are particularly interesting, as they comprise the wild horse, the yák, or long-haired bull, whose tail furnishes the Indian *chaori*, the shawl-wool goat, whose fine under-fleece is woven into the beautiful Kashmirian shawls, and the púrik sheep, of which some twenty specimens have been exhibited in the Zoological Gardens of London.

WILD ANIMALS.

The wild animals of Ladák are both numerous and interesting. "The high hills are a refuge for the wild goats, and the rocks for the conies."* The elevated plains of the Indus and the lofty table-lands of Rukchu abound with the wild horse, the marmot, and the hare: while the snowy mountains and rugged glens teem with many varieties of the wild goat, sheep, and deer, some of which are most probably still unknown.

The *Kyang*,† which has been called a horse by some, and an ass by others, is the *Equus hemionus* of Pallas, and the *Equus Kyang* of Moorcroft. The animal when

* Psalm civ. 18.

† The male is called simply *rKyang*, and the female *Mo-rKyang*. See Plate VI. for four views of the Kyang's skull.

full grown is about fourteen hands high : the facial line is highly arched, like that of the zebra and quagga, and the ears (like theirs) are longer than those of a horse, but much shorter than those of an ass. A line of black hair extends along the whole of the back, but there are no cross stripes across the withers as in the ass. The tail has a long tuft of hair at the end like the zebra. The general colour is reddish-brown on the back and sides, and white on the stomach. Moorcroft* remarks, that it is certainly not the *gorkhar*, or wild ass of Sindh, and I can vouch that it is quite different from the gorkhar of the Bikanar and Baháwalpur desert. Trebeck,† who saw herds of them on his trip to Chibra, to the south-east of Lé, states his opinion of the Kyang's shape as follows. "The form, from the fore to the hind leg and feet, to a level with the back, is more square than that of an ass, his back is less straight, and there is a dip behind the withers and rounding of the crupper, which is more like the shape of the horse. His neck is also more erect and arched than that of the ass." The following are the dimensions of a skull in my possession.

	Ft.	In.
Greatest length	1	9¼
" depth	0	10
" breadth	0	8½
	lb.	oz.
Weight of upper jaw	5	0½
" lower jaw	3	15½
Weight of skull	9	0

Lastly, the Kyang *neighs* like a horse, which in my judgment is conclusive that he does not belong to the

* Travels, I. p. 311.

† In Moorcroft's Travels, I. p. 443.

genus *Asinus*, but is very nearly allied to the *Equus caballus*. If the Kyang is a different genus from the *Equus hemionus* of Pallas, he should be called *Equus Tibetanus*. A living specimen of the animal has been sent to England by the Hon. Mr. Thomason, the Governor of Agra, but as the naturalists of Europe have not, I believe, yet had an opportunity of examining the skeleton, I have given several careful drawings of the skull of a Kyang, which I shot in 1846, at an elevation of 17,000 feet, on the summit of the *Nakpo Gonding* Pass, to the north of the *Chomoriri* Lake. This skull has forty teeth; and there is now no trace of any premolar teeth in the upper jaw, such as have been found in other specimens, and which led Mr. Hodgson to give the Kyang the new name of *Equus polyodon*,* or rather *Asinus polyodon*.

The wild yák, called *Brong* or *Dong*,† is said to inhabit the grassy plains on the upper courses of the Sutluj and Sangpo. The people generally believe in their existence, but I could neither procure any of their horns, nor find any person who had actually seen the living animal. Vigne‡ was informed that the wild yák was to be found "on the northern slopes of the Himálaya that descend upon the plains of Yarkand." Mr. Blyth§ quotes Wood to the same effect. My brother‖ also mentions that wild yáks are to be found "to the north and east of Garo," that is, in the district of Gnári. As the tame yák has been domesticated from time

* Journal As. Soc. Bengal, XVI. p. 354. Note by Blyth.

† *hBrong*. The female is called *hBrong-hBri*, which is commonly pronounced *Dong-di*.

‡ Vigne's Travels in Kashmir, Ladák, II. p. 277.

§ Journal As. Soc. Bengal, XI. p. 282, note.

‖ Ditto ditto, XII. p. 222.

immemorial, the existence of wild herds in the same country may perhaps be doubted; but the general prevalence of the belief is worthy of being recorded.

The largest of the wild sheep is the *Nyan* or *Ovis Ammon* of naturalists. It is found only in the most inaccessible places, near the snow-limit. Specimens of the horns may generally be seen along with those of the ibex and shá (*Ovis montana*) on the religious piles of stones called *Mané*, where they are placed by the shepherds as votive offerings. The *Nyan* of the Tibetans is closely allied to the Kachkar of Badakshán and Chitrál. Mr. Blyth has, however, distinguished them by separate names, calling the latter *Ovis Polii*, after Marco Polo, who gave the first description of the animal.

Another species of wild sheep is the *Ná*. Vigne* calls it *Sná*, and describes it as of "the size of an ordinary sheep; of a dull brownish-gray colour, with curved, smooth, and four-sided horns." Csomo de Körös calls it a "large sheep-like deer." It is apparently the same as the *Náhur* of Nepal, and the *Ovis Náhur* of Hodgson and Blyth.†

A third species of wild sheep is the *Shá*,‡ which I have seen browsing in large flocks on the mountains, on the left bank of the Indus below Lé. The animal is as large as a stag, with strong wiry hair of a reddish-brown colour on the back, gradually changing to white on the stomach. The chest is covered with a long fringe of

* Travels, II. p. 280. The name is written *rNa*, in Tibetan. See also Csomo de Körös, Dict. in voce.

† Journal As. Soc. Bengal, XVI. p. 360.

‡ *Shá-ba*, and the female *Shá-mo*. Csomo de Körös calls the *Shá*, a stag (Dict. in voce); but the real stag is called *Shu*. The horns of the *Shá* are shown in Plate VIII.

Plate VII

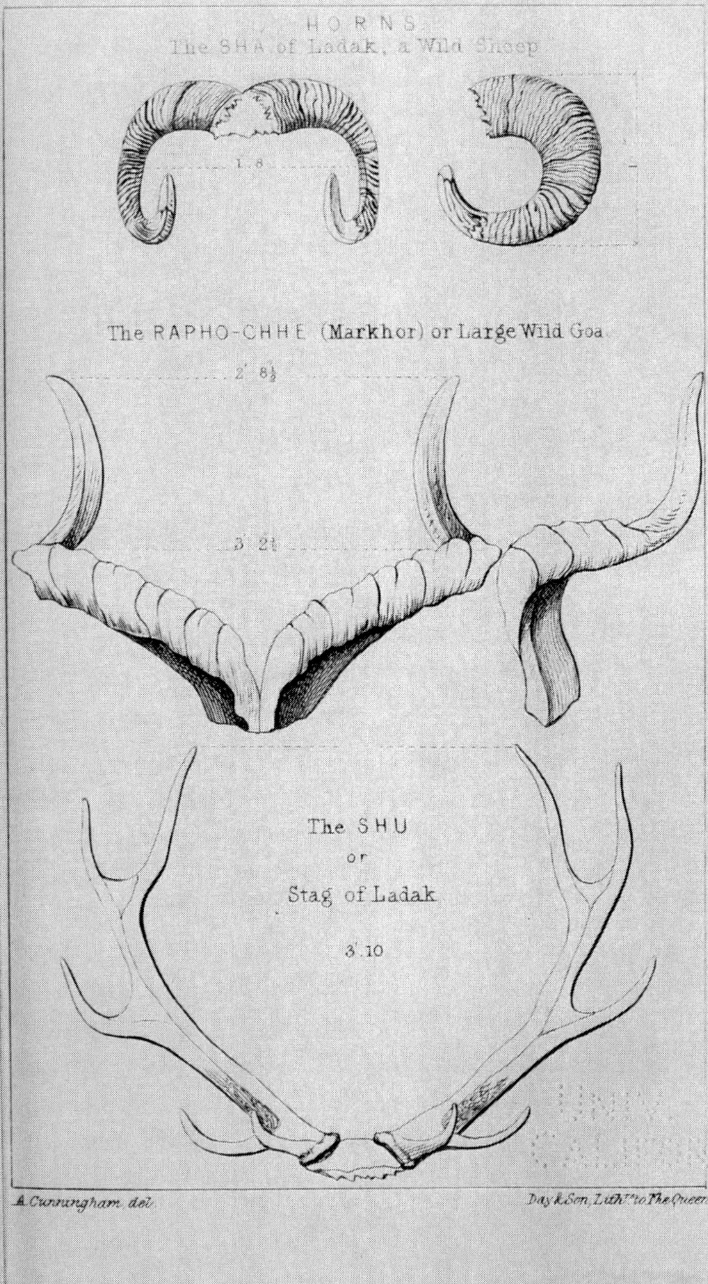

A. Cunningham del. Day & Son, Lithrs to The Queen

dirty black hair. The massive horns, which touch at their bases, are curved backward and downward, the tips being turned forward, upward, and inward. Each horn thus forms about three-quarters of a circle. The *Shá* is the *Ovis montana* of naturalists. The horns of a specimen, which I obtained on the banks of the Indus, below Lé, have the following measurements.

	Ft.	In.
Length of horn	2	4¼
Base of horn, greatest depth	0	3¾
„ „ breadth	0	3
Extreme interval	1	8
Interval between tips	1	0½
Greatest circumference	0	10½
Weight ... 12 lbs.		

The age of this specimen was nearly seven years, the *rugæ* of the third year being the boldest and most deeply marked.

The wild goat called *Rápho-chhé*,* or the "great goat," is the *Már-khor*, or "snake-eater" of the Musalmáns. It is common in Balti, and in Badakshán and Chitrál; but I was unable to procure any specimen of its horns in Ladák. A pair obtained by Colonel Bates in Balti is represented in Plate VII. These horns meet at the base, rise straight upward, then turn backward and again upward. The following are the measurements:—

	Ft.	In.
Length of horn	3	9
Circumference of base	0	11
Breadth of widest face	0	4
Perpendicular rise	2	3⅓
Extreme width	3	2½
Width from tip to tip	2	8⅓

* *Rá-pho-chhé*, or simply *Rá-chhe;* the female *Rá-mo-chhe.* Mr. Vigne says that *Rawa* means a horn, and *chægho*, great; but *rárácho* is simply a "horn," and not a "great horn." See Plate VII. for a pair of horns.

No specimen of this magnificent goat has, I believe, yet been obtained by any naturalist, nor have I heard of any traveller who has seen the animal. I would suggest that it might be called *Capra megaceros.*

Another species of wild goat is the Tibetan ibex, or *Skyin.** Mr. Vigne procured a pair of horns that were four feet three inches in length. In his opinion the Skyin "is larger than the European ibex, and the horns are longer, more curved, and more tapering." The Skyin frequents the most inaccessible rocks, and the animal, when shot, is frequently much mutilated by its headlong plunge down some precipitous cliff. Vigne states that between one and two hundred of them are killed in Balti during the winter, when they are forced to descend into the valleys.† In Ladák they are also snared at night, and shot in the grey dawn of the morning, when they venture down to the streams to drink. They are killed for the sake of the soft under-fleece, which, in Kashmir, is called *Asali Tus.*‡ This is an exceedingly fine and soft wool of a light brown colour, which is exported to Kashmir, where it is used as a lining for shawls, woollen stockings, and gloves. It is also woven into a very fine cloth, called *Tusi,* of a soft and delicate texture, which is much prized for its warmth. The high price of the Tus is caused by the difficulty of procuring the animal, and by the uselessness of the hair. The person who separates the hair from the wool of the domestic shawl-

* *Skyin;* the female is called *Dan-mo.* In Kullu and Spiti, the Skyin is called Kyin; and Spiti is called Piti, but the spelling in Tibetan always preserves the initial *s.*

† Vigne's Travels, II. p. 279.

‡ اسلي توس means simply "genuine *Tus,*" or the wool of the *wild* goat; *Tus* means "nature."

goat is paid by the hair itself, which is manufactured into coarse blanketing for tents, and twisted into ropes. But the hair of the wild goat is short, wiry, and coarse, and the cost for picking is charged to the price of the Tus, or fine wool. Moorcroft says that neither the domesticated shawl-goat, nor the Vigogna,* furnishes a wool so full and rich to the feel, nor has so fine a material ever yet graced a British loom.

The frequent occurrence of ibex-horns on the temples of Kanáwar, Láhul, and Chamba has often suggested to me the idea that a similar religious feeling amongst the Greeks may have prompted the dedication of real ox-skulls, perhaps of animals that were slain in sacrifice, in the ancient Hellenic temples. In process of time, when the rude posts became Doric pillars, and the rough ends of the sloping beams were carved into triglyphs, the real ox-skulls were supplanted by their sculptured representations, which afterwards adorned the metopes of the Doric frieze. At least it seems difficult to account for their frequent representation on any other supposition.

The *Shu* or Tibetan stag has been described by Mr. Hodgson† from a specimen obtained near Phári, in Tsáng, the central province of Tibet. A second specimen was procured from the district of Chúmbi, to the south of Phári, where the country is more wooded and less arid than most other districts of Tibet. In 1839 I procured a most magnificent pair of stag's horns from the upper glens of the Lidar valley, in Kashmir; and in 1847 I obtained a second but smaller pair from the same valley.‡ The former pair had six snags on each horn, and was

* Transactions Roy. As. Soc. I. p. 53.

† Journal As. Soc. Bengal, XIX. p. 466; and XIX. p. 518.

‡ See Plate VIII.

therefore a genuine *Barah-singha* (twelve-horned). The latter specimen agrees in all respects, save that of size, with those described by Mr. Hodgson. One of his specimens was procured from the most southern part of Tibet, where the climate is less rigorous and the country more wooded. My specimens were obtained in the upper course of the Lidar river, in the eastern end of Kashmir towards Ladák, where the climate may be called half-Tibetan from its dryness. The horns of my Kashmirian specimen are represented in Plate VII. Their dimensions are the following, which I have placed beside those of Mr. Hodgson's Tibetan specimen.

	Kashmirian.			Tibetan.	
	Ft.	In.		Ft.	In.
Length of horn	3	4½	...	3	10½
Girth above burr	0	7½	...	0	7¾
Chord of arc, or bend of horn	0	10	...	1	0½
Basal interval between horns	0	3½	...	0	4½
Interval between extreme snags	3	5	...	3	9
" " " tips	2	0	...	2	6½

The Musk deer, called Lá,* is found both in Tibet and in Kashmir, but I had no opportunity of procuring any specimens. Vigne mentions the Kashmirian Lá, and states that Dr. Falconer thought it was a new species.

Other wild animals of Tibet are the leopard, the bear, the wolf, the fox, and the dog. The leopard, wolf, and fox, are described by Mr. Hodgson, and noticed by Vigne.† Moorcroft ‡ adds the ounce and the lynx. The

* *gLá-ba*, or simply *gLá*; and the female *gLá-mo*.

† Journal As. Soc. Bengal, XI. p. 275, and Vigne's Travels, II. p. 281. The leopard is called *Zig* (*-gZig*); the bear, *Dom;* the dog, *Khyi;* and the fox, *Mikpa* (*dMig-pa*); from *dMig*, a hole; it is also called *dByi*.

‡ Travels, I. p. 312.

dog is mentioned by Mr. Hodgson only, who describes it as a rare animal of a pale wolf-like colour.

The hare, called *Ri-bong*, is abundant amongst the rocks on the grassy plains of Rukchu. It is called Ri-bong, or the "hill-ass," on account of the length of its ears.* The Botis do not eat hares, as they consider the animal as a species of donkey. In 1846 I shot five in half an hour in one of the glens to the eastward of the plain of Kyung. They sit behind the rocks, with their long ears pricked, and half their heads just raised above the stone. When roused they run from rock to rock, reminding one of the words of the Psalmist, "The rocks are a refuge for the conies." The Ri-bong is as large as an English hare, has longer ears, and is of a bluish-grey or slate-colour. It is the *Lepus pallipes* or "white-foot" of Mr. Hodgson, who gives the following dimensions of his specimen.†

	Ft.	In.
Length from head to tail	0	11
„ of tail	0	4
„ of head	0	4¾
„ of ear	0	4¾

Mr. Hodgson describes a second species of Tibetan hare under the name of *Lepus oïostolus*, and he refers to Moorcroft as his principal authority for this variety.‡ But on a reference to Moorcroft (I. 225), I find that the hares shot by Trebeck and himself on the plain of Rukchu, were of a "bluish-white colour, and not much larger than English rabbits." Both in 1846 and in 1847 I shot these bluish-coloured hares on the plains of

* Ri-bong, and also Phyi-pa. *Ri-bong* means the "hill-ass." The Hindus also liken the ass to a hare, by naming the wild ass *Ghor-khar*, or the "horse-hare."

† Journal As. Soc. Bengal, XI. p. 288.

‡ Ditto ditto, XI. p. 288.

Rukchu, and I feel satisfied that they are the same as the *Lepus pallipes* of Mr. Hodgson; and the more so, as several that I shot were fully as large as any English hare. Moorcroft evidently saw only one species, as he refers to the Rukchu hares a second time.*

The smaller species of hare, or *Lagonys*, is extremely common all over Tibet. It is the *Lepus alpinus* of Pallas. I have shot them near the summit of the Lânak Pass, 18,750 feet above the sea, and on the very crest of the Pir Panjál Pass at 12,000 feet. The table-lands of Rukchu, and the plains along the Yunam River, are literally honey-combed with their burrows. The Tibetan *Lagonys* is named *Shippi*, or the "whisperer," and is thus closely allied to the "calling hare" of America.

The marmot of Tibet, according to Mr. Hodgson,† is of two distinct species, the large and the small, which he has distinguished by the names of *Arctomys Tibetensis*, and *Arctomys hemachalanus*. The former obtains a length of two feet, with a tail of six inches. The latter does not reach more than thirteen inches in length. I have seen only the larger animal, which is common on the sandy plains of Rukchu. Moorcroft‡ mentions that he obtained the skin of the squirrel in Ladák; by which I believe that he meant the Arctomys.

Of the *Mustelidæ*, or weasel tribe, I am acquainted with only one species,—the *Mustela*, or true weasel. I saw one specimen of it in 1846 near the Polokonka Pass, at an elevation of 16,000 feet; and in 1847 I shot one close to the crest of the Lánák Pass, 18,700 feet. The

* Travels, I. p. 312.

† Journal As. Soc. Bengal, XII. p. 409.

‡ Travels, I. p. 312.

skin and skull were preserved by Dr. Thomson, in whose collection they have been carried to England. The length of body was about seven or eight inches, the legs short, and the nose long, and the whole of a light sandy colour.

Mr. Hodgson* has described a second species of *Mustelidæ*, in the Tibetan polecat, and he refers to a third in the Tibetan badger.

BIRDS.

The larger birds of Ladák are not many, and few of them, I believe, are peculiar to the country. The gigantic *Chakor*, or snow-pheasant, is found in Láhul and Spiti, and also in Kanâwar, but only near the snow. The common Chákor, *Rekpa*,† is abundant throughout the cultivated part of the country. Moorcroft invariably identifies the Chákor with the Francolin, or Greek partridge. According to Griffith,‡ Perdrix *Francolinus* is the black partridge of India, and Swainson§ calls it the Francolin *Chætopus*, and associates it with the grey partridge of India (Chæt. Pondicerianus).

The eagle (*Cha-nak*,‖ or the "black bird") and the kite (*Chákor*, or the "white bird") are common enough, and so is the large raven. Smaller birds also are numerous, but I had no opportunity of procuring specimens. On the western side of the Lánák Pass, about 16,500 feet, I saw a hoopoe.

* Journal As. Soc. Bengal, XVIII. p. 448.

† *sReg-pa*, pronounced *Rekpa*.

‡ MS. note by Griffith in his copy of Swainson's Birds.

§ Swainson's Birds, II. p. 344.

‖ *Bya*, generally pronounced *Cha*, is simply a bird. *Bya-nag*, is the "black bird;" and *Bya-dKar*, means the "white bird."

The water-fowl, *Chhu-cha,** swarm on the lakes and on the still waters of the Upper Indus. I have shot the wild goose, *Nang-gyod,* on the Thogji Chenmo and Chomoriri lakes, at 15,000 feet, and Colonel Bates and I shot three teal on the Suraj Dal, or small lake at the head of the Bhága River, at an elevation of upwards of 16,000 feet. I have shot both ducks and teal on the banks of the Indus below Hanlé, and in the swamps of Chachot just above Lé.

REPTILES.

The only reptile that I saw in Ladák was a single species of lizard, from four to seven inches in length. I noticed them on the lofty table-land between Gurkhyam and Hanlé, at an elevation of 15,000 feet. I captured one lizard as a specimen, but it managed to make its escape before I reached Hanlé.

FISH.

" Fish† abound in all the streams; but the chariness of life which is taught by the religion of Buddha, prevents their being caught." We procured fish from fourteen to fifteen inches in length in the stream at Hanlé, at an elevation of 15,000 feet, and again in the Puga rivulet at the same height. They were a kind of trout. Opposite the villages of Múd and Nyimo I observed fish jumping in the Indus. Vigne‡ mentions that the fish in the Indus at Skardo were all of one species of Himálayan trout, the largest weighing between two and three pounds.

* *Chhu-bya,* the " water-bird."

† Moorcroft's Travels, I. p. 313. Fish are called *Nya.*

‡ Travels, II. p. 282.

MOLLUSCA.

The only existing mollusk I observed in Ladák was the *Lymnæa auricularia.* In Plate IX. I have given three specimens, from Pitak and Nubra in Ladák, and from Skardo in Balti. Beside them I have placed for comparison a specimen of the same mollusk from Kashmir; and above them two extinct specimens from the old lacustrine formations on the banks of the *Thogji Chenmo* and *Pangong* salt lakes. The superior size of the Kashmir specimen is perhaps no more than might be expected from the greater mildness of the climate; but that of the extinct species is most remarkable. The largest existing specimen from Pitak measures only six-eighths of an inch in length, and rather less than five-eighths in breadth; whereas the extinct specimens are upwards of an inch in length, and more than three-quarters of an inch in breadth.

These fresh-water fossil shells are found in a fine yellow sandy clay, many feet above the present level of the salt-water lakes. When they existed, the lake of Thogji Chenmo must have been a noble sheet of fresh water, upwards of forty miles in length by about twenty miles in extreme breadth, covering the whole plain of Kyung, from the foot of the Thung-Lung Pass to the rocky glen of the Sumgyel (triple junction) River. These fossil shells are now lying in myriads in the narrow pass between the old bed of the Thogji Lake and the plain of Kyung, and they are equally numerous in the upper part of the plain of Kyung.

At what period these vast plains were covered with water will be an interesting subject of inquiry for the geologist; but the mind gets bewildered in trying to pierce the infinite obscurity of bygone ages. One point alone seems clear; that when all these lakes existed, more moisture must have been evaporated, and more snow must have fallen as well as more rain; and the humid atmosphere would have produced a milder climate more favourable to animal and vegetable life. The hills would, perhaps, have been clothed with trees, and the still waters of the magnificent lakes would have teemed with myriads of *Lymnæa*, of which only the shells now remain. But the gradual wearing down of the water-courses, and the continual bursting of the lakes, have nearly dried up all the primeval waters of Ladák; and the consequent loss of moisture has occasioned the present general scarcity of rain and snow, and that extreme dryness of atmosphere which has caused the total dearth of trees. The only sheets of water that now exist are landlocked and salt.

A second extinct species of shell is a bivalve (*Cyclas*); but as all the specimens that have been found were preserved inside the *Lymnæa*, they are necessarily small; it is now perhaps impossible to determine exactly whether they are river or lake shells.

Fossil shells are also found in the fine clay deposits near Skardo, of which I have given a specimen in Fig. 4, Plate IX., which contains a *Planorbis* and a *Luccinea* (or perhaps a small *Lymnæa*). One specimen of the existing Planorbis of Skardo is given in Fig. 9.

DOMESTIC ANIMALS.

The domestic animals of Ladák are ponies, asses, oxen, sheep, goats, and dogs. The Argons, or mixed race of half-Kashmiris half-Botis, resident at Lé, now keep a number of common fowls, but they have only within the last few years been introduced from Kashmir.

Ponies.—The ponies, according to Moorcroft,* who was a good judge, are "small, active, and hardy, but not numerous nor much used." At least one-half of the ponies used in Ladák are brought from Yarkand; but they are all geldings. The asses are small, and only equal to half-pony loads.†

Oxen.—The oxen are the *Yák*, or Chaori-tailed bull, and the yák cow, *Brimo* or *Dimo*, and their hybrid produce with the common cattle.

The *Yák* ‡ is short, but broadly and strongly built, with a small head, short horns, and a wild-looking eye. His long black hair reaches close to the ground before it is cut, and he has usually a shaggy and savage appearance. The *Yák* is used chiefly for carrying loads, as he is generally too intractable for the plough. The cow is kept only for milk.

The most valuable hybrids are the *Dso* bull and the *Dso-mo* cow, which are the produce of the male yák and the common cow. The *Dso* is used, throughout Ladák, for the plough as well as for carrying loads, as he is much more tractable than the yák and quite as strong. The *Dso-mo* yields much more milk than the yák cow, and of a much richer quality. The milk is used chiefly for butter, of which almost every Ladáki consumes a certain quantity daily in his tea, in the same way as milk is used in England. The *Dso* is a very handsome

* Travels, I. p. 309.

† Ponies of all sizes are called *Tá* (in Tibetan *rTa*). Asses are called *Bong*.

‡ The Yák (in Tibetan *gYag*) is the *Bos grunniens*, or grunting ox. The bull is called *Pho-gYag*, or *Pho-yak*; and the cow *hBri-mo*. See Plate XLII.

animal, with long shaggy hair, mostly black and white, but frequently reddish-brown and white, and sometimes altogether white. The hair is cut annually like that of the yák, and is used for the same purposes. The price of a good *Dso* varies from sixteen to twenty rupees.

The other hybrids are little valued. The *Drepo* or *Drelpo* is the male produce between the common bull and the *Dso-mo;* but it is inferior in strength, and the *Dremo,* or female, does not yield more milk than a common cow. The cross between the yák and the *Dsomo* is still less valued. Other crosses are few and accidental; as the produce of all these hybrids quickly degenerates.*

The number of neat cattle I had no accurate means of ascertaining; but as amongst the encampments I generally found that there was about one yák for every ten sheep, the present number may be estimated at about 25,000. Their total value, at the average rate of sixteen rupees each, will be Rs. 3,40,000, or £34,000.

Sheep.—The Ladáki sheep are of two distinct kinds, the tall black-faced *Huniya,* which is used chiefly for carrying burdens, and the pretty diminutive sheep of *Purik,* which is used only for food. All sheep are called by the general name of *Luk;* a flock is called *luk-khyu;* the shepherd, *luk-pa* or *luk-dsi;* and the sheepfold, *luk-ra.*†

The common sheep is the *Huniya,* which, with the exception of the pretty little Purik breed, is almost the only kind of sheep to be found throughout Tibet. This fine sheep is much larger than any of the Indian breeds,

* Moorcroft, I. p. 309, and my brother, Capt. J. D. Cunningham, in Journal As. Soc. Bengal, XIII. p. 221, both say the same thing.

† *Lug,* pronounced *Luk, Lug-khyu, Lug-pa, Lug-rDsi, Lug-ra.*

Plate VIII.

The PURIK SHEEP.

Day & Son lith. to the Queen

the height averaging from twenty-seven to thirty inches. It might, therefore, with advantage be crossed with the common small sheep of our hill provinces. Nearly the whole of the traffic of Ladák is transported on these sheep. They are food, clothing, and carriage, and form the principal wealth of the people of Ladák. I have seen a single flock of six hundred sheep, entirely laden with wool; and in one day I have counted as many as from five to six thousand sheep laden with shawl wool and common wool, borax and sulphur, and quantities of dried apricots, all making their way to the hill provinces on the south-west. The *Huniya** is, therefore, much prized; and a man's wealth is generally estimated by the number of his sheep. The average price is two rupees and a half (or five shillings), but fine strong rams are worth from three to four rupees.

The whole trade of Ladák does not exceed 30,000 small maunds of sixteen seers each, equivalent to the same number of sheep-loads. But the large importation of grain, which took place yearly before the population had been thinned by disease, emigration, and war, must have employed some 400,000 sheep. Of these, probably about one-half belonged to the Ladákis, and the other half to the hill people of Káshtwár, Chamba, Láhul, Kullu, and Kanáwar. After making a due allowance for lambs, I should estimate the former number of sheep at upwards of 300,000, or rather more than twelve sheep per house. At present the number is not so great, probably not more than 250,000. At the rate of 2 seers (4 lb.)† per sheep, the annual produce of wool

* *Huniya* is the Indian term, of which the Tibetans have made *Hunhi-yi*. The sheep is called *Huniyi-luk*.

† The English sheep yield an average of 4 lb. each, and even the little Purik sheep of Ladák yield 3 lb. See Moorcroft, I. p. 310.

would be about 400,000 seers, or 25,000 small maunds, of which about 5,000 maunds are exported. The remainder is consumed in the country; which gives an allowance of one maund per house, or of 2½ seers (5 lb.) annually, for each individual for clothing and other purposes. This is probably correct, as each person possesses at least the following amount of woollen garments.

One blanket 7 × 5 feet, weighing	4 lb.
One whole fleece, for a cloak	4 „
Two fleeces for bedding and stuffing of pillows ...	8 „
A woollen choga, or coat	5 „
Cap, waistband, stockings, boots	3 „
Seers 12=	24 „

Allowing a change of clothing about every five years, the annual consumption of wool will be two seers and two-fifths for each person, or 300,000 for the whole population. To this must be added the number of blankets used by the rich and consumed in the manufacture of bags for the conveyance of grain and other produce. *Atta* (coarse flour) is always carried in skin bags: but I would estimate the number of blanket bags at about one-half of the whole. The number of sheep employed in carriage being 200,000, the quantity of blanketing will be 100,000 yards, weighing 17,500 seers. The total produce and consumption may therefore be thus stated.

	Maunds.	Value.
Wool, exported	5,000	... Rs. 10,000
„ for home consumption	20,000	... 40,000
Total produce ...	25,000	... Rs. 50,000
	or 800,000 lb. ...	£5,000

The value of the sheep at an average price of two rupees and a half each, will be Rs. 6,25,000, or £62,500.

The Purik sheep attracted the particular attention of

Moorcroft,* whose account of them has been published in the Royal Asiatic Society's Transactions. He was so impressed with the value of this breed, that he collected a small flock for transmission to England: but unfortunately just as he was leaving Ladák the whole flock of sixty-seven was carried off by the chief of Hasora.† It was Moorcroft's opinion that the British cottager might keep three of these sheep with more ease than he now supports a cur-dog; and that every small farmer might maintain fifteen or twenty of them without any extra expense: as they would be entirely supported on that kind of produce which now runs wholly to waste or is thrown out on the dunghill. The Purik sheep will eat crumbs and parings of all kinds. Apricot-skins, turnip-peelings, pea-shells, and tea-leaves are eagerly picked up by this domestic animal; which, as Moorcroft has also noticed, will not disdain to nibble a bone. It will also eat grass, straw, chaff, and leaves. I brought a small flock of twenty from the Purik district to Simla, from whence they were despatched to England by the Governor-General. The Court of Directors presented them to Prince Albert, by whom they were first exhibited in the Zoological Gardens, and afterwards distributed to different persons interested in the breeding of sheep.

This pretty little sheep when full grown is not larger than a South-down lamb of five or six months: but "in the fineness and weight of its fleece, and in the flavour of its mutton it is equal," says Moorcroft, "to any race hitherto discovered." It gives two lambs within twelve months. It is twice shorn during the year, and the total clip yields fully three pounds of wool, of which

* Transactions Royal As. Soc. I. p. 49; and Travels, I. p. 310. The name is written *Pu-rig* and *Bu-rig*, but always pronounced Purik.

† Travels, II. p. 92.

the first clip in Moorcroft's estimation was "fine enough for tolerably good shawls." The Purik sheep is much prized for the flavour and delicacy of its mutton; and in the western districts of Ladák, scarcely any other meat is eaten. In Lé, the average price of a fine Purik sheep is about two rupees, but in their native district they can be procured at one rupee each, and at this price I purchased the little flock that was sent to England. The accompanying sketch of these animals was published in the *Illustrated News*.* The total number of this particular breed cannot be more than one-tenth of the whole, or about 25,000. The flocks may be thus distributed throughout the different districts.

	Huniya.		Purik.
In Drás	25,000	...	—
Suru	25,000	...	—
Purik	25,000	...	25,000
Kánji, Wanlá ...	25,000	...	—
Ladák proper ...	75,000	...	—
Nubra	25,000	...	—
Zanskar	20,000	...	—
Rukchu	5,000	...	—
	225,000	+	25,000
Total ...	250,000		

Goats.—The common domestic goat† of Ladák is the well-known shawl-goat, which thrives only in the most elevated districts. It is bred in Nubra, Zanskar, and Rukchu; but the finest wool is brought from Ruthog and Ngári, which formerly belonged to Ladák, and from Chang Thang, or the southern and mountainous districts of Kotan. The fleece of the shawl-kid is soft, curly, and beautifully glossy. It is used as a lining for cloaks by the more wealthy, and is exceedingly warm and comfortable. The shawl-goat is only shorn once a

* Plate IX. † All goats are called *Ra-ba*, or simply *Rá*.

year, and the wool is at once separated from the coarser hair. The hair is manufactured into blanketing for tents, coarse sacking, and ropes for home consumption. The wool is exported to Kashmir, and to Núrpúr, Amritsar, Lahor, Ludiana, Ambála, Rampur on the Sutluj, and Nepál. To Rampur and Nepál the wool is exported direct from Ruthog and Ngári, but Lé is the entrepôt between the other shawl-marts and the wool-producing countries. In Lé the wool is roughly cleaned, by which process it loses two-fifths of its weight. The picker receives the hair as the price of his labour.*

Between Lé and Kashmir only one fixed duty, of half a rupee per maund of sixteen seers, is now charged; but in former days, before Gulab Sing's acquisition of Kashmir, the duties, or rather exactions, were numerous and vexatious. The packages were made up in pony-loads of from sixty to seventy seers each, on which the charges were as follows:—

	Rs.	a.	p.	
By the Ladák government	5	0	0	
Duty levied at Drás	0	3	0	
„ Gagangir	1	0	0	
„ Gonda Sarsuig ...	0	8	0	
„ Kandarbal... ...	0	5	6	
„ Mahriána	0	8	0	
Total ...	7	8	6	Kash. Rs.
or	4	11	0	Comp.'s Rs.
The present duty is only ... Rs.	2	0	0	
showing a difference of	2	11	0,	or of 5s. on every load.

* The fine shawl-wool is called *Le-na;* the common wool, *Bal;* and the hair, *sPu.* The Tibetans are not ignorant of cotton, which they call *shing-bal*, or "tree-wool," for the same reason that the Greeks called it ξυλινον, or "tree-flax." The Tibetan names of *Lena* and *Bal*, are the same as the Latin *lana*, and the English *wool.*

In Kashmir the wool is sold by the trader to the regular wool-merchants at an average price of Kashmiri Rs. 4. 8 a., or of Company's Rs. 2. 10 a. per seer. It is then made over to the cleaners, to be cleared from the dirt and grease which still remain in it. This is effected by steeping it in a mash of rice for several days, disposed in alternate layers of wool and mash. The rice is first soaked for three or four days in water until it begins to smell; the water is then poured off, and the rice is bruised into a mash. After the wool has been soaked for a short time, it is pulled lightly but briskly into pieces, and rubbed between the hands. The mash is squeezed out, and the wool is left perfectly clean. The cleaning costs one and a quarter Kashmiri rupee per seer, or three-quarters of a Company's rupee.

The hair is next separated from the fine wool by the tedious process of picking by hand. Even after the wool is woven into cloth, many people are employed to pick out the dark-coloured hairs by hand; and the wool itself is separated into two kinds, the white and the brown, which are spun into thread. This work is all done by the poorer classes. One seer of uncleaned wool yields

Of White wool	...	$20\frac{1}{4}$	Rs. weight, or	$\frac{1}{4}$th.
Brown wool	...	$5\frac{1}{4}$	„	$\frac{1}{16}$th.
Common wool	...	$54\frac{1}{2}$	„	$\frac{11}{16}$ths.

The common wool is manufactured into the soft stuffs called pattu.

The thread is purchased from the *wool-merchants* by the *thread-merchants*, who pay according to fineness, and afterwards sell it to the *shawl-merchants*, by whom it is made over to the *dyers*. The prices of the undyed threads are—

	Weight.		
Of very fine white single thread	1¾	Rupee for	1 Rupee.
" " double "	1½	"	"
" light brown (*phiri*)	5¼	"	"
Fine white silky (*reshami*)	3¾	"	"
Very fine brown (*khudrang*)	3	"	"
Fine ditto ditto	4½	"	"

The thread-merchants are contented with the usual custom (*dasturi* of India) of half an anna in each rupee, or about six per cent.

I have now traced the gradual additions in price of the shawl-wool from the time that it leaves the hands of the producer, at one rupee per seer, until it is spun into thread and sold to the shawl-merchant at ten times the original price. About one-third of this increased price might be avoided by cleaning the wool more thoroughly in Ladák, and by the direct purchase by the shawl-merchant from the producer.

The intervention of three different traders, the Ladáki, and Kashmiri wool-merchant and the Kashmir thread-merchant, between the producer and the manufacturer, enhances the price by at least six per cent. each, or about twenty per cent. altogether.

The average quantity of shawl-wool exported to Kashmir is the same as in Moorcroft's time, about 800 loads, or 3,200 small maunds of sixteen seers each; and about the same quantity is exported to all other places. The average price in Ladák is about two rupees per seer, or Rs. 2,04,000 (£20,400). Of the 6,400 maunds exported, about 4,000 maunds are imported from Chang-thang, Ruthog, and Ngári; and the remaining 2,400 maunds are the home produce of the highlands of Nubra, Ladák, Zanskar, and Rukchu. As the usual yield of fine wool for shawls and *pattus* is half a seer, the total number of goats in Ladák must be about 80,000. The average price of a shawl-wool goat is four rupees, and the total value of the flocks of Ladák Rs. 3,20,000, or £32,000.

Dog.—The domestic dog* of Ladak is the well-known shepherd's dog, or Tibetan mastiff. They have shaggy coats, generally quite black, or black and tan; but I have seen some of a light-brown colour. They are usually ill-tempered to strangers; but I have never found one that would face a stick, although they can fight well when attacked. The only peculiarity that I have noticed about them is that the tail is nearly always curled upward on to the back, where the hair is displaced by the constant rubbing of the tail.

II.—VEGETABLE PRODUCTIONS.

I.—TREES.

The vegetable productions of Ladák are few and unimportant. The trees consist of willow, two varieties of poplar,† a kind of tamarisk, the pencil-cedar, and the *Elæagnus Moorcroftii.*‡ The tamarisk and the pencil-

* The Tibetan name for a dog is *Khyi.*

† *gShol-po* and *dByar-pa.*

‡ Capt. Madden, in the Horticultural Society's Journal, has quoted a passage from Moorcroft, to the effect that "a few willows and poplars are the *only trees* in Ladák," and he then produces the authority of Capt. H. Strachey to show that Moorcroft was wrong. But the fact is, that Moorcroft is right *in what he does say*, for either Capt. Madden or Capt. Strachey has misquoted him. In his Travels, I. p. 267, Moorcroft distinctly states that willows and poplars are the *only timber-trees* in Ladák; and in I. p. 306, he repeats the same thing. But in both places he says *timber-trees;* and he is right; for the *Shukpa* (*Shug-pa*) is too small a tree to yield timber, although, if not held sacred, it might yield wood for boxes. Capt. Madden should have recollected that the *Ser-shing* had been first described by Moorcroft, and was therefore named *Elæagnus Moorcroftii.*

cedar (*Shukpa*) are indigenous; the others are all regularly planted. The plane-tree has been introduced into Skardo, where its size and beauty have obtained for it the name of *Shing-Gyal*, "the prince of trees." The poplar is the most valuable wood in the country, as its long straight bole is particularly adapted for bridges, and for the rafters and beams of houses. It is generally planted in straight rows. The willow abounds in all the water-courses, but generally in the state of a pollard, as its supple twigs and branches are extensively used for baskets of all kinds and hurdles. These two trees were first met with at Gya, at a height of 13,500 feet. They furnish the only fire-wood procurable in Ladák; but wood is too valuable in this barren country to be thus wasted, and the principal fuel used by the people is short Tibetan furze, called *Dáma*, and dried dung of all kinds. The Elæagnus is an ornamental tree with a yellow flower, from which it derives its name of *Ser-shing*, or yellow tree. It is the Persian *Sanjit*. The tamarisk is abundant in the narrow glen of the Rulang-chu, or Puga rivulet, below the hot springs, where they attain fifteen and sixteen feet in height, the warmth of the water, 66°, being favourable to their growth.

The fruit-trees are the apple, the apricot, the walnut, the mulberry, and the vine.* The apricot is the only one found as high as Gya, 13,500 feet. The vine and apple make their first appearance at Bazgo and Sáspul, the walnut at Sáspul, and the mulberry at the monastery of Tamisgong. The apples, which are plentiful along the Indus, are of large size and good flavour. The apricots are large, but not so well flavoured as those of Balti. The grapes are much inferior to the splendid fruit of

* The vine is called *Gun*, *rGun*.

Kashmir, but they had a peculiarity which was new to me; the same bunch would yield large grapes an inch and a half in length, and small round seedless grapes like black currants. The latter are dried in the sun, and find their way to the Zimla bazaar, where they are kept by the merchants in large earthenware jars, duly labelled as "fine Zante currants," and sold at the rate of two rupees a pound, the proper price being about one quarter of a rupee per pound. The cherry is found in the warm districts.

II.—GRAINS.

The crops consist of bearded and beardless barley, common wheat and buck-wheat, peas, turnips, and mustard. In the southern province of Spiti, wheat* grows at a height of 13,000 feet (at Lárá and Lidang above Dangkhar). In the valley of the Indus it first appears at Ugshé and Chimra, between 11,000 and 12,000 feet. Buck-wheat† generally affects the same elevations as common wheat. Both kinds of barley‡ are grown at an elevation of 15,000 feet; at Hanlé, at the Korzo Gonpa, on the bank of the *Tshomoriri* lake, and above Gyihbar in Spiti.

Peas§ are cultivated at Gyihbar and Loxar, the loftiest villages in Spiti, between 14,000 and 15,000 feet, and at Miru, in the Gya valley, from 12,500 and 13,500 feet. Mustard also is found at the same elevation; at Gyihbar in Spiti, and at Gya and at Miru in Ladák proper. Turnips are grown at 15,000 feet at the Korzo Gonpa, on

* Wheat is called *Gro*, which in some districts is pronounced *To*.

† *Bro*, by many pronounced *Do*.

‡ *Nas* is the name for all kinds of barley. *Nas-karmo* is white barley, and *Nak Nas* is black barley.

§ *Honma*, which is spelt *Sronma*.

the banks of the Chomoriri lake, but they are small and hard. The turnips at Lé and at Tamisgong are good and palatable.

III.—CULTIVATION.

All cultivable land is called *Zhing*,* and this term is also generally used for a field of any kind. Good rich land is called *Zhing-zang;* stony land is called *Ri-zhing*, that is literally, "hilly land;" and meadow land is called *Thang-zhing*, that is, "plain land." All the cultivable land in Ladák lies along the courses of the small streams, and in patches on the banks of the great rivers. In the bed of the Indus especially there are large tracts of grass-land which are never brought under cultivation, but are kept solely for the grazing of cattle.

Landlords are called *Zhing-pa* and *Zhing-dag*. The poor cultivate the lands themselves, but the wealthy employ regular labourers. The *Glapa*,† or labouring man, holds the plough (*thong* or *shől* ‡), while the *Glapa-mo*, or labouring woman, breaks the clods or digs the upturned earth. The women also irrigate the fields, and cut the crops. The ploughman, *Thong-pa* or *Moba*, and the diggers, *Ko-pápo* and *Kopámo*,§ are usually paid by the month (*da-phok* ||). Yáks are employed in drawing the plough, which is of wood, the share being only tipped with iron; but many of the fields are dug by the hand with a peculiarly-shaped mattock, *ko-byed*,¶ of which

* *Zhing*, arable land; *Zhing-bZang*, rich land; *Ri-Zhing*, hilly land; *Thang-Zing*, plain land.

† *Gla-pa*, a labouring woman is called *Gla-pa-mo*.

‡ *Thong* or *Shol*, or sometimes *Thong-shol*.

§ *Thong-pa* or *rMo-ba*, a ploughman. The diggers are *rKo-pa-po* and *rKo-pa-mo*.

|| *Zla-Phogs*, pronounced *Da-Phok*, "monthly pay."

¶ *rKo-byed*, called also *Tog-tse*.

the handle forms a very acute angle with the blade. After ploughing, the fields are prepared with manure, *lúd*,* which consists either of *Yák-lúd*, yák's dung, or of *Lúk-lúd*, sheep's dung. Occasionally they use cow-dung, *Yák-chi* or *Ba-chi*. But in a country where fire-wood is so scarce as not to be obtainable by any but the richest classes, all kinds of dung are in daily use as fuel, and but little can be spared for enriching the land.

In a dry country like Ladák, where it seldom snows and scarcely ever rains, the harvest is entirely dependent upon artificial irrigation. The waters of the smaller streams are arrested by dams (*chhu-lon*), and conducted with considerable skill and care from terrace to terrace, and from field to field. I was particularly struck with the laborious irrigation bestowed upon the rich lands of Sáspul, and with the bold ingenuity displayed in the aqueducts of Kambo and Hardas. The former is a small village on the left bank of the Purik river (the Waká-chu). The latter is on the left bank of the Drás river. The Kambo aqueduct is only about one mile in length, but the Hardas aqueduct is nearly three miles long. These canals, which are conducted several hundred feet above the villages, are mostly built up with a retaining wall, and puddled with clay to hold the water. In a few places the rock itself was excavated to form a passage for the water, but in other places, where the hill was too precipitous, or the rock was too hard, the water was passed along hollow poplar and willow trunks, which were supported by uprights standing on ledges of the rock, or on huge pegs driven into its crevices.

The land in Ladák is all measured by the *Khál*, or

* *Lúd*, dung. Cow-dung is called *gYag-lChi* or *Ba-lChi*.

*Bhára-khál-kyi,** which is a field that requires one khál of seed. The produce is likewise reckoned in kháls. This word khál means simply a load or burden of any kind, and is apparently the same as the Indian *khára*, or *khári*, which is a measure of twenty bháras; while the *kharika* is that sized field which requires a *khári* of seed. In the Hindu Himálayas, a *bharao* (bharava†) is that sized field which requires a *bhára* of seed. Thus, in each country the estimate is made according to the most usual means of transport. In Tibet and in the Botiyan Himálayas, where sheep are almost the only means of transport, all estimates are made in the khál, or *luk-khál*, that is, a sheep's load of from 12 to 16 seers each (24 to 32 lb.). In the Hindu Himálayas, where men or women carry everything, all measures are reckoned in the *bharao*, or man's load (*bhára*) of 32 seers (64 lb.). In the plains of India, where *gáris*, or carts, are used, the reckoning is made by the *khári*, which is a load of 20 *bháras*, equal to 12 or 15 cwt.

When the term *khál* is used alone, a sheep's load is always intended, for all other loads are distinguished by a prefix, as *Yák-khál*, an "ox-load;" *Ta-khál*, a "horse-load." The common khál, or sheep's load, is equal to 5 battis of 2½ seers or 5 lb. each, or 8 battis of 2 seers or 4 lb. each, or just about half a bushel; and as in England the usual quantity of seed per acre is about two bushels, or one cwt., the size of a khál of land will be equal to a quarter of an acre, or one rood. But as the seed is much more broadly sown in Ladák than in

* *Khál* or *Bhára-khál-kyi*. The occurrence of *bh* shows that *Bhára* is a word of Indian origin. *Khál-hBo* is a "khál measure."

† *Bhárava*, from *Bhára*, a load.

England, I should estimate the khál of land at about one-third of an English acre, or even more.

The seed is sown in May, and the crops are cut in September, before the first fall of snow. On the 16th of September, 1846, on the bank of the Tshomoriri lake, at an elevation of 15,000 feet, I found the Lamas of the Korzo Gonpa (monastery) cutting a field of unripe barley. The sky was very cloudy and threatening, especially to the southward, and the poor Lamas expected snow, which, if it fell upon the standing crop, would, they said, destroy it. The crop was all cut by the evening, and removed, and the next day it snowed without intermission for twenty-four hours. The crops are either pulled up by the roots or cut close to the roots, with a *zorpa*, or sickle, to get as much straw as possible for the winter fodder of the cattle. When cut, it is generally spread out on the ground to ripen and dry, but occasionally it is loosely bound in sheaves.* The return varies according to the quality of the soil and the quantity of manure. In Drás, Moorcroft heard that it was " about twenty for one ;" but according to my informants, the best lands in Ladák Proper, at Sabu, near Lé, and at Sakté, in the Chimra valley, do not yield more than ten-fold ; while the poorer lands give a return of only five or six-fold, or on an average eight-fold. But the richer lands, in the Suru valley, and on the Waká and Drás rivers, which enjoy a milder climate and a moister atmosphere, generally yield from ten to fifteen-fold. The average return for the whole of Ladák may therefore be estimated at about ten-fold, or perhaps less.

Two ears of bearded barley from Lé gave a return of

* A sheaf is called *Chhun-po.*

fifty grains each, and the same number of ears of beardless barley, from the banks of the Tshomoriri lake, gave a return of forty-five grains each. Moorcroft, however, mentions that the Hasora wheat grown in Ladák yields from forty to seventy grains in each ear.* From these statements it is clear that not more than one-fourth of the seed can germinate. Much of it is, no doubt, eaten by the vast flocks of pigeons and chakors, which abound in Ladák; but the greater proportion, perhaps, rots. Many of the young plants must be destroyed by the night frost; for in most of the districts of Ladák it freezes almost every night, even during the month of June.

The total produce of Ladák may be ascertained approximately in the following manner. In 1847 I obtained the census and other statistical details of 142 villages in the different districts of Ladák, containing 1,890 houses, with 20,815 *kháls* of cultivable land, or just 11 *kháls* per house. As the total number of landed or paying houses† in Ladák is 18,000, the whole amount of cultivable land throughout the country may be reckoned at 198,000 kháls, or about 66,000 acres. Each khál requires 16 seers of seed, and yields about ten-fold. The total available produce for food is therefore only nine-fold, or about 28,512,000 seers, equal to 1,000,000 bushels, which, with the former population of 165,000, would not give more than 7 chittaks (14 oz.) of food to each person daily, while the average consumption is at least 8 chittaks (1 lb.). The deficiency is about 24 seers for each person; which, at the rate of 16 seers per

* Travels, I. p. 275.

† In Ladák no houses are taxed except those which have lands attached to them.

rupee,* would entail an annual outlay of Rs. 1. 8 a. (about 3s.), or a total importation of Rs. 2,47,500 worth of grain. This sum, divided over the whole adult male population of about 40,000, shows an annual expenditure of six rupees per man; or, if divided amongst the whole number of 24,000 houses, about ten rupees per house. This sum was defrayed entirely by the profits of the carrying trade, of which the Ladákis have an entire monopoly between Yarkand and Kashmir.

With the present population of 125,000 people, the land would yield fully enough for home consumption, or 9 chittaks (1 lb. 2 oz.) daily for each person; but scarcely more than three-fourths of the lands are now under cultivation. The present annual produce is, therefore, not more than twenty-two millions of seers, or somewhat less than 800,000 bushels, which will yield only 7¾ chittaks (15½ oz.) of food for each person daily. The deficiency is half an ounce daily for each individual, or about 5½ seers annually, equal to 5½ annas (about 9d.). The whole annual importation is, therefore, only 687,500 seers, in value about Rs. 43,000. This sum divided over the whole adult male population of 30,000 persons, shows an annual expenditure of Rs. 1. 6 a., or if divided over the 18,000 houses, about Rs. 2. 6 a. 2 p. per house.

There is a curious custom in Ladák, which has a counterpart in the *arwan* of India and the *neck* of England. At every harvest the farmer selects a small bundle of the finest ears of barley, which he fastens round

* This was the rate in Lahul in 1846, and at Lé in 1847; but in the grain-growing districts I was informed that wheat was sold at thirty-two seers, and even at thirty-six seers per rupee. The individual expense of each family or house was therefore perhaps not more than half of the sum stated above.

the neck of a pillar in the largest room of his house. At Gya, I was told that the first cuttings were thus dedicated on the occasion of every harvest. Moorcroft* was informed that it was the custom "to consecrate the two or three first handfuls of each year's crop to a spirit who presides over agriculture." The necks of pillars would appear to have been the usual in-door place for the deposit of votive offerings of every kind; for Captain Turner,† when leaving *Tashi-Lhunpo*, bound a white scarf round the capitals of each of the four columns of the apartment which he occupied. He did this "in conformity with the custom of those regions." At Lé, Moorcroft saw ears of wheat: at Gya, Bazgo, and Sáspul, I noticed only ears of barley. Perhaps different places may have different customs, as wheat is used in England and barley in India for the same purpose; but as no wheat is grown at Gya, the use of barley was there a matter of necessity. In India, the first cuttings of barley (*arwan*) are brought home to be eaten by the family, and presented to the houshold gods and Brahmins. The grain is mixed with milk and sugar, and tasted seven times by each member of the family. The festivity of the season is proverbial.‡

Phula, phula, kyun phiré? Ghar Arwan áya.
Jhuka, jhuka, kyun phiré? Piyáda áya.

Why so very, very glad?
Because it's harvest-home.
Why so very, very sad?
The collector 's come.

---

* Travels, I. p. 318. † Turner's Tibet, p. 329.

‡ Sir H. M. Elliot's Glossary. Every page of this valuable work teems with most interesting information regarding the history of India, and the manners and customs of its people.

In Devonshire, the "neck" consists of the finest ears of wheat, which are selected and tied up in a small sheaf by some old man, who stands in the midst of the reapers holding the "neck" with both hands. It is possible that the name may be derived from the sheaf having once been carried home and fastened round the neck of a pillar or wooden post, as in Ladák.

In Scotland, the farmers have a custom similar to one which prevails amongst the Botis of Spiti, Hangorang, and Kanáwar. The Scotch farmer weaves the first-cut corn into a threefold plait, which he places over his chimney-piece until the next harvest. The Boti peasant fixes three or more ears of barley outside his own door, and makes a votive offering of three or five, or some odd number of ears to his native divinity in the village *Thákûrdwára.**

All these various customs would seem to have a common origin in the celebration of the harvest season, which in every country has been a time of rejoicing. The *adwan* and *juri* of the Hindus and the harvest-home of the English are similar to the private *ambarvalia* of the Romans. So also the votive offerings of the Tibetans were consecrated for the same object as the *lustratio* of the Romans. The former offered his first cuttings of corn with a prayer for a plentiful harvest, the latter performed their lustrations (ambarvalia) immediately before the sickle was put to the corn, to obtain the blessing of the gods on the fields which were thus lustrated.

* Gerard's Kanáwar, p. 98, and Capt. J. D. Cunningham's Notes on Moorcroft and Gerard, in the Journal of the Bengal Asiatic Society, vol. xiii. p. 246.

III.—MINERAL PRODUCTIONS.

The mineral productions of Ladák are more interesting to the geologist than important to the economist. The most striking geological features, and the principal localities of some of the prevailing rocks, have already been noticed in my description of the mountains: but the more useful minerals still remain to be mentioned.

Slate.—"The use of slates,"* says McCulloch, "is entirely European. From the Hellespont to China there is not a single slated house." This statement is correct, as far as my observation goes in the *plains* of India, where slates cannot be procured, but in the *hills* the use of slates is very common. The best slates that I have seen are those of the clay-slate formation, in the *Dhaola-Dhar* range, between Kangra and Chamba. There are quarries on both sides of the range. The roof of the great temple at *Mahila*, on the Rávi, is roofed with large slates, which are nailed to the planking in the usual manner. On the south sides of the range, the use of slates is universal. All the houses in the large towns of Kangra, Tira, and Jwála-Mukhi, are roofed with slates of a very fine description. All the temples, and many of the houses in the districts around Simla, are also roofed with slates, but of an inferior kind. In Mandi and Kullu, however, the mica-slate formation yields very large thin slates of an excellent description. In Láhul and Ladák the clay and mica schists could be split into slates of a smaller size; but the extreme scarcity of timber prevents the construction of large rooms, and for small ones the people find that flat roofs are the simplest and the most commodious.

* M'Culloch's Commercial Dictionary, art. SLATE.

Lime.—The most prevalent rock in Ladák is limestone. In Spiti, the whole formation is of this rock, excepting near Losar, where it changes into clay slate. It forms the range that divides Rukchu from Zanskar, and again changes into clay slate near the junction of the Sum-gyel rivers.

It pervades Zanskar, and is found on both banks of the Indus; in the Photo Lá and Hánu passes. It occurs at both ends of the Pangkong lake, and extends from Sassar to the crest of the Kárákoram range. Notwithstanding this general prevalence of the rock, the scarcity of wood is so great that none but the wealthy can afford to use lime mortar in their houses.

Marble.—For ornamental purposes none of the Ladáki limestones that I have seen would be considered of any value;* but the fossiliferous limestone of Kashmir takes a very high polish, and the splendid pillars of the Shálimar are the only beautiful things now remaining in that once celebrated garden.

Gypsum.—This useful mineral is found at the sulphur-mines, on the banks of the Puga rivulet, either in pure white flakes regularly disposed, or in a compact rock, with crystals of sulphur attached to it, and thin veins of nearly pure sulphur desseminated through it. It occurs also on the right bank of the Spiti river, below Losar, at the celebrated cave of Amaranáth, in Kashmir, and on the banks of the Shigar river, in Balti.† No use whatever is made of it by the people.

Clay.—Extensive deposits of the finest clays of all

* Mir Izzet Ullah, however, mentions a striped marble-like Sulimáni stone as occurring in the bed of the Shayok river, between Chong-Ulang and Dong-Bailák.—Quart. Orient. Magazine, 1825, p. 113.

† See Vigne's map for Gypsum.

EXTINCT and EXISTING SHELLS, from Ladak, Balti, and Kashmir.

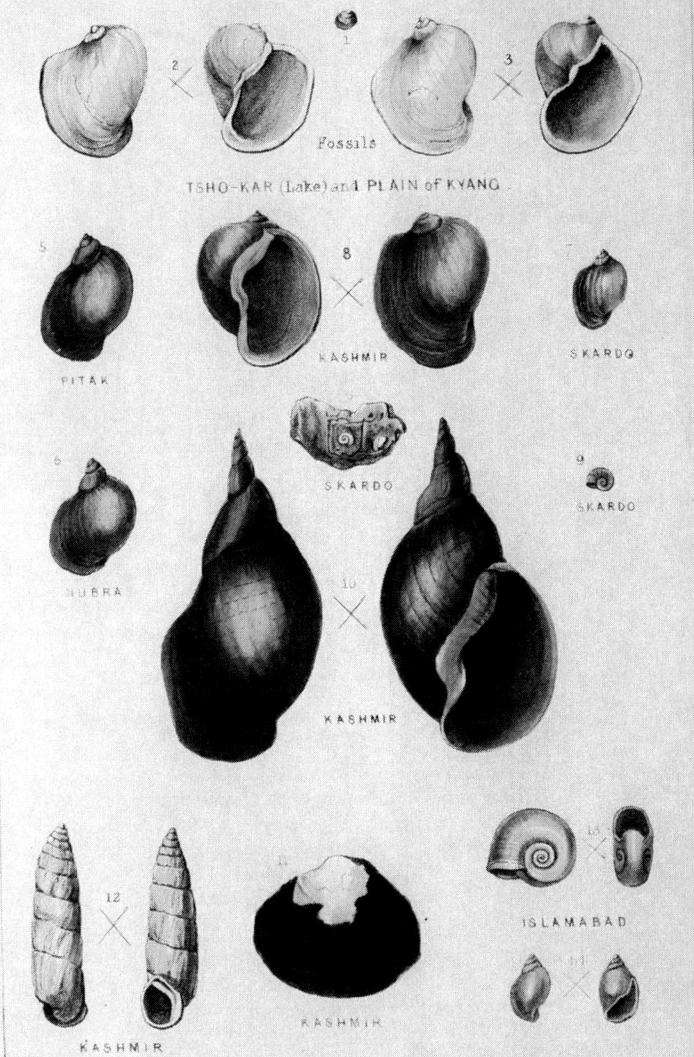

A. Cunningham del. Day & Son Lith^rs to The Queen.

colours are found throughout Ladák. They are all lacustrine formations, and are seen adhering to the sides of ravines, and attached to steep cliffs that have once been washed by the great rivers. In the gap between the monastery of Pitak and the end of the granite range, to the west of Lé, there is an immense mass of indurated clay, disposed in horizontal layers of different shades, but chiefly of a pale yellow and light lavender colour. Beyond Pitak the same clay strata occur again in a recess of the hills on the right bank of the Indus. But the most remarkable deposits of clay are immediately below Lama-Yúrrú, where a pale straw-coloured clay is seen in all places in the bed of the stream, in small patches on the summits of detached rocks, and in large masses overlying the slate to a height of at least one thousand feet above the present bed of the stream.* A similar coloured clay occurs in a ravine of the Yunam river, just above the Yunam lake. At different places in the Nubra valley, Dr. Thomson observed similar deposits of bluish-coloured clay; and near Skardo he found one containing fossil remains of Planorbis and Succinea. Near Rámu-Serai, in Kashmir, I found beds of highly indurated clay, mixed with boulders, which rose to a height of 150 feet above the plain. This lacustrine formation would alone prove the existence of a vast lake, that once covered the whole valley of Kashmir to a depth of about 200 feet.

Steatite was found by Vigne on the banks of the Drás

* The Lamas of this place have a tradition that a lake formerly existed on the spot, that the rock was cut through by Naropa, a Lama from Brigúng, near Lhasa, and that the present monastery of Yung Dung Gonpa was built by him. Lámá Yúrrú is the Kashmirian name of the place. All clays are called *rDsa-ma*.

river, near the Taskyum bridge,* and on the left branch of the Shigar river, in Balti.

Gold is found by washing the sands of the Indus and of the Shayok river; but the washings are entirely carried on by Mussulmans from Balti, as the Buddhists of Ladák have long been prohibited from the search. The prohibition is said to have originated in the fears of the Gyalpo lest the people should neglect their fields in the tempting pursuit of gold. The crowds that have flocked to the recent "diggings" in California and Australia have fully justified the fears of the Gyalpo. Gold is also found in Chang-thang, but its collection is prevented by a superstitious belief that the lumps of native gold "belong to the genii of the spot, who would severely punish the human appropriation of their treasures."† The sands of the Indus have long been celebrated for the production of gold. Pliny‡ says, "*Fertilissimi sunt auri Dardæ;*" and this is the case even at the present day; for the sands of the Indus, in the Dardu country, are said to be more prolific than those of any other part of the river. But the gold of the Indus was known at a still earlier date; for Megasthenes relates that the Indian ants dug gold out of the earth, not for the sake of metal, but in making burrows for themselves.§ These Indian ants are no doubt the

* Travels, II. p. 392, and map. † Moorcroft, I. p. 314.

‡ Lib. VI. c. 19. The conclusion of the passage is curious and suggestive, *Setæ vero argenti,* that is, "the country of the Dardæ produced most gold, but that of the *Setæ* the most silver." As we know that silver is not found in India, the *Setæ* can be no other than the *Seths,* or "bankers," in whose hands the wealth of India has been for ages. It seems probable that many of the Indian nations, enumerated by ancient authors, may have been only different trades and professions.

§ Arrian, Indica, XV.

marmots (*Arctomys*) and rat-hares (*Lagonys*) of Tibet, which in making burrows "throw up the earth wherein the ore is contained, from which the Indians extract gold." On the plains along the banks of the Indus and Shayok, the marmots still throw up the earth mixed with gold-dust, from which the Indians of Balti occasionally extract a few grains of gold. Megasthenes confesses that he had not seen the animals themselves, but only their skins, which had been brought by the Macedonian soldiers into Alexander's camp. The skin of the marmot is the commonest of all the furs now brought to India.* Its Tibetan name is *Phyi-pa* or *Chipa* (or *Chupa*), which was probably confounded by Alexander's soldiers with the Indian *Chúntá*, the name of the large ant; or *Phyi-pa* may have been confounded by the Indians themselves with *Pippilaka*, the Sanscrit and Bengali name of the large ant.†

The same story of the ants as big as foxes is told by Herodotus; and Professor H. H. Wilson‡ has aptly illustrated it by a passage from the Mahábhárata, which relates that "the people who dwell under the pleasant shade of the *Kichaka-venus* (a kind of willow) and along the Sailodá river, between the Meru and Mandara mountains, the Khasas, Prádaras, Páradas, Ekásanas, Arkas, Kulindas, Tanganas, and Paratanganas, brought to Yudhishthira lumps of gold, a *drona* (64 lb.) in weight, of the sort called *paippílika*, "or ant gold," which was so called because it was exfodiated by the

* The same holds good to the eastward, for Mr. Hodgson says, "In the extensive peltry trade carried on between Nepál and Tibet, no skin is more commonly met with than that of the marmot."—Journal As. Soc. Bengal, X. p. 777.

† *Phyi-pa*, commonly pronounced *Chi-pa*.

‡ Journal Roy. As. Soc. VII. p. 143.

pippílaka, or common large ant." This belief, however erroneous, as the learned professor observes, was neither extravagant nor irrational. A yet earlier mention of the gold of Alpine India is that of Ctesias; but he distinctly states that it was not obtained by washing, as in the river Pactolus.* Gold is called *Ser*, gold-dust *Ser-dul*, and the gold-washer *Ser-pa*. This name I believe to have been the origin of the classical *Seres*. In Tibetan *Serki-yul* means the "gold country;" and as the affix *yul* can be omitted at pleasure, the names of Serki and Serika are almost identical.†

Copper.—According to Moorcroft, "some copper-mines are said to have been discovered towards Kashmir."‡ This statement is probably correct, as Jacquemont found copper ore in the Lidar valley, on the south-west side of the range which divides Kashmir from the Ladáki district of Suru. If any trust can be put in a name, I should suppose that copper (*zangs*) had been found in *Zangskar*, but I could not learn that it had been discovered there.

Lead and *Iron* are, according to Moorcroft, found in pits in the mountain districts remote from Lé.

Plumbago is found in Balti; but the specimens which I procured are of an inferior description. They are gritty, and will not mark paper without scratching; but as they were most probably taken from the long-exposed surface, good black lead may still perhaps be found in the same place.

Sulphur, called *Muzi*, is obtained only at Puga, in

* Fragments of Ctesias by Lion. Indica, XII. Ἔστι δὲ καὶ χρυσὸς ἐν τῇ Ἰνδικῇ χώρᾳ, οὐκ ἐν τοῖς ποταμοῖς εὑρισκόμενος καὶ πλυνόμενος, ὥσπερ ἐν τῷ Πακτωλῷ ποταμῷ.

† *gSer*, gold; *gSer-rDul*, gold dust.

‡ Travels, I. p. 313.

Ladák; but the sulphur of Chang-thang is so easily obtainable, that the Puga mine is almost neglected. The bed of the small rivulet Rulang-chu, which traverses the glen of Puga, is full of hot springs, varying in temperature from 80° to 148°. The hottest springs are strongly impregnated with sulphuretted hydrogen. The sulphur itself is found on the left bank of the rivulet, where a small hole has gradually been excavated by the shepherds. It occurs in pure transparent crystals attached to the gypsum, or in thin opaque laminæ disseminated through the rock. The quantity exported is very small, but I was informed by the shepherds that as much as 100 small maunds (of 16 seers each) are sometimes mined. In 1847 I saw twelve sheep-loads (or twelve maunds) of sulphur that had been taken from this mine; but I feel satisfied that the average quantity of sulphur annually mined cannot be more than fifty maunds, and is probably much less. No duty is taken at the mine; and the export duty, which is only a quarter of a rupee per maund, can often be evaded.

Borax, in Tibetan *Tshalé*, is thrown up in the form of boracic acid by the hot springs of lowest temperature in the valley of Puga. The banks of the rivulet, for about two miles in length, are quite white with the saline matters that are continually being precipitated. These salts are chloride of soda and borate of soda. They are carefully scraped from the surface, as the under-coating is only the refuse of former years. Those of a faint pinkish hue, inclining occasionally to green, are preferred; but these colours entirely disappear as the salts become dry. This impure mixture is the tincal of commerce, from which the borax (borate of soda) is obtained in India in the shape of crystals, by solution and evaporation.

Soda.—The banks of the Thogji Chanmo lake, in Rukchu, are incrusted with masses of saline matter; and in passing round its southern end, the crisp, hardened surface of salt yields and crackles beneath the feet of the traveller. The lake is commonly called *Tsho-kar*, or the White Lake, by the Botis, and *Khaori Talao*, or Salt Lake, by the Hindus of Bisahar, Chamba, and Kullu. The salt is natron, or sub-carbonate of soda. No use is made of it.

Magnesia.—The salts deposited on the banks of the great Tshomoriri lake are common salt and muriate (hydrochlorate) of magnesia. These salts do not occur in any great heaps, like those on the Tsho-kar; but as the Tshomoriri lake is sixteen miles in length, a considerable quantity might no doubt be obtained annually along its forty miles of shore.

Salt, in Tibetan *Tshá*, is found on the banks of the Tshomoriri lake, in combination with the magnesia. I was informed that no use whatever was made of it, as rock salt (from Lahor) was procurable without difficulty.

Garnets of an inferior description, and of a dark brown colour, were found at Puga by Dr. Thomson in a coarse grit stone rock. The natives were not aware of their existence.

Momiai, a mineral substance of a dirty brownish-black colour, is found in Balti. It has a strong unpleasant smell, and it burns with a thick black smoke, leaving a considerable quantity of dark-coloured ashes. It is probably petroleum, the quantity of ash perhaps arising from the admixture of some foreign substance, employed either to collect or to solidify the native liquid. The common *momiai* of Indian medicine is of course a manufactured article; although not made, as generally asserted, of the melted fat of Abyssinian boys, who have been roasted for the purpose. The *momiai* of Balti is said to be a natural product. The original *momiai* was only mummy,* which, at one time, was held in much repute, even in Europe.

* The name of *Momiai* موميائي is derived from *Momia* موميا, or Mummy.

IX.—COMMERCE.

I.—HOME TRADE.

The artificial productions of Ladák are confined to the manufacture of blankets and coarse woollens, chiefly for home consumption, and of black mohair tents, made from the hair of the yák or grunting ox, which form the only habitations of the nomadic population. Both blanketing and sacking can be purchased in Lé, the former only in small quantities, the latter in almost any quantity, as there is a constant demand for it for bags for the conveyance of goods. The blanketing is manufactured in pieces one foot wide and eleven to fifteen yards in length. The price varies from two to three rupees each, according to fineness. The quantity of blanketing and of sacking annually expended in Ladák on the carrying trade amounts to about 120,000 yards, in the manufacture of which 20,000 small maunds (or 640,000 lb.) of wool are consumed. The total value of the manufacture is only Rs. 7,500 or £750.

II.—FOREIGN TRADE.

The foreign trade of the country, in home produce, is confined to four natural productions,—wool, borax, sulphur, and dried fruits, of which only the first is of any consequence, and even that is not of sufficient importance to deserve more than a slight notice.

Wool, in Tibetan *Bal*, is the chief product of Ladák. It is of two kinds: goat-wool, or *Le-na*, which is used for shawls, and sheep-wool, or *Bal*, which is used for blanketing and coarse clothing, and for stuffing pillows and bedding.

The quantity of home-produced shawl-wool annually exported from Ladák averages 2,400 small maunds, or 76,800 lb. The value in Ladák is the same amount in rupees (Rs. 76,800), at the rate of two rupees per seer. The shawl-wool is exported to Kashmir, Nurpur, Amritsar, and Rampur.

The commoner sheep-wool is produced in much greater quantities, and the general amount of export (5,000 maunds) more than doubles that of the finer wool. The value at eight seers per rupee is only 2,000 rupees.

Borax.—The borax and sulphur-mines are found together at an uninhabited spot named Puga, on the Rulang-chu, a small stream which is full of hot springs, and which joins the Indus on its left bank,   miles above Lé. Puga stands in N. latitude 33° 12′, and E. longitude 78° 16′, at an elevation of 15,264 feet above the sea. The borax is ejected in the bed of the stream by the numerous hot springs at various temperatures, from 80° upwards. The salt (borate of soda) is found along both banks of the rivulet for about two miles, in conjunction with chloride of soda. It is in a damp state, owing to the vapours emitted by the hot springs. In collecting the borax, the surface of the salt, which is generally of a light pink creamy hue (sometimes inclining to green), is carefully scraped and collected in bags. When dry, it is of a dull white colour. In this state it is collected by the shepherds, who pasture their flocks on the rich summer grass of the plains of Rukchu. The quantity of this borax annually exported is stated at 500 maunds, or 16,000 lb.; the value, at the rate of sixteen seers per rupee, being only Rs. 500.

Sulphur.—The Puga sulphur-mine is situated at a short distance from the stream, at the foot of a gypsum cliff. The mineral occurs chiefly in the form of thin laminæ disseminated throughout the rock; but in all the fissures there are numerous detached crystals, quite transparent and of all sizes, from that of a grain of sand to one-eighth of an inch. In detaching the sulphur, the crystals are mostly reduced to powder and partially mixed with the gypsum rock; and in this state it is carried to the markets of Nurpur, Kangra, and Rampur. The vague statements of the shepherds make the annual supply about 500 maunds, or 3,200 lb., but I should think that it rarely amounted even to one-half of that quantity.

Dried Fruits.—These consist of apricots and small seedless raisins (commonly called currants). I have no means of making even a guess at the amount of this export, but the quantity must be considerable. I never found a single trader or shepherd without numerous bags of them; and I have procured them in all the bazaars in the hill states from Kashmir to Kangra and Simla. In the Simla bazaar they are sold at from two to two and a half seers per rupee.

The whole value of the foreign trade of Ladák, in home produce, does not exceed Rs. 80,000 or £8,000.

III.—FOREIGN TRADE IN FOREIGN PRODUCE.

The chief source of wealth in Ladák is the carrying-trade, or transport of foreign produce from one country to another through its own territories. This trade it owes entirely to its centrical situation between Kashmir and India on the south, and the Chinese provinces of Yarkand, Kotan, and Káshgár on the north. It is the entrepôt between Kashmir, where the shawls are manufactured, and the Chinese provinces of Ruthog and Chang-Thang, where the shawl-wool is produced. It supplies north-western India with tea, shawls, wool, and borax; and the Musalmán provinces of China with opium, saffron, brocades, and shawls. These are the staples of the trade through Ladák, but the number of smaller articles that are interchanged is very great, and as the detail may be interesting, I subjoin a list which I prepared at Lé from the accounts of the Yarkandi and Kashmiri merchants. Many of them are quack medicines of very doubtful properties; but the most curious items are undoubtedly the export of sugar to Yarkand, and its after-import in the shape of sugar-candy. The *Gur*, or coarse sugar, of Kashmir is carried a long journey of two months and a half to Yarkand, where it is refined and crystallized: and the sugar-candy is again carried over the same long journey back to Ladák and Kashmir. The Yarkandi sugar-candy is certainly very white; but it is surpassed in colourless transparency by that of Bikaner.

List of Chinese articles brought to India.

Shawl-wool from Chang-Thang and Ruthog.
Churas or Bang, an intoxicating extract of hemp.

Silver in bars or ingots, called *Kuru* and *Yámbu.**
Felts of various kinds.
Suklát, a kind of camlet made of camel's hair.
Tea, both green and black.
Sugar-candy.
Russia Leather, called Bulgár.
Sable-skins, called Kúndúz.
Gúma, or black leather.
Kimsan, or golden-coloured leather, about eight inches wide.
Ságri, or green leather.
Láka, a peculiar cloth made of hemp-bark.
Velvets, both coarse and fine.
Mashru, or coarse silk cloths of three kinds—
1. Bádsháhi.
2. Alchinbar, made at Alchi or Ilitsi.
3. Kotani, made at Kotan.

Siling, a soft and fine silky woollen of two kinds—
1. Shirún, and 2. Gorún.

Parcha Samsún, coarse cotton cloths.
Parcha Zukh, ditto ditto.
Silk, both raw and manufactured.
Gold.
Gold thread, called Zirri, both genuine and false.
Silver.
Silver thread.
Turquoises, from Persia, through Bokhára.
Carpets, from Kotan.
Rewand-Chini, or rhubarb.†
Chob-Chini, or China-root.
Gol-i-Dál-Chini.
Zedaary, Nirbisi from Nepál.
Coral, Múnga.
Musk, Mushkanáfa.
Tobacco.
Raisins.
Pistachio Nuts, Pista.
Soap.

---

* *Kuru* is the Turki name; the Tibetans call them *Yam-bu.*

† Dr. O'Brien informs me that China-root is much used as an excellent substitute for sarsaparilla. Dr. O'Shaughnessy states that it is largely imported into Calcutta from the eastward.—See the Bengal Dispensatory, p. 645.

Bádián-khitai, Chinese aniseed, which is bruised and put into tea.
Mamira, a yellow root said to be a cure for bad eyes.
Galer-patthar (neck-stone), good for swollen necks.
Mulhatti, liquorice-root, used for coughs.
Daryâhi.
Ponies.
Salt, from the lakes of Chang-Thang.

List of Indian articles carried to Yarkand.

Láki, goat-skins dyed red, from Nurpur.
Cottons, flowered (chicken).
Ditto, coarse (ghára).
Ditto, thin (gaji).
Chintzes of all kinds.
Silk, *lungi* of Multán.
Shawls, mostly coarse.
Jámiwár, or shawl-cloth figured in breadths.
Brocades, mostly coarse.
Turbans.
Opium.
Indigo.
Heron-plumes, Kalgi, generally made of the feathers of the jungul fowl.
Shoes, from Nurpur.
Pearls of all sizes up to one hundred rupees each.
Otter-skins.
Turmeric.
Cardamums.
Ginger.
Cloves.
Black Pepper.
Honey.
Tamarinds, dry.
Sherbet, lemon.
Coarse Sugar, Gúr.
Narcachor, the root of a reed, used both as a scent and as a medicine. It is the common *Narkat* or *Nalkand* (Curcuma Zerumbet).*

---

* In Hindustáni نرکٹ, नर्कट, *Narkat*; in Sanskrit नलकाण्ड or नलकांड, *Nala kánda*, or river-reed. It is plentiful in the Sindh at

Túrbad, Convolvulus Turpethum, or Turbith, a purgative root.
Hábilistan.
Khurma or *Chhuhára*, dates.
Salt.

CHINESE IMPORTS FOR INDIA.

Shawl-wool.—The principal article of Ladáki trade between the Chinese provinces and India is shawl-wool, of which about 3,200 maunds are annually sold to the Kashmiris, and an equal quantity to the traders of Nurpur, Rampur, Amritsar, and Ludiana. Of this, some 2,400 maunds are the produce of the country, and the remainder, amounting to 4,000 maunds, or 128,000 lb., is obtained from Chang-Thang and Ruthog. As the average value of shawl-wool in Ladák is 2 rupees per seer, or 1 rupee per lb., the total value of the annual import of shawl-wool is Rs. 1,28,000, or £12,800. The whole is again exported.

Sheep's wool is imported only in small quantities, as the country itself supplies more wool than it consumes. About 1,000 maunds are said to be brought annually from Ruthog, of which the value in Ladák, at the rate of 8 seers per rupee, is only Rs. 500. It is all exported again.

Charas, or Bang, is brought from Yarkand. About 500 maunds are imported annually, at the average price of three rupees per seer. The whole value of this article is therefore Rs. 24,000, or £2,400. About 300 maunds of charas are consumed in Ladák, and the remaining 200 maunds are exported to the neighbouring countries.

Tobacco is imported largely from Yarkand, the annual supply being stated at 4,000 maunds, or 128,000 lb., of

Narwar or Nalwar; and it is possible that the name may have been derived from this celebrated fort.

which the whole is consumed in the country. This amount allows one pound for each individual, which is somewhat more than the quantity annually consumed in England: * which in 1842 was twenty-two millions of pounds, amongst twenty-eight millions of population, or three-quarters of a pound each. This difference arises no doubt from the difference of habits, as the use of tobacco is only partial in England, while in Ladák it is universal. The average price of tobacco at Lé is one rupee per seer, and the value of the whole import is Rs. 64,000, or £6,400. Small quantities of tobacco are also imported from Bisahar and Kashmir, but I could not ascertain the amount.

Borax is imported from Chang-Thang, to the amount of 2,500 maunds, or 80,000 lb., annually. Its price in Chang-Thang is one rupee for four maunds, or sixty-four seers. In Ladák it averages about thirty-two seers per rupee, and in the lower hill bazaars it is sold at sixteen seers per rupee, in its original impure state. The total value of the import is Rs. 1,500, or £150.

Sulphur is also imported from Chang-Thang; but the quantity is small, not exceeding 400 maunds, or 12,800 lb. Its price is usually one anna per seer, and the whole value of the import only Rs. 400, or £40.

Opium is the chief article of trade between India and China, through Ladák, as it is between India and China generally. The annual supply was stated at 500 maunds, or 16,000 lb., which, at the average rate of fifteen rupees per seer, amounts to Rs. 1,20,000, or £12,000 worth. The stated quantity is most probably less than the truth, as the total amount of opium that was destroyed at Yarkand in 1840, after the imperial edict of 1839, is

* M'Culloch's Commercial Dictionary.

said to have been worth one lac of *kurus*, equal to Rs. 166,00,000, or £1,660,000! This vastly exaggerated amount, which was repeated by several people, was most probably the round sum total of all the confiscated opium throughout the Chinese empire,* although my simple informants fully believed that this enormous quantity had been destroyed at Yarkand alone. The imperial edict is now as little respected on the western frontiers as it is on the eastern sea-coasts; from which politicians may learn how vain and useless is the attempt to thwart the wishes of a whole people. The drug produced in our hill states is of a superior quality, and as it is much prized by the Chinese, the land trade in opium is yearly on the increase.

Shawls of inferior descriptions are taken to Yarkand in considerable numbers. The finest shawls, such as we see in India and in England, are only manufactured to order; but the commoner shawls of coarser material and large patterns are preferred in the Yarkand market, on account of their cheapness. Their prices range from Rs. 50 to Rs. 300 per pair: the average being about Rs. 100. The number of shawls annually exported amounts probably to 500 pairs: but this number is only an average of the widely different statements of the merchants—some of whom said 200 pairs, and others

* The value of the Opium destroyed may be thus stated—

Indian Opium, 20,000 chests, at Rs. 625 each =	£1,250,000
Turkish Opium, 1,000 chests, at Rs. 800 each =	80,000
	£1,330,000

This sum is equal to more than 80,000 *kurus*, and might, with the additional value of the Ladáki opium, be commonly stated in round numbers at one lac (100,000) of *kurus*.

1,000. The value of 500 pairs of shawls is about Rs. 50,000, or £5,000.

Brocades are another article regarding which I found great difficulty in obtaining any definite information. The commoner kinds, ranging from Rs. 50 to Rs. 300 each, are preferred for the Yarkand market. Perhaps about 400 may be exported annually, which at an average price of Rs. 100 each, are worth Rs. 20,000, or £2,000.

Láki, or skins of red leather.—These are goat-skins tanned and coloured at Nurpur. There is a great demand for them all over the hills, but more particularly in Ladák and Yarkand, where bright-coloured leathers are generally employed in the manufacture of boots, and of bridles and trappings of horses. About 200 maunds, or sheep-loads (6,400 lb. weight) of these skins are said to be annually imported into Ladák; which at the mean rate of one pound per skin, and of one rupee each, are worth Rs. 6,400, or £640. Half of this quantity (100 maunds), or 3,200 skins, worth Rs. 3,200, or £320, are exported to Yarkand.

Spices to the value of about Rs. 1,000, or £100, are said to be annually imported into Ladák, of which the greater part, or Rs. 800 worth, are carried to Yarkand.

Saffron is supplied entirely by Kashmir. The quantity varies; but the usual supply is said to be twenty maunds, or 640 lb.; which, at the rate of forty rupees per seer, is worth Rs. 12,800, or £1,280. The whole is exported to Yarkand.

Cloths of all the coarser sorts, and a considerable number of flowered cottons and bright-coloured chintzes, form an important article of Ladáki trade. The annual amount is about 100 maunds, or 3,200 lb., in value Rs. 10,000, or £1,000. A small quantity is used in

Ladák for the bordering of skull-caps, but the remainder is exported to Yarkand.

Tea is more or less drunk by everybody in Ladák, and a considerable quantity is therefore imported both for home consumption and for the supply of Kashmir and the Punjáb. The gross annual import is said to be 1,000 maunds, or 32,000 lb.; which, at the rate of three rupees per seer, is worth Rs. 9,600. About 200 maunds (6,400 lb.) is exported, leaving only 800 maunds, or 25,600 lb., for the use of the people of Ladák. This will not give more than three ounces to each person; but there is good reason for believing that a considerable quantity of Chinese tea is smuggled into Ladák; and we know that the black tea of Bisahar is now largely imported to be mixed with the Chinese tea. The average supply for each individual cannot therefore be less than half a pound. In England it reaches a pound and a quarter for each person.*

DUTIES.—IMPORTS AND EXPORTS.

YARKAND.

On Imports.	Rs.	a.	p.	On Exports.	Rs.	a.	p.
On Charas, per maund	2	4	0	On Cloths, Láki, &c.			
„ Wool	2	4	0	per maund ...	0	4	0
„ Tea	0	8	0	„ Opium	0	4	0
„ Cloths	0	8	0	No other duties are now taken on exports to Yarkand.			

KASHMIR.

	Rs.	a.	p.		Rs.	a.	p.
On Cloths, per maund	1	0	0	On Wool, per maund	0	8	0
„ Saffron „ ...	3	0	0	„ Tea, per dama ...	1	0	0
„ Brocades, per piece	0	8	0	„ Langa and Siling,			
„ Shawls, per pair	0	8	0	per piece ...	0	2	0
„ Tobacco	0	4	0				
„ Ghi	0	4	0				

* M'Culloch's Commercial Dictionary.

On Imports.	Rs.	a.	p.	On Exports.	Rs.	a.	p.
On Sugar-candy ...	1	4	0				
„ Spices	1	4	0				
„ Opium	2	8	0				
„ Otter-skins ...	2	8	0				

BISAHAR.

On Imports	Rs.	a.	p.	On Exports	Rs.	a.	p.
On Opium, per maund	1	4	0	On Charas, per maund	0	10	0
„ Spices	0	10	0	„ Gold and Silver, per yámbu ...	0	8	0
„ Cloths	0	10	0				
„ Iron	1	0	0				

NURPUR.

On Imports	Rs.	a.	p.	On Exports	Rs.	a.	p.
				On every pony-load ...	3	0	0

ZANSKAR.

On Imports	Rs.	a.	p.	On Exports	Rs.	a.	p.
On Láki, per maund	2	2	6				
„ Ghi	0	4	0				
„ Honey	0	2	0				
„ Opium	2	8	0				
„ Otter-skins ...	2	8	0				

The following tables show the annual amount and value of all the imports and exports of the trade of Ladák, with the total amount of duty levied on each article.

IMPORTS FROM THE CHINESE TERRITORIES.

Articles.	Quantity.		Value.			Duty.		
	Maunds.	lb.	Rate per Seer.	Rupees.	£.	Rate per Maund.	Rupees.	£.
Shawl-wool	4,000	128,000	2 0 0	1,28,000	12,800	0 8 0	2,000	200
Wool	1,000	32,000	0 2 0	2,000	200	0 8 0	500	50
Tea	1,000	32,000	3 0 0	48,000	4,800	0 2 0	2,000	200
Charas	500	16,000	3 0 0	24,000	2,400	2 4 0	1,125	112½
Tobacco ..	4,000	128,000	1 0 0	64,000	6,400	0 4 0	1,000	100
Borax	2,500	80,000	0 0 6	1,250	125	0 4 0	625	62½
Sulphur ..	400	12,800	0 1 0	400	40	0 4 0	100	10
Total ..	13,400	428,000		2,67,650	26,765		7,350	735

IMPORTS FROM THE INDIAN TERRITORIES.

Articles.	Quantity.		Value.			Duty.		
	Maunds.	lb.	Rate per Ser.	Rupees.	£.	Rate per Maund.	Rupees.	£.
Opium.......	500	16,000	15 0 0	1,20,000	12,000	2 8 0	1,250	125
Shawls, pairs	500	—	100 0 0	50,000	5,000	0 8 0	250	25
Brocades, pcs.	400	—	50 0 0	20,000	2,000	0 8 0	200	20
Láki........	200	6,400	32 0 0	6,400	640	2 2 6	431	43
Spices	—	—	—	1,000	100	0 15 0	100	10
Saffron	20	640	40 0 0	12,800	1,280	3 0 0	60	6
Cloths	100	3,200	—	10,000	1,000	1 0 0	100	10
Total ..	820	26,240		2,20,200	22,020		2,391	239

EXPORTS TO THE INDIAN TERRITORIES.

Articles.	Quantity.		Value.			Duty.		
	Maunds.	lb.	Rate per Ser.	Rupees.	£.	Rate per Maund.	Rupees.	£.
Shawl-wool*	3,200	102,400	2 0 0	1,02,400	10,240	0 8 0	1,600	160
Ditto †	3,200	102,400	2 0 0	1,02,400	10,240	0 12 0	2,400	240
Total ..	6,400	204,800		2,04,800	20,480		4,000	400
Wool ‡	5,000	160,000	0 2 0	10,000	1,000	0 2 0	625	62½
Ditto §	1,000	32,000	0 2 0	2,000	200	0 2 0	125	12½
Total ..	6,000	192,000		12,000	1,200		700	70
Tea	200	32,000	3 0 0	9,600	960	0 4 0	800	80
Charas	200	32,000	3 0 0	9,600	960	0 10 0	125	12½
Borax	3,000	96,000	0 0 6	1,500	150	0 4 0	750	75
Sulphur....	500	16,000	0 1 0	500	50	0 4 0	125	12½
Total ..	16,300	521,600		2,38,000	23,800		6,550	655

* Exported to Kashmir. † Exported to other places.

‡ Home produce. § Imported from Chang Thang.

EXPORTS TO THE CHINESE TERRITORIES.

Articles.	Quantity.		Value.			Duty.		
	Maunds.	lb.	Rate per Ser.	Rupees.	£.	Rate per Maund.	Rupees.	£.
Opium	500	16,000	15 0 0	1,20,000	12,000	0 4 0	125	12½
Shawls, pairs	500	—	100 0 0	50,000	5,000			
Brocades, pcs.	400	—	50 0 0	20,000	2,000			
Láki........	100	3,200	32 0 0	3,200	320	0 4 0	25	2½
Spices	—	—	—	800	80			
Saffron	20	640	40 0 0	12,800	1,280			
Cloths	100	3,200	—	10,000	1,000			
Total ..	720	23,040		2,16,000	21,600		150	15

TOTALS OF IMPORTS AND EXPORTS.

	Value.		Duty.	
	Rupees.	£.	Rupees.	£.
Imports.				
From the Chinese Territories ...	2,67,650	26,765	7,350	735
„ Indian „ ...	2,20,200	22,020	2,391	239
Total Imports ...	4,87,850	48,785	9,741	974
Exports.				
To the Indian Territories ...	2,38,000	23,800	6,550	655
„ Chinese „ ...	2,16,000	21,600	150	15
Total Exports ...	4,54,000	45,400	6,700	670

The total amount of duties thus collected is Rs. 16,441. This, with the addition of other small duties on Chinese silks, salt, iron, and copper vessels, will amount to about Rs. 18,000, which was the acknowledged amount of the duties collected in Ladák both before and after Gulab Sing's conquest. I have therefore some reason to believe in the general accuracy of the statements which I received from the merchants, although perhaps not one of them may be strictly correct. Statistical questions are particularly puzzling to ignorant men, who are unaccustomed to deal with large numbers, and when they get beyond hundreds begin to talk of lacs. I found too, that the statements of the Kashmiris were generally false, and I believe wilfully so; at least the returns which they gave me of the numbers of people and *khâls* of land in the different villages of Drás, were undoubtedly manufactured for the occasion. Thus every house had exactly one man, one woman, and one boy, and every village possessed exactly three *khâls* of land. But the mis-statements of the Botis arose, I believe, generally from ignorance, as I never could find any obviously manufactured statistics, like those of the Kashmiris. I have already noticed the close agreement between the sum of my detailed accounts of the import and export duties, and the gross amount of Rs. 18,000, which was universally said to be the total amount of all the duties collected in Ladák. I will now add another fact that will most probably tend to increase the reliance which the first would induce us to place in the general accuracy of these details. A considerable quantity of silver in ingots, or bars, is annually brought into Ladák by the Yarkandis, thus proving that the value of the merchandise which they import is less than that which they export. Now these details exhibit precisely the same fact, as I will now show.

IMPORTS FROM YARKAND.

Shawl-wool	Rs. 28,000
Tea	48,000
Charas	24,000
Tobacco	64,000
	164,000
Add ponies, sugar-candy, drugs, skins, turquoises	16,000
	180,000
Exports to Yarkand	216,000
Excess of Exports	Rs. 36,000

This sum is equal to upwards of 216 silver ingots, called *yámbu* and *kuru*, each of which is worth Rs. 166. The fact that Yarkandi bullion is constantly being brought into the Ladák market is further proved by the duty of half a rupee, which is levied on each ingot when it is exported to Bisahar.

All merchandise is called *Tshong*, and the merchants or dealers *Tshong-pa;* as, *Bal-Tshong*, a wool-merchant; *Chhang-Tshong*, a spirit-dealer. Merchants are also called *Don-thun*, or "Ware-gatherers;" but the usual term is *Tshong-pa*. The chief, or head merchant, is *Tshong-pon*. Any regular gathering of merchants, such as annual meeting at Garo, is called *Tshong-dus*, a fair; and the friendly glass, which is partaken together after the completion of a bargain, is named *Tshong-chhang*, "the mercantile glass."

COINS, WEIGHTS, AND MEASURES.

In Ladák one meets with the coinage, as well as with the merchandise, of all the surrounding countries. The golden *tilás* of Bokhara and Kokand (or Kokan), the sycee silver and pierced copper coins of China, the thin silver pieces of Nepál, the copper dumps of Bisahar, the almost pure rupees of the Moguls of Delhi, the Nának-sáhi and Govind-sáhi rupees of Ranjit Sing, and the broad rupees of British India, bearing the head of the Queen of England. The only native coin is the silver *Jud*, or *Jao*, which is worth one quarter of a rupee.

The *Tilá* is the common gold coin of the Mahomedan countries, and is worth six rupees in Lé.

The Chinese silver ingot, called *Kuru* by the Yarkandis, and *Yámbu* by the Tibetans, is a plain bar of pure metal, weighing Rs. 156½. In 1847 it was valued at Rs. 166. These lumps of bullion are often bent in the middle into the shape of a horse-shoe. They are then called *Tá-Mikma*, or horses' hoofs.

The Nepál coins are of silver, each being worth half a rupee, or two *jaos* of Ladák. The coins of several of the Nepál Rajas are still current in Ladák. They consist principally of the currency of the Gorkha chiefs; but a few specimens of the Newár sovereigns are still to be found. One which I obtained belongs to *Jaya Ranajita Malla Deva* of Bhatgaon, and is dated in the year 842 of the Newár era, equivalent to A.D. 1711.

The Mogul rupees have very nearly been superseded by the *Nának-sáhi* and Company's rupee. In Moorcroft's time they would appear to have been plentiful, and more particularly the coinage of Muhammad Shah.* Even in 1839 I found the Mogul coinage prevalent in Kullu, Láhul, and Chamba; where I obtained two rare specimens of the pageant kings *Rafi-ud-Darját* and *Rafi-ud-Daulat*.

The *Jao* or *Jud* of Ladák is coined at Kashmir. It

* See his Travels, I. p. 353, where he mentions the price of Bisahar tea at fifteen Muhammad Sháhi rupees per Pakka maund.

is a thin irregular-shaped piece of silver, about the size of a shilling, with a Persian inscription on each side. On the centre of the obverse is the name of *Mahmud Shah*, surrounded by a circle of large dots. The inscription on the reverse is difficult to read, but the upper line is certainly *Bután*, which is the Kashmiri name of Ladák. The second, or middle line, is perhaps *Zarb;* and the two together form *Zarb-i-Butan*, "struck in Batan." Below is the word *sanh*, or *sanat*, and a figured date, which looks like 878, but of what era it is impossible to say.* As the coins bear the title of Mahmud Shah, they cannot date earlier than A.D. 1687, when the Gyalpo of Ladák was nominally converted to Muhammedanism, after the expulsion of the *Sokpos* by the troops of Ibrahim Khan, the governor of Kashmir under Aurangzeb. The coins which I possess all bear the same date; and, as they are but little worn on the surface, they cannot have been minted for any great length of time. The date, which I should have expected to find on these coins, is the Hijra year 1099, equivalent to A.D. 1687, which was the year of the Gyalpo's conversion.

The gold coins in use are called *Ser-jao*, or "golden jao," or simply *Ser-ki-dong*, or "golden coins." All coins are called *Dong*, or *Dong-tse*. The silver coins are named *Nul-ki-dong*, or simply *Nuk-dong*, and the copper coins *Zangi-dong*, or *Zang-dong*.† Ready money, or cash, is called *Marba*, or *Markyang*.

The weights of Ladák are the *Batti* and the *Man*, or *Maund*. The Batti is equal to two Indian seers or

* See Plate XIV. for a sketch of one of these coins.

† *gSer-kyi-Dong*, golden coin; *dNul-kyi-dong*, silver coin; and *Zangs-kyi-dong*, copper coin.

thirty-two chitaks. The name is no doubt derived from the Hindi word *Battis*, "thirty-two."* Indeed the measure itself, as well as the name, is Indian, and the Ladákis most probably derived it from the neighbouring hill states. The man or maund is equal to eight battis, or sixteen seers, and is therefore the same as the small maund of India.

The only other Ladáki measure with which I am acquainted is the *Khál.* This term has already been explained with reference to the measurement of land, in my account of the vegetable productions. The *Khál*, which is the universal measure for all kinds of heavy produce, but more especially for grain, is of two kinds: the *Dek-khál*, or the "weight khál," and the *Shor-khál*, or "measure khál."† The common *Khál*, whether by weight or measure, is the well-known quantity of a sheep's load, *Luk-khál*, which is equal to eight battis, or one maund of sixteen Indian seers, or thirty-two pounds English.‡ This is usually named simply *khál*, but when the larger measures are mentioned, the prefix is always used, as *Tá-khál*, the "horse khál," which is equal to four maunds, or 128 lb.; and the Yak-khál, which is the same.

* In Hindi बत्तीस.

† *hDegs-khal* and *gShor-khal* or *Pre-bu*.

‡ Trebeck's valuation is the same. See Moorcroft's Travels, II. p. 70.

X.—GOVERNMENT.

I.—NATURE OF GOVERNMENT.—VARIOUS OFFICERS.

THE government of Ladák was formerly a mild despotism under a ruler who bore the title of Gyalpo.* The conduct of affairs was generally intrusted to the prime minister, or *Kahlon;* and the king was well satisfied both with his minister and with his subjects, if the former gave him sufficient means† for the enjoyment of his royal pleasure, and if the latter never disturbed his quiet ease with their complaints. The king literally did nothing, except when roused to exertion by some unusual occurrence. His subjects could behold his royal presence only by the presentation of an offering in money, according to their circumstances. But this was a costly pleasure; and the mental abstraction of the Buddhist prince was rarely disturbed by the curiosity, or loyal zeal, of his people. Occasionally an ambitious prince would arise, who (like Singhé Namgyal) retained

* The ruler was usually called *rGyal-po,* or the emperor; aud the queen was called *rGyal-mo,* or the empress. In writing more formality was used, and the ruler was either entitled *rGyal-po-chen-po,* "the great emperor," or he was designated by his own name *Singgé-rNam-rGyal,* "King Singge."

† The prime minister was always the Gyalpo's treasurer, or keeper of the privy purse.

the whole power in his own hands. The apparent power of the prime minister was absolute, but his real power was much curbed by the wide-spread authority of the monastic establishments, and by the partial independence of the petty *Gyalpos* and district *Kahlons.*

In Great Tibet the *Kahlons* of the four chief provinces of *Ngári, U, Tsáng,* and *Khám,* were elected by the civil power in subordination to the Grand Lama, while the inferior *Kahlons,* and all other petty officers of state, were elected by the four chief *Kahlons.* But in Ladák the prime minister's office was almost hereditary; that is, it was restricted to a member of one of the families of the principal *Kahlons,* or governors of districts. The choice was determined, as in other countries, either by royal favour and successful intrigue, or by greater popularity and superior abilities. Possession, however, gave so firm a grasp of power, that the office was usually retained in one family for several generations. The Kahlon of Moorcroft's time was the Kahlon or petty Gyalpo of the Chimra valley; and the power remained in the hands of his family until the final settlement of Zoráwar Sing, at Lé.

Many of the principal nobility of Ladák were petty chiefs of valleys, which had once been independent. Thus there was a *Gyalpo* in Nubra; another in Gya; a third in Spiti; a fourth in Zanskar; a fifth in Paskyum; a sixth in Soth; a seventh in Suru; and an eighth in Hembabs, or Drás. The chiefs of Paskyum and of Soth distinguished themselves by their protracted resistance on the first invasion of Ladák by Zoráwar Sing.

The prime minister was simply styled *Kahlon,* or "the minister," or *Bangki-Kahlon,* "the chief minister,"* while his deputy was usually known by the addition of his own name, as *Kahlon-Rigsen*, "minister *Rigsen*," or by prefixing the term *Nono*, as *Nono Kahlon*, "the younger, or deputy minister."† The other Kahlons were distinguished by the names of the districts over which they ruled, as *Kahlon-Bazgo*, "the governor of Bazgo."

The next great officers were the *Lonpos*,‡ or governors of towns, and the *Kharpons*,§ or commanders of forts. The former were distinguished by the names of their respective towns; as *Lé-pon*, "the governor of *Lé*;" *Gar-pon*, "governor of *Garo*." In Lé, also, there were the *Mak-pon*,‖ or "commander-in-chief," and the *Chagsot*,¶ or "lord high treasurer;" the *Shogam-Chagsot*,** or "head collector of taxes;" as well as the *Shakspon*,†† or "chief justice;" and the *Khrimpons*,‡‡ or "magistrates." Lastly there was the *Káká-Tádsi*,§§ or "head master of the horse;" and the *Chagsi-Goba*, or Kotwál, an office equivalent to that of mayor.

* This is the "Banka khalun" of Moorcroft (I. pp. 238—249). The true title was *dBang-kyi-bKah-bLon* or *Bangki-kahlon*, that is, "the powerful minister."

† *No-no* is the usual term of respect which is used in addressing any young man of the higher ranks, and when prefixed to *Kahlon* it means the younger or deputy minister. Moorcroft (I. pp. 334, 335) gives the term, without the title, as the usual designation of the deputy minister, just as we should say "the deputy" instead of the deputy chairman. *Nono* is also applied to all under-officers, as *Nono-Chagsot*, the "under-treasurer;" *Nono-Shakspon*, the "deputy justiciary."

‡ *bLon-po*, "the manager, arranger, or governor." Moorcroft (I. p. 255) calls him *Lompa*.

§ *mKhar-dPon*, the "fort-chief." ‖ *dMag-dPon*, the "war-chief."

¶ *Phyag-mDsod*, pronounced *Chag-sot*.

** *Shogam*, "a duty, a tax." †† *gShags-dPon*, "justice-chief."

‡‡ *Khrims-dPon*, "law-chief."

§§ *Gá-gá-rTá-rDsi*, "head master of the horse."

The inferior officers were the *Mipons*,* or *Gobas*† (that is, literally, the "head men" of the villages), and the *Shogampa*, or provincial collectors of taxes and customs.

The *Gobas* (who were also called *Grongpons*,‡ or "village chiefs") were directly responsible to the *Kahlons*, or *Gyalpos*, of their respective districts, in all criminal matters, and in most accounts of revenue; although the *Mipons*, or head men, of some of the principal towns, rendered their accounts direct to the *Chagsot*, or lord high treasurer of Lé. But these exceptions were, I believe, only made in the cases of such villages as were set apart for the particular maintenance of the queen, or of some members of the royal family. The *Chagsot*, or lord high treasurer, rendered his accounts to the *Kahlon*, or prime minister, who kept the privy purse of the king and his family.

The titles of the different functionaries varied in different districts; but the most common were those which I have just given. The petty *Gyalpos* and provincial *Kahlons* were frequently called *Depons*,§ or "district chiefs," a name which recalls the Sanscrit *Dés-pati*, and the Greek Δεσποτης. Among the Mahomedans of Ladák (both the pure Kashmiris and the hybrid Argons), the petty chiefs are invariably called *Chho*; as *Gya-pa-chho*,‖ "the *Gyalpo* of Gya."

* *Mi-dPon*, "man-chief or head man."

† *hGo-ba*, emphatically the head man, from *hGo*, "the head, the top of anything."

‡ *Grong-dPon*. In Great Tibet, and in some parts of Ladák, this word is pronounced *Tongpon*. The Lamas more especially adhere to the pronunciation of Lhasa.

§ *sDé-dPon*, "district-chief."

‖ *mChhog*, "the head, the chief."

II.—RELATIONS WITH SURROUNDING STATES.

The few questions of foreign polity that the government of Ladák had to deal with were simple and easy. They were chiefly confined to political relations with Balti and Rudok; to commercial ties with Yarkand and Kashmir; and to the religious connection with Lhasa. The last was a national bond of union between two people speaking the same language, and holding the same faith; and the presents which were annually sent to Lhasa, by the Gyalpo of Ladák, were an humble offering to the Dalai Láma, as the head of the Buddhist religion, and not an extorted tribute to the emperor of China as lord paramount.

The difficulties of the passage of the Karakoram mountains prevented the Chinese governors of Yarkand and Kotan from attempting the conquest of Ladák; and the poverty of the country offered no temptation to the Mahomedan rulers of Kashmir. The Ladáki relations with these states were therefore friendly. With Rudok on the east there has been a long peace. The boundary is well defined by piles of stones, which were set up after the last expulsion of the *Sokpo*, or Mongol hordes, in A.D. 1687, when the Ladákis received considerable assistance from Kashmir. With Balti on the west, however, there existed a continual state of border-plundering, accompanied with fire and sword, which occasioned frequent references, and which created and kept up unfriendly feelings between the two states. The difference of religion greatly added to the natural antipathy of neighbourhood; and two centuries ago these two causes combined to lure Ali Sher and the Mahomedans of Balti to the invasion and partial conquest of Ladák.

III.—ADMINISTRATION OF JUSTICE.

The administration of justice in Ladák was truly patriarchal. When any one was injured or aggrieved, he proceeded straight to the *Gyalpo* or *Kahlon* of his district, or to the *Goba* of his village, and represented his case. An assembly of five, or of seven elders* of the community was then called to hear and to decide upon the case. In the capital the proceedings were conducted with the observance of more form. The complainant made his case known to the *Lonpo*, or mayor, who reported it to the *Kahlon*, or prime minister. The *Shakspon*, or chief justice, was then directed to assemble a regular court, composed either of five or of seven members, according to the importance of the case. The members were selected, as in the provinces, from amongst the *Gatpas*, or "elders;" but to them were joined two or more *Khrimpons*, or "sitting magistrates," whose duty it was to expound the *Yul-khrim*,† that is, the "law of the land," or civil law. The *Shaks-khang*,‡ or "court of justice," was opened and closed by the sounding of the *Khrim-dung*,§ or "trumpet of justice," and the sentence of the court (excepting in capital cases) was carried into execution without delay.

* *rGad-pa*, pronounced *Gatpa*, an "old man," an "elder." The number of members points to a common origin with the universal and still prevailing *Panchayet*, or "assembly of five," throughout India. Five must have been the ancient number, as even a single arbitrator or umpire is now called "*Panch*."

† *Yul-khrims*, "land-law." In Ladák this word is pronounced *Yul-khrim*, but in Great Tibet it is corrupted to *Yul-thim*.

‡ *Shags-khang*, "justice-hall."

§ *Khrims-dung*, "justice-trumpet;" there was also a *Khrims-rNga*, "justice-drum."

The punishments were few in kind, being only stripes, fines, and imprisonment, and in extreme cases, banishment or death; but they were numerous in degree, apportioned to the amount of guilt. The punishment of death was seldom awarded, and still more rarely executed. In cases of sacrilege, such as spoliation of temples, or in horrible cases of murder, the criminals were either crucified, or thrown into the Indus, bound hand and foot and weighted with stones. But the more usual punishment for murder was banishment, or rather ignominious expulsion from society, preceded by stripes and branding, and accompanied by every indignity that could be imagined by the ingenious malice of men, or that could be perpetrated by the elaborate mischief of boys. The brand was made of iron, and was about one inch in length. It bore a dog's head, with the inscription, "dog-marked—expelled." Thus after being well flogged and branded, the unfortunate criminal was drummed out of society, followed by hooting crowds,* who pelted him with stones and dirt.

For the murder of a child, a woman was sentenced to the loss of one hand, and to expulsion with the same indignities as above.

In cases of killing in a scuffle, the custom of Great Tibet was to bind the homicide to the corpse, and at the end of twenty-four hours to cast the living and dead together into the river. I did not hear of this custom in Ladák; but as commutation of punishment is almost

* The expression used by my informant was *ho-ho*, that is, the man was *ho-ho-ed*, or hooted. The brand of a dog was also used in Kashmir as a mark of disgrace at least nine hundred years ago. In the *Raja Taringini* it is related that Reja Saugráme, in A.D. 948, punished the Brahman Chakramela by marking his forehead with the "paw of a dog" (*Swapádena*).

always procurable for money, it is probable that the sentence of the law may have been death, although in practice the culprit was permitted to compromise by stripes, imprisonment, and fine. Such a course was in strict keeping with the precepts of their religion, which is averse to the taking of any animal life.

The two modes of capital punishment were *drowning* and *crucifixion*. In the former the culprit was bound hand and foot, and thrown into the Indus with a stone fastened to his neck.* In the latter mode the criminal was conducted to the *Songsa*, or "place of execution," by the *Shetma*, or "executioner." The *Sal-shing*,† or "crucifix," was a St. Andrew's cross fixed to an upright stake. The culprit was stripped naked; his hands and feet were bound to the extremities of the cross, while his head was secured to the upright stake by his own hair. In this position he was either quickly tortured to death by boiling oil, or was slowly allowed to expire under all the agonies of thirst and physical suffering. It is worthy of notice that in both of these modes of capital punishment, the shedding of blood was studiously shunned; for the sentence of crucifixion was carried out by *binding*, instead of nailing, the criminal to the cross. I presume, therefore, that there must have been some religious repugnance to putting a culprit to death by any mode that involved the shedding of blood. Mutilation of one or of both hands was, however, occasionally employed.

* Fra Orazio, p. 291. The same punishment was carried into effect in the same manner in Great Tibet. The culprit was "getta al fiume con un gran sasso al collo."

† *gSal-shing*, "clear wood." For what reason such a name was given to the stake, it would perhaps be difficult to discover. Perhaps it was intended for the tree that *cleanses* from guilt.

For *Theft* and other crimes, the punishment (*chhad-pa*) was threefold: 1st. *Lús-chhad,* that is, "corporal punishment," or stripes; 2nd. *Nor-chhad,* "property punishment," or fine, which was nearly always taken in goods at a ruinous valuation; 3rd. *Tson-chhad,* "prison-punishment," or imprisonment.

The corporal punishment was the same for man and woman. The culprit was placed full-length on the ground, and received the awarded number of stripes on the bare posteriors. This punishment, however, could always be avoided by the payment of a commensurate fine. The punishment by fine was always enforced, except in cases of poverty and absolute inability; but the culprits were made to pay in person by a double amount of stripes for what they were unable to pay in money or in goods.

In cases of imprisonment the culprits were confined in the *Tson-khang*, or jail, secured with fetters (*skrog*), and superintended by the *Tson-dsi,* or jailer. Theoretically food was allowed during the term of imprisonment; but practically, both in the provinces and in the capital, the prisoners' friends were obliged to supply food to save them from starvation.

In cases of common theft, the stolen property, if recovered, was restored to its owner, and a fine, equal in value to the amount of the stolen goods, was levied on the thief for the benefit of the state. If the property was not recovered, a double fine was levied, one half being given to the robbed party, and the other half to the government. This was the punishment for a first offence. For a second offence the sentence was loss of the left hand; for a third offence, loss of the right hand;

and for a fourth offence, death by drowning. These at least were the allotted punishments, and, with the exception of the last, they were generally carried into effect in all cases of robbery of public property or of church goods. But in cases of private robbery the usual influences had their weight. Near relationship might sway the judges to a milder sentence; or a fair bribe, judiciously bestowed, might induce the chief Láma of the monastery of Hémis to interfere, by an appeal to the king's mercy, which it was unusual to refuse. A direct appeal could also be made to the king by the prisoner's relatives, on the presentation of an offering of four or five rupees, if the criminal was a poor man, or of fifty to a hundred rupees, if he was a rich man.

For *Adultery*, where the woman was the guilty party, the paramour, as in Europe, was fined according to his means, or received an equivalent corporal punishment, while the husband had the option of taking back the woman, if he chose to do so. Or if he did not wish to keep her, he could retain her dowry. When the husband was the guilty party, the wife could demand back her dowry.

Common disputes, involving blows and abuse, were settled at once by fines and stripes.

In doubtful cases, where the evidence was unsatisfactory, a decision was obtained either by casting lots, or by ordeal. In the latter case, the accused had either to draw a red-hot iron through his hand, or to take a stone out of a pot of boiling oil without injury. In Great Tibet both of these ordeals are practised; but the latter is rendered much more complicated and difficult by the immersion of two stones, one black and the other white, in the boiling oil.* The extraction of the *white* stone, with an uninjured hand, is held as a complete proof of innocence; while the extraction of the *black* stone, with uninjured hand, is equivalent to the Scotch verdict of "not proven," of which the accused receives the benefit.

The foregoing is a concise account of the practical laws of Ladák under its native rulers. Amongst a people who were averse to the taking of any animal life, the sentence of death was but seldom enforced; the last case of capital punishment, which was executed in 1845, being the only one during thirty years; and I suspect that even this sentence would not have been carried into effect but for the stern and unbending firmness of *Magna*, the dogra thanadar of Lé. The culprit was a blacksmith of Chachot, who had been repeatedly punished by imprisonment, fines, and stripes, for pilfering the gilt leaves of books from the monasteries and the gilded pinnacles of the *Chodtens*, or mausolea. His last exploit was the entire removal of the copper-gilt pinnacles from the *Chodtens* attached to the large monastery of Hémis. The thanadar was proof against all appeals for mercy, chiefly, I believe, with a view to conciliate the religious brotherhood of Hémis, and partly as a stroke of policy in a newly-conquered country, to exhibit a marked example of unflinching firmness in the execution of the law. As a Hindu, Magna Thanadar was quite indifferent in the matter of life or death. The unfortunate thief was therefore bound hand and foot,

* Fra Orazio, del Regno del Thibet, p. 290. The Capuchin father declares that the Tibetans can save their hands from injury by the use of some secret art (si servono d'un certo secreto, o per arte magica).

and, with a stone fastened to his neck, was cast headlong into the Indus from the Chachot bridge.

The laws of Ladák still continue in force under the rule of Mahárája Guláb Sing, with the single exception of death for the slaughter of kine. This punishment was early carried into effect in some eight or ten cases in the different districts of Ladák. In 1841 and 1842 at Nubra, Chachot, Lé, and Nyimo, single individuals were put to death, and their bodies exposed on gibbets, by Jhandu, the thanadar of Lé, for killing and eating kine. All these were Musulmáns from Balti. In Drás, where all the population are Mahomedans, several were put to death by Gusáun Thanadar for the same cause. The skeleton of the man gibbeted at Lé, in 1841, was still nearly perfect in October 1847, when I saw it.

IV.—REVENUE.

The chief sources of revenue in Ladák were a tax on property and a duty on merchandise. The tax, called *Khral*, *Thang*, or *Shá*,* was levied on the dwellings and not on the lands; for as the lands did not produce sufficient food for the sustenance of the people, the establishment of a land-tax would have been absurd. The mass of the people obtained their living by the *transport* of wool and other goods *through* their own country, to and from Yarkand and Kashmir. The duties, called *Shogam*, were imposed on merchandise, both imports and exports, and the whole revenue thus obtained was called *Thob-thang*.

The tax on houses was collected partly in kind, *Brú-*

* *Khral*, pronounced *Thal* in some districts, *Thang*, and *dPya*, the last being pronounced *Sha* or *Cha*.

khral, and partly in money, *Nul-khral*.* The collectors, called *Shangudpapo*,† transmitted their various quotas, at stated periods, to the *Chag-dsot*, or lord high treasurer, at Lé, where they were all deposited in the *Ter-dsot*,‡ or treasury. The poorer classes, who were unable to pay either in money or in kind, were obliged to pay by bodily service as labourers. They were appropriately named *Kanggro*, or "foot-goers," that is, porters or labourers on foot, in contradistinction to the others, who were called *Lagdon*, or "hand-doers," that is, payers by hand.

The duties were collected at the custom-houses (*Sho-gamgyina*) by the *Shogampas*, or customs-officers; and the tolls on the high-roads were taken by the *Láchanpas*, or toll-gatherers. These duties were taken partly in kind and partly in money, and generally in equal portions. The gross annual collections usually averaged Rs. 18,000.

The tax on houses was regulated according to their size. For a large or "full-sized" house (*Khang-chhen*) there was a charge of seven rupees; for a middle-sized or "half-house," three and a half rupees; and for a small or "quarter-house," one and three-quarter rupee.§ Under the *Gyalpo's* rule there were reckoned 18,000 paying houses, of which

400	of large size paid Rs.	7 each	=	Rs. 2,800
1,600	middle	,,	$3\frac{1}{2}$,,	=	5,600
16,000	small	,,	$1\frac{3}{4}$,,	=	28,000
18,000	houses paying		... ...		Rs. 36,400

* *hBru-khral*, "corn-tax," and *dNgul-khral*, "money-tax."

† *dPya-sNgud-pa-po*, pronounced as in the text, *Shangudpapo*.

‡ *gTer-mDsod*, called also *gTer-mTsong* and *rTsis-khang*.

§ *Khang-chhen*, "house-large;" the middle size were called *Khang-phyed*, "half-house," and the smallest size were named *Phyedi-phyed*, "half of half," or quarter.

Each house, therefore, paid a mean rate of two rupees per annum; but, partly from various remissions of taxes, and partly from the inability of the poorer classes to pay, excepting by bodily service, the total amount of house-tax rarely exceeded Rs. 30,000.

But besides the 18,000 paying houses, there were about 4,000 houses alienated for the support of the numerous monasteries, and about 1,000 for the maintenance of the queen and the various members of the royal family. The Gyalpo also had his own villages, which contained about 1,000 houses more. The whole number of dwellings in Ladák was therefore about 24,000.

Under the Dogra rule, although the number of inhabited dwellings has diminished, yet the number of paying houses is still about the same, as all the crown villages have been appropriated by the government. The assessment is, however, different, as a much greater number of houses have been taxed at the higher rates. I could not obtain any precise information as to the number of houses included under each rate; but as the gross amount of collections was generally estimated at nearly Rs. 50,000, the following scale must be a close approximation to the truth. The mean rate is two and a half rupees per house.

1,000	houses of large size	at Rs. 7 each	=	Rs. 7,000
5,000	„ middle	„ 3½ „	=	17,500
12,000	„ small	„ 1¾ „	=	21,000
18,000	houses paying	... ...		Rs. 45,500

There were besides two other sources of income which contributed to swell the revenue of the state; namely, a tax on the brokers who transacted all commercial affairs between the different merchants both home and foreign;

and the annual amount of presents received from the various *Kahlons*, *Lonpas*, *Kharpons*, and other officers of government. The former generally amounted to nearly thirty-five *kúrús* of silver, which, at Rs. 166 per *kúrú*, are equal to Rs. 5,700.* The value of the presents was usually about Rs. 5,000.

The gross revenue of Ladák, collected from all sources under its native rulers, was as follows:

House-tax	Rs. 30,000
Customs	18,000
Tax on brokers	5,700
Presents or fees	5,000
	Rs. 58,700

to which must be added,—first, the amount alienated for the support of monasteries, or about Rs. 8,000, valuing each of the 4,000 houses at the average rate of two rupees each: secondly, the amount derived from the crown villages of about 2,000 houses, equal to Rs. 4,000 more, or in all to Rs. 12,000. The total revenue was, therefore, Rs. 71,700, or about £7,000 sterling.

Out of the gross collections made for government, one-half of the customs, and one-half of the tax on brokers, were the perquisites, or salary, of the *Kahlon*, or prime minister. The net amount received by the *Gyalpo* was therefore just so much less than the above Rs. 58,700, or only Rs. 46,850; this, with the produce of the crown lands, amounted to nearly Rs. 49,000. But his actual income was nearly double this amount, for he was the chief trader in his own dominions; and as all his traffic passed duty free through Ladák, he always realized between forty and fifty thousand rupees a year. His

* *Kuru* is the Yarkandi name for the "ingot" of silver, which the Tibetans call *Yam-bu*.

average income from all sources thus amounted to about one lac of rupees, or nearly £10,000 per annum. In addition to his regular income, both public and private, the Gyalpo enjoyed the royal prerogative of drawing his food from those districts, which, possessing no chiefs of their own, were immediately dependent on the supreme government. He was supplied with corn and butter, wood and grass, for four months in the year, by Nubra; for two months by Rukchu; and for four months by Tangtse. Certain villages also supplied the royal table with apricots, apples, and grapes.

The various charges defrayed by the state were few in number, and small in amount, as all the principal public officers had the privilege of trading duty free, while the inferior servants of government enjoyed various perquisites which were equivalent to salaries. The paid officers of the state were the *Lonpo*, or governor; the *Shakspon*, or lord chief justice; and the different *Khrimpons*, or magistrates of Lé; besides the *Káká Tádsi*, or master of the horse, and the *Chagdsot*, or lord high treasurer. I could not ascertain the amount of their individual salaries, but the gross amount of civil charges was estimated at Rs. 20,000, or £2,000 per annum, and which I believe to be near the truth. The military charges were nothing, as each family or house was obliged to furnish one soldier whenever called upon to do so, and to feed him during his term of service.

Under the present rule of Mahárája Guláb Sing, the revenue of Ladák may be estimated as follows:

Tax on houses	Rs. 45,500
Customs	18,000
Tax on brokers	5,700
Presents or fees	5,000
Monasteries	6,300
	Rs. 80,500

or about £8,000 sterling. The last item is the gross amount derived from a heavy tax which has been imposed on all the *gonpas*, or monasteries, throughout the country. The sums paid by the different religious establishments were thus stated to me—

Monastery of Hemis (with Hanlé)	Rs. 900
„ Chimra	900
„ Thigsé	500
„ Pitak	500
„ Gáwan	900
„ Láma Yúrrú	900
Twenty-five smaller monasteries at Rs. 60 each =	1,500
	Rs. 6,300

The charge incurred in the maharaja's government of Ladák, I found it impossible to ascertain with any degree of precision, as it was a delicate subject to make inquiries about. From various sources I could only learn that the country is divided into districts, over each of which is appointed a thanadar on a small salary, varying from Rs. 200 to Rs. 500 a month. There are five of these thanadars in Ladák, each independent of the others, and accountable only to the maharaja himself. The principal of them is Basti Rám, the thanadar of Lé, a shrewd and intelligent man, and a tried soldier. He is a native of Káshtwár, and was a petty officer under Zoráwar Sing on the first invasion of Ladák. He was present at the surrender of Skardo, the capital of Balti; and he was one of the few survivors of Zoráwar Sing's unfortunate expedition into Great Tibet in the winter of 1841, A.D. His quickness and experience, combined with a frank and easy manner, secured him the confidence of the maharaja; and after successfully ruling the district of Zanskar during a very turbulent period, he has now obtained one of the highest posts in the maharaja's service, in the governorship of Ladák Proper, of which the capital is Lé. His personal salary is only Rs. 500 a month, but he is permitted to trade on his own account to a limited extent; and his profits, together with the presents which he receives from merchants and others, amount to a very handsome income, which was estimated vaguely at Rs. 20,000 a year. But the maharaja himself is the chief trader in his own dominions, more particularly in the two staple articles, the export of saffron, and the import of wool. I have therefore strong doubts whether Basti Rám can realize more than ten or twelve thousand rupees yearly. But even this sum, when added to his personal salary, will yield him a respectable income of Rs. 18,000, or nearly £1,800 a year.

There are five thanadars, who are placed in the following districts, over which they exercise military command as well as civil authority. 1. Ladák; 2. Zanskar; 3. Kargyil; 4. Drás; 5. Nubra. The salaries of these officers, at the average rate of about Rs. 300 a month, amount to Rs. 18,000 per annum.

The number of troops garrisoned in Ladák was variously stated to me by different individuals at from 600 to 800 men; of whom about 200 are stationed at Lé, and in different parts of the district of Ladák Proper. The others are divided among the remaining districts. At Lé also there are thirty artillerymen with a battery of four guns.

The military expenses were estimated at between thirty and forty thousand rupees a year; and as the pay of the soldier is nominally five rupees a month, this sum (Rs. 36,000) would support a force of 600 men. But the men do not receive more than two or three rupees in cash, the remainder being made up to them by "billets" for food wherever they may be quartered. The cost of each soldier to the state was therefore generally estimated by the people at only four rupees a month. At this rate a body of 700 men could be supported for Rs. 33,600, which would be increased to Rs. 35,000 or Rs. 36,000 by the pay of the petty officers.

The whole expenses of the government, both civil and military, therefore, amounted to between Rs. 50,000 and Rs. 60,000; thus leaving a surplus of about Rs. 25,000 for transmission to the maharaja. This surplus was not however remitted in cash, but in goods, which consisted chiefly of wool from Chang-thang, and of cloths and tea from Yarkand.

V.—MILITARY RESOURCES.

In Ladák there was no regular army; but every family or house throughout the country was obliged to furnish one ready-armed soldier at the call of the government. The *Kahlons*, *Lonpos*, and *Gobas*, also furnished quotas of from ten to four men each. At the last general mustering in 1834, the number of armed peasants, collected to oppose Zoráwar Sing, amounted to 22,000. The same number is said to have been collected when the *Gyalpo* was at war with Ahmed Shah of Balti. Indeed it is scarcely possible that a greater number of "armed" men could have been collected, as each house throughout Ladák possessed only one weapon, and the number of houses was not more than 24,000. I have every reason to believe in the correctness of these numbers, as my information was derived from various sources; from Jemadar Basti Rám, and other officers of the maharaja, as well as from *Lamás*, *Gobas*, and Mahomedans of Ladák. The difference between the number of houses and that of the armed men actually collected together is only 2,000, a number so small that it may include all absentees from sickness and other causes, as well as all the guards required at Lé and in the provinces for the personal service of the Gyalpo, and for the security of the state treasure.

On a call to arms, the soldiers (*Makmi**) were told off for the cavalry and infantry branches by the very simple process of selecting all those who had horses (or rather ponies) for the cavalry (*Táhipung*†), and leaving the remainder for the footmen, or infantry (*Kangthangipung*). Their arms were swords, matchlocks, and bows and arrows. Many had shields (*Go*‡), and some few had helmets (*Mog*§). They were assembled by beat of drum (*Thab-nga*‖).

The army (*Pung*, or *Makpung*¶) was placed under the control of a *Makpon*,** or commander-in-chief, who was either a member of the royal family, or one of the principal *Kahlons*.

Other titles were conferred upon the different *Kahlons*

* *dMag-mi*, pronounced *Makmi*, a "war-man," or "soldier," from *dMag*, battle. Compare the Greek μαχη with the latter, and μαχιμος with the former.

† *rTa-hi-dPung*, from *rTa*, a "horse."

‡ *Go*, a "shield," or any defensive armour.

§ *rMog*, a "head-piece," a "helmet."

‖ *hThab-rNga*, a "war-drum."

¶ *dPung*, or *dMag-dPung;* the latter is also commonly contracted to *dMung*.

** *dMag-dPon*, "battle-chief," or *dMag-hGo*, "war-chief." *Makpon* is the family title of the Hasora chief. He must therefore be of Tibetan origin. It is curious that *Go-Mag-go*, which so much resembles Gog-Magog, should mean "civil and military chiefs."

and *Gobas*, according to the numerical strength of the quotas furnished by their respective districts and villages. Thus the Kahlon who brought a few hundreds was dignified with the title of *Stong-pon,** "chief of a thousand," or colonel; a wealthy Goba who could muster from 50 to 100 men, was styled *Gyapon,*† "chief of a hundred," or captain; while an inferior Goba who was attended by only four or five men, was called *Chu-pon,*‡ "chief of ten," or serjeant.

The camp (*Maggar*§), which was pitched without any regularity, consisted almost entirely of black tents made of yák's hair. The Kahlons and some others had white blanket tents, but these were so few in number as not to affect the general sombre appearance of the camp. When, however, the cooking commenced, and volumes of smoke began to issue from the open roofs of the tents, now ascending in fantastic curls, and now whirling rapidly round and spreading a milky canopy over the black tents, the Boti camp wore a very picturesque appearance. During the day little was heard but the busy hum of men preparing their food or cleaning their arms, but towards evening the whole air frequently rang with noisy brawls and angry squabbles, which gave but too convincing a proof of the powerful influence of their favourite *chang*.

All disputes in camp were settled at once by stripes or fine, according to the sentence of an assembly of officers, whose decisions were final. These assemblies

* *Stong-dPon,* commander of one thousand.

† *b,rGya-dPon,* commander of one hundred.

‡ *bChu-dPon,* commander of ten.

§ *dMag-sGar,* a "military camp," to distinguish it from the common encampment of the Nomads, *sGar*.

were exactly the same as our drum-head courts-martial; and their sentences were accordingly termed *Makkhrim*,* or martial law.

The soldiers were obliged to find their own food. Each man was therefore generally attended by another male member of his house or family, who carried the joint provisions on his back during the daily marches, while the soldier carried his arms. Occasionally they relieved one another. In case of a casualty also the state had a substitute at hand, while the family preserved the arms and clothes, and (if he had one) the horse of the defunct, all of which would otherwise have been lost.

Although these bodies of undisciplined militia were not deserving of the name of an army, yet they were generally strong enough to repel all attacks of their immediate neighbours of Balti, Rudok, and Chumurti, who were as poor and as unsoldierly as themselves; while the great poverty of the country, and the extreme rigour of the climate, were sufficient to deter the effeminate Kashmiris from even thinking of such a project without a shudder. In fact, there is no record of any invasion of Ladák by the Kashmiris; on the contrary, the Raja Taringini relates the entire conquest and occupation of Kashmir by the Boti *Rinchana*, or, as he is more commonly called in Kashmir to this day, *Ratanjo*,† about the middle of the fourteenth century. Rinchana was the son of *Bakhtán Bhot;* that is, he was probably of the *Yasan* family, which still bears the title of *Bakhto*. Being driven from his native country, he naturally fled

* *dMag-khrims*, "war-law."

† *Jo* or *Cho* is the Tibetan *mChhog*, the common title of a chief amongst the Boti Mahomedans.

to the Botis of the east, which will account for his entering Kashmir by Gagangir on the Drás road, as related in the Raja Taringini.

The forts of Eastern Ladák were nearly all castellated monasteries, the defence of which was intrusted to the unwarlike monks, assisted by a few of the armed peasantry, who performed the duty by turns, under the command of one who was dignified with the title of *Kharpon*, or governor.* In Western Ladák there were several castles belonging to petty chiefs, such as Paskyum and Soth, which were better calculated for defence. The monastic castles were mostly perched on high rocks quite destitute of water, and it was a part of the daily duty of the garrison to fetch water for the monks. Had any of these castles possessed a proper supply of water, their generally inaccessible positions would have rendered them safe against all common attacks. I have seen the monasteries of Hanlé, Hémis, Thigsé, Shé, Lé, Pitak, Phyang, Bazgo, Láma Yúrrú, Hesku, Kharbu, Thakshé, and Mulbil, as well as the ruined forts of Balukhar and Paskyum. The monasteries are all built on steep cliffs, more or less high, with stone walls coloured white and red, and surmounted with an endless number of small flags. They are generally difficult of access, and always picturesque. Perhaps the most remarkable is that of Thakshé, on the right bank of the Kánji river. It is perched on a lofty isolated cliff, bluff and overhanging on the north side, and with a precipitous slope of about 65° on the south side. The only ascent is by a very steep pathway.

* *mKhar-dPon*, "fort-chief." A fort is also called *rDsong*, and the governor *rDsong-dPon*. Every commandant of a castle, or military post, even if his garrison does not amount to more than four men, is dignified with the title of *Kharpon*.

The fort of Paskyum, on the left bank of the Waká-chu, commanded the passage of the river, which is there unfordable. It stood about 100 feet high, on an alluvial flat, overhanging the river; but it was easily taken by Zoráwar Sing, and afterwards destroyed. The fort of Sod was held out by the *Gyalpo* in person for ten days; but it was at last, after some loss, taken by assault, when it shared the same fate as Paskyum.

The best "means of defence" possessed by Ladák consisted in the general inaccessibility of the country during one half of the year, when the passes were closed by snow; and to the power of breaking down the bridges over the Indus, and other unfordable streams, during the summer. The latter was not, however, resorted to on Zoráwar Sing's invasion, excepting in the solitary case of the bridge at Paskyum; the destruction of which, by the Banka Kahlon, delayed the advance of the invaders for one day. The reason assigned for not breaking down the Khallach bridge, over the Indus, was, because its destruction would have stopped the traffic with Kashmir during one entire season. But the traffic was virtually stopped by the war; while the destruction of the bridge would have saved all the rich villages on the right bank of the Indus, as well as the capital itself, for a whole year. But the energetic Zoráwar was marching rapidly on, while the listless Botis were debating; and the bridge was passed, and the enemy had reached Bazgo, within twenty miles of the capital, before the helpless Gyalpo had decided upon what to do. Decision was then too late, as there was no alternative but flight or submission. The first, although a virtual relinquishment of the country, would have been manly and honourable; but the Gyalpo chose the more humiliating alternative of actual surrender. Such was the fate of a country which might have been saved by a hundred resolute soldiers at the bridge of Khallach. But the indolent votaries of an almost worn-out faith were no match for the more active and energetic worshippers of Mahadeo and Párbati.

Under the government of Maharaja Guláb Sing, the country is held by a few garrisons of tolerably well-appointed infantry, who are quartered in the different forts erected by Zoráwar Sing and his successors. The forts that I have seen are those of Lé, Kargyil, and Drás, besides the bridge-head at Khallach. They are all built on the same kind of plan, and in similar situations on the banks of streams, that they might insure an unfailing supply of water, without which the strongest fort would be untenable.

The new fort at Lé is built upon the open plain, and on the edge of the Lé rivulet, at somewhat more than a mile to the south-west of the city. I saw it to great advantage on my visit, as the thanadar Basti Rám had kindly deputed his son to attend me. Everything, therefore, was prepared. The interior was trim and orderly; the guns were clean and bright; and the men were all dressed in respectable uniforms, which appeared too new to have been much worn. The walls are built of huge sun-dried bricks, and are nearly thirty feet in height. In the interior the barracks, as well as the store-rooms, are built against the walls all round, and their flat roofs form the terre-plein of the ramparts. Each room is furnished with a door. The guns are four brass three-pounders, all in good order, and well set up on substantial carriages. They are manned by thirty well-dressed artillerymen. Altogether I was as much pleased with the orderly appearance, as with the judicious situation, of this fort.

The new fort of *Kargyil* is situated on the left bank of the Suru river, immediately above the junction of the *Waká-chu.* It is a square of about sixty yards, with round towers at the angles, and a square tower with a small outwork in the middle of the river-front. This work forms a difficult entrance, and at the same time insures a supply of water. The walls are loopholed throughout, and the garrison can sweep the bridge over the Suru river with deadly effect. The position was admirably chosen, as it completely commands the high-road to and from Kashmir.

The new fort of Drás is similar to those of Lé and Kargyil. It is situated on the left bank of the Drás river, and commands the passage of the valley.

The bridge-head of Khallach is on the right bank of the Indus. It consists of a square loopholed tower, built of large sun-dried bricks, with an inclosure surrounded by a high loopholed wall. The garrison of twelve men is furnished from Lé, and is relieved every three months. This work completely commands all approach to the bridge on each bank of the river.

In my opinion, the measures which the maharaja has taken for the maintenance of his power in Ladák are judicious and effective. Many people grumble; but the dissatisfaction is principally confined to the upper classes, who have lost all their power; and to the Kashmiri Mahomedans, a despicable race, who are ever wishing for change, and who, if they were under the British to-morrow, would long for the Chinese on the next day. To the lower classes the change of government has in some respects been a very decided benefit; for although they may now pay *directly* a larger amount than formerly to the state, yet indirectly they pay a less sum, as there is now only *one* duty throughout the country, in place of the numerous charges which were formerly exacted by all the district *Kahlons* and petty *Gyalpos*. They have also the advantage of excellent roads, which is a benefit duly appreciated by a people whose principal means of livelihood are derived from the transport of merchandise. For these good roads, as well as for the almost complete extinction of theft, the Ladákis are indebted to the active zeal of Zoráwar Sing and his successors. Such are some of the advantages which have resulted from the conquest of the country by an energetic people.

VI.—POSTAL ESTABLISHMENT.

The postal arrangements throughout Ladák are simple and effective; but the transmission is generally slow. The *Goba* of each village is bound to furnish a courier to carry the post from his own to the next village on the road. Along the high-roads the couriers are all horsemen, *Tázampa*,* and the post is carried at the rate of from twenty to thirty-five miles a day. The former is the usual rate; the latter is the express rate when any government business is urgent. Thus letters sent from Kashmir usually reach Lé, a distance of 220 miles, in ten days; but when the despatch is urgent, it generally reaches in six days.

All officers of government make use of the village couriers for the conveyance of orders or intelligence;

* *rTá-zam-pa*, "horse-bridge."

but merchants always send special couriers of their own. The poorer classes have no correspondence; and the limited intercommunications of the upper classes, amongst whom each family has generally one member in government employ, are all conveyed by the Tázampas.

XI.—PEOPLE.

I.—POPULATION.

In A.D. 1822 Moorcroft* estimated the population of Ladák at about 165,000 persons, of whom he thought that not less than two-thirds were females. But Csoma de Körös,† who resided for some time in Zanskar, shortly after Moorcroft's visit, says the people of Ladák consisted of 20,000 families. Now, by an accurate census of the two Botian districts of Lahul and of Spiti, it appears that the average number of persons in one family is 6·7. As the different climates of these two districts exhibit the extremes of the Ladáki climate, the mean of the two may be taken as fairly representing the true number of persons in each house or family throughout Ladák. At this rate the 20,000 families of Csoma de Körös would amount to no more than 134,000 persons; to whom must be added about 12,000 lamas and nuns, who dwell apart in the monasteries and convents; thus making the whole population of Ladák (between 1820 and 1830) not more than 146,000 persons. But this estimate is certainly too low.

The information which I obtained in 1847 was derived from various independent sources, all of which agreed

* Travels, I. p. 320.

† Journal As. Soc. Bengal, I. p. 121. Geographical notice of Tibet.

in stating that the total number of houses was formerly 24,000, of which only 18,000 paid the house-tax. At the rate of 6·7 persons per house, the lay population would have been 160,800, and the whole population 172,800. But as the result of Moorcroft's inquiries gave a rate of little more than six persons per house, a mean rate of about six persons and a half per house may be taken as the nearest approximation to the true rate. This rate will give a lay population of 156,000, and a total population of 168,000 persons. As this number agrees so nearly with Moorcroft's estimate, it may be assumed to be tolerably correct.

In stating the number of professed religionists at 12,000, I have been guided only by the vague statements of the people. Some asserted that the number of lamas and nuns formerly amounted to 20,000; but the more general reckoning was only ten or twelve thousand. The total amount of population (between 1820 and 1830) was therefore most probably about 165,000 persons, as estimated by Moorcroft.

The correctness of this estimate seems to be borne out by the following statement. In 1834, when the Gyalpo called upon all the people to join in repelling the invasion of Zoráwar Sing, he is said to have collected a body of 22,000 men. As the number of houses was 24,000, and as each house was bound to furnish one soldier, the number of fighting men should have been 24,000. But the difference is fully accounted for by the ascertained loss of 14,000 persons by small-pox just before the invasion; for as one-fourth of these must have been grown-up males, the number of soldiers collected ought not to have exceeded 21,500; and making allowances for illness and other causes, was probably not more than 20,000 men. The extra number would have been made up by the quotas of the different kahlons, lonpas, and gobas, who were obliged to furnish from ten to four men each.

Since Moorcroft's time, however, the population has very much decreased, partly owing to the ravages of disease, but chiefly to the destructive effects of war. In the summer of 1834 the small-pox broke out in Ladák with such fatal virulence that 14,000 persons,* or more than one-twelfth of the whole population, were carried off. Amongst a filthy people, who never wash, and who only change their garments when the cloth has rotted piecemeal off their persons, the mortal effect of such a contagious disease as small-pox cannot be wondered at.

But the ravages of disease were almost forgotten in the more deadly destructiveness of war and its attendant miseries. They who survived the small-pox had only to lament the sudden loss of near and dear relatives; but they who escaped death in the war had also to bewail the pillage of their property and the destruction of their houses. By the wholesale plunder of the metal images belonging to the monasteries, the invaders gave a rude shock to the pious minds of the whole people, while they secured the bitter enmity of the lamas by an extensive resumption of monastic lands.

Such was the effect of these severe and impolitic measures, that no less than three-fourths of the lamas,

* About 10,000 died before the conquest. Dr. Henderson, who was then in Ladák, gave both physic and advice, but nothing availed to check the disease. Zoráwar Sing *is said* to have vaccinated great numbers by force, of whom no less than 4,000 died. My informant was a Musalman who hated the present maharaja, and I doubt the truth of his statement about the compulsory vaccination.

or about 9,000 persons, are said to have left their native land, and to have found refuge in the numerous monasteries of Great Tibet.

During the wars from 1834 to the close of 1841, it is said that about 15,000 Ladákis perished, and that about 1,000 (who were chiefly Musalmans) emigrated to Balti and the neighbouring districts. Of the 4,000 Ladákis who accompanied Zoráwar Sing on his inroad into the Lhasan territory, it is well known that nearly the whole perished in the snow. A few made their way back to Ladák; and some four or five hundred, who were made prisoners, are said to be most strictly confined at Lhasa.

In 1847 I found, by a census of 1,890 houses, that the average number of persons per house was 4·147; but as a very considerable number of people were absent from their homes, the true rate per house could not have been less than five persons, or about the same as that of the district of Spiti, which I ascertained to be 5·3 persons per house. The number of inhabited houses is said to be 23,000, which at this rate, and allowing the present number of lamas and nuns to be only 3,000, will make the total amount of the population 124,900, or in round numbers, 125,000 persons. The decrease in the population, since Moorcroft's time, is, therefore, not less than 40,000 persons. The causes of this decrease are the following:—

	Persons.
Carried off by small-pox in 1834	14,000
Lamas emigrated	9,000
Perished during the wars	15,000
Emigrated (chiefly Musalmans)	1,000
Total decrease	40,000
Moorcroft's census	165,000
Present census	125,000

Including Spiti and Láhul, the present population is therefore not more than 4·333 persons per square mile.

The census of the two districts of Spiti and Láhul is as follows:—

—	Villages	Houses.	Males.			Females.			Total Persons	Persons per House.	Houses per Village.
			Men.	Boys.	Total.	Women	Girls.	Total.			
Spiti ..	38	262	460	226	686	503	218	721	1,407	5·3	6·9
Lahul ..	43	594	1,033	1,470	2,503	1,389	945	2,334	4,837	8·1	13·8
Total ..	81	856			3,189			3,055	6,244	6·7	10·8

Neither of these districts is so well peopled as Ladák, the number of persons per square mile being 2·58 in Láhul and only ·608 in the barren and rocky Spiti.

In 1847 I made a census of most of the villages along my route through Ladák, which embraced about one-twelfth part of the whole country.

The following table shows the relative numbers of males and females in the Buddhist country of Ladák, compared with the same in the various Musalman districts on the Indus.

—	Villages	Houses.	Males.			Females.			Total Persons	Persons per House.	Houses per Village.
			Men.	Boys.	Total.	Women	Girls.	Total.			
Ladák ..	142	1,890			3,646			4,192	7,838	4·147	13·3
Balti, &c.	158	6,406			13,662			13,387	23,394	4·235	34·4
					17,308			17,579		4·181	23·85

In the Buddhist country it will be observed that the females outnumber the males, while the reverse is the case in the Musalman districts along the Indus. This is just what might have been expected from the different habits of the people. The Musalmani girl is married at ten or twelve years of age, and becomes a mother before she has acquired either the strength or stature of a woman; while the Ladáki girl is rarely married before she is about seventeen or eighteen years of age. The advantage of this practice is best appreciated by a reference to the tables of longevity, which show that for every Balti woman who reaches the patriarchal age of threescore years and ten, there are no less than three Ladáki septagenarian ladies. That this difference is not due to the climate, or to particular customs which might affect both sexes, is further shown by the same tables; from which we learn that for every Balti man who reaches seventy years of age there are only two Ladákis. The difference must therefore be due to some cause which affects the women only; and this cause I presume to be the very early marriages of the Musalmani females.

II.—ORIGIN.

The Botis, or Bhotiyas,* are usually considered as a distinct race of people, chiefly I believe on account of their peculiar language. But this peculiarity must have been partly produced by their isolated position, and partly by the few wants of a poor people; as both of these causes must have operated against the introduction and naturalization of foreign words. Regarding their origin, therefore, nothing but a conjecture can be hazarded. Judging from their language and features, which have much in common with those of the Chinese, the Botis must be pronounced to be an offshoot of the great Mongolian race; and all differences, both physical

* *Bhotiya* is the Hindu name. The Tibetans call themselves *Botpa*, *Bod-pa*. The name is most probably derived from their profession of Buddhism, *Bauddha* being the designation of a Buddhist.

and moral, may be easily accounted for by the severe cold and extreme dryness of the Tibetan climate, and by the former intimate connection of the people with the Caucasian Hindus of India for many centuries during the flourishing period of Buddhism.

The great mass of the people of Ladák are all of one race or caste. They intermarry and eat together, and are all eligible as members of the national priesthood. But in the northern provinces of Ladák there is a numerous class called *Bem*,* or "low," which includes all the dancing-women and their attendant musicians, all smiths and carpenters, and in fact handicraftsmen of every kind. In Lé itself, and in Chachot, there are small colonies of Kashmiris, whose connection with the native Botis has produced a mixed race called Argon.† These same hybrids between the Kashmiris and the native races are also found in Kashgar, Yarkand, Aksu, and Kotan.

III.—PHYSICAL DESCRIPTION.

Of the physical characteristics of the Botis, little has been made known beyond the facts that they have "a strongly-marked Tartarian or Mongolian countenance, and that they are superior both in vigour of body and in stature to the other Mongolian races of Kalmaks and Tungusis."‡ Their peculiarly Tartarian physiognomy must be considered as a presumptive proof of their

* The men are called *hBems-pa;* the women *hBems-mo*, or *Bem-mo*.

† This is probably the Turki word *Arghun*, ارغون, "fair;" the mixed race of half Kashmiris being much fairer than the people of the country.

‡ Prichard, Natural History of Man, p. 217.

Mongolian origin. Their superiority in bodily strength is perhaps owing partly to the bracing climate of their elevated country, and partly to the former infusion of Hindu blood. I have had practical proof of this superiority amongst the Botis of Láhul, Kanáwar, and Spiti. In 1846 the short Láhuli women carried with the greatest ease, day after day, the roof of my tent, which the taller and finer-looking men of Kullu and Simla refused on account of its weight. Again in 1847 the Kanáwari and Spiti women carried loads at which the pampered Simla coolis had grumbled. I have repeatedly seen a box weighing sixty pounds carried by girls of sixteen and eighteen years of age over the high passes of Kanáwar.

Regarding their alleged superiority of stature I am rather sceptical. But as no detailed accounts of the average heights of the different Mongolian races are accessible to me, I can only quote the statement of Pallas, that the Kalmaks are "generally of a moderate height," and "rather small than large." The following table shows the stature of the Boti race in different parts of Ladák and Balti, according to the average measurements of from five to seven persons of each sex in many different villages, always including the tallest and shortest men and women that could be found.

TABLE OF STATURE.

	Districts.	Men.			Women.			Landlords.		
		Tallest.	Shortest.	Average	Tallest.	Shortest.	Average.	Tallest.	Shortest.	Average
		ft. in.	ft. in.	ft. in.	ft. in.	ft. in.	ft. in.	ft. in.	ft. in.	ft. in.
Buddhists.	Rukchu	5 1·5	5 0·0	5 0·9	5 0·0	4 1·0	4 8·2	5 3·0	5 1·0	5 2·5
	Spiti	5 6·5	5 0·0	5 2·4	5 2·5	4 1·0	4 8·9	5 7·5	5 4·0	5 5·7
	Nubra	5 7·0	5 4·0	5 2·7	4 7·0	4 0·0	4 9·8			
	Ladák	5 5·0	4 10·0	5 1·4	5 4·0	4 1·0	4 10·1	5 9·0	5 2·0	5 5·3
	Average			5 1·8			4 9·2			5 4·5

	Districts.	Men.			Women.			Landlords.		
		Tallest.	Shortest.	Average	Tallest.	Shortest.	Average.	Tallest.	Shortest.	Average
		ft. in.	ft. in.	ft. in.	ft. in.	ft. in.	ft. in.	ft. in.	ft. in.	ft. in.
	Chhorbad......	5 8·0	4 8·0	5 0·9	5 0·0	4 4·0	4 9·3			
	Khapolor......	5 7·0	4 6·0	5 0·7	5 2·0	4 2·0	4 9·1			
	Keris	5 5·0	5 0·0	5 2·9	4 11·0	4 8·0	4 10·6			
	Parguta	5 9·0	4 10·0	5 3·5	5 4·0	4 4·0	4 8·5			
	Skardo........	5 11·0	4 9·0	5 2·3	5 0·0	4 6·0	4 9·7			
	Shigar	5 5·0	4 4·0	5 0·4	4 11·0	4 8·0	4 9·4			
	Rongdo	5 7·0	4 9·0	5 2·1	5 0·0	4 7·0	4 9·7			
	Average			5 1·8			4 9·5			
	Average of Botis			5 1·8			4 9·35			
Botis.	Upper Kanáwar	5 6·0	4 11·0	5 1·9	5 1·5	4 4·5	4 9·0	5 8·0	5 4·0	5 5·9
Botis.	Middle Kanáwar	5 6·0	4 9·0	5 2·0	5 5·0	4 9·0	4 11·1	5 8·0	5 0·0	5 5·3
Botis.	Lower Kanáwar	5 9·2	4 11·0	5 4·1	5 6·0	4 10·0	5 1·2	5 7·0	5 7·0	5 7·0
	Average			5 2·0			4 9·7			5 6·1

In this table the effect of the admixture of Hindu blood will be seen at once in the superior stature of the people of Lower Kanáwar.* Those of Middle Kanáwar also occasionally intermarry with the Hindus; for I found a woman, named Charanu, a native of Saráhan, near Rampur, who was wedded to two husbands in the village of Kala, opposite Labrang, in Middle Kanáwar. In fact the people of Kanáwar generally are called Kanets, a name which is said to designate a people of mixed race. The proper name of the country is therefore most probably *Karanáwara*, the country of *Karanas*, or people of mixed race, a name usually applied to the offspring of a degraded Khsatriya and a Khsatriya

* The Botis are shorter than the Kirghiz of Wakhan and Pamer who were measured by Wood.—Oxus, pp. 338—372.

	Tallest.	Shortest.	Average.
Men	5 5·5 ...	5 2·0 ...	5 3·2
Do.	5 7·2 ...	5 1·7 ...	5 4·5
		Mean ...	5 3·85

female. The same name is applied by Marco Polo to another mixture of the same races—Tartars and Indians. There are indeed Kanets in other parts of the Himálayas, but only in those districts which border upon Ladák; as in Bisahar, Kullu, Chamba, and Kashtwar.

The average stature of the Botis of Ladák appears to me to be very short indeed when compared with that of their Hindu and Chinese neighbours; but that this is chiefly, if not wholly, the effect of poor food and of privation of all kinds, is proved by the average stature of the landlords, or head men, of the different villages. These never carry burdens on their backs, are better fed, and better clothed; and (when they travel) usually ride from one place to another, instead of toiling up and down the steep and rugged passes of their native mountains. This shows the beneficial effect of wholesome food and of comparative comfort even in the most rigorous climate.

The stature of the women seems to be particularly low. This is not, however, shown in the averages, which exhibit a difference of only four inches between the men and the women. But the number of very short women is much greater than that of very short men. In Ladák I saw only six men that were under five feet in height; of whom two were four feet eleven inches; three were four feet ten inches; and one was only four feet nine inches. Amongst the women of Ladák, however, I saw no less than ten that were under four feet five in height. Of these, one was four feet four and a half; two were four feet four; one was four feet three; two were four feet two; one of forty years of age was four feet one and a half; and three were only four feet one inch in height. I am unable to say positively what may be the cause of the great number of very short women; but I am inclined to attribute it partly to the system of polyandry which prevails among them. This system is, I believe, almost universal amongst the mixed race of Kanetis throughout Kanawar and the other Kaneti districts, but as far as I could learn it is not so prevalent amongst the pure Botis of Ladák. The custom has therefore most probably been borrowed from the polyandrous Hindu race of Himálayan Kshatriyas, amongst whom it has been preserved for at least twenty-five centuries, since the Pandavan brothers jointly espoused the princess Draupadi.

The great differences observable in the stature of the Musalmán races of Shigar on the north and of Skardo on the south, must no doubt be attributed to the mixture of other races; of the diminutive Kirghiz of Pamer with the first, and of the tall Kashmiri with the second. The people of Shigar were once, I believe, pure Kirghiz.

In general the Botis have short, squat, stout figures, with broad, flat, ugly faces; but occasionally amongst the better classes I have seen both men and women who were well made and well featured, and with a fine rosy colour in their cheeks. Indeed, I have even seen a few of the women that were really handsome, with good regular features and fine figures. But in general they are all, both men and women, not only ugly but hideous, and more especially the old women. Dr. Gerard's amusing description of these people is too graphic to be omitted.* "In figure they are stout, waddling, and dumpy; * * * in face they are not beautiful, even when young; when past their climacteric, very unseemly; and when old, a picture of horrid ugli-

* Asiatic Researches, XVIII. p. 249.

ness. Not regardless of the aid of artificial charms, their hair, glistening with rancid oil, hangs loosely round their sunburnt necks. Sometimes it is woven into tresses which braid the contour of the face; but it is commonly unregarded, and blows out in the wind, giving them a shaggy appearance like wild beasts." Gerard's travels were confined to the southern districts of Láhul, Spiti, and Rukchu; in which the climate is much more rigorous than in the districts along the Indus, where apples, grapes, and walnuts are cultivated with success; and where alone I saw the fine-looking women mentioned above.

The face of the Boti is broad, flat, and square, with high cheek-bones, large mouth, and narrow forehead. The nose is broad and flat, and generally much turned up, with wide nostrils, and with little or no bridge. The eyes are small and narrow, and the upper eyelids usually have a peculiar and angular form that is especially ugly. The eyes are nearly always black; but brown, and even blue eyes, are seen occasionally. The inner corners are drawn downwards, by the tension of the skin over the large cheek-bones; the eyelids are therefore not in one straight line, parallel to the mouth, as is the case with Europeans, but their lines meet in a highly obtuse angle pointing downwards. This gives an appearance of obliquity to the eyes themselves that is very disagreeable. The ears are prominent, very large, and very thick. They have also particularly long lobes, and are altogether about one-half larger than those of Europeans. The mouth is large, with full and somewhat prominent lips. The hair is black, coarse, and thick, and usually straight and crisp. Bushy heads of hair are sometimes seen, but I believe that the frizzly appearance is not due even in

Nomadic BOTI of LADAK, Hanle

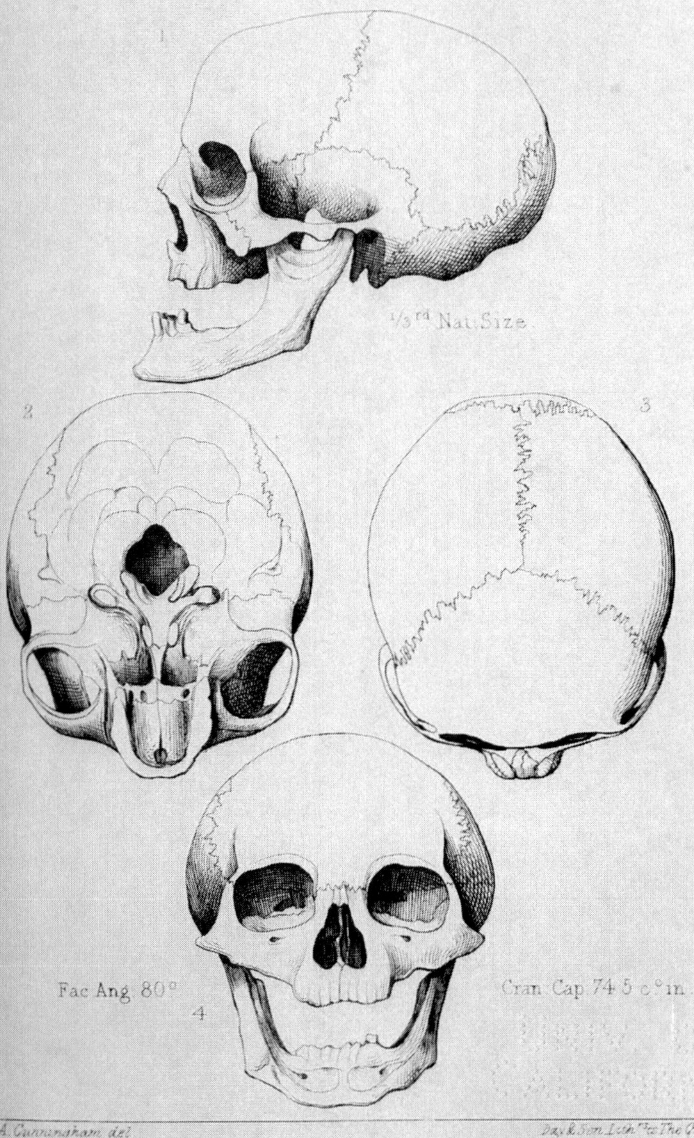

A. Cunningham del.

Day & Son Lith^rs to The Queen

Settled BOTI of LADAK, Lé.

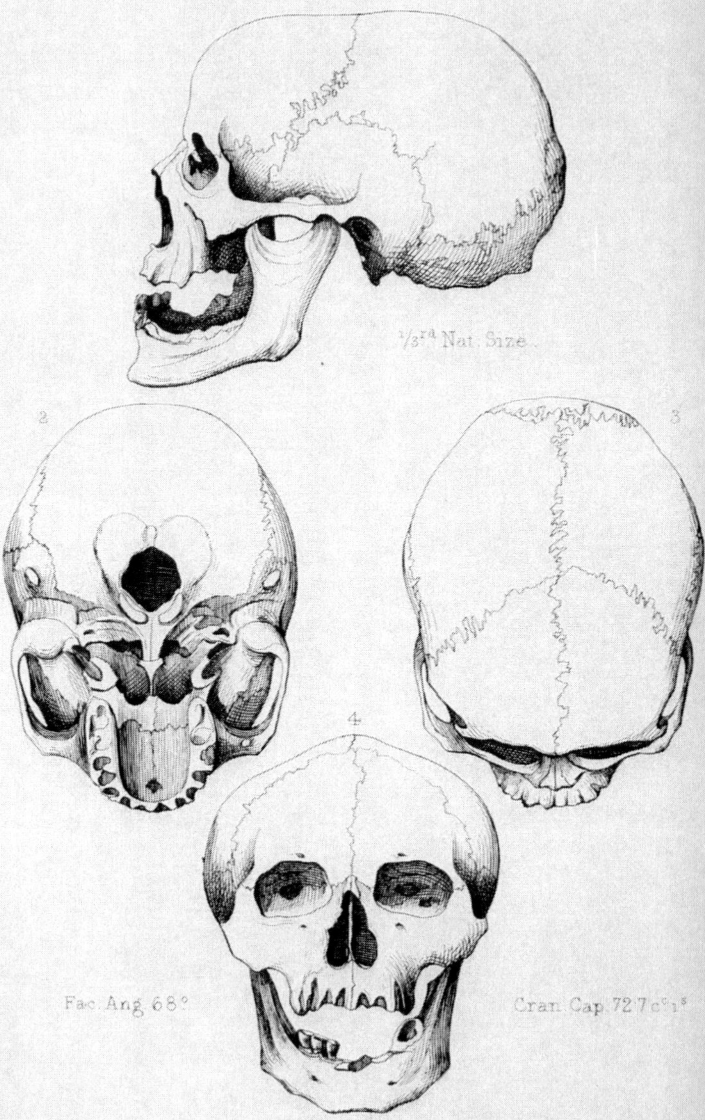

A. Cunningham del.

Day & Son, Lithrs to The Queen.

part to any natural tendency to curl, but solely to the tangled and thickly agglomerated matting of the hair, consequent upon its never having been combed or washed from first to second childhood.

In the accompanying plates* I have exhibited four different views of two Botian skulls which I procured at Hanlé and at Lé. The first is a specimen of the nomadic dwellers in tents, the second of the settled inhabitants of houses. There is a considerable difference in the shapes of these two skulls, but I believe that the Lé specimen is a departure from the usual type; its elongated form being most probably due to some malformation at the time of birth. This is I think fully proved by the continuation of the longitudinal suture from the top of the cranium down to the nose. As a second skull from Lé, which I have in my possession, resembles very closely that of the nomadic Boti of Hanlé, this cranium may be taken as a very good specimen of the Ladáki type of Boti.

The characteristics of this type are almost the same as those of the Mongolian. The more striking are a round and globular shape of cranium, and a great lateral extension of the zygomatic arches, coupled with a narrow forehead, which gives what Prichard has called a pyramidal form to the front view of the skull; that is, if lines be drawn from the outside of the cheek-bones touching the temples, they will meet in a point at a short distance above the head. This form is quite different from that of the European skull, in which the width of the forehead is often greater (but I believe never less) than that of the cheek-bones. In other respects these Boti skulls appear to resemble very closely

* Plates X. and XI.

those of the civilized Chinese. Indeed, if the statements of their own historians* are to be credited, that the Chinese originally came from the Shensi forests of the frontiers of Tibet, we can scarcely come to any other conclusion than that they were originally of the same stock as the people of Tibet, or in other words, that they were actually Botis. The Mongolian origin of the Chinese and of the Botis is, I believe, universally admitted; and I would attribute the differences between them and the present nomadic Mongols partly to the early civilization of the Botian race, and partly to the admixture of Hindu blood. The form of the skulls in my possession, and more particularly of the frontal bone, also shows a considerable affinity to the Hindu race. In corroboration of this view, I am happy to quote the opinion of M. D'Halley,† who says, "Peut-être que les Bhots sont des Hindus modifiés par leur mélange avec des Mongols."

The following table exhibits the facial angle, the cranial capacity, and the present weight of the four Botian skulls, three of which are in my possession.

Skulls.	Facial angle.	Cranial capacity.	Weight.	
		Cubic in.	lb.	oz.
No. 1 from Hanlé	80°	74·5	1	4·44
2 " Lé	68°	72·7	1	6·44
3 " Lé	73°	70·0	1	7·46
4 " Balti	75°	72·0	1	2·40
	74°	72·3	1	5·18

The facial angle in these specimens ranges from 68°

* Prichard, Natural History of Man, p. 227.

† Des Races Humaines, p. 128, note.

to 80°; but as there is good reason for supposing that the skull which yields the lower number has been a malformation, I would deduce the mean facial angle from the other three skulls, which agree with each other in general appearance. This would fix the facial angle of the Botis at 76°, which is somewhat less than the European average of 80°, but at the same time it is a considerable improvement upon the Mongolian and Kalmuk average of 70°. That some individuals may occasionally approach the Caucasian standard, we have an example in the cranium of the nomadic Boti of Hanlé, which has a facial angle of 80°.

The amount of the cranial capacity is another distinguishing characteristic of different races. In this respect the Botis are remarkably deficient, but perhaps not more so than might be expected from the small size of the race generally. Taking the average height of Europeans at five feet and a half, and the average capacity of their skulls at eighty-eight cubic inches, then the cranial capacity of a Boti five feet in height should be ten-elevenths of the other, or eighty cubic inches. But the average of the three Botian skulls in my possession falls much below this number; that of the most capacious being only seventy-four cubic inches and a half.

The three Botian skulls now described agree very closely, in their respective weights, with that of a Chinese, recorded by Prichard, which weighed 1 lb. 7½ oz. Had the teeth been perfect, the agreement would have been still more close: for No. 1 has but half a tooth; No. 2 has only three teeth, while No. 3 has twelve teeth.

The true average would therefore most probably range

from 1 lb. 7 oz. to 1 lb. 8 oz. These skulls are all thin and smooth, and of compact texture, excepting only the jaws, which appear to me to be rather massive for the size of the head.

Of the configuration of the Boti skeleton, I can give but little positive information. The shoulders are square and broad, and the trunk is rather long in proportion to the stature. I obtained the pelvis* belonging to No. 1 cranium, which has a longitudinal axis of 3·75 inches, and a transverse axis of 3·6 inches, with a form inclining to the square. According to Professor Weber, as quoted by Prichard, this shape prevails generally amongst people who resemble the Mongolians.

The Botian tribe would, therefore, seem to possess the same physical characteristics, both in outward form and in their bony structure, as those which distinguish the Mongolian race generally, with only some slight modifications, which are most probably due to their connection and occasional mixture with the Caucasian race of India.

For the sake of comparison I have given sketches of two Kashmirian skulls,† one male and one female, which I procured in the city of Kashmir. The differences are very striking; but more particularly the oval shape of the skull, the flattened form of the zygomatic arches, and the narrowness of the jaws; all of which peculiarities are characteristic of the Caucasian race. The measurements of my Kashmiri skulls are as follows:—

* See Plate XII. † Plates XIII. and XIV.

Plate XII.

Pelvis from Hánlé

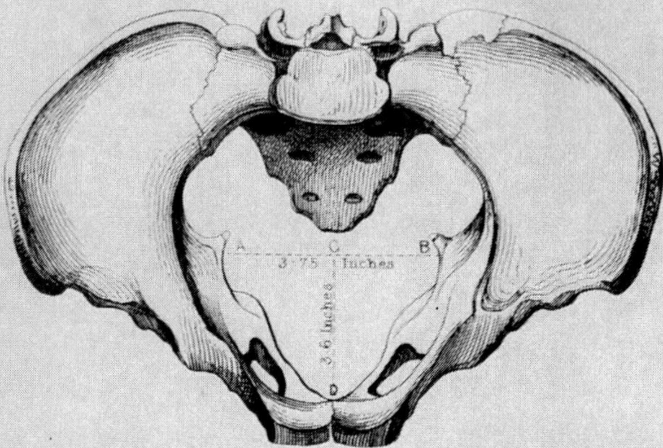

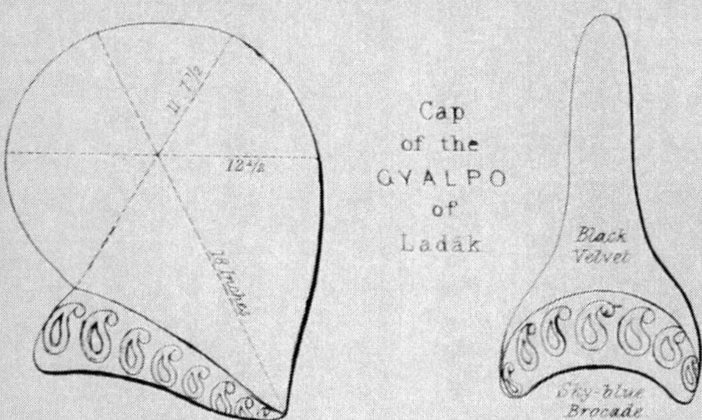

Cap of the GYALPO of Ladák

The JAO of Ladák (6)

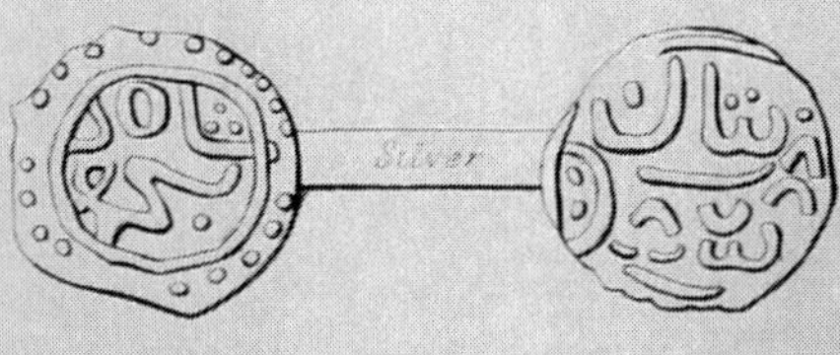

Cunningham del. Day & Son, Lithrs to The Queen

Plate XIII

Male KASA of KASHMIR City

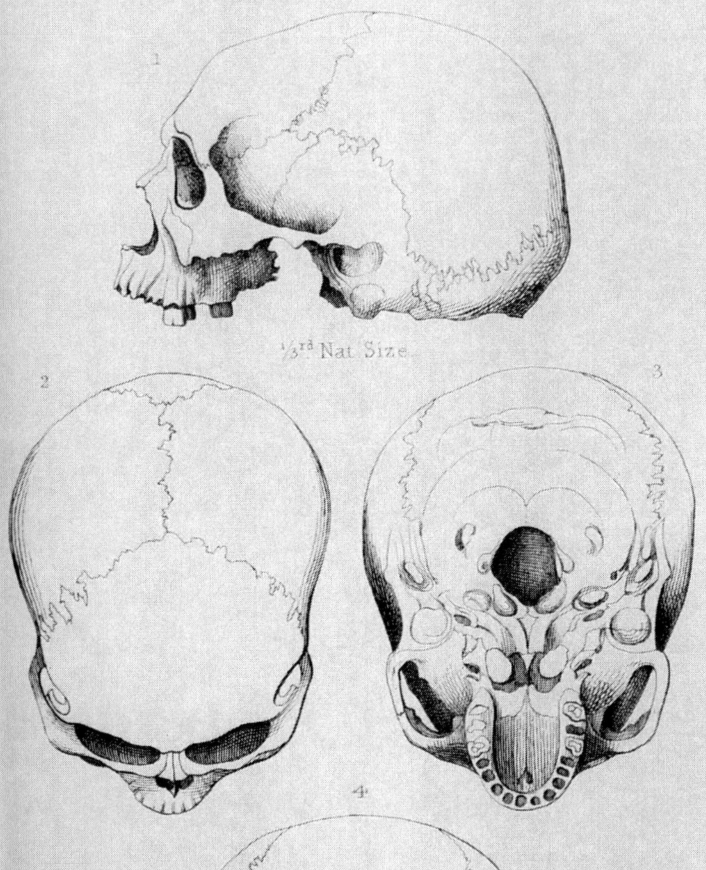

A. Cunningham del.

Day & Son Lithrs to The Queen.

Plate XIV.

Female KASA of KASHMIR City

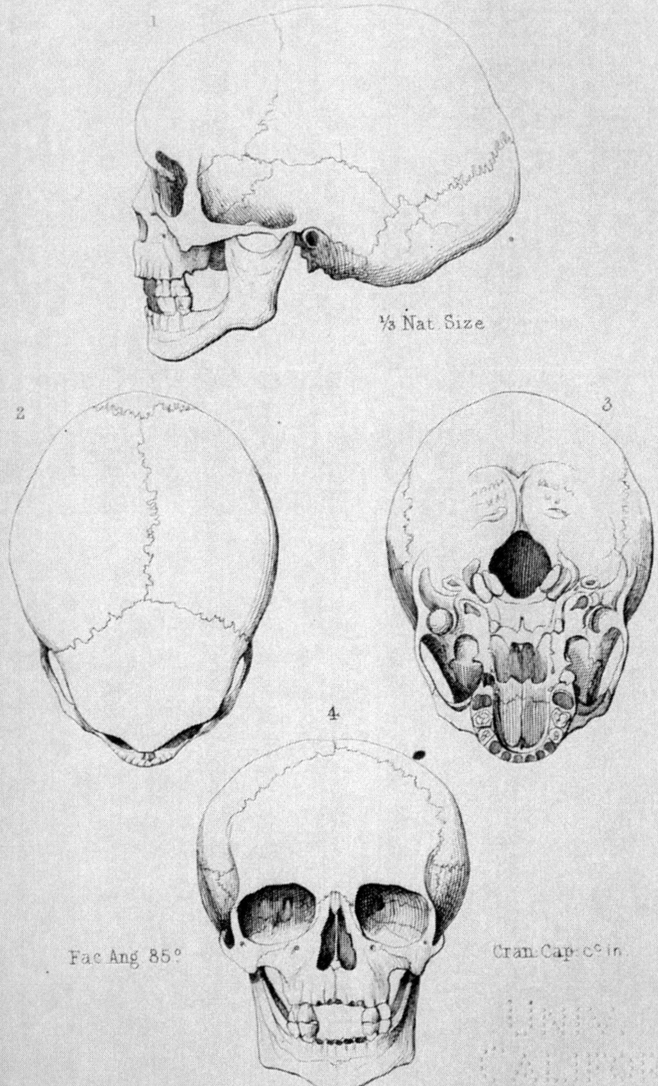

A. Cunningham, del.

Day & Son, Lithrs to The Queen.

	Facial angle.	Cranial capacity.	Weight.
			lb. oz.
Male	73·5°	97	1 14·4*
		Cubic in.	
1st Female	85°	68	1 5·2
2nd Female	84°	67·5	
Average Female	84·5°	67·75	

LONGEVITY.

One of the most interesting subjects of inquiry which I pursued daily in Ladák was the extreme ages attained by the oldest people in all the villages in my route. To test the value of the information thus collected, I have added to the following table the number of persons per cent. of each sex who reach the respective ages of seventy, eighty, and ninety years throughout the whole of Great Britain. The table requires little explanation. The first and second columns give the actual number of males and females in the several villages where the ages of the people were ascertained. It is necessary that this should be stated, as it will at once account for the great per-centage of females in Rukchu who had passed the patriarchal age of seventy. The number is 2·45 per cent., or three out of 122. But the general average is still much below that of Britain; and I feel satisfied that the whole table gives a very fair approximation to the truth. I have added a column showing the duration of life in Balti and the small Musalman states on the

* This very large skull wants the lower jaw, and has only three teeth in the upper jaw; but the bone of the skull averages about one quarter of an inch in thickness. The whole weight, if complete, would be nearly 2½ lb.

Indus. The differences between this and the average of the Ladákis can only be accounted for by the general dissoluteness of all Musalmáns, and the consequent spread of loathsome and fatal diseases.

TABLE OF LONGEVITY PER CENT.

	Numbers.		70 to 80.		80 to 90.		90 to 100.	
	Males.	Females.	Males.	Females.	Males.	Females.	Males.	Females.
Rukchu	113	122	0·880	2·459	0·880	0·820	—	—
Spiti	686	751	1·157	1·164	0·291	0·693	—	—
Ladák	1,342	1,492	0·745	0·670	0·447	0·268	0·074	—
Purik........	867	883	1·268	0·905	0·807	0·792	0·115	0·113
Nubra	788	1,030	1·269	2·336	0·507	0·777	0·127	0·194
Average	3,796	4,278	1·064	1·507	0·586	0·670	0·063	0·061
Balti, &c.	13,662	13,387	0·537	0·527	0·184	0·175	0·070	0·022
Great Britain			2·218	2·401	0·700	0·756	0·059	0·074

I heard of only one person who was more than 100 years of age. She was an old nun of Sakté, in the Chimra valley, whose sons were seventy and eighty years old. She was said to be 110 years of age. I had no means of ascertaining the rate of mortality; but different people stated the annual number of deaths at Lé at from twenty-five to fifty, or about forty persons. As the population of the capital is nearly 4,000 persons, the annual mortality will be rather more than one per cent. The population of the country, except in times of war or disease, remains nearly stationary; but this is not owing to any unhealthiness of climate, but to the system of polyandry, which most effectually checks any increase. In 1822 the number of houses in Spiti was 267,* and in 1847 the number was 262.

* Trebeck in Moorcroft, II. p. 71.

Plate XVII.

A. Cunningham Del.

Zang-bo. Chang-jok.

Men of PIN in SPITI.

IV.—DRESS.

The men of Ladák wear a cloak* of woollen, thick and warm. It is usually white, or rather it has once been white; for as the people only wash themselves once a year, and never wash their clothes, their cloaks are always of a dirty hue. Round their legs, from knee to ankle, they have coarse woollen leggings† (of felt), fitting tightly, or else wrapped close round the leg and secured by a garter,‡ which is wound spirally round the leg from the ankle upwards. The garter is generally black, but sometimes red. On their heads they wear either quilted skull-caps, as filthy as their cloaks, or caps of sheep-skin with the wool inside, and with a large flap behind, which covers the back of the neck as well as the ears. Those in better circumstances have fur caps of the same shape. Their boots are of felt, with soles of sheep or goat-skin, which are turned up all round and sewn to the felt. The upper part of the felt boot is open to the front, and is allowed to fall over, something in the manner of the boots worn in England in Charles II.'s time. The lamas have red boots, and the others mostly have theirs ornamented with small bits of coloured cloth in the front.§

The Ladáki women wear a black woollen jacket with a large striped woollen petticoat of many colours, generally green, blue, red, and yellow, reaching below the mid-leg. Over all they wear a sheep skin with the wool inside, secured, or rather skewered, in front by a large

* The cloak is called *La-pa-sha*.

† The legging is called *rKang-Phying*.

‡ The garter is called *rKang-gDub*.

§ See Plates XVII. and XXIII. for the men's dress.

iron or brass needle. The poorer classes have the outside of the skin plain, but those in better circumstances cover it with coarse woollen baize, either red, blue, green, or yellow, with a broad border always of a different colour. The upper classes cover this sheep-skin cloak either with brocade or with silk. Their heads are always bare, the hair being arranged in a border of narrow plaits, which hang round the head like a long fringe. From the forehead, over the division of the hair, they all wear a long narrow band of cloth studded with coarse many-flawed turquoises, which hangs down behind as low as the waist, and is usually finished off with a tassel of wool or a bunch of cowrees. The ears are covered by semicircular woollen lappets, fastened to the hair and edged with brown or black fur, generally of the otter-skin, called Kunduz. These ear-flaps are always red, the inside being woollen, and the outside brocade. These are made coarse or fine according to circumstances; for the Ladáki women seem to pride themselves upon the style and material of these lappets just as much as European ladies do upon the fashion of their bonnets.*

The dancing-women wear similar dresses, but they sometimes also have long gowns, of different colours, instead of the jacket and petticoat. Their heads are always covered, either with a coloured and quilted skull-cap, or with a circular, flat-topped, stiff woollen hat, something like a short shako without a peak. These are ornamented with cornelians and turquoises.† All

* See Plates XV. XVI. XVIII. XIX. and XXII. for the women's dress of Kanáwar, Spiti, and Ladák.

† Plate XXII. Moorcroft, I. p. 328, remarks that "a Ladáki female in full costume would create no small sensation amongst the fashionable dames of a European capital."

Women of Lower KANAWAR

Women of Upper KANÁWAR

HANGO SUNGNAM LIMO

Height 4f. 9 — Height 4f. 10

DANGKHAR — Sang. Ram — SHE

SPITI — SPITI — LADAK

Plate XIX

A. Cunningham Del.

Day & Son Lithrs to the Queen

Landlords Wives.

From NURLA in LADAK.

classes of women wear, besides, a profusion of necklaces, made of cornelian, turquoises, or amber, and they have also massive ornaments of silver and brass, studded with turquoises. Both men and women wear in their waist-cloths or girdles a *Chakmak* (or leather case ornamented with brass, containing flint, steel, and tinder), and the men, besides, usually carry a knife or dagger in their girdles. The women likewise carry a brass spoon, a convex brass mirror, and a case of coarse needles attached to their girdles; to these may be added a small metal or wooden cup or quaigh, a single or double flageolet, a metal spoon, and plate, all of which are stuffed into the slackened breast of the dress, next the skin, along with a ball of wool, a coil of rope, and a few unleavened wheaten or barley cakes.

V.—FOOD.

The food of the common people usually consists of thick barley cakes, or of barley-meal moistened with water, with a broth of turnips, either fresh or dried, according to the season, to which are added a few peas, and a seasoning of salt and pepper. Meat is seldom tasted by the poorer classes excepting upon occasions of rejoicing, at a birth or marriage. Tea is now, I believe, coming into common use, although I never myself saw any of the labourers drinking it. Amongst the upper classes tea is drunk two or three times a day. It is made in a strong decoction with soda, then seasoned with salt and churned with butter, until it acquires the colour and consistency of thick rich cocoa or chocolate. Wheaten cakes are eaten with it in the morning, either plain or with butter and sugar. The same meal is repeated in the middle of the day, with any fruits that may be in season,—apples, grapes, and apricots, or with the last dried. In the evening they usually have rice, and a broth of turnips, or of sheep or goat mutton, for since the occupation of the country by the Hindu Dogras, Yak's flesh is no longer to be had in Northern Ladák. Even in the British district of Spiti, the Yak is now a sacred animal, as our Government have made over the district to the Hindu raja of Bisahar.

All classes are exceedingly fond of spirituous liquors, although they have nothing better than their own indigenous *Chang*. This is made from fermented barley and wheat flour, and has a most disagreeable sour smell, like that of bad beer, and a thick appearance like dirty gruel. This is the usual beverage; but it is sometimes distilled, by which process a clear spirit is obtained, something like whiskey, but of a most villanous flavour.

VI.—SOCIAL CUSTOMS.

The most remarkable social institution of the Botis is the system of polyandry, which is strictly confined to brothers. Each family of brothers has only one wife in common. The most usual number of husbands is two, but three and even four husbands are not uncommon. This system prevails of course only among the poorer classes, for the rich, as in all eastern countries, generally have two or three wives, according to their circumstances. Polyandry is the principal check to the increase of population, and however revolting it may be to our feelings, it was a most politic measure for a poor country which does not produce sufficient food for its inhabitants.

The Botis are very social people in their habits, and every event is made the pretext for a feast, which usually ends in great uproariousness, and frequently in general drunkenness. Huge bowls of *Chang* form the chief attraction of an entertainment, and the song * and the laugh abound, until the liquor is finished. On these occasions they prefer merry or drinking songs. The singer is often accompanied by a fiddler, and sometimes by a drum. Exhibitions of female dancers frequently form a principal part of an entertainment; but the performers are more remarkable for their costume than for their graceful movements. The principal occasions on which these entertainments are held, are births, marriages, and deaths. The ceremonies are the following:

The birth-feast, *Tsas-Ton*, is held one week after the mother's confinement, when all the relatives assemble at her house to celebrate the child's birth. All the guests make presents to the mother, according to their means, of pieces of cloth and food, and occasionally of money. The party then dines, and the entertainment ends with a bowl of chang. The mother remains at home for one month.

The naming-feast, *Ming-Ton*, which answers to our christening, is held just one year after the birth. The child is then taken before some great lama, to whom an offering is made of a rupee or a quantity of wheat or barley, according to the means of the parties. The lama pronounces a name, and the relatives retire to the usual entertainment of dinner and chang.

The marriage-feast, *Bag-Ton*, is a much more formal business. When betrothed, the bridegroom proceeds to

* A drinking-song is appropriately called *Chang-gLu*, a "liquor-song."

the bride's house with a bowl of chang, and the relatives discuss the wedding-day and the spirits together. After the bridal day has been fixed, the bridegroom is obliged to send a portion of food and chang daily to his elect. After the end of fifteen or twenty days all the relatives of both parties assemble together to ask the bridegroom what present he will make to the mother of the bride. The bridegroom makes an offer, generally of a few rupees (one to ten), according to his means and the ardour of his love. A poor man will give a pot of chang and a silver *jao* (sixpence) to his bride's mother, while the thriving man will give a present of ten rupees. About ten or fifteen days after the "asking," the relatives of both parties assemble at the bride's house, and conduct the lady in state to the bridegroom's house, where prayers are read by a party of lamas, and the couple are declared man and wife. The whole party then sits down to dinner and chang, of which the supply on these occasions is always ample. The entertainment lasts for several days, according to the means of the bridegroom, and the assembled lamas read prayers every morning to the half-sober guests.

The funeral-feast, *Shid-Ton*, varies according to the rank and circumstances of the deceased. For a rich man, a large party of lamas assemble, and read prayers daily until the body is burned, which does not usually take place for fifteen or twenty days. For a poor man, only a few lamas meet together and read prayers for four or five days (never beyond a week), while the body remains in the house. During this time a piece of cloth is fixed over the doorway as a sign of mourning. The lamas are regaled with food and tea daily; and, when the body has been burned, they are presented with the clothes and cooking-vessels of the deceased.

When a great man dies, such as the Gyalpo or any of the Kahlons, his corpse is kept in the house for fifteen or twenty days, while the assembled lamas read prayers daily. The number of the lamas depends on the means or pride of the relatives. The body is then carried to the *Pur-khang*, or place of cremation, and after being burned in a metal vessel, the ashes (*Pur-thal*) are carefully collected and made into an image of the deceased. A *Chhorten*, or pyramid, is erected on the spot for the reception of an urn or funeral vessel (*Pur-Gom*), in which the following articles are deposited with the figure:—

1. Wheat, barley, rice, and peas.
2. Pearls, coral beads, turquoises.
3. Gold, silver, copper, iron (either in money or vessels).
4. Rolls of prayers and holy writings.
5. Pieces of the holy Shúkpá, or pencil-cedar, and of sandal-wood, both white and red.

The body of the great lama is interred in a coffin (*Pur-Gam*), dressed in the usual clothes, with the knees brought up to the chin, and corded together in as small a compass as possible, and in a sitting posture. Beside the body are placed the deceased's plate and cup, his rolls of prayers, his praying-cylinder, and all his religious instruments, together with the grains, minerals, and metals, usually deposited with royalty. To these are added images of Shakya Thûbba, Jámya, and Chanrazik, and a figure of the lama himself. The coffin is deposited in a *Chhorten*, before which, for some time, food and water are offered daily, and a light is kept burning every night.

These details may appear trifling, but they are really of great value for the illustration of Indian Buddhism. In some of the topes or Chaityas, near Bhilsa, Lieut. Maisey and myself found both precious stones and precious metals deposited with the relics of Sáriputra and Maha Mogalána, the right and left hand disciples of Buddha. On some of the relic-boxes we found inscriptions giving the names and patronymics, and occasionally the titles, of the holy men whose relics were enshrined. These short epitaphs are still used in Ladák, where they are called *Dur-chang*, or tomb-inscriptions.

In the lofty districts of Rukchu and Chang-thang, where no wood is procurable, and where burning with the Tibetan furze would be a tedious operation, the bodies of the dead are always exposed on hills to be eaten by vultures and wild dogs. Trebeck* states that the faces of the dead are covered when thus exposed; but my informants, both at Rukchu in 1846, and at Hanlé in 1847, were silent on this point. The Hanlé hill was literally covered with bones, from amongst which I obtained the skull and pelvis of the most perfect skeleton.

In Great Tibet the bodies of the dead are cut into small pieces by professional corpse-butchers, or pinkers (*découpeurs de mort*), and given to the dogs. This is called the "terrestrial funeral." The bones after being bruised in a mortar with parched corn are made into balls and thrown to the dogs and vultures. This is the "celestial funeral;" and these two are considered the most fortunate modes of disposing of the dead.†

* Moorcroft's Travels, II. p. 49.

† Nouv. Jour. Asiatique, tom. iv. 1829, pp. 254, 255, Father Hyacinthe's translation from the Chinese.

The favourite amusement of the Botis, both of Ladák and of Balti, is *Polo,* in which all parties from the highest to the lowest can take a part. I saw the game played at Mulbil, in a field 400 yards long and eighty yards broad, which was walled round for the purpose with a stone dyke. There were twenty players on each side, all mounted on ponies and armed with sticks about four feet long, and bent at the lower end. One player took the ball and advanced alone into the middle of the field, where he threw up the ball and as it fell struck it towards one of the goals. The goals were formed of two upright stones placed about twenty-five or thirty feet apart. When the ball was driven through a goal, one of the successful party was obliged to dismount and pick it up, for if the opposite party should have driven it back before it was picked up, the goal did not count. The game consisted in winning a certain number of goals, either five, seven, or nine. Numerous musicians were in attendance, who made a most lively din whenever a goal was won; and the noise was increased by the cheers of the successful party.

The game is a very spirited one, and well calculated for the display of bold and active horsemanship.* Accidental blows occur frequently, but the poor ponies are the principal sufferers. The game was once common in India under the name of *Chaogan,* but it is now completely forgotten. The old chaogan-grounds still exist in every large town in the Panjáb hills; in Bilâspur, Nadon, Shujanpur, Kangra, Haripur, and Chamba, where the goal-stones are still standing. The game is

* It is well and tersely described by Vigne as "hockey on horseback." Mr. Thornton calls it "*cricket* on horseback;" but it has nothing whatever in common with cricket.

repeatedly mentioned by Bâber; but after his time it gradually became obsolete. It was introduced by the Musalman conquerors, and the very first king, Kutb-ud-din Aibak, was killed by a fall from his horse when playing at chaogan in A.D. 1210.* The Pathán kings of India still continued to join in the game down to the time of Sikander Lodi, in A.D. 1498, when "one day, while the king and his court were playing at chaogan, the bat of Haibat Khan Shirwani by accident came in contact with the head of Suliman, the son of Darya Khan Lodi, who received a severe blow. This was resented on the spot by Khizr Khan, the brother of Suliman, who, galloping up to Haibat Khan, struck him violently over the skull. In a few minutes both sides joined in the quarrel, and the field was in uproar and confusion. Mahmud Khan Lodi and Khan Khanan Lodi interposing, endeavoured to pacify Haibat Khan, and succeeded in persuading him to go home quietly with them. The king, apprehensive of conspiracy, retired immediately to the palace; but nothing more transpiring, he made another party at the same game a few days after."†

VII.—HOUSES—PUBLIC AND PRIVATE.

The finest buildings in Ladák are the monasteries, which are always placed on heights more or less lofty, and which generally have a very picturesque and imposing appearance. Many of them would be places of some strength if they possessed water; but I am not aware of a single monastery that has even one day's supply. The outer walls of the monastery are formed by

* Briggs's Ferishta, I. p. 199. † Idem, p. 574.

A. Cunningham Del.

Day & Son Lith^rs to the Queen.

The Monastery of HANLÉ, in Rukchu

the dwellings of the monks, and the interior, if large, is divided by other buildings into several open courts. One room, more spacious and much more lofty than the rest, is set apart as a temple for the performance of daily service. The outer walls are generally white-washed; and the battlements are ornamented with broad bands of red, and surmounted with numerous small flags that flutter in the breeze and give a lively appearance to the whole place. Outworks are sometimes added for the purpose of defence. These are generally plain curtain-walls connected by square towers crowned by machicoulis.*

The generality of the houses throughout Ladák are so much alike that a description of one will serve for all. The houses usually consist of two or three stories and sometimes of four. The foundations and lower parts of the walls are built of stone, the upper walls of large sun-dried bricks, 20×10×6 inches. In the better houses some of the rooms are of considerable size, twenty-five feet long and eighteen broad; but they are always very low, the highest not exceeding seven and a half or eight feet. The roofs of these large rooms are always supported by plain wooden pillars. The roof is formed of poplar spars five or six inches in diameter, peeled white, and laid only one to one and a half feet apart. The beams are covered in with small straight pieces of poplar branches about one inch in diameter, peeled white, and placed touching each other. Generally they are laid straight across the beams; but sometimes at different angles, in the alternate intervals, so as to form a pattern like herring-bone. The whole is then covered with a layer of leaves and a thick coat of well-beaten

* See Plate XX. for a view of the monasterv of Hanlé.

clay. The floors are generally of earth, but the better sort are paved with small slit pebbles, about the size of turkeys' eggs, set in clay with the flat surfaces upwards. They form a clean, hard, smooth, and lasting floor.

The principal room generally has a balcony towards either the south or the west, from ten to twenty feet in length, and usually about two feet and a half in width, where the family sit to enjoy the sun in the winter season. The doors are mere rough planks of wood, joined together by wooden tenons, and sometimes strengthened by cross bars fastened with wooden pins. Purdahs or wadded curtains are also used as an additional means of excluding the cold wind; but when the doors are shut, there is only a dim light admitted into these apartments through one or two loopholes, which are closed with small shutters at night. If supplied with glass windows and fireplaces, many of these houses would form very comfortable residences; but at present they must be wretched habitations for the winter.

The houses of the poorer classes are generally of two stories: the lower story being appropriated to their cattle. The roofs are much more coarsely made, and the rooms are small and very low, being sometimes under six feet in height. In Ladák, the upper story is usually reached by a flight of earthen steps; but in Lahul, by the sloping trunk of a tree notched into steps.

The royal palace at Lé is a large fine-looking building, that towers in lofty pre-eminence over the whole city. It is 250 feet in length and seven stories in height. The outer walls have a considerable slope, as their thickness diminishes rapidly with their increase of height. The

Plate XVI.

Palace at LÉ

upper stories are furnished with long open balconies to the south, and the walls are pierced with a considerable number of windows. The beams of the roof are supported on carved wooden pillars, and covered with planks painted in various patterns on the outside. The building is substantial and plain; but its size and height give it a very imposing appearance.*

* See Plate XXI. for a view of the palace at Lé.

XII.—HISTORY.

I.—UNDER NATIVE RULERS.

"The earlier history of Ladák is that of Tibet in general, as it originally formed one of the provinces of that kingdom, governed as to temporal matters by an independent prince, and in spiritual affairs by the Guru Lama, or chief pontiff of Lhása." Such was Moorcroft's opinion;* and such also is that of the present inhabitants: and there can be no reasonable doubt that such was the usual position of Ladák, although its political dependence was more nominal than real. Under vigorous rulers, such as Palgyi-Gon in the tenth century, and Singgé Namgyal in the seventeenth century, its entire independence was asserted and upheld. But the original dependence at some distant period is, I think, clearly proved by the acknowledged descent of the Ladáki princes from Khri-Tsaupo, the first recorded king of Great Tibet.

The earliest historical notice of Ladák is that of the Chinese pilgrim *Fa-Hian*, in A.D. 400.† At that time

* Travels, I. p. 336.

† *Fo-kwe-ki.* French translation by Remusat, &c., p. 26. *Fo-kwe-ki.* English translation by J. W. Laidlay, p. 27, note 1. This translation is enriched by many valuable notes, both geographical and religious. It should be in the possession of every one who takes any interest in the ancient history of India.

the country had a king, and a numerous clergy, all of whom were strongly attached to the popular Buddhistical doctrine of the "*Lesser-advancement*," which consisted of outward observances, both moral and religious. The ceremonial of the *quinquennial assembly*, which was originally established by Asoka, about B.C. 250, was duly performed with much rude magnificence, and with becoming gravity. Buddhism was then the prevailing religion of Ladák; and there seems good reason to believe that it had been firmly rooted there for upwards of 400 years, since the first century before the Christian era, when the Buddhistical doctrines were first *widely* spread throughout Tibet by the preaching of 500 Kashmirian missionaries.*

In the tenth century, when the empire of Great Tibet was finally broken up, several of the outlying districts were separated by ambitious chiefs, and erected into independent kingdoms. Thus Purang was occupied by Tashi-Degon, and Ladák by Palgyi-Gon.† From that time down to the end of the sixteenth century, no historical records now exist in Ladák itself, although it is possible that a copy of the royal genealogy may yet be found at Lhása. Csoma de Körös was certainly misinformed regarding the existence of a book at Lé containing the "names of the kings that successively reigned in that principality."‡ For, during the invasion of Ladák in the beginning of the seventeenth century, by Ali Mir, the Musulmán chief of Skardo, all

* Klaproth's Chinese Chronology, in Prinsep's useful Tables, p. 128. It was however first introduced about B.C. 240.

† Csoma de Körös, Kings of Tibet. Prinsep's useful Tables, p. 131. See also Deguigne's Hist. des Huns, &c. tom. i. p. 165.

‡ Note appended to his list of Tibetan kings. Prinsep's useful Tables, p. 132.

the temples and monasteries of the country are said to have been destroyed, and their libraries thrown into the Indus. To this cause the Lamas attribute the entire want of all historical documents prior to that time; and their only record accordingly begins with the conquest of the country by *Chovang-Namgyal*,* a descendant of *Khri-Tsampo*,† the first king of Tibet. No date is given: but as his brother's son was a contemporary of the emperor Jehángir, this conquest could not have taken place much earlier than A.D. 1600, or perhaps about 1580.

During my stay in Ladák I had a copy of the existing history of the country transcribed for me in the original Tibetan. The historical portion of this work is brief, as the greater part of the volume consists of the Lamaïc ideas of the cosmogony and theogony. When in Ladák I had the principal historical parts read and explained to me, of which I made notes at the time; and I had also an abstract prepared by a Munshi in Urdu. From these I have now arranged the only interesting parts of the history, extending over a century and a half, during which period Ladák was conquered three different times.

Chovang-Namgyal, a descendant of the ancient kings of Tibet, being expelled from Lhása, took refuge in Ladák, where he established himself about A.D. 1580. He afterwards extended his conquests into the neighbouring districts of *Changmarangi, Lodang, Purang, Gugé, Lhojumlang, Lungti, Shigar, and Khabkar*.‡ He

* *Chho-dVang-rNam-rGyal*, that is, king Chovang.

† *Khri-rTsam-po*, pronounced *Thi-Tsanpo* in Great Tibet.

‡ The names of these places are thus written in Tibetan: *Byang-dMa-rangis, bLo-dang, Bu-rang*, or *sPu-rangs, Lho-hJum-lang, Lung-ti, Shi-dKar, Khab-dKar*. Purang lies to the S.E. of Ladák, and Shigar

then returned to the capital to make preparations for the invasion of Yarkand by the Nubra road. On hearing of his intentions, the chief men of Nubra at once waited upon Chovang at Lé, to tender their submission, and a trustworthy officer was despatched to receive charge of the district. After this, Chovang imposed a yearly tribute of one hundred golden *tillas** upon the landlords of *Kukiwála*, and upon those of *Rudok* a yearly tribute of 207 golden *tillas*, besides one horse and ten unicorns.† He also levied a considerable sum from the neighbouring districts.

Having acquired a large sum of money by these conquests, Chovang Namgyal resolved upon erecting an image of Buddha, under the name of *Sankya-Bidung*, or the "replete with extreme holiness." When the image was finished, all the people assembled to make their offerings, and a great feast was celebrated upon the occasion. Some time afterwards, about A.D. 1600, when he was meditating the erection of other images, he was prevented by death, and having no children, he was succeeded by his brother.

The new king, named *Jámya Namgyal*,‡ upon his

to the N.W. of it. The ambitious Chovang therefore would seem to have aspired to the conquest of *Ngári*, and of *Balti*, as well as to that of Ladák. But the historian has most probably dignified some successful plundering expeditions with the name of conquests.

* A *tilla* is worth about six rupees. The proper name for the gold coin is *sir-jao*, or a golden *jao*.

† In the original, *bSe-ru*, an animal with one horn. Csoma de Körös calls it a kind of deer (see Dict. in voce). Klaproth has a long note upon this animal (see Nouv. Journ. Asiat. tom. vi. pp. 229, 230, 231). He states that Mr. B. H. Hodgson's *Chiru* of southern Tibet is the same as the *Seru;* of which I think there can be no doubt. Mr. Hodgson himself assigns the animal to the "open plains of N.E. Tibet," but he has published no description. See Journ. As. Soc. Bengal, IV. p. 522.

‡ *hJam-dVyangs*, "sweet harmony."

accession, received the usual offerings of submission from all the Ladákis, excepting only a petty chief of Purik who was in the interest of Ali Mir, the Gyalpo of Balti. Chovang Malig, the head chief of Purik and the elder brother of the rebel, applied to Jámya for a small force to coerce the refractory chief. The king assented and accompanied his troops to the Purik district, where they were suddenly overtaken by a violent snowstorm. The royal troops were dispersed; and the king and many of his principal followers were taken prisoners by the rebel and sent to Skardo,* where they were confined. The remainder of the troops were permitted to return to Ladák.

Ali Mir, the ruler of Skardo, taking advantage of the helpless state of the country, immediately marched upon Lé with a large force, and took possession of the whole of Ladák.† The temples and monasteries were burned;‡ the images of Buddha and of his various personified emanations were destroyed by the bigoted Mahomedans; and all the religious and historical books were thrown into the Indus. The conquest was complete; and arrangements having been made for the future government of Ladák, Ali Mir marched back to Skardo.

Shortly after his return, the conqueror released Jámya, the imprisoned Gyalpo of Ladák, and gave him one of his daughters in marriage. No reason is assigned for

* *Skar-mDo*, pronounced *Skardo*, "the starry place," or "starry fort."

† This conquest is also recorded in Vigne's brief historical notice of Balti (Kashmir, II. p. 253); but the chief of Skardo is there called Ali Sher, and not Ali Mir. Ali Sher is the true name, as all the petty chiefs of the Balti district claim their descent from him.

‡ The buildings in Ladák are readily burned down, as all the walls are bonded together with timber, which in so dry a climate is readily ignited.

a proceeding so foreign to the usual tyrannical bigotry of a Musalmán. It is probable that Ali Mir, finding it difficult to retain Ladák as a permanent province of his kingdom, thought it more politic to secure by a display of apparent generosity, even the lukewarm friendship of the king of Ladák, than to encounter the active hostility of a whole people.

Jámya's return was hailed with joy by his people, who all hastened to present their offerings of submission and congratulation, and to beg that he would restore the temples and images of Buddha, and procure new copies of their sacred books from Lhása. All this he was able to effect by his prudent management, as well as to extend the boundary of his dominions to *Tanchi.*

By the Baltian princess, Jámya had two sons, named *Singgé Namgyal* and *Norbu Namgyal.* The former was married to the daughter of *Chovang Gyalmo,** who bore him two sons, named *Navang Namgyal* and *Tanjin Namgyal.* On this occasion the king sent a costly present of money, gold, silver, pearls, and coral to the temple of *Joborinché,* at *Brakpipulka,*† near *Lhása.* He also ordered to be copied in letters of gold, silver, and copper, the two books called *Gyatokisangsum,*‡ after which he is said to have died of grief or chagrin upon learning that two temples of Buddha still remained

* *rGyal-mo,* a "queen." She must have been one of the petty princesses of the country.

† *hBrag-p,hi-sbrul-ku,* pronounced *Brakpipulka.* The neighbourhood of Lhása is literally a vast suburb of temples. The names of many are given by Father Hyacinthe in his translation from the Chinese, but I can find no mention of *Joborinché.* See Nouv. Journ. Asiat. tom. iv. pp. 294-5-6.

‡ *rGya-tog-gSeng-gSum,* the "three secrets of *Gyatok.*" The lamas read "*two*" to me; but as *gSúm* means "*three,*" there are probably three books of this name.

unfinished. His reign probably extended from A.D. 1600 to 1620.

Jámya was succeeded by his eldest son *Singgé Namgyal*, who, feeling emulous of the military fame of his uncle *Chovang*, began his reign by conducting an expedition into the districts of *Gugé*, *Kiprok*, and *Tipichangyap*, from which he carried off many cattle and other property of the zamindars. During his reign a monk, named *Staktshang-Raspa*, who had travelled through *Gyagarnag*, *Urgyan*, and *Kháché*,* arrived at the village of *Tamosgang*,† in Ladák, where he made and consecrated an image of Chamba.‡ To this image he attached five monks for the performance of daily service, and having seen the complete establishment of the worship, he gave away in alms all that he possessed and departed.

After this Ahmed Khán, the chief of Balti, with the assistance of Jehángir Shah, invaded Ladák with a very large force; but *Singgé Namgyal* having collected his own troops to oppose them,§ the invaders were defeated

* *rGya-gar-nag*, literally the "white and black plains," that is, India and China. *U-rgyan*, the country of mixed races, perhaps the Indo-Persian district of *Udyána*, and the valley of the Kábul river. *Khá-chhe*, Kashmir.

† *gTang-mo-sgang*, on the right bank of the Indus below Lé. It is now the most populous village in Ladák.

‡ *Byams-pa*, pronounced *Chamba*, the "Clement." This saint is now very popular in Ladák. He is the future Buddha, MAITREYA.

§ Jehángir reigned from A.D. 1605 to 1628. The defeat of the Baltis may therefore be placed about A.D. 1625. This defeat is confirmed by the chronicles of Skardo, which (according to Vigne, *Kashmir*, II. p. 253) refer the loss of Ladák to the reign of Ahmed Khan, the son of Ali Sher. The subsequent invasion of the Lhásan territory probably took place in 1630. It is at least certain that these events could not have occurred later than 1630–1635, because in 1640 the celebrated and

with great slaughter at *Kharbu.** After this victory the king returned to his capital, and then proceeded at once against the people of *Gugé*, *Chaprang*, and *Lomostang*, who had taken advantage of the Muhammadan invasion to rebel against the authority of Ladák. They were quickly reduced by the active Singgé, and at the same time he took the opportunity of adding the neighbouring district of Rudok to his kingdom. Flushed with success, Singgé Namgyal next determined to attack Lhása itself; but when he had advanced as far as *Sri Kirkir*,† he was met by a deputation from the people of the country, headed by *Deba-Changpa*, with several mule-loads of gold, silver, tea, and other articles as a peace-offering. On receipt of this present, Singgé Namgyal consented to evacuate the Lhásan territory. Accordingly he fell back to Lomostang,‡ and afterwards took possession of the districts of *Purang*, *Gugé*, *Zanskar*, *Spiti*, *Purik*, *Mangyumla*, *Sedakh*, and *Shakyamcho*.§

ambitious Grand Lama *Navang-Lozang* had conquered the whole of Tibet.

* *Khar-bu.* There are two places of this name in Ladák, the larger of which is situated on the left bank of the Kanji river. The other stands on the right bank of the Drás river. The battle must have been fought at the former place, because it is on the high road from Balti to Lé, whereas the Kharbu of Drás is out of the way.

† *Shi-ri-Kyir-kyir.* This means a "winding or whirling stream," and is probably the river *Sekor* of our maps, which joins the *Tsangpo* about half-way between Lé and Lhása. *Kyir-kyir*, "circular," is evidently the same word as the Latin *circulus*, and the Greek κυκλος.

‡ This is probably the Stang of our maps on the right bank of the Sutluj, and on the high road between Spiti and Garo.

§ *Purang*, a district of Ngári to the west and south of the Mánasarovar lake, and the *Pruang* of Capt. H. Strachey's map. *Gu-gé* is also a district of *Ngári* to the west of *Purang;* its chief places are Chaprang and Toling. The districts of Zanskar and Spiti are well known. *Pu-rig* lies upon the Kanji and Waká rivers, to the eastward of Suru; its chief places are Kharbu and Paskyum. *Mang-yum-la* is certainly the district

Singgé Namgyal had three sons, named *Deldan Namgyal*, *Indra Namgyal*, and *Tenchhog Namgyal*, amongst whom, by the advice of the lama *Thunshak*,* he divided his dominions. To Deldan he gave *Ladák*, *Purik*, *Rudok*, and *Mangyum*, as far as *Dáh*, on the Indus; to Indra he gave the district of *Gugé;* and to Tenchhog he gave *Spiti* and *Zanskar*. By this division of his territories the province of Ngári was finally alienated from Ladák, and was soon after lost by the family of Indra Namgyal to the Lhásan authorities.† Singgé Namgyal reigned from about A.D. 1620 to 1670.

Singgé Namgyal was succeeded by his son Deldan Namgyal in the government of Ladák, Rudok, and the

of Katakshe or *Mang-khar*, on the Indus, which still includes the large village of *Dah*. Katakshe usually belonged to Balti. *Sed-kha* and *Shag-kyar-r Gyam-chho* are unknown to me.

* *Thun-shags;* in Sanskrit *Amsgha Siddha*.

† It is to this petty state that Moorcroft alludes when he says that "Chanthan was formerly subject to independent princes, but their authority gradually merged into the supremacy of the chief pontiff at Lhása." (Travels, I. p. 364.) According to the information obtained by my brother, Capt. J. D. Cunningham (see Journal As. Soc. Bengal, XIII. p. 231), it would appear that the Gyalpo of Gugé was killed in a war with the Ladákis. The invaders were however expelled by a force from Lhása, which the last chief had asked for, and the Lhásan authorities afterwards retained the province in their own hands. A treaty was then formed with the ruler of Ladák, who married the daughter of the Lhásan commander, and received the district of Spiti as the bride's dowry. This is stated to have taken place about the beginning of the last century, or about A.D. 1720, that is, some fifty or sixty years after the division of his territories by Singgé Namgyal, and the foundation of the principality of Gugé by his son Indra Namgyal. As the district of Spiti is said to have belonged to Gugé, the family of Then-chhog Namgyal must have been dispossessed by that of Indra Namgyal some time beforehand. According to the above account also, the Spiti district must have been alienated from the kingdom of Ladák from about A.D. 1660 to 1720, when it was reconquered by the Ladáki ruler Delek Namgyal.

western districts of Purik, Suru, and Hembabs. He began his reign with a display of great zeal in the cause of religion by constructing a large image of gold and silver in the village of Shé.* He also built a lofty tomb with a pinnacle of gold and silver, to the memory of his father, and constructed a wall around the monument of his mother. He erected temples at Zanskar, Pushbuz, and Tumnuz, each at a cost of Rs. 10,000. In the fort of Lé, also, he set up an image of Chandra,† and appointed several priests for the performance of daily worship. In the same place too he consecrated a silver image of Chanrazik, the god of the dead.‡

The appointment of *Shakya-gya-cho* to the post of chief minister having produced a revolt in the district of Purik, the minister with a large force marched in person to Kharbu, where, having seized the principal officers, he returned to Lé and imprisoned them in the fort of Hemis. About a year afterwards the people of Chigtan, Shako, and Sôd,§ rebelled against the government. The minister was again despatched to quell the disturbance, which he effected without any difficulty; and *Thai Sultán*, the author of the rebellion, being

* This image, which still exists at Shé, has now lost all its gilding. It is a colossal copper figure of *Shakya Thubba*, or Shakya in a *squatting* posture. *Shé* is on the right bank of the Indus, a few miles above Lé.

† *lCham-hdré.* Moorcroft calls this image by the name of *Chamba* (*Byams-pa*, the "Clement"), but his description of it differs somewhat from the paintings of Chamba which I possess. (See Moorcroft's Travels, I. p. 343.)

‡ *Spyan-ras-rigs*, pronounced *Chan-razik.* It is equivalent to the Sanscrit *Avalokita* or *Avalokiteswara*, the "seen." This image is also described by Moorcroft, and most accurately (I. p. 342).

§ *Chigtan*, *Sha-rkar* or *Shako*, in the Suru valley. *Sôd*, near Paskyum in Purik.

seized at the village of Karchu,* was sent as a prisoner to Lé.

After this the minister with a large army invaded the district of Khapalor, one of the dependencies of Balti. On his way he took possession of the district of Chhorbat; and at Thorchekhar, near Khapolor, he received the submission of Hatim Khán, Sultán Khán, and Ali Khán, the chiefs of the district.† But the chiefs of Karchu and Balti having obtained aid from the Mahomedan governor of Kashmir, advanced against the invaders, whom they encountered at Sariru.‡ The Ladákis, under their leader *Parak Namgyal*, gained a signal victory; the Kashmiris having lost many of their officers as well as their colours and drums. In consequence of this victory, the chiefs of Karchu and Balti tendered their submission, and became tributary to Ladák.

But this success was shortly followed by an alarming invasion of Sokpos.§ Under their leaders, named *Galdan Chobar Jongar* and *Lobzang Sherab*,‖ these marauders routed the Ladáki troops at *Dalang-*

* This place is the chief town of the Suru district. It is the same as Moorcroft's Lang-kartsé.

† *Kha-po-lor* and *hChhor-hBad* are both upon the Sháyak river, and were both dependencies of Balti until the Dogra conquest in 1840. *Tho-rche-mKhar* is perhaps the *Hajacha* of Vigne's map, which lies immediately to the eastward of Khapolor. Hatim Khan was the chief of Pargutu, and Ali Khan of Keris.

‡ *Sa-ri-ru*, position unknown.

§ *Sog-po*, the people of the *Sog* tribe. They are the *Sákas* of the Hindus, the Σακαι and Σαγαραυκαι of the Greeks, and the *Mogals* of the present day, who, under the celebrated Janghez Khan, only a few centuries ago, spread terror throughout Europe. Their country is called *Sog-yul*, and also *Li-yul*, or Brass-land.

‖ *dGah-ldan-Chho-dBar*, with the affix of *hJong-hGar*. The name of the other leader was *bLo-bzang-She-rab*.

Kharmar, and pursued them as far as *Lung-Khung;* but being afterwards worsted by the Ladákis, they retired to their own country. In the following year, however, they again invaded Ladák, and having again defeated the Gyalpo's troops, at *Balaskya*, they took possession of the village of *Chang-la.** Here they were joined by the people of Gugé, and having advanced as far as Sakti, near the pass of Chang-la, they halted while the Ladáki troops retreated upon Lé. This took place in the year of *Chhumo-phag-lo*, or the "water-hog," the sixtieth year of the Tibetan cycle, equivalent to A.D. 1685-86.

After this the Sokpos took possession of the whole country as far as Nyimo,† excepting only the forts of Tashigang, Baku, and Chimra.‡ Having failed in an attempt upon the fort of Tumnuz, they encamped at Bazgo,§ where they halted for six months. During that time repeated skirmishes took place between the two armies; and the Sokpo chief, Galdan Jongar, tried in vain to destroy a bridge by throwing stones upon it. These events occurred in the year of *Shingpho-byi-lo*,‖

* *Byang-la*, pronounced *Chang-la.* From this and the following mention of the village of Sakti, it appears that the Sokpos invaded Ladák from the side of Ruthog (or Rudok) by the Chang-la pass. The Sakti fort was in fact dismantled by the Sokpos. (See Moorcroft, I. p. 427.)

† *Nyi-mo*, on the right bank of the Indus, about twenty miles below Lé.

‡ Chimra is most probably the village of *Chum-ri*, at the junction of the Chang-la rivulet with the Indus.

§ *Baz-go*, a large village on the right bank of the Indus, about twenty-four miles below Lé.

‖ In the original this date is written *Shing-pho-khyi-lo*, or the "wood-dog-year," which is the eleventh of the Tibetan cycle, and equivalent to either A.D. 1637 or 1697, neither of which is admissible. I have

or the "wood-mouse," the first year of the Tibetan cycle, which is equivalent to A.D. 1686-87.

The Ladákis now implored the aid of the Muhammadan governor of Kashmir, who, with the permission of Aurang Shah (the emperor Aurangzeb), despatched a force of 600,000 men (most probably about 6,000) under Nawáb Fateh Khán, Murid Khán, Lashkar Khán, Kahgán Sultán Khán, Yahia Khán, and Jahángir Khán, to the assistance of the Gyalpo. They crossed the Indus at *Khallach,** by two wooden bridges; and at *Thanskya-tanag* they encountered and completely defeated the Sokpos. The Musulmáns pursued them as far as *Pitak,*† and having taken that fort, they put the garrison to death, whilst the main body of the Sokpos took refuge in the fort of Lé. After this the invaders having agreed to quit Ladák, retired to Kashún, on which the Mahomedans returned to Kashmir, accompanied by *Jig-bal Namgyal,* the younger son of the Gyalpo. This happened in the year of *Shingmo-lang-lo,* or "the wood-ox," which is the second of the Tibetan cycle, and equivalent to A.D. 1687-88.

In the following year, however, the Sokpos again invaded Ladák, and destroyed the fort of Lé. But, afterwards, through the mediation of a lama, named *Brug-pa-Pham-Bangpo,* the Sokpos agreed to retire on receiving possession of the district of Rudok. A large stone was then set up as a permanent boundary between

therefore made a slight correction by changing *khyi* to *byi,* which is fully justified by its tallying with the other recorded dates.

* *Khal-lach.* The principal bridge across the Indus, on the high road from Kashmir to Lé, is still at this place.

† *Pi-tag,* a small rock-fort on the right bank of the Indus, only four miles from Lé.

the two countries, the line of demarcation being drawn from the village of *Dechhog* to the hill of *Karbonas*.

This invasion of Ladák by the Sokpos is thus related by Moorcroft.* "About a century and a half ago the Kalmak Tartars invaded Ladák and occupied Lé, and the Raja flew to Kashmir and implored the aid of Ibrahim Khan, the governor of that province in the reign of Aurangzeb. With the permission of the emperor, and on the condition that the Raja became a Musalmán, Ibrahim Khan led a body of troops into Ladák, expelled the Tartars, and replaced the Raja on the throne by the title of Akabal Mahmud, conformably to his new faith. A mosque was erected in Lé, which is still kept up. The son and successor of the Raja reverted to the national creed, and the apostasy was overlooked at Delhi in consideration of the encouragement given to Mahomedanism in the country, and a small annual tribute or present paid to the governor of Kashmir, as the representative of the emperor." A similar account is given by Mir Izzet Ullah,† who says, however, that the title given to the Raja was *Akabet* Mahmud Khan, and that "the Hakims at Kashmir still address the raja of Tibet by that designation." Izzet Ullah farther states that the Raja "coins the *Júd*‡ in the name of Mahmud Shah." This last fact seems to be conclusive of the Gyalpo's apostasy; and I may add that the Dogra soldiers always called the last Gyalpo by the name of Akabet Mahmud Khán. The people, however, both lamas and laymen, whom I interrogated upon this subject, stoutly denied that the Gyalpo had

* Travels, I. pp. 336, 337.

† Quarterly Oriental Magazine, No. V. p. 109.

‡ "Four *júds* make one rupee."—Izzet Ullah.

ever become a Musalmán, although they acknowledge that from that time Ladák had continued to pay tribute to the governors of Kashmir. The real truth no doubt is, that the chief made an open profession of the Muhammadan faith in the presence of the Musalmán troops at Lé; but after their retirement to Kashmir he naturally reverted to his own creed. It is probable that the Gyalpo's younger son, Jigbal, who accompanied the Musalmán troops on their return to Kashmir, may have become a Musalmán; and that the governor may have been satisfied with the real conversion of the son, and the permanent establishment of a masjid at Lé.*

Deldan Namgyal had several sons, one of whom, *Jigbal*, accompanied the Muhammadan army to Kashmir. Another, named *Banchak*, proceeded to Lhása with the Sokpos, at the request of their leader. Of a third, called *Thuptan*, nothing is related. A fourth, named *Delek*, succeeded his father, who abdicated in his favour, and afterwards resided in the fort of Stuklakté. The reign of Deldan Namgyal probably extended from A.D. 1670 to 1705.

Delek Namgyal married the princess, or Gyalmo, of Lomostang, by whom he had five sons: 1st, *Nyima;* 2nd, *Navang;* 3rd, *Dechok;* 4th, *Choltan-grub;* and 5th, *Chortan.*† Delek Gyalpo probably reigned from A.D. 1705 to 1740. It was during his reign that the district of Spiti was re-annexed to the kingdom; and it was

* Vigne (II. p. 253) says that "the name of the first Ali Sher Khan, or Shah Murad, is still to be seen upon a mosque at Lé." Moorcroft, however (I. p. 337), refers the building of the masjid to the period of the Gyalpo's conversion, and so does Izzet Ullah.

† These names are written thus: 1st, *Nyi-ma;* 2nd, *Nga-dVang;* 3rd, *bDe-skyong;* 4th, *Chho-dVal-ton-grub;* 5th, *Chho-rtan.*

perhaps towards the end of his reign, or more probably in the beginning of his successor's reign, that Ladák was invaded and conquered by Murád, the chief of Balti,* who reigned from about A.D. 1720 to 1750.

From that time down to A.D. 1834, when the country was conquered by the Dogras under Zoráwar Sing, the general of Raja Guláb Sing of Jammu, the history, as related to me, was uninteresting. I find, however, that Vigne† mentions an invasion of Balti by an army of Ladákis, during the reign of Ali Sher, the father of Ahmed Shah, the last chief of Balti. The invaders were defeated and obliged to surrender. As this must have happened not more than twenty or twenty-five years prior to Moorcroft's visit to Ladák, it is strange that he makes no mention of it. Vigne's account is farther confirmed by the existence of a tree, which was pointed out to him on the Ladáki frontier near Khallach on the Indus, which was said to have grown from a stick planted there by Ali Sher Khan on his return from a victory in Ladák.‡

When Moorcroft visited Ladák in 1822, the Gyalpo paid an annual tribute to the governor of Kashmir, with which Ranjit Sing was probably contented. But the recent conquest of Kashmir, and the threats of the Sikh governor, had even then alarmed the Gyalpo, who made a tender of his allegiance§ to the British Government, which, unfortunately for the prosperity of

* Vigne's Kashmir, II. p. 253. † Kashmir, II. p. 254.

‡ Kashmir, II. p. 254. It is possible, however, that this may refer to the conquest of Ladák by the first Ali Sher Khán.

§ Moorcroft's Travels, I. p. 420. I agree with Professor Wilson, Preface, p. xxxix, that "a friendly footing in Ladák would be highly favourable for establishing a beneficial trade with Tartary and Turkistan."

Ladák and the commerce of British India, was refused. From that time the Gyalpo lived in continual apprehension of an invasion of his territory by the Sikhs from Kashmir; but the governors of that district were too frequently changed, and too closely watched by the emissaries of the Jammu brothers, to be able to carry out such a design, even if they had formed it. For Raja Dhyán Sing, who was omnipotent in the Sikh durbar, was resolved that no one but his elder brother Raja Guláb Sing should obtain possession of Ladák and Balti. The invasion of these countries was therefore postponed until Guláb Sing had consolidated his power in his newly-acquired territory of Káshtwár,* which he had lately wrested from its hereditary chief.† Accordingly, in 1834, when the power of the Jammu brothers had been extended over all the hill states lying between the Jehlam and the Ravi, excepting only Kashmir, a large body of Dogra troops under the Vazir Zoráwar Sing invaded Ladák from the Káshtwár valley. The following account of this invasion was kindly dictated, at my request, by Mehta Basti Ram,‡ now governor of Lé, who was one of the principal officers of the expedition. As an authentic record of an interesting event, of which no other account exists to my knowledge, I should have

* *Káshtavára*, abounding in wood.

† The representative of this family is now a Christian residing at Simla. He formerly lived at Ludiana, where he was converted by the American missionaries.

‡ Mehta Basti Ram is a Hindu rajput of Káshtwár. He was the governor of Takla-khar, or Takla-kot, near the source of the Sarju or Ghágra river, at the time of Zoráwar Sing's defeat and death, when he made his escape to the British provinces of Almora. He speaks in high terms of the kindness shown to him by the British resident, Mr. Lushington.

preferred giving the narrative almost literally, but I found that in this shape it would entail the insertion of too many foot-notes, which would have completely distracted the attention of the reader. I have therefore re-written the account entirely, and have given the Tibetan names, which my knowledge of the localities enabled me to do without much difficulty. The narrative was of course dictated in the first person, for which I have throughout substituted the name of "Dogra" and "the Dogra troops."

II.—CONQUEST OF LADÁK BY THE DOGRAS.

1. The chief officers engaged in this expedition under the Vazir Zoráwar Sing, were, 1st, Mia Rai Sing; 2nd, Mehta Basti Rám; 3rd, Mirza Rasul Beg; 4th, Rána Zálim Sing; 5th, Singhé Mankotiah; 6th, Mian Tuta; 7th, Sirdar Uttam Sing; and 8th, Vazir Khojah Bhunjah.

2. The Dogra troops marched from Káshtwár, and entered the Ladák territory by the pass at the head of the Suru valley,* where, on the 16th of August, 1834, they were opposed by the Boti leader Mangal, at the head of 5,000 men. The Dogras advanced to the attack up a hill, which was obstinately defended for a whole day, and at last succeeded in dislodging the Ladákis with a loss of only six or seven killed, and five or six wounded; whilst the enemy lost thirty killed, and as many wounded. They encamped on the north side of the hill for the night, and on the next morning marched to Suru, where they halted for eight days. During that time the Vazir

* This pass was described to me as being extremely easy on the northern side, but very steep and difficult on the south.

prohibited his troops from cutting the corn, which was then ripe, and his politic conduct was rewarded by the immediate submission of the zamindars, who came over to him in a body, and placed themselves under his protection. The Vazir then built a small fort,* which he occupied for a month. He next advanced to *Shakhar*,† where there was a fort belonging to Thai Sultán, and having reinstated the zamindars of Janguri and Shakhar in their villages, he made a summary settlement of the district by imposing a tax of four rupees upon each house.

3. Leaving thirty-five men in the fort and ten men over the bridge, the Dogras advanced by *Langkarchu* ‡ and *Manji* to the bridge of Paskyum, where they were again opposed by the Ladákis. The struggle was desultory and protracted, the Dogras losing only seven killed, while the Botis had fifty or sixty killed, and a greater number wounded. By a skilful manœuvre the Ladákis effected their retreat across the bridge, § which they then broke down. On the following day, however, the Dogras managed to cross the river on inflated skins without opposition; on which the chief of the place abandoned Paskyum, and fled to the fort of Sôd, ‖ where, with the zamindars of the district, he determined to hold out.

* This is the fort in Vigne's map called "Kilah Suru Kurri," belonging to Guláb Sing.

† *Shá-mKhar*, the fort of *Sha*.

‡ The Lang-kartse of Moorcroft. The true name I believe is "*Lung-karj-chu*," or the "valley of the Karj river." The bridge here mentioned is that which was crossed by Moorcroft on his journey to Drás.

§ The Waká-chu is not fordable at Paskyum, and the bridge is within musket-range of the fort, and of numbers of houses on the northern bank of the stream.

‖ *Sôd*, the Soth of Moorcroft, who mentions an interview that he had with the Raja at Paskyum.

4. The Dogras advanced towards the place and raised a battery against it; but after ten days' firing nothing had been effected, although they had lost forty men in killed and wounded. The Vazir, who had remained behind at Paskyum, then ordered Mehta Basti Rám, with a party of 500 men, to make a vigorous assault upon the place. Accordingly, early the next morning, whilst it was still dark, the attack was begun by a discharge from the battery, under cover of which the Dogras advanced rapidly to the assault. By daybreak they had gained possession of the place, and had captured the Gyalpo. Altogether the number of prisoners taken at Paskyum and at Sôd amounted to 6,000 men. A whole month was then wasted in fruitless negotiations with the zamindars of the district, who would not agree to the terms of settlement proposed by the Vazir.

5. In the mean time Akabat Mahmúd Khan, the Gyalpo of Ladák, with the *Banka Kahlan* * and four chiefs, named Gapaju, Dorje Namgyal, Chang or Chovang Nabdan,† the Kahlon of Bazgo, and Rahim Khan, of Chachot, accompanied by a force of about 22,000 men, arrived at Mulbil. From thence they despatched envoys to the camp, who at first talked boldly, and tried to frighten the Dogras, but they afterwards

* *bKah-bLon*, the prime minister; but the term is also applied to the chief men of all the districts. At this time the Kahlon of Chimra was the prime minister.

† This man accompanied the unfortunate expedition of Zoráwar Sing into the Lhásan territory. After the Vazir's death he was made prisoner and carried to Lhása, where he is said to be now kept in rigorous confinement. His wife, a buxom-looking dame, who manages the estate of Bazgo, informed me that she had sent several persons to Lhása, not one of whom had been able to communicate with her husband.

declared their readiness to agree to honourable terms, and proposed that some respectable and confidential agents should be sent back with them to treat with their chiefs regarding the terms of accommodation. To this the Vazir consented, and after having feasted the envoys and placed turbans on their heads, he deputed Mehta Basti Rám, with some other Dogra officers and a guard of 500 matchlock-men, to accompany them. When the men were ready to start, the Vazir was requested not to send so large a party, as their number would be more likely to alarm than to pacify the minds of their countrymen. Accordingly only five men, with two respectable zamindars, named Gola and Nanda, were sent with the envoys. On their arrival in the Ladáki camp, these men were treacherously seized by the chiefs, and despatched under a guard of 500 men to the bridge of Darkech. One of the men, however, a Suwar, named Ratan Sing, managed to escape, and returned to the Dogra camp. In the mean time Banka Kahlon, by a circuitous route, attacked the Dogras in their rear, and made many prisoners, who were thrown bound into the river in sight of their comrades. On this the Vazir, seeing the danger of his situation, ordered a retreat, which with some difficulty was effected to Lang-Karchu, in the Suru valley, to the fort of Thai Sultan. There the Dogras remained unmolested for four months, procuring a precarious subsistence by plunder alone.

6. At the end of that time Banka Kahlon with his 22,000 men advanced towards Langkarchu; but the Vazir, having received intelligence of their movements, despatched a party of 100 men to oppose them, when they were within one kos (one mile and a half) of the place. Now the straggling manner in which the Dogras

were obliged to wade through the snow, and the unsoldier-like way in which their tents were scattered over the open country completely deceived the Ladákis as to the real number of their enemies. They were, besides, quite exhausted with their long and fatiguing march through the snow; and therefore, instead of attacking the Dogras at once, they halted for a consultation, which ended in the whole body sitting down to prepare their evening meal of tea and wheaten flour. On seeing this the Dogras attacked them with their swords, and after five or six were killed on each side, and several were wounded, Banka Kahlon and the other Ladáki leaders became alarmed, and fled with numbers of their men. The remainder of the Dogras, who had hitherto held aloof, now rushed to the attack, and completed the rout of the Botis; 400 Ladákis, in attempting to escape along the bank of the river, were overwhelmed by the fall of a snow-bed, and 1,200, who had been concealed behind a hill, were made prisoners, along with Moru Tádsi,* the Káhlon of Bazgo, and his son Gyurmed.† The Dogras lost three of their leaders, namely, Uttam Vazir, Hazru Vazir of Una, and Surtu Rana, with twenty men, and between fifty and sixty wounded.

7. After this victory the Dogras were again enabled to advance to Paskyum by making use of their prisoners for the carriage of their baggage. From thence they marched by Shergol to Mulbil, where they halted for fifteen days, and then proceeded by Kharbu to Lama-

* *Mo-ru-rTá-rDsi*, or *Moru*, master of the horse. Vigne (Kashmir, II. p. 352) calls him Marut Tanzin. He was the Káhlon of Chimra, a district to the S.E. of Lé, on the Rudok road. See Moorcroft's Travels, I. p. 425.

† *hGyur-med*, pronounced *Yurmed* in Great Tibet.

Yurru, where they were met by an envoy with a letter from Sultán Akabat Mahmud Khán,* suing for peace. Eight months,† he said, had now elapsed in the vain struggle for independence, and that, if the Vazir would promise faithfully that he should not be seized, he would himself come to treat about the terms of peace. To this the Vazir at once assented, adding that the king need not be under any alarm, as the Dogras wanted nothing more than the payment of a regular tribute to their master, Maharaja Guláb Sing. On this the Gyalpo advanced to Bazgo, and intimated his wish to have an interview, provided the Vazir would not bring a large body of men with him. Accordingly the Vazir, Zoráwar Sing, with Mehta Basti Rám and 100 men, waited upon the Gyalpo, whom they found encamped upon the plain of Bazgo,‡ with a party of 2,000 men. The Gyalpo received the Vazir kindly, and begged that he would move his camp to Bazgo, which was soon afterwards done.

8. When ten days had elapsed, the King wished the Vazir to accompany him to Lé, but with only a small party, lest the inhabitants should become alarmed. Zoráwar Sing assented, and started for Lé with only 100 men. Soon after their arrival the Vazir waited upon the Gyalpo, and was preparing to make his usual offering

* This is the name by which the Dogras always knew this chief. They had received it from the Muhammadans of Káshtwar, who of course used no other name for the descendant of one who was said to have been converted. The Gyalpo's real name was Tonduk Namgyal.

† As the advance was made in the middle of August, 1834, the defeat of the Ladákis must therefore have taken place in the middle of April, 1835. Vigne (II. p. 353) says the spring of 1835.

‡ Bazgo is a very picturesque place situate on the right bank of the Indus, twenty miles below Lé.

of a *Sadka* of Rs. 100 * to the Gyalpo's son, named Chang-raphtan, then only seventeen years of age, when the prince, mistaking the action either for an insult or for treachery, drew his sword. His followers did the same, and the Dogras also drew their swords. On this the Gyalpo fell upon his knees and clasped the Vazir's hands, while the prince and his followers retired into the fort of Lé. Some horsemen carried the intelligence to the Dogra camp at Bazgo, when 5,000 men started at once for Lé, which they reached the next morning.

9. For four months † the Vazir remained at Lé, when it was finally arranged that the Gyalpo should pay Rs. 50,000 for the expenses of the war, and a yearly tribute of Rs. 20,000. Of the first, a sum of Rs. 37,000 was paid at once, partly in cash and partly in jewels. The balance the Gyalpo promised to pay in two instalments, the first of Rs. 6,000 at the end of one month, and the second of Rs. 7,000 at the end of four months. The Vazir then fell back to Lama Yurru.

10. At this place he heard that the chief of Sod had recaptured his fort, and had put to death the Dogra garrison of fifty-five men. By forced marches the Dogras reached Sod; but the enemy having dispersed, they halted there for thirteen days. Thence they marched thirty-seven and a half miles ‡ in two days to Suru, where they surprised the Botis by a night attack. Thirteen of the enemy were taken prisoners and hanged

* A bag of money waved around the head by the person who presents it.

† As the march from Suru to Lé, with ten days' halt at Bazgo, must have occupied nearly a whole month, the Vazir could not have left Lé until the middle of October, 1835.

‡ Twenty-five *kos*, each kos being as nearly as possible one mile and a half.

upon trees; while by a promise of fifty rupees for every head the Dogras obtained 200 prisoners, who were at once beheaded. After this the zamindars of the district tendered their submission.

11. Here it was discovered that this rebellion had been excited by Mihan Sing, the Sikh governor of Kashmir, who had even sent a servant of his own, named Jala Sing Gopi, with fifty men, to the assistance of the chiefs of Suru and Sod.

12. Leaving Suru the Vazir marched in ten days to Jasku * or Zanskar, the chief of which, together with all the zamindars, waited upon him, and agreed to pay a tax of three rupees and a half for every house.

13. Intelligence now arrived that an insurrection had broken out in Lé; that the Gyalpo, at the instigation of Mihan Sing, the Sikh governor of Kashmir, had closed the roads to the merchants;† that he had confiscated the property of Moru Tâdsi and the Banka Káhlon, and that he had imprisoned and tortured his Munshi Daya Ram, on suspicion of his being a partisan of the Dogras. This news distressed the Vazir very much; and his anxiety was further increased by the difficulty of finding a guide, who would conduct him by the direct route to Lé, upon which he had determined to march at once. Every one professed entire ignorance of any direct route, until at length a man named

* *Zangs-mKar*, which the Dogras invariably call *Jasku*, and which is the *Zanskar* of our maps.

† Mihan Sing's intention was undoubtedly to force the whole trade through Kashmir, which otherwise, owing to the occupation of Ladák by the Dogras, would have been turned into other channels leading through Káshtwár, and the Dogra territories dependent upon Jamu to India. The amount of duties upon merchandise in transit through Kashmir had already fallen off from this cause.

Midphi Sata offered his services, to whom the Vazir gave a present of a pair of golden bracelets, worth Rs. 500, besides two rupees a day, and the promise of the district of Zanskar in perpetuity.

14. With twelve seers of wheaten flour, and a bag of barley upon each horse, the party, under the direction of their guide, marching from forty-five to sixty miles * a day, in ten days reached the village of Tsumur,† where they most unexpectedly heard that the wife and son of the Gyalpo were then residing. A party of 500 horsemen was sent forward to capture them; but they received early intelligence of the movement, and fled to Lé. On this the Gyalpo waited upon the Vazir at Chachot,‡ and expressed his sorrow and contrition for what had occurred. The Vazir demanded why he had so shamefully broken his promises, and added, "Although

* From thirty to forty kos a day; but this is impossible in such a country. The probable length of each day's march cannot be estimated at more than thirty miles, which would give a total distance of 300 miles in ten days. The exaggeration, however, is natural to men in such circumstances. This march must have taken place in the end of November, 1835, at a season of the year when the winter's snow has already set in throughout Ladák, and when all the higher passes are finally closed. Their route was therefore most probably up the Zanskar river, and over the Lunga Lách and Thung-Lung passes to the Indus below Gya. By this route they would have travelled about 300 miles. I know of no other route that would be passable in November. The direct route to Gya from Zanskar is open but for a few months, and that which lies down the course of the Zanskar river, and over the Singé Lá to Lama Yurru, is closed in October. Besides which, the distance by either of these routes would not have been even 150 miles.

† This is no doubt the large village of *Chumri* or *Chimra*, on the right bank of the Indus, opposite to Marchalang, and on the high road leading to Rudok. This position must have been chosen by the raja's family for the convenience of escape into the Chinese district of Rudok.

‡ Chachot is on the left bank of the Indus, between Chumri and Lé. It is the Chushut of Moorcroft.

we conquered your country with 10,000 men, we did not place a single man of our own over any of your districts, but left you in sole charge of the whole kingdom." The Gyalpo was much ashamed, and promised to be faithful for the future.

15. On the next day the Dogra troops, accompanied by the Gyalpo, proceeded to Lé, where the Vazir demanded the balance of the tribute, amounting to Rs. 13,000, besides the additional expenses of the army. To pay the first, the Vazir was obliged to take the property of the royal ladies; and in lieu of the second, the Káhlon, Achu Ganpu, offered tea and wool, gold and silver utensils, and other goods, which were accepted. The government of the country was then bestowed upon Moru-pa Tâdsi, the Káhlon of Banka, while the Gyalpo was allowed a jaghir.* A fort was erected outside the city of Lé, and Dalel Sing was appointed thanadar of the place with a body of 300 men. After this Zoráwar Sing proceeded to Jammu, taking with him the son of Moru Tâdsi, and some other respectable men, as hostages for the good behaviour of the new king.†

16. Before leaving Lé, the Vazir had ordered Lakpat Rai‡ and Basti Ram to proceed against Baldé.§ Ac-

* This was the large village of Tok, on the left bank of the Indus, opposite to Lé. It is still held by the Gyalpo's grandson, although three-fourths of the perquisites formerly attached to it have been resumed.

† This must have taken place in the spring of 1836, according to the narrative, soon after which Vigne appears to have visited Lé, where he found that the new king, called "Marut Tanzin," was installed, while the old king "was living at Tok, over the river, opposite to Lé."—Vigne's Kashmir, II. p. 354.

‡ Lakpat Rai was the governor of Kashmir in 1846, and was killed in the early part of the rebellion of Shekh Imám-ud-din.

§ Baldé or Paldér, the Phaldam of Moorcroft, is the chief place in Zanskar.

cordingly they marched with fifteen hundred foot-soldiers by the Zanskar road to Baldé, where they were opposed by Budhi Sing Mithania, the chief of the district. Victory declared for the Dogras, with a loss of eighteen or twenty men killed on their side, and about twenty or twenty-five on that of the enemy. After a halt of seventeen days, they proceeded towards Jammu, leaving a garrison of twenty men in the fort of Chatrgarh.*

17. Maharaja Guláb Sing and the Mia† were both very much displeased with the Vazir Zoráwar Sing for having made over the country to Moru Tâdsi, who had no claim to it. The Vazir replied that Moru Tâdsi belonged to the royal family of Ladák; but that since his elevation was displeasing to the Maharaja, he would depose him on his return to Lé. One year after this, news was brought that the new king had revolted, that he had killed the thanadar of Baldé and his twenty men, that twenty others had been made prisoners; and that the Dogra troops throughout the country were beleaguered in their different forts.

18. On hearing this, the Vazir started at once with a body of three thousand infantry, and in two months reached the district of Baldé; but owing to the swollen state of the river he was unable to accomplish anything for two months more.‡ At the end of that time, when the river had become passable, the Dogras attacked the

* Chatrgarh is on the right bank of the Chanáb river.

† Uttam Sing, the eldest son of Guláb Sing, a fine soldier-like young man, was killed at Lahor, along with No Nihál Sing, by the falling of a gateway.

‡ The swollen state of the river points to the months of July and August. The capture was, therefore, most probably made in September.

fort of Chatrgarh, which they carried by storm with a loss of fifteen men on their own side, and of twenty on that of the enemy. Some twenty or thirty prisoners that were taken, had their ears and noses cut off, which frightened the people so much that they immediately tendered their submission.

19. Leaving a garrison in the fort of Chatrgarh, the Vazir again marched into Zanskar over the hills.* On this march twenty-five men died from the severe cold, and ten men lost their feet and hands in the snow.† On reaching Zanskar the Dogras found that the people had fled; but during a halt of two months everything was arranged satisfactorily. After that, Rai Sing and Mia Tota, with about 1,000 men, advanced towards Lé, on which Moru Tâdsi, the new Gyalpo, who was formerly Káhlon of Banka, fled with precipitation from the capital. Being closely pursued, he was nearly overtaken, when, by the resistance of some of the more trustworthy of his followers, he was enabled to continue his flight. He was at length captured at the village of Tábo,‡ in Spiti, after a loss of six or seven men on

* Their route lay over the high pass which leads from Chatrgarh to the Baldé district of Zanskar. This pass was crossed by Dr. Thomson, in June, 1848, who found the boiling point to be 180·3°, at a temperature considerably below freezing. The height of the pass must therefore approach very nearly to 19,000 feet. On the Zanskar side there was a glacier extending down to 14,500 feet. The loss of so many men by the frost is therefore quite credible.

† As the fort of Chatrgarh did not fall until September, the crossing of this pass could not have taken place until October, when, from its extreme height, it would of course have been covered with fresh snow.

‡ Tábo is on the left bank of the Spiti river, and within five miles (by the road) of the British frontier of Upper Kanáwar. The Banka Káhlon's intention was, no doubt, to cross the Spiti river by the Pog Jhula, which is only five miles from Tábo. In another hour, therefore, he would have been safe.

each side; on which he was taken back to Lé and imprisoned.

The old Gyalpo, Akabat Mahmud, and the new one, Moru Tâdsi, were both brought before the Vazir, who deposed the latter, and reinstated the former, upon the old terms of Rs. 23,000 yearly tribute, but with the stipulation that the expenses of the troops which occupied the country should also be defrayed by him.

The Vazir then again proceeded to Jammu, where he remained for a whole year,* after which he returned to Ladák with 5,000 men, for the purpose of seizing Moru Tâdsi, the Káhlon of Banka, and Chang Nabdan, the Káhlon of Bazgo, both of whom had been plotting against the Gyalpo Mahmud Khan.†

They had been in correspondence with Ahmed Shah of Balti, whom they wished to engage in a general rise against the Dogra authority. The Balti chief imprudently lent too willing an ear to their overtures, and by a subsequent act furnished the long-looked-for pretext for invasion, which Zoráwar Sing was but too glad to seize upon. Early in 1835 Ahmed Shah being dissatisfied with his eldest son Muhammed Shah, had formally disinherited him by the inauguration of his younger brother Muhammed Ali. On that occasion Muhammed Shah fled to the camp of Zoráwar Sing in Suru, and claimed his protection. This the wily Vazir readily granted; but not wishing to embroil himself with the chief of Balti while the campaign in Ladák was still before him, he contented himself with giving promises

* From different statements in the narrative, Zoráwar Sing's residence at Jammu must have been during the latter half of 1838 and the beginning of 1839.

† Basti Ram's narrative ends here. The remainder of this history has been compiled from other information.

of future assistance to the Balti prince. After a time the prince returned to his father; but the reconciliation could not have been very cordial, for early in 1840 the prince fled to Lé, and sought refuge with the Gyalpo, whom he believed to be a puppet of the Dogra chief. The real authority was not, however, in the Gyalpo's hands, but in those of his two ministers, the Káhlon of Banka and the Káhlon of Bazgo; and as they were anxious to have Ahmed Shah on their side during their intended outbreak against the Dogra authority, they suggested to him the propriety of sending a party to seize his son, to which no resistance would be offered. Ahmed Shah at once agreed to this proposal, and a small party of fifty men was allowed to carry off the Balti prince to Lé.

III.—CONQUEST OF BALTI.

When Zoráwar Sing arrived in Zanskar and heard of the flight of Muhammed Shah, he sent strict orders that the prince should be treated with kindness and respect, intending, perhaps, to use him as a tool for the furtherance of his master's view upon Balti. But shortly after, when he heard of the prince's seizure by a party of Balti troops, he determined at once upon the conquest and annexation of that principality. A letter was, however, first addressed to Ahmed Shah, informing him that his son, who had sought the Maharaja's protection, had been forcibly carried off by a party who had invaded the Ladák territory, and that, unless the prince was sent back again, the Dogra troops would enter Balti and force his release. To this letter Ahmed Shah deigned no reply.

Accordingly, in the end of the year 1840, the Vazir assembled an army of 15,000 men, and a large body of Ladákis, for the conquest of Balti. Ahmed Shah also prepared himself for the struggle, and was joined by a large party of discontented Ladákis, who, after crossing the Indus, destroyed the bridge, to delay the advance of the Dogras. Zoráwar Sing was obliged, therefore, to march down the right bank of the river, which he followed steadily for twenty-five days, receiving the submission of the chiefs of Khatakchau and Khapolor, but without finding any place where the army could be crossed. He then detached Mia Nidhân Sing, with a body of 5,000 men, by way of Shigar, to look for a road, and to collect provisions, which had now become very scarce in the Dogra camp. But the Baltis kept a good look-out, and had early intelligence of this movement. Mia Nidhân Sing was allowed to advance unmolested for about fifteen miles, when his party were surrounded and attacked by thousands, and he himself was cut off with nearly the whole of his detachment.

About 400 men only managed to find their way back to the Dogra camp with the tale of their defeat. At the same time the winter set in with a heavy fall of snow,* and as provisions were extremely scarce, the Dogra troops became so much dispirited, that their discipline was seriously affected. With an impassable river in their front, and certain starvation both from cold and hunger, whether they retreated or remained in their present position, the majority of the troops paid no attention to orders, and of the few who still obeyed, none did so with alacrity.

* Vigne, II. p. 266, states that there are occasional winters of great severity.

The Dogra army had halted in this position for fifteen days, exposed to frost by night and to hunger by day. Many had sought shelter from the snow amongst the overhanging rocks, and there they sat listless and vacant, and utterly indifferent whether they should be cut off by the sword of the enemy, or be frozen to death by the cold. The Vazir saw the desperate state in which he was placed, and roused himself to discover a passage across the river, but after several hours' vain search he returned in the evening wearied and desponding. Upon this Mehta Basti Rám and some others, to the number of about forty, determined to make a last effort to extricate themselves from their difficulties. At midnight, with only one companion, Basti Rám examined the bank of the river for several miles, while his party kept up a smart fire upon the Botis on the opposite bank, to distract their attention. At length they discovered a place where the river was frozen over sufficiently thick to bear a man's weight, save about twenty feet in the middle, where the ice was thin. Then, sending for assistance, they cut down trees and placed them over the weaker parts of the ice, and by five o'clock in the morning the Indus was passable.

Intelligence was sent at once to the Vazir, by whose order this small party of forty men was the first to cross the Indus; but they had been so benumbed by their night's work, and by their previous exposure, that ten of them sank down exhausted, and afterwards lost their hands and feet, and eighteen others were unable to get through the snow. Basti Rám was then left with only twelve men, which the Botis perceiving, they moved to attack him; but, in the mean time, Zoráwar Sing, having roused a number of his men, pointed out to them that the river was passable, and that it had already been crossed by some of their more adventurous fellow-soldiers. Upon this a number of Dogras advanced gladly to the attack. The Indus was rapidly passed, and the small party of daring men, after a smart fight, was safe. The Botis retreated, leaving 200 men dead on the field, and 100 men wounded. The Dogras lost only 25 killed, and 15 or 16 wounded in the action; but they had about 500 men more or less disabled by the loss of hand or foot during the exposure to the snow of the last few days.

The retreating Botis were pursued, and slaughtered for nine miles, as far as Marwan, where the victorious Dogras pitched their camp. The Vazir halted there for a few days to re-organize his troops, and to reward those who had distinguished themselves in the last action. To Mehta Basti Rám he gave Rs. 500 and a pair of gold bangles, and to thirty-two others of his party he gave similar presents of less value, to some Rs. 100, to some Rs. 50, and to others Rs. 40, according to their deserts.

Zoráwar Sing then advanced to Skardo, and after some desultory firing, the fort was surrendered by Ahmed Shah for want of water.* He was shortly afterwards deposed by Zoráwar Sing, who installed his eldest son Muhammed Shah in his room, on the promised payment of an annual tribute of Rs. 7,000. But the astute commander, who had profited by his experience in Ladák, would not leave this new conquest to the doubtful faith of a son of Ahmed Shah. A small garrison of trustworthy soldiers was placed in a new fort on the bank of the river, to confirm the faithfulness of the new king, and Ahmed Shah and his favourite son

* Ahmed Shah retired to the fort before Zoráwar's arrival, having first set fire to his own palace.

were carried off as prisoners to Ladák. In this campaign the invaders lost about 200 men, and the Botis about 300 men.

Previous to the conquest of Skardo, the old king of Ladák, Tonduk Namgyal (or Akabat Mahmud), had been accused of having intrigued with Ahmed Shah for a simultaneous and organized rising of the Tibetans of Ladák and Balti. He may, perhaps, have been wrongfully accused; but as his feelings must naturally have inclined him to think favourably of any enemy of the Dogras, it would have been impolitic to have left him behind, as the absence of the conquering troops might have tempted him to rebel. Zoráwar Sing therefore carried Tonduk Namgyal with him on his expedition against Skardo. The old man had outlived the downfall of his country; he had survived close personal restraint and bitter indignity; but when his last hope was cut off with the fall of Skardo, he gave way to despondency, and being attacked with small-pox, he died within a month after the annexation of Balti to the Jammu viceroyalty of the Sikh dominions. On the death of Akabat Mahmud, his grandson Jigmet Singgé Namgyal, a mere boy, was acknowledged as Gyalpo by Zoráwar Sing. The father of this lad, Prince Chovang (or Chang) Raphtan Namgyal, fled first to Hundar in Nubra, and afterwards to Spiti, on the deposal of Akabat Mahmud. In October, 1837, he reached Sarâhan, in Bisahar; and in April, 1838, he came to Kotgurh, where he resided until his death in 1839. He was then about twenty-one years of age. His wife, a daughter of the Káhlon Chovang Tandup, remained in Ladák with her young son Jigmet Singgé.

IV.—INVASION OF TIBET.

Elated with his success, Zoráwar Sing now threatened the neighbouring states, and even talked of invading Yárkand. But the Lhásan provinces of Rudok and Ngári were more accessible; and the unscrupulous conqueror revived the old claims of Ladák to those districts which had been alienated since the time of Singgé Namgyal. It was enough for him that the monasteries were known to possess vessels and instruments of gold and silver for the service of religion; and that the country produced the finest shawl-wool. The plunder of the first would enrich himself and his soldiers, and the acquisition of the latter would be highly pleasing to his master, as it would throw the whole trade in shawl-wool into the hands of the Jammu Raja.

In the month of May, 1841, with an army of 5,000 men, he advanced up the valley of the Indus, and plundered the monasteries of Hanlé and Tashigong. His troops penetrated to Rudok and Gáro, both of which submitted without striking a blow. The conqueror then passed the sources of the Indus, and established his head-quarters on the Sutluj at Tirthapuri, in Gugé, the principal place in the holy district of Lake Manasarovara. The whole country was now occupied by parties of Dogra and Ladáki soldiers. Basti Rám was stationed at Takla-Khar, on the Karnali or Gogra river, close to the frontiers of Kumaon and Népal. Rahim Khán, a half-blood Musalmán of Chachot, was placed over Spiti, while Ghulám Khán, his son-in-law, was employed in the congenial occupation of plundering the monasteries and temples. This work he executed with iconoclastic fury. The gold and the silver were reserved for his master; but the plastic images of clay, the books and the pictures, excited the religious bigotry of the Musalmán, and were indiscriminately destroyed.

The news of this invasion was speedily carried to Lhasa; and about the 7th of November, Zoráwar Sing first heard of the approach of a Chinese force. He at once detached a small party of 300 men, under Nono-Sungnam,* to oppose the advance of the Chinese; but the detachment was surrounded at Kar-dam-Khar, to the south of the Ráwan-Hrad lake, and almost cut to pieces. The Nono himself escaped, and was again detached on the 19th of November, with a larger force of 600 men, under the joint command of himself and Ghulam Khán; but this party was also surrounded and cut to pieces, and the leaders were both made prisoners.

Zoráwar Sing, still treating the Chinese with contempt, although they numbered about 10,000 men, or three times the strength of his own force, at once advanced from his position at Tirthapuri with the whole of his available troops. The two armies first met on the 10th December, and began a desultory fire at each other, which continued for three days. On the 12th Zoráwar Sing was struck in the shoulder by a ball, and as he fell from his horse the Chinese made a rush, and he was surrounded and slain. His troops were soon thrown into disorder, and fled on all sides, and his reserve of 600 men gave themselves up as prisoners. All the principal officers were captured, and out of the whole army, amounting with

* *No-no* is the title given to a younger brother. Nono Sungnam (or Sodnam) was the younger brother of Chang Raphtan, the Káhlon of Bazgo.

its camp-followers to 6,000 men, not more than 1,000 escaped alive, and of these some 700 were prisoners of war.

The Indian soldiers of Zoráwar Sing fought under very great disadvantages. The battle-field was upwards of 15,000 feet above the sea, and the time mid-winter, when even the day temperature never rises above the freezing-point, and the intense cold of night can only be borne by people well covered with sheepskins and surrounded by fires. For several nights the Indian troops had been exposed to all the bitterness of the climate. Many had lost the use of their fingers and toes; and all were more or less frost-bitten. The only fuel procurable was the Tibetan furze, which yields much more smoke than fire; and the more reckless soldiers had actually burned the stocks of their muskets to obtain a little temporary warmth. On the last fatal day not one-half of the men could handle their arms; and when a few fled, the rush became general. But death was waiting for them all; and the Chinese gave up the pursuit to secure their prisoners and plunder the dead, well knowing that the unrelenting frost would spare no one. A few men made their way to their brethren at Takla-Khar; but that garrison was so dismayed by the defeat, that they fled precipitately, even over the snowy mountain-range, near the head of the Kali river, into the British province of Kumaon. But even in this unopposed flight one-half of the men were killed by frost, and many of the remainder lost their fingers and toes. These few, and the prisoners, form the whole number that escaped with their lives.*

* In this very month, and in the same year, 1841, the British army, of about the same strength, was destroyed at Kabul.

Amongst the prisoners were Ahmed Shah, the ex-ruler of Skardo, and his favourite son Ali Muhammed, whom Zoráwar Sing was afraid to leave behind. The old man was treated with kindness, and even with distinction; but his heart was broken, and he pined and died in a few months. Other prisoners of distinction were, 1st, *Rai Sing*, Zoráwar's second in command, for whose liberation Maharaja Guláb Sing wished the Governor-General to intercede with the Lhásan authorities.

2nd. *Chang-Nabdan*, the Káhlon of Bazgo, whose wife, a buxom rosy-cheeked dame, came crying to me in 1847 at Nyimo, to do something for her husband's release. She had written every year to him by different persons, but had never got any reply, as no communications were allowed with the prisoners.

3rd. *Nono-Sungnam*, the brother of the last. These two brothers were considered particular friends of the invaders, and were therefore treated more harshly than the multitude.

4th. *Ghulám Khán*, the active plunderer and desecrator of the Buddhist temples, was tortured with hot irons. His flesh was picked off in small pieces with pincers; and, mangled and bleeding, he was left to learn how slow is the approach of death to a wretch lingering in agony.

During the winter the Chinese re-occupied the whole of the Gáro territory, and early in the spring of 1842 a body of about 3,000 men advanced into Ladák, and laid siege to the new fort at Lé.* They were joined by the boy-king Jigmet Namgyal, and the unwarlike Tibetans

* The people of Balti also rose; but they were soon reduced by a small force under Vazir Lakpat, who destroyed the fort and palace, to prevent the chance of another insurrection.

once more began to dream of independence. But after a short reign of six weeks, Dewán Hari Chand and Vazir Ratanu advanced with fresh troops, and the Tibetans were rudely awakened from their dream of liberty by the musketry of their old enemies, and the 3,000 would-be heroes who had talked of invading Kashmir, fled ignominiously towards Rudok. There they recovered themselves, and taking up a strong position, they determined to await the approach of winter, and then join in a general rising against the Indian invaders. But the simple Tibetan was no match for the wily Indian, and the Lhásan commander was soon made a prisoner by stratagem. The strong position of the Tibetans was shortly afterwards turned; and the Lhásan Vazir was glad to be permitted to retire on the single condition that the old boundary between Ladák and China should be re-established.

In the autumn of 1846, during the rebellion of Shekh Imámuddin in Kashmir, there was a slight disturbance in Zanskar, which was promptly repressed by the Vazir Basti Ram, who is now one of the confidential servants of Maharaja Guláb Sing. Since then the whole country has been quiet; and the passive Tibetans have yielded to a power which they find it unsafe to resist. The neighbouring districts of Gilgit and Chalás have been added to the Maharaja's kingdom; and the same prince, whose dominions only twenty years ago were limited to the petty state of Jammu, now rules undisputed master of Kashmir and Western Tibet, from the sources of the Shayok to the head of the Gilgit river.

XIII.—RELIGION.

I.—EARLY RELIGION OF TIBET.

THE religion of Tibet is a modified form of Indian Buddhism. This faith was first introduced into Ladák during the reign of Asoka, upwards of 2,000 years ago, when that great follower of Buddha was propagating his new religion with all the zealous ardour of a proselyte. In 241 B.C., at the close of the third synod, numerous missionary teachers were despatched to all the surrounding countries to spread the peaceful doctrines of Sakya Muni. The *Thero-Majjhantiko* (Sanskr. *Sthavira Madhyamika*) was deputed to Kashmir and Gandhara ;* and, upwards of six centuries afterwards, the people on the Indus still attributed the spread of Buddhism "beyond the river" to some Sramanas (or ascetics) who came with sacred books, 300 years after the Nirvana of Buddha,† or in B.C. 243. The agreement of these dates gives to the two events the relation of cause and effect, the conversion of the people having been the result of the mission.

The spread of Buddhism in Ladák was followed by its introduction into China, about the beginning of the

* Mahawanso, p. 71. † Fo-kwe-ki, c. VII.

Christian era, and into Great Tibet in the middle of the seventh century.

Previous to the occupation of Tibet by Khri-Tsampo, in about 250 B.C., there is nothing known of its history, excepting the fact that the people were of the Bon or Pon religion, which, like that of the Indian *Tirthakaras*, was an epicurean atheism. According to the Mogul author Sanang Setzen, Khri-Tsampo was an Indian prince of the Litsabyi (or Lichhavi) race, who, being conquered in war, had sought refuge in Tibet, where he was hospitably received, and afterwards proclaimed king by the people, who are called the *Debchin Bonbo* of heaven, and the *Yang Bonbo* of earth.* Csoma de Körös repeats a similar story, with the addition that Nya-Khri-Tsampo, "being defeated in battle," fled to Tibet, where he was acknowledged as king by the *Pons*. The date of 250 B.C., assigned to this event by Csoma, makes the Lichhavi prince a contemporary of the great Buddhist king Asoka, by whom he was most probably expelled from India; for the Lichhavi family had been the leading people in the community of Vaisáli for many centuries, during which time they distinguished themselves by their fierce opposition to the Buddhists. They opposed Sakya himself in argument, and were silenced, but not convinced by him. The Lichhavis of Vaisáli professed entire belief in Swasti, from which they derived their name of *Swástikas*, or followers of

* M. Schmidt supposes that these terms indicate the people of the mountains and valleys. They may, however, denote only different sects; the one affecting heavenly aspirations, the other leaning to earthly objects. *Debchin* is most probably Tibetan,—the "blissful,"—which is used by the Tibetans as an equivalent of the Sanskrit *Sugata*, the "well-gone," or blessed, an epithet of former Buddhas. *Yang* may be the Tibetan *Yangs*, great, vast.

the "mystic cross," which was a monogrammatic sign, formed of the letters *su* and *ti*. The combination *suti* is the Pali form of the Sanskrit *swasti*, which is compounded of *su*, well, and *asti*, it is. Wilson gives the meaning of "so-be-it;" but both versions equally imply complete resignation under all circumstances, which was the chief dogma of the fatalist *Swástikas*. These followers of the mystic cross held the doctrine of eternal annihilation after death; from which they derived their Tibetan name of *Mu-stegs-pa*, or "Finitimists."* According to the Tibetans, they were indecent in their dress, and grossly atheistical in their principles. They called themselves *Tirthakara*, or "pure doers;" and the synonymous name of *Punya*, "the pure," was carried with them into Tibet, where it became celebrated for ages, and where it still survives as *Pon* amongst the Finitimists of the eastern province of Kham

According to the Chinese, the founder of the doctrine of the *Tao-sse*, or Rationalists, was *Laotze*, who lived from about B.C. 604 to 523. He was therefore a contemporary of Sakya Muni, by whom he is said to have been worsted in argument. By the Tibetan Buddhists he is called Sen-rabs;† but this perhaps signifies nothing more than that he was of the race or family of Sena. His faith continued paramount in Great Tibet for nine centuries, until Buddhism was generally introduced by Srong-Stan in the middle of the seventh century. But the followers of the *Yung-drung-pa*, or "mystic cross," were still powerful; and in A.D. 899 Buddhism was formally abolished by *Lang Tarma*, and was not again

* Csoma de Körös, Grammar, p. 192.

† Id. ibid. p. 181.

introduced for more than seventy years, until, in A.D. 971, it was finally restored, and has since continued to be the dominant religion of Tibet.

The great spread of the *Pon-gyi-chho*, or Pon religion, can be best appreciated by the traces of its former existence in the widely distant regions of Arakan and Ladák. The people of Arakan give a long line of fifty-five *Pun-na* princes * as their earliest sovereigns, a dynasty which must have reigned for at least 600 years. In Ladák the great monastery of *Lama Yurru* is still called *Yung-druny-Gonpa*, or the "monastery of the mystic cross." The establishment of this monastery is attributed to Naropa, a Lama from Brigung, near Lhasa; but it seems more probable that the name of *Lama Yurru* was derived from the Lama, because he had suppressed the faith of the mystic cross (*yung-drung*), and had established the Lamaïc doctrine of Buddhism.

But Buddhism was the prevailing religion of Ladák from the conversion of the people by Asoka's missionaries down to A.D. 400, when Fa Hian visited India. At that time he found Buddhism flourishing in the little state of *Kia-chhe*, or Ladák, as well as in Kotan and other small states to the northward of the Tsung Ling, or Karakoram. The king of *Kie-chha* (Kha-chan, or "Snow-land)" still celebrated the great quinquennial assembly † of the Srámanas which had been established by Asoka. The ceremony, which lasted for one month, was conducted with becoming gravity, and closed by the

* Journ. As. Soc. Bengal, XIII. p. 31,—Captain Latter.

† In the Gyalpo's time, the Lamas assembled annually at Lé, in the month of *Táng-po* (March), and were dismissed with presents. They now assemble at Hemis, in June. In this monastery there are still 160 Lamas.

distribution of presents amongst the Srámanas. As Fa Hian noticed nothing unusual in these proceedings, we may conclude that the Buddhism of Ladák was the same as that of India. The number of Srámanas was more than 1,000, all of whom were satisfied with the study of the "Lesser Advancement," as laid down in the *Vinaya*, or "Precepts of Discipline," which comprised only the lowest class of Sakyas precepts. But though the Buddhism of the people of Ladák was perfectly orthodox in A.D. 400, yet Fa Hian noticed a peculiarity in their practice, which was unknown to the Indian Buddhists. "The Srámanas," he says, "make use of revolving cylinders, the efficacy of which is not to be described."* These were no doubt the prayer-cylinders which are seen in the hands of the Indo-Scythian princes on their coins, and which may still be found in every Lama's hand throughout Ladák.

II.—TIBETAN SYSTEM OF BUDDHISM.

The religion of the Tibetan Buddhists is contained in a voluminous work called the *Kah-Gyur*, or "Translation of Precepts," because it is a version of the precepts of Sakya, made from the Indian language. It is also frequently called *De-not-sum*, which is a mere translation of the Sanscrit *Tripitaka*, or the "Three Repositories," because it contains the three great divisions of the Buddhist doctrines: the *Vinaya*, the *Sutra*, and the *Abhidharma*. But the Tibetan version is more generally divided into seven distinct classes, of which the last treats of the mystical doctrines of the Tantrikas. These seven divisions are the following:—

* Fo-kwe-ki, c. V., note,—"objet circulaire et tournant."

—	Tibetan.	Sanskrit.	English.
1	Dul-va	Vinaya	Discipline.
2	Sher-chin	Prajnáparamitá ...	Transcendental Wisdom.
3	Phal-chhen ...	BuddhavataSangha	Baudha Community.
4	Kon-tsek	Ratnakuta ...	Pile of Gems.
5	Do	Sutranta ...	Aphorisms.
6	Nyang-Dás ...	Nirvana	Final release from Existence.
7	Gyut	Tantra	Mystical Doctrines.

The three divisions are as follows :—

—	Tibetan.	Sanscrit.	English.
1	Dul-va	Vinaya	Discipline.
2	Do	Sutranta	Aphorisms.
3	Chhos-non-pa ...	Abhidharma ...	Supreme Law.

In this division the *Do* comprises all but the first two of the seven classes. The doctrines contained in these works are of course the same as those of the Indian Buddhists, but the names have been translated instead of being transcribed.

Sakya Muni, the founder of the Buddhist faith, is usually called *Chom-dan-das*, or "he who has been victorious," by the Lamas, but *Shakya Thubba*, or the "mighty Sakya," by the people. The Buddhist Triad, called in Sanscrit *Ratna Trayáya*, or the Three Gems, is styled Kon-chhok-tun, or the "Three Supremacies," by the Tibetans, who give the following names to the different members of the Trinity.

1. Buddha is *Sangya-Konchok*, or the "Supreme" Intelligence.

2. Dharma is *Chhos-Konchok*, or the "Supreme" Law.

3. Sangha is *Gedun-Konchok*, or the "Supreme" Congregation.*

A Buddha, or one who has obtained Buddhahood, is styled *Sangya;* a Buddhist, *Sangya-pa;* and the Buddhist religion, *Sangya-kyi-chhos*. The whole Buddha community, in Sanscrit *Sangha*, is called *Gedun*, and is divided into the same number of classes as in India.

1. The Bodhisatwa, or True Intelligence, is called *Chang-chhub*, the perfect or accomplished, and *Chang-chhub-Sempah*, "Perfect Strength of Mind;" because he is supposed to have accomplished the grand object of a Buddhist's life, by the perfect suppression of all bodily desires, and by complete abstraction of mind. As the Bodhisatwa was often styled *Arhanta*, or *Arhata*, the "venerable," so the *Chang-chhub* is frequently called *Pa-chom-pa*, or "he who has subdued his enemy."

The *Pratyeka*, or "Individual Intelligence," is called *Rang-sangya*, or "Self-intelligence;" and his other name of *Anayámi* is translated by *Phyir-mi-hong-ba*, or "he who turneth not out of the way."

The *Sráwaka*, or "Auditor," is called *Nyan-thos*, or the "Listener," and his Sanskrit title of *Srota-panna* is rendered by *Gyun-du-zhug-pa*, or "one who has entered the stream" that leads to happiness.

In the earliest periods of Buddhism the worship of the people was confined to the holy triad of *Buddah*, *Dharma*, and *Sangha*. Much pious reverence was shown to the relics of former Buddhas, as well as to

* The Tibetan names of the Triad are thus spelt:—1. *Sangs-rGyas-dKon-mChog*. 2. *Chhos-dKon-mChog*. 3. *dGé-mDun-dKon-mChog*.

those of Sakya himself, and his principal disciples. Even so late as A.D. 400, we find Fa Hian recording the devotions paid to the relics of Ananda, Sáriputra, and Mogalána. But previous to this time I know of no mention of the great Dhyáni Bodhisatwa, *Padma Páni*, who is the regent or present lord of this world, nor of the equally celebrated Bodhisatwas *Manju Sri* and *Avalokiteswara*. These two are first noticed by Fa Hian;* but he is quite silent regarding *Padma Páni*, and the whole of the elaborate system of Dhyáni Budhas and Bodhisatwas, which are, I presume, the invention of a much later date.

In Ladák at the present day, though the people still reverence Shakya Thubba, or the great Buddha (Sangya Konchhog), yet their worship is equally given to *Padma Páni*, *Jámya*, and *Chanrazik* (or Padma Páni, Manju Sri, and Avalokiteswara), and though they still confirm an oath by appealing to the *Kon-chhog-Sum*, or "Three Supremacies," of the Buddhist triad, yet, when they undertake any enterprise, or begin a journey, their prayers for success are almost invariably addressed to Padma Páni.

The system of Dhyáni Buddhas and Bodhisatwas, which has long been known throughout Tibet, was first made known to the European world by Mr. Hodgson.† The self-existent Adi Buddha, by five spontaneous acts of divine wisdom (*jnyán*), and by five exertions of mental reflection (*dhyán*), created the Pancha-Dhyáni Buddha, or "Five Celestial Buddhas," whose names are as follows:—

* Fo-kwe-ki, c. VII.

† Hodgson's Buddhism, p. 40.

—	Sanscrit.	Tibetan.
1	Vairochana	Nam-par-snang-dsat.
2	Akshobya	... ...
3	Ratna Sambhava	... ...
4	Amitábha	Hod-pag-med.
5	Amogha Siddha	Tung-shak.

Each of these Buddhas again, by the mere exertion of his inherent *jnyán* and *dhyán*, is said to have created a Bodhisatwa. The invention of the *Pancha Dhyáni Buddha Sáktis*, or female energies, which are known both in Nepal and in Tibet, must therefore belong to a later period.

The Buddha Sáktis are the following :—

—	Sanscrit.	Tibetan.
1	Vajra Dateswari	... ...
2	Lochaná	Nang-Salma.
3	Mamukhi	... ...
4	Pandará	Kos-kar-chen.
5	Tárá	Grolma.

The five Dhyani Bodhisatwas are the following :—

—	Sanscrit.	Tibetan.	English.
1	Sámanta Bhadra...	Kuntu-Zang-po ...	Supreme Happiness.
2	Vajra-Páni ...	Lag-na-Dorje ...	Sceptre-bearer.
3	Ratna-Páni ...	... ...	Jewel-bearer.
4	Padma-Páni ...	Chakna-Padma* ...	Lotul-bearer.
5	Viswa-Páni ...	... ...	World-bearer.

The *Lokeswaras* (*Jigten-Bangchuk*†) are also acknow-

* *Phyag-na-Dorje*, pronounced *Chakna-Dorje*.

† *hJig-rTen-dBang-Phyug*, " the Lord of the World."

ledged in Tibetan Buddhism. All these are celestial beings, the spontaneous emanations from the Divinity, who have never been subject to the pains of transmigration. Inferior to them are the created or mortal beings, who are divided into six classes, named *Droba-Rikdruk*, the "six advancers or progressors," because their souls progress by transmigration from one state to a better state, until they finally attain absorption into the divine essence; after which they are no longer subject to transmigration. These six classes are—

1. *Lhá*, "Gods," equivalent to the Hindu *Sura* and *Deva*.
2. *Lhá-ma-yin*, or *Lhá-min*, "Demi-gods or Titans," equivalent to the Hindu *Asura* and *Daitya*.
3. *Mi*, "Man;" the Sanskrit *Manushya*.
4. *Dudro*, "Brutes;" in Sanscrit *Tiryyaka*, "crookedly," because they walk a little out of the right path.
5. *Yidok*, "Goblins;" in Sanscrit *preta*.
6. *Myalba*, "the damned;" in Sanscrit *Náraka*.*

It is one of the most essential dogmas of the doctrine of transmigration that the disembodied soul is incapable of receiving either reward or punishment. Hence the belief in other grades of mortal beings, both superior and inferior to man. The good man, after death, is supposed to be raised to the dignity of a *Lhamayin*, or demi-god, while the bad man is degraded to the state of a *Dudro*, or brute. These different orders of beings were not the invention of the Buddhists, for they existed long before the rise of Buddhism, and were the offspring of man's yearning for a future and better state. Like as in India, where the Brahmans have declared all the ancient

* The hells are divided into eight cold and sixteen hot hells, which are favourite subjects of representation with the Chinese and Tibetan painters. The punishments are *not everlasting;* finite sin is expiated by finite punishment; and when the expiation is completed, the person is born again. See also Fra Orazio, Nouv. Jour. As. tom. XIV. p. 410.

village *Thakurs* and *Debis* to be only so many different forms of Mahadeo and Parbati, so in Tibet the Lamas have craftily grafted into their system all the ancient gods and spirits of the former inhabitants. Hence, though Buddhism is the prevailing religion of the country, yet the poorer people still make their offerings to their old divinities, the gods of the hills, the woods, and the dales. Some of these divinities are the following:—

1. *Rihi-Lhá* ... ... Mountain Gods, or Oreades.
2. Chhubi-Lhá ... ... River Gods, or Naiädes.
3. Shinggi-Lhá ... ... Tree Gods, or Dryades.
4. Zhi-Lhá* ... ... Family Gods, or Lares.
5. Zhing-Lhá ... ... Field Gods, or Leimoniades.
6. Khyim-Lhá ... ... House Gods, or Penates.

In after-times the mystical system of the Tantrists was engrafted on the Buddhism of Nepál and Tibet; and the pictures of the prevailing red and yellow sects are filled with representations of the three-eyed destroying *Vargchuk* (Iswara), and of his blood-drinking spouse *Chang-Summa* (the three-eyed goddess *Trilochana*). These doctrines were named *Nang-pa*, the esoteric or orthodox, in contradistinction to the Phyipa, exoteric or heterodox. With them, I believe, originated the filthy system of Buddha Saktis, or female energies of the Pancha Dhyani Buddhas, in which the *yoni*, or female symbol, plays a prominent part.

* *gZhis-Lhá*. *Lha* is the generic name of God; hence, Buddha is called *Lhá-yi-Lhá*, the "God of Gods." The similarity of this name to the Roman *Lar*, and to the old Arabic *Ilah*, God, is very striking. I may notice here, that the usual translation of the Musalmán Kalimeh, لا اله الا الله *La Ilah ila Allah*, "there is no God but God," is a manifest truism. The true translation is, "there is no God but *Allah*."

III.—DIFFERENT SECTS—LAMAS.

During the palmy days of Indian Buddhism, the faith of the Tibetans most probably partook of all the different fluctuations of belief that prevailed in India. The most ancient religious sect that is now known is the *Nyimapa*, all of whom wear red dresses. Most of the Lamas in Ladák and Ngari are of this sect. In the middle of the eighth century *Urgyan Rinpoche* (the gem of Urgyan, or Padma Sambhava) was invited into Tibet by Khrisrong De-tsan. He is said to have been an incarnation of the Dhyáni Buddha Amitabha (*Hod-pag-med*). He was the founder of a new sect, who differ from the *Nyimapas* chiefly in their worship of this incarnation. In the eleventh century Tibet was visited by *Chovo-Atisha*, a Bengali Pundit, who infused new vigour amongst the votaries of Buddhism. His pupil *Bromston* founded the Rareng monastery, and originated the *Káhdampa** sect, or those who are content with the observance of the "precepts" (*kah*), without caring for the acquirement of the higher branches of transcendental wisdom. The followers of these three sects all wear red dresses. Another sect, the *Sákyapas*, also wear red; but I know nothing of their peculiar tenets.

In the middle of the fourteenth century appeared the great Lama *Tsong khapa*. Some say that he was an incarnation of Amitábha (*Hod-pag-med*), and others of Manju Sri (*Jámya*). He was born in 1355, and died in 1419. He built the temple of *Gáhldán*, and was the first great abbot (*khánpo*), who occupied the Gáhldán

* *bKah-gDams-pa*, "followers of the precepts."—Csoma, Grammar, p. 197.

chair, which has been filled by a succession of abbots down to the present day.

The earlier abbots or patriarchs were the following :*—

1.	Tsong-kha-pa	born	1355 A.D.
		founded Gáhldán	1407
2.	Darma Rinchhen	born	1417
3.	Gelek Paldan	„	1429
4.	Zhalu Lekpa	„	1436
5.	Logros Chhos	„	1448
6.	Baso Chhosgyan	„	1461
7.	Logros Tanpa	„	1471
8.	Mon Lampal	„	1478

Previous to the establishment of the *Gáhl-dán* chair by Tsongkhapa, there would appear to have been no great patriarchs, or head abbots, of the Lamaïc priesthood; but the principle being once established, the attainment of this rank became an object of ambition, and the great abbots of *Gáhldán* were soon eclipsed by the superior piety, greater learning, and more active zeal of the abbots of *Tashi-Lhunpo*.† But the fame of Tsongkhapa was confirmed. He had established the annual feast of " intense supplication," which is still observed, and had originated the great sect of *Gelukpa* (the virtuous), which are distinguished from the older sects by a yellow dress. This sect is now the most numerous in Tibet, and both the *Dalai Lama* of Lhasa and the *Tashi Lama* of Tashi-Lhunpo belong to it. Tsongkhapa's memory is still venerated throughout Tibet. Pictures of him are hung up in all the temples, and the holy impressions of his hands and feet are said to be preserved

* Csoma's Chronology. Grammar, p. 181.

† *bKra-shis-Lhun-po*, the " mass of glory." It is pronounced *Tashi*, and is a very common man's name. Lhun-po is the English word " lump;" and the Greek Ο-λυμπο-ς.

in butter* in the western chamber of the Potála monastery.

Gedun Tub-pa ("the perfect Lama"), the founder of Tashi-Lhunpo, was born in A.D. 1339. He built the temple in 1445, and died in 1474. Before his death he had supplanted the abbots of *Gáhldán* in the estimation of the people, and his successors have enjoyed the reputation which he established: for previous to his time the great abbots of Gáhldán had been elected by the choice of the Lamas; but the bold and original mind of *Gedun Tub-pa* devised the present system of a perpetual incarnation. He himself was said to be an incarnation of the celestial Bodhisatwa Padma Páni; and at his death he relinquished the attainment of Buddhahood, that he might be born again and again, for the benefit of mankind. He died in 1473, and in 1474 his successor *Gedun Gya-tsho* (the Ocean of Lamas) was discovered as an infant by the possession of certain divine marks. The fifth in succession, *Navang Lozang Gyatsho*, founded the hierarchy of Dalai Lamas at Lhasa, in 1640, and made himself master of the whole of Tibet. In 1643 he rebuilt the Potála monastery, and in 1650, after repeated solicitations, he paid a visit to the Emperor of China. The inscription of the Emperor Khang-hi, engraved on stone, calls the grand Lama of Lhasa, who had been reigning in 1642 (that is, Navang-Lozang), the *fifth* Dalai Lama. But he was in fact the *first* Dalai Lama, although he was the *fifth* Tashi Lama who had

* Nouv. Journ. As. 1830, p. 169. Father Hyacinthe. The prints of the Grand Lama's hands were eagerly sought for by the people.—Turner, 459. Several of my pictures have these prints on the back. I have also a *sanad*, or grant, by the Emperor Akbar, which bore on the back the print of his royal hand.

occupied the chair of Tashi Lhunpo. Since his time there have been two great Lamas, the one called the Dalai Lama, occupying the chair at Lhasa, and the other called the Tashi Lama, filling the chair at Tashi Lhunpo. Precedence is given to the Dalai Lama, both in writing and in conversation; but their influence is pretty equally divided. Both chairs are filled by a succession of supposed incarnations, and generally the elder of the two is the most influential. The succession from *Gedun Tubpa* down to the present day is the following:

—	Written Names.	Spoken Names.	Date. A.D.	Remarks.
1	dGe-hDun-Grub-pa	Gedun-Tubba	1389	Born. Founded Tash Lhunpo 1445.
2	dGe-hDun-rGya-mTsho ..	Gedun-Gyatsho ..	1474	
3	bSod-nams-rGya-mTsho ..	Sonam-Gyatsho ..	1541	Visited Altun Khán.
4	Yon-tan-rGya-mTsho ..	Yontan-Gyatsho ..	1587	
5	Nag-dVang-bLo-bZang ..	NAVANG LOZANG ..	1615	Established himself a Dalai Lama; 164 conquered Tibet; an visited the Empero of China 1650.
6	Rin-chhen-Tshangs-dByangs	Rinchhen Tshang Chang	1690	?
7	bLo-bZang-skal-lDan ..	Lozang-Kaldan	1725	?
8	bLo-bZang-hJam-dPal ..	Lozang-Jampal ..	1760	A minor in 1774.
9	Lung-rTogs-rGya-mTsho ..	Luntok Gyatsho ..	1790	?
10	Tshul-khrims-rGya-mTsho ..	Tshul-thim Gyatsho ..	1817	?
11	dGe-dMu-reGya-mTsho ..	Gemure Gyatsho ...	1835	Nine years in 1844.

But besides these two great Lamas of the yellow sect of Gelukpa, there is a third great Lama in Bhutan, called the *Dharma Raja*, who is the head of the *Dukpa* sect, all of whom wear red dresses. Dharma Raja is his usual title amongst the people of Bhután, but amongst the Tibetans he is generally called *Jigten Gonpo** (Lord of the World). The Dalai Lama is called *Gyalba Rinpochhe*,

* See Plate XXII.

JIGTEN-GONPO,

The Dharma-Raja of Bhután.

Day & Son, Lith[rs] to The Queen.

the "Gem of Majesty," and the Tashi Lama is called *Panchen Rinpochhe*, the "Gem of Learning."

All who have taken the vows of celibacy are called by the collective name of *Gédun*, the clergy. A monk is styled Lama, and a nun Ani. But the followers of the Gelukpa sect are divided into several classes. The lowest grade is the *Getshul*, or neophyte, and the *Gétshulma*,* or novice. The professed monk is called *Gelong*, and the professed nun *Gelongma*.

The principal sects in Tibet have already been mentioned, but there are some others deserving of notice. Of these the principal is the *Karmapa*,† or "believers in the efficacy of works." They are the same as the *Kármmikas* of Nepál. The *Kahgyudpas* are "believers in the succession of precepts." They are satisfied with the observance of the *Do* (sutras or aphorisms), and care not for the attainment of the esoteric doctrines of the *Sherchin* (Prajnáparamitá), or "transcendental wisdom." The *Brikhungpa* sect derives its name from the district of Brikhung. I know nothing of their tenets. All the above sects were offshoots of the Gelukhpa, and accordingly they wear yellow dresses. The Dukpa sect wear a red dress. They are numerous in Bhutan, and are found all over Tibet. I know nothing of their peculiar tenets; but from the name of the sect, *Dad-Dukpa*, which means "faith in the thunderer," I should suppose that they pay especial reverence to the holy *Dorje* (*Vajra*, or thunderbolt) which descended through the air, and fell at Sera in Tibet. A picture which I possess of the great Lama *Skyobba Jigten Gonpo*, of the red sect, represents him with the *Dorje* in his right hand.

* See Plate XXIV.

† *Karma-pa*, naturalized from Sanscrit.

It seems probable, therefore, that the name of the sect was derived as I have supposed.

IV.—DRESS—RITUALIC INSTRUMENTS.

Most of the Lamas in Ladák wear a red coat with sleeves and long skirts secured by a red girdle. All wear red boots. Most of them are bareheaded, but the higher Lamas wear semicircular red caps. One great Lama, the abbot of Lama Yurru, wears a peculiar hat, formed of bands that diminish in width by steps towards the top.* Most Lamas have their heads shaved, or the hair cropped short; but the abbot's hair was uncut. The pictures of the grand Lamas, both yellow and red, represent them without hair. This agrees with the practice of the Indian Buddhists, who were obliged to shave their heads. The Dharma Raja, or great Lama of the red sect, wears a semicircular red cap similar to those of the Ladáki Lamas.† His right arm is bare, but the rest of his person is clothed in ample red garments, suitable to a cold climate. The *Sanghati*, or kilt, and the *uttara-sanghati*, or cloak, of the Indian Buddhists, are formed into a coat with sleeves and skirt, and over this is worn a robe or blanket. In all the pictures the *antara-vásaka*, or "inner vest," is represented beneath the other dress. This is no doubt shown purposely, to prove that the great Lamas, according to the command of Sakya, never lay aside their inner vests.

The Dalai and Tashi Lamas wear the same description of dress, but of a yellow colour. But all of them have transgressed the holy precept not to wear any ornamented

* See Plates XXIII. and XXIV.

† See Plates XXII. and XXIII.

Abbot High Lama

of LAMA YURRU.

Plate XXV.

Dublo, aged 39
a [illegible] Lama

Churmgjok, aged 22
a [illegible] ([illegible] Sect.)

Plate XXV.

The DRIL-BU, or Bell.

A. Cunningham Del. *Day & Son Lithrs to the Queen*

clothes, for they have yellow and red brocades, spangled with flowers of gold. The Dalai and Tashi Lamas wear peculiar conical caps with long lappets.

The ritualic instruments are three: the bell, the sceptre (or thunderbolt), and the prayer-cylinder.

The bell, *drilbu*,* is used during the performance of daily service, but for what purpose I could not ascertain. It is represented in the left hand of the great Lama Skyobba Jigten, of the red sect, and it is placed on the throne at the feet of the great Dalai Lama Navang Lozang. The bell represented in the accompanying plate is formed of a very white brittle-looking metal. On the upper part are the syllables *tan*, *man*, *lan*, *ban*, *man*, *tsun*, *pan*, *bDrin*; which may, perhaps, be intended to represent eight notes of the bell. Inside, in three places, are the monosyllabic interjections *aum! ah! Hun!* The outside is chiefly ornamented with representations of the *dorjé*, or sceptre.

The sceptre, *dorjé*, is the vajra of the Indians. This holy instrument is said to have flown away from India, and to have alighted at Sera, in Tibet. That it was looked upon in India, from a very early time, as an object of reverence, or as an emblem of power, is proved by its being placed in the right hand of a raja in the Sánchi bas-reliefs,† which date as high as the beginning of the Christian era. It is also sculptured on the rock at Udegiri, where it is represented in one of the hands of Durga, who is slaying the Bhainsâsur. This sculpture is as old as the seventh or eighth century.

In Tibetan it is called *sera-pun-dze*, and the annual festival which has been established in its honour is one

* *Dril-bu*, a "little bell." See Plate XXV.

† Eastern gateway, right pillar.

of the principal religious ceremonies. The Lamas carry the sceptre in procession from Sera to Potála, where they present it before the Dalai Lama, who makes a salutation to it. They next take it to the Chinese officials, and then to the Káhlons, or ministers, all of whom make suitable presents of money; after which it is carried back to Sera with the same solemnity.

The accompanying plate * represents one of these instruments, in my own possession, of full size, together with sketches of the old Indian vajras, from the sculptures at Sánchi and Udigiri.

The prayer-cylinder, or *mani-chhos-khor* (the precious religious wheel), is a very ingenious instrument, and does great credit to the genius of the Tibetans. The body of the instrument is a metal cylinder, about three inches in height, and from two to two and a half inches in diameter. The axis is prolonged below to form a handle. The cylinder is filled with rolls of printed prayers and charms, which revolve as the instrument is turned round. Every Lama carries a *chhos-khor*, which he keeps perpetually turning by a gentle motion of the hand, assisted by a cubical piece of iron fastened by a chain to the outside. As every revolution of a prayer is equivalent to its recitation, the *chhos-khor* is a very ingenious instrument for multiplying the number of a man's prayers.

In the accompanying plate† I have represented two of these instruments, of half-size. One of them has the sacred sentence, the holy *sadakshara mantra*, or " six-syllabled charm," *Aum! Mani-padme, hun!* engraved once on the outside; the other has the same sentence twice repeated, in raised letters of silver.

* See Plate XXVI. The name is written *rDo-rjé.*

† See Plate XXVII.

Plate XLI.

The DORGÉ, Sceptre or Thunderbolt.

A. Cunningham. del.

Day & Son. Lith.rs to the Queen

Plate XXVII.

The MANI-CHHOS-KOR, or Prayer-Cylinder.

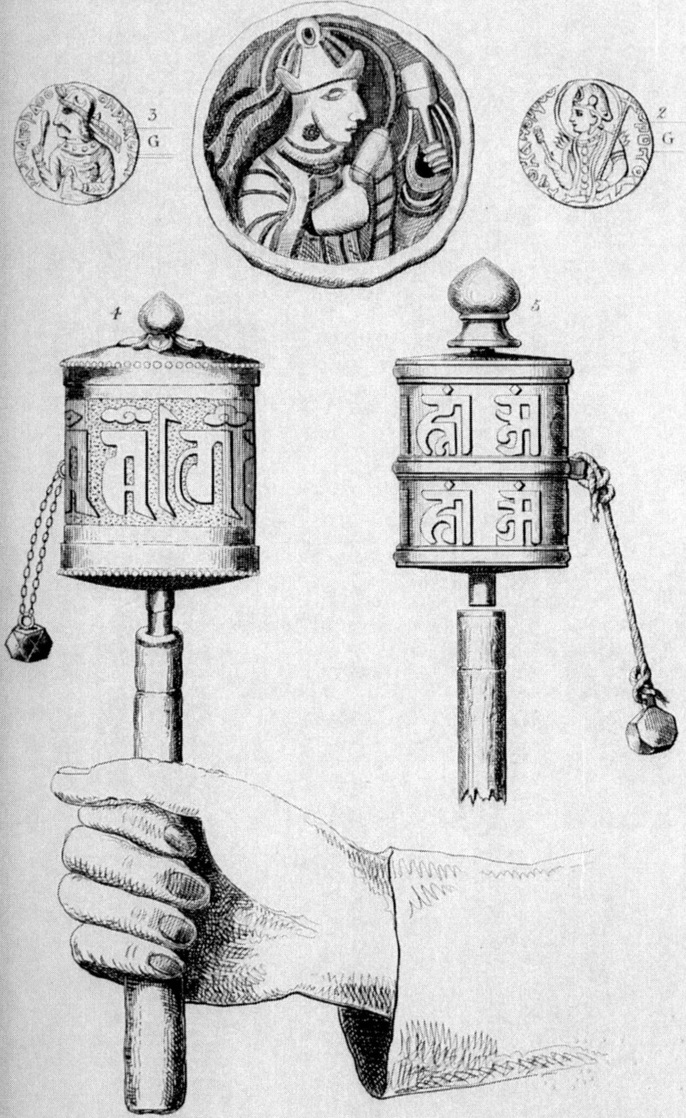

A. Cunningham, Del.

Day & Son Lithrs to the Queen.

The earliest mention of the prayer-cylinder is by the Chinese pilgrim Fa Hian,* in A.D. 400, who saw it in the hands of the Srámanas of *Kic-chha* (Ladák). Klaproth states that this instrument is not mentioned in any Indian books; and I can vouch that I have never seen it represented on any piece of Indian sculpture. It was, however, in very early use in North-western India, where it was introduced by the Indo-Scythian princes about the beginning of the Christian era. On the gold coins of Hoërki, or Hushka, the Indo-Scythian prince is generally represented holding the prayer-cylinder in his right hand.† The same object is no doubt represented on the large medallion in the accompanying plate; but the figure holding it is most probably the chief patriarch of the Buddhist religion.

These instruments are found of all sizes and in all positions. Cylinders, about one foot in height, are placed in rows around the temples, and are turned by the votaries before entering. Larger cylinders are found near villages, turned by water, which keeps them perpetually revolving day and night. The device is so ingenious as to induce a hope that it may be adopted in Roman Catholic countries, where the time now spent in telling beads and reciting pater-nosters and ave-marias might be more profitably employed in worldly matters, while the beads were told, and the prayers were repeated by machinery. An ingenious mechanist might form small prayer-boxes, which could be wound up to produce a certain number of revolutions of an inclosed pater-noster or ave-maria; and thus any number might be got through during the night. Indeed, I am not sure that Roman

* Fo-kwe-ki, c. V.

† See Plate XXVII.

Catholic watches might not be invented for the perpetual revolution of pater-nosters.

V.—RELIGIOUS BUILDINGS—IMAGES.

The principal religious edifices are the following :—

1. *Gonpa,* or "monastery." This word signifies a solitary place; because monasteries were originally built, according to the directions of Sakya Muni, far from the bustle and disturbing influences of cities. The monasteries have already been described. Convents are only separate monasteries walled off from the rest of the buildings. Both are called *chhos-né;* but the common term is gonpa.

2. *Lhákhang,* "God's house or temple." All the temples that I have seen consist of single rooms, square and unadorned outside, and filled with images and pictures inside. The images are generally about half life-size, made of unburnt clay and painted. In the larger temples the images are of metal and of colossal size. A temple is also called *Tsang-khang,* or "holy house."

3. *Lábrang,* a "lama's house." Where no monasteries exist, the lamas live in separate houses. I mention this because Alexander Gerard supposed that the *Lhá-khang* (God's house) was the same as the *bLá-brang* (lama's residence).

4. *Chhod-Ten,** in Sanscrit *Chaitya,* an "offering-receptacle." This is properly a dedicatory building or pyramid erected in honour of Shakya Thubba, or of some one of the holy Buddhas or Bodhisatwas. It is

* *mChhod-rTen,* sometimes pronounced *Chhorten.*

Plate [illegible]

The CHHODTEN, or Mausoleum.

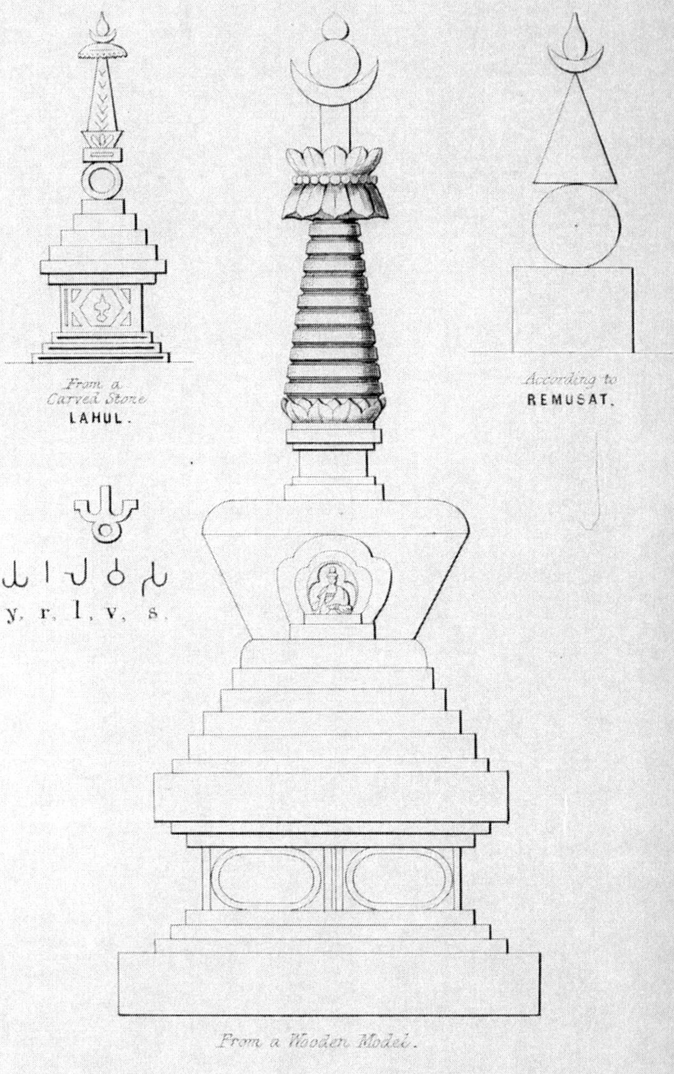

From a Carved Stone LAHUL.

According to REMUSAT.

From a Wooden Model.

A. Cunningham del. Day & Son lith. rs to the Queen

sometimes called *Chhos-ten*, or the "holy receptacle," but the proper name is *Chhod-rten*, the "offering-repository," because offerings are made to the shrine. The figure in the accompanying plate* is taken from a wooden model in my own possession. The basement, which is square, is surmounted by four steps, on which stands the dome or principal part of the edifice. Originally this was a plain hemisphere, but the form was gradually altered until it assumed its present shape of an inverted and truncated cone. The dome is surmounted by a lofty pinnacle, crowned by the holy emblem of *Chhos-Konchok* (or *Dharma*). This symbol is a monogram formed of the four radical letters (in old Pali) which represent the four elements; and the whole is typical both of the material frame of man, and of the material universe.† The radical letters are *ya*, air; *ra*, fire; *va*, water; *la*, earth; to which is added the letter *s* for Mount Sumeru. The pair of eyes delineated on the basement show that this *Chhod-Ten* was dedicated to the supreme Buddha, *Sangya-Konchok*, the "eye of the universe."

5. *Dung-Ten*, a "bone-holder," or relic-repository. This is the genuine *Stupa*, or tope of India, prepared for the reception of a relic. It is a funeral building or pyramid, erected either over the corpse of a lama, or over the ashes of a king or person of consequence. It is similar in shape to the *Chhod-Ten*. The deposits usually placed in these mausolea have already been described.

* See Plate XXVIII.

† According to the Chinese, as quoted by Remusat (Fo-kwe-ki, c. XIII. note 6), the whole pyramid represented the "five elements;" but they are wrong, for it is only the pinnacle which is an emblem of *Dharma*, or the material elements. See my work on the Bhilsa Topes.

Mani,* a dyke or pile of stones. The *Mani* is a stone dyke from four to five feet in height, and from six to twelve feet in breadth. The length varies from ten and twenty feet to nearly half a mile. A mani which I measured near Bazgo was 823 paces, or nearly half a mile, in length. A second mani near Lé was somewhat longer, or 880 paces, or 2,200 feet. Moorcroft states its length at 1,000 paces, but these were most probably the paces of a native, of little more than two feet each. The surface of the mani is always covered with inscribed slabs. The most usual inscription is the holy six-syllabled mantra, *Aum ! mani-padme, hun !* But other formulæ also occur; such as *Aum ! Vajra Páni, hún ! Aum ! Vagiswari, hún !* &c. These are generally inscribed in Tibetan characters, but sometimes also in mediæval Devanagari letters, called *Lantsha*. These slabs are votive offerings from all classes of people for the attainment of some particular objects. Does a childless man wish for a son, or a merchant about to travel hope for a safe return; does a husbandman look for a good harvest, or a shepherd for the safety of his flocks during the severity of winter, each goes to a lama and purchases slate, which he deposits carefully on the village *mani*, and returns to his home in full confidence that his prayer will be heard.

Tshá-khang, an "image-room." *Tshá* is the little medallion figure of a lama, which is made of a portion of his ashes mixed with clay. In every *Lhákhang*, or temple, there is a small room or cupboard set apart for the reception of these medallions. In a temple at Nako I saw about one hundred cubic feet of them. A very perfect specimen in my possession is one inch and three-

* *Ma-ni*, a word naturalized from Sanscrit.

eighths in diameter. The lama is represented seated on the ground, with his left hand in his lap and his right hand raised in the attitude of teaching. The figure is gilt. On the back of the medallion is stamped the word *Tshá*, "medallion." The grand lamas are represented by more precious images of life-size. Two statues of the Tashi Lama, which Turner saw, were respectively of gold and of solid silver gilt.

The following is a general description of the images and paintings of the principal Buddhas and Bodhisatwas who are worshipped by the Tibetan Buddhists.

Shakya-Thubba, or Buddha, is always represented seated. His right hand usually rests on his right knee, and his left hand in his lap, holding his alms-dish. In one picture, however, he is represented holding his alms-dish in both hands. His body is always coloured yellow, usually gilt, and his hair is short, curly, and blue. At the large village of Shé, near Lé, there is a colossal copper-gilt statue of Shakya Thubba of the following dimensions.

	Feet.	Inches.
Height of image, seated	37	1
Breadth across the shoulders	7	4
Breadth from knee to knee	12	0
Length of ear	4	3
Diameter of alms-dish	2	3
Circumference of throne	81	0

This image was erected by the Gyalpo Deldan Namgyal, about A.D. 1680.

Chhos-Konchok, or Dharma, is represented seated. She has four arms, two raised in the attitude of prayer, the third holding a necklace or garland, and the fourth a lotus. Her colour is white.

Gédun-Konchok, or Sangha, is represented seated;

the right hand resting on the right knee, and the left hand holding a lotus.

Chamba, the future Buddha Maitreya, is represented seated with both hands raised, the fingers forming the *Pad-kor*, or lotus-shape. His body is yellow, and his hair short, curly, and blue.

Jámya, or Manju-Sri, is also represented seated, with his right hand raised and holding a flaming sword, and his left hand carrying a lotus. His body is of a yellow colour.

Chanrazek, or Avalokiteswara, is represented standing. His right hand rests by his side, and his left holds a lotus. His body is white.

Lagna-Dorjé, or Vajrapáni, is represented standing; his left hand empty, and his right hand carrying a lotus. His body is yellow.

Thunshak, or Amogha Siddha, is represented seated, with his left hand in his lap, and his right hand raised in the attitude of teaching. His body is green.

Grolma, or Tárá, the Sákti or female energy of Amogha Siddha, is also green. She is represented seated, her right hand resting on her knee, and her left hand holding a lotus.

The Tántrika, *Vargchuk*, or Iswara, is a favourite subject with the Tibetan painters and sculptors. He is always represented as *Chan-sum-pa* (or Trelochana, the "three-eyed"). His body is usually blue, but sometimes red. His loins are covered with a leopard's skin, and a snake is generally wound round his waist. He carries either a *Dorjé* (vajra, or "thunderbolt"), or a sharp-cutting sword in his right hand, and is generally exhibited trampling human beings beneath his feet. He is also represented frantic with anger, his eyes staring,

Eastern Pillar, called CHOMO, at Dras.

A Cunningham del.

his nostrils dilated, and his mouth wide open, while his whole body is surrounded by flames. Such is the male divinity of the Tántrists.

The Tántrika, *Todde-Phag-mo* (or Káli), is represented of a blood-red colour, with a garland of skulls round her neck. Her right hand holds the Vajra, or thunderbolt, and with her left hand she carries a cup of blood to her mouth. She is also represented as *Chan-sum-má* (or Trelochaná, the "three-eyed"), and is surrounded by a circle of flames. She carries a long sceptre surmounted by skulls and the holy *Dorjé.*

The Tibetan Lamas are unrivalled amongst Orientals as modellers in clay and workers in metal. A small medallion, about two inches square, which I possess, contains five figures surrounded by leaves and flowers of exquisitely delicate workmanship. It is formed of baked clay, but the edges are as sharp as if the work had been done by an European artist in plaster of Paris. Equally good is a figure of Shakya Thubba.

On the side of the road, between the hamlet of Styalbo and the village of Drás, there are two pillars of granitic mica-slate, which the people call *Chomo*, or "The Women," but which, I believe, have no connection whatever with Tibetan Buddhism, as the nearly obliterated inscriptions are in Kashmiri *Tákri*, and not in Tibetan characters.

The Eastern Pillar has one principal figure, a four-armed female, and two attendant females, one on each side, and each with one leg bent. They all wear necklaces, earrings, armlets, and anklets. On the pedestal are several small kneeling figures with their hands raised and joined together in attitudes of prayer. This pillar is six feet nine inches high, one foot six inches broad, and one foot thick.*

The Western Pillar has the same principal figure, also a four-armed female, with two attendant females on each side. This pillar is six feet high, two feet nine inches broad, and one foot thick.†

From the style of these figures, as well as from the nature of the alphabetical characters, I have no hesitation in stating my opinion that they are Brahminical statues erected by some Kashmirian Hindus. This opinion is strengthened by the fact that there is a third undoubted Hindu pillar standing close to them, which I believe to be a *Sati* pillar. On one side is sculptured a horseman, which is the usual emblem, placed on the pillar of a *Rajputni Sati*, to denote that her husband was a soldier. On the back of the pillar there is an inscription of eight lines in Kashmirian *Tákri*, which I am unable to translate satisfactorily. The words are the following :‡

Pra
Lokeswaram cha Maitré-
-yam pratishtáptantasram A-
-tabhavatumanya matwanvapra
Adathárábha U (*la*) *maiyatre* (*ma*)
(*ndra ?*)
Aswáchaptakaye
gadrá
dram Alá.

---

* See Plate XXIX. † See Plate XXX. ‡ See Plate XXX.

Plate XIX

Western Pillar, called CHOMO, at Drás

A. Cunningham Del. Day & Son lith^rs to the Queen

VI.—RITES AND CEREMONIES.

The religious service of the Lamas is performed at three fixed periods of the day; at sunrise, noon, and sunset. The service consists of the recitation or chanting of portions of the *Do* (Sutras, or "Precepts") or of the *Dulva* (Vinaya, or "Rules of Discipline"), accompanied by the solemn sound of several musical instruments. These are:—1st, large sliding trumpets, five and six feet in length, called *Chhos-Dung*, or "holy trumpets;" 2nd, large drums, *Chhos Ná;* and 3rd, large brazen cymbals, *Bul-chhal.* Sometimes also a conch, *Dung-kar*, is used. The musical sounds are slow and prolonged, and the effect is exceedingly solemn and even melancholy. During the performance of the service incense is kept regularly burning, and offerings of fruit and grain, and even of meat, are made to the figures of *Shakya Thubba* (or Buddha), *Chanrazik* (or Avalokiteswara), and *Jámya* (or Manju Sri).

Moorcroft, who frequently witnessed the daily service of the Lamas, thus describes it.* "The religious service of the Lama, which is performed daily at the *Gon-pas*, or temples attached to monasteries, consists chiefly of prayers and chanting, in which the formula '*Aum! mani-padmé, hun!*' is frequently repeated; and the whole is accompanied with the music of wind instruments, chiefly harmonizing with tabrets and drums. Amongst the former is a sliding trumpet of large size, which is upheld by one man whilst blown by another, and has a very deep and majestic intonation; a hautboy, the reed of which is surrounded by a circular plate covering the mouth, and the conch shell, with a copper

* Travels, I. p. 344.

mouth-piece; metallic cymbals, much more mellow and sonorous than others, complete the band."

But the religious service of the Lamas is not confined to the recitation of the *Dulva* and the *Do*, or to the frequent repetition of the six-syllabled *mantra*, "*Aum! Mani-padmé, hun!*" They occasionally proclaim aloud the numerous titles of the supreme Buddha; and recite, with endless repetition, the different mystical sentences peculiar to the various Bodhisatwas, and to the Tántrika Sáktis, or female energies of the Dhyáni Buddhas. They also recite mystical sentences from the Tantras, to deprecate the wrath of the furious Káli (*Chandá*, the angry goddess).

The following are specimens of these *mantras*, or mystic sentences. They are all in the Sanskrit language:—

1. The Mantra of *Shakya Thubba* (Buddh'a).

Namah Sámanta Buddhánam! Sarva-klesha nishuddhana;
Sarvva dharma vahiprapta; gagana sama sama, swáhá!

"Glory to the chief Buddhas! Reliever of all suffering!
Master of all virtue! Equal, equal to the Heavens! adoration!"

2. The Mantra of *Kuntu-Zangpo* (Samanta-bhadra).

Namah Sámanta Buddhánam! Sámantanugati, varaja,
Dharmanirgati, mahá, mahá, swáha!

"Glory to the chief Buddhas! acquirer of distinction, best-born,
Who goeth forth with virtue; great, great adoration!"

3. The Mantra of *Champa* (the future Buddha).

Namah Sámanta Buddhánam! ajitanajaya,
Sarvva Satwayasháyanugata, Swáhá!

"Glory to the chief Buddhas! conqueror of the invincible,
Possessor of the fame of all purity, adoration!"

4. The Mantra of *Chakna-Dorjé* (Vajra-Páni).

Namah Sámanta Vajránám! Chanda Maha-roshana,-hun!

"Glory to the chief Vajras; fierce and greatly-angry, *hun!*"

5. The Mantra of *Jámya* (Manju-Sri).

Namah Sámanta Buddhánam! hé, hé, hé! Kumáraka, Vimukti, Sathirthati, smara, smara, pratihana, swáhá!

"Glory to the chief Buddhas! hé, hé, hé! Young Prince, Emancipation, Communion, Memory, Memory, Great Prowess, Adoration!"

6. Mantra of *Chanrazik* (Avalokiteswara).

Namah Sámanta Buddhánam! Sarvva Tathágata, Avalokita, Karaná, Máyá; Rá-rá-rá! Hun! Jáh! Swáhá!

"Glory to the chief Buddhas! Universal Tathágata, Avalokita, The Merciful, the Compassionate: Rá-rá-rá! Hun! Jáh! adoration!"

7. Mantra of *Grol-ma* (Tárá).

Namah Sámanta Buddhánam! Karnodbhavé! Túri, taráni, Swáhá!

"Glory to the chief Buddhas! offspring of mercy! By whom existence is traversed, adoration!"

The above are the mystic prayers offered up to the supreme Buddha by the different Bodhisatwas and others, whose names they bear. But there are numerous other *mantras* addressed to the Bodhisatwas themselves, as in the following specimen, which is taken from an actual Tibetan stereotype wooden block in my own possession:—

8. *Aum! Vagiswari Mun! Aum! Mani-padme, hun! Aum Vajrapáni, hun!*

(the same repeated).

Aum! amaráni-jivantiye, swáhá!

Aum! Vajra-krodha, háyagriba, hu-lu, hu-lu, hun, phat.

"In the name of the Triad! O, divine lord, *Mun!*
In the name of the Triad! O, Lotus-bearer, *Hun!*
In the name of the Triad! O, Sceptre-bearer, *Hun!*"

(the same repeated).

"In the name of the Triad! O, immortal Being, adoration!
In the name of the Triad! O, wrathful *Vajra*, flame-necked, *hu-lu!—hu-lu!—hun!—phat!*"

This is addressed to the supreme Buddha (Bhageswara), to the celestial Bodhisatwas, *Padmapáni* and

Vajrapáni (the lotus and sceptre bearers), and to the Tántrika divinity Iswara. Other *mantras* are:—

9. *Aum! Sarvva Vidya, Swáhá! aum! Sarvva vidya! Swáhá!*
Aum! áh! Guru sumati-jnyán Siddh, hun-hun!
"In the name of the Triad! Universal Wisdom, adoration!"
(the same repeated).
"In the name of the Triad! ah! Teacher of Supreme Intelligence, Holy-one, *Hun-hun!*"

10. *Aum! Muné, Muné, Mahá-Mune, Sakya-Munaye, Swáhá!*
Aum! Mani-padme, hun! Aum! Chanda Mahá-roshana, hun, phat!
Aum! Táre, tuttáre, turé, Swáhá!
Aum! Mohi, mohi, mahá-mohi, Swáhá!
Aum! Mati, mati, Smriti, Swáhá!
Aum! Maitri, Maitri, Mahá-Maitri, Arya-Maitri, Swáhá!
Aum! Vagiswari, Mun! Aum! Mani-padmé, hun! Aum! Vajrapáni, hun!

"Aum! O, Muni, Muni, Great Muni, SÁKYA-MUNI, adoration!
O, Lotus-bearer, *hun!*—O, fierce and greatly-angry, *hun-phat!*
O, TARA, * * * * * adoration!
O, Pleasure, Pleasure, Mighty Pleasure, adoration!
O, Intellect, Intellect, Understanding, adoration!
O, MAITREYA, Maitreya, Great Maitreya, venerated Maitreya, adoration!
O, Divine Lord, *Mun!* O, Lotus-bearer, *hun!* O, Sceptre-bearer, hun!"

These are, however, sensible productions compared to the gibberish of others, of which the following is an untranslateable specimen:—

11. *Bhyoh, rakmo-bhyo! rakmo-bhyo-bhyò!*
Rakmo thun-bhyo! khala rakchhenmo!
Rakmo, abya-tabya, thun-bhyo!
Ru-lu, ru-lu, hun, bhyo, hun!

This potent charm I found repeated twenty-seven times on a roll of paper, inside an image of Shakya-Thubba. How deplorably low must be the religious belief of those who hope to weary Heaven into compliance with their wishes by the importunate reiteration of such gibberish!

XIV.—LANGUAGE.

I.—ALPHABET—PRONUNCIATION.

THE alphabetical character of the Tibetans is the Devanágari that was current in India in the seventh century. It was introduced into Tibet from Kashmir by Thumi Sambhota.* The alphabet is called *Ka-ga* (or A B C), because *k* and *g* are the first letters. There are thirty consonants, arranged in eight classes, as follows:—

1.	ka ...	kha ...	ga ...	nga
2.	cha ...	chha ...	ja ...	nya
3.	ta ...	tha ...	da ...	na
4.	pa ...	pha ...	ba ...	ma
5.	tsa ...	tsha ...	dsa ...	wa
6.	zha ...	za ...	ha ...	ya
7.	ra ...	la ...	sha ...	sa
8.	'ha ...	á		

The 1st, 2nd, 3rd, 4th, and 7th, correspond with the arrangement of the Nágari alphabet, excepting only in the omission of the second set of aspirates, *gh*, *jh*, *dh*, and *bh*. The hissing palatals of the 5th and 6th classes are almost peculiar to the Tibetan language. The *tsa* and *dsa* are, however, in constant use by the Kashmiris.

The vowels are five, *a*, *i*, *u*, *e*, *o*, which are pronounced as in Italian. The vowel *a* is inherent in every consonant, excepting the few silent prefixes. The other vowels

* Csoma's Grammar, p. 178.

are formed by marks placed either above or below the consonants.

The Tibetan language is written syllabically, the different syllables being separated by a small wedge-like point, called *Tsheg*, thus ٧. The sentences also are divided by signs or marks of punctuation, called *Shad.* Thus, one mark, །, is equivalent to a comma; a double mark, །།, to a colon; and four marks །། །། to a full stop. The semicolon is formed by joining the intersyllabic point *Tsheg* to the single punctuation mark *Shad*, from which it receives its name of *Tsheg-Shad.* It is formed thus༔, and is almost the same as our own semicolon.*

Of the Tibetan language I am not confident to speak; but, as far as my knowledge of it enables me to offer an opinion, I should say that it has no affinity with any of the surrounding dialects. A few words are of course the same as in Sanscrit; such as *khar*, a fort (Sanscrit, *garh*). But for every word similar to Sanscrit I think that I could point out one similar to English; thus, *brang* means to bring; *kyan* is a "can;" *thwore* is "to-morrow;" *skyur* is "sour;" *dal* means "dull;" *tuk* is "thick;" *bal* is "wool;" *lhunpo* is a "lump;" *tsem* is a "seam;" *dir* is "here;" and *der* is "there;" *tar* is "tired;" *rog* is a "rogue" (the crow being called *cha-rog*, or the "bird-rogue"); *yahba* is a "yawn;" and *ikhug* is a "hiccough." The last two are, however, imitative sounds. But there is another resemblance between English and Tibetan, which is of a totally different kind. This is the difficulty of ascertaining how to pronounce a word from its spelling. A foreigner is

* The marks of punctuation are called *rKyang-shad*, the comma; *gZhis-shad*, the colon; *bZhi-shad*, the full stop; and *Tsheg-shad*, the semicolon.

puzzled with our *plough*, *dough*, and *slough* or *enough*, and with our *rite*, *write*, *right*, and *wright*. But the Tibetans are equally capricious in their pronunciation. *Spyan* they pronounce *shan* and *chan*, *phyag* they pronounce *chhag*, and *byang** they pronounce *chang*. Then again, they pronounce *do* (two), *bDo* (abundance), *mDo* (a short treatise or district), *hDo* (an answer), *rDo* (a stone), and *sDo* (danger), all in the same manner. And these, again, are confounded with the several words that are spelt with *t* and *th*.† It is in fact equally difficult to know how to spell a word from its pronunciation as to pronounce one from its spelling. In correct speaking, the silent initial letters should be rapidly sounded; and they are so by the more learned Lamas, *but by them only*. It is true that Vigne writes *Erganak* for *rGyanak* (the "black plain," the Tibetan name of China); but Moorcroft wrote *Guinnak*. Again, the pronunciation varies in different districts: thus, the compounds in *kh*, as *khy*, and *khr*, are pronounced *thy* and *thr* in Lhasa. *Khyi*, a dog, is called *thyi;* and *khrimpon*, a judge, is called *Thimpon;* but in Ladák they are pronounced as they are spelt. In Lhasa the final *s* in *Shags* is silent, as *shak*, justice. In Ladák it is pronounced *Shaks*. One of the most violent mispronunciations is *Tashi* for *bKra-shis*, as in *Tashi-Lhunpo*. Another is *U*, for *dBus*, the name of a district in Central Tibet. In the time of Ptolemy, however, this word must have been pronounced according to its spelling; for there can be no reasonable doubt that the people, whom he calls *Dabasæ*, are the inhabitants of *Dabus*, now *dBus*.

* In Kanâwar, however, the word is pronounced *Byang*, as in *Byangi*, wool, from which comes Chang Thang.

† So also *dMigs*, object; *dMig*, a hole; *Mig*, an eye; *rMig*, a hoof; *rMigs*, a worm; are all pronounced *Mik*.

II.—FORMER LIMITS OF THE TIBETAN LANGUAGE.

The Tibetan language is now confined to the mountain valleys of the Tsangpo and Indus, and to the upper courses of the Sutluj, the Sarju, and the Chenáb. But in ancient days it probably extended over the greater part of the Cis-Himálayas,* as I can trace by the Tibetan names of the smaller streams. All the larger rivers have been re-named by the Brahmans; but the smaller streams still retain their old names. Thus I find, within a few miles of Simla, the *Andre-ti*, or water of the Andar village; the *Ghail-ti*, or water of the Ghail valley; the *Khanyao-ti*, or water of the Khanethu district; and the *Gumo-ti*, or water of the Gumo valley. Other names are the *Chahi-ti*, the *Manyao-ti*, the *Chigaun-ti*, and the *Wal-ti*, all of which preserve the Tibetan word *ti*, "water." It is, perhaps, idle to speculate at what period the Tibetans could have possessed the present districts of Bisahar, Kyonthal, and Sarmar; but it must have been many centuries ago, before the Khasas† were driven into the hills by the conquering Hindus.

In Kanâwar, where the Indian and Tibetan languages meet, there are two dialects, which partake more or less of the one or of the other. The *Milchang*, or common language of Lower Kanáwar, is so called by the people of

* Pliny, VI. c. 17, Scythæipoi Caucasum montem (appellavere) *Graucasum*, hoc est *nive candidum;* and Isidor (according to Wilford) states that *Kroakasis* means "white" in the eastern tongue. Now, the only eastern language which approaches these words is the Tibetan, in which *Kar-khá-chan*, pronounced *Kar-khá-tsan*, means "white-snow-full-of," which is exactly Pliny's "nive candidum."

† The Kanets of the hills are all Khasas; and in Chamba, Kullu, and Kanâwar, they interpose between the Hindus and Tibetans.

Bisahar; the Kanâwaris themselves call it *Milchanang*. This name is most probably only the Tibetan word *Mingchang* (pronounced *Milchang*), "notorious or very common, vulgar." This dialect prevails over Lower Kanáwar, and along the left bank of the Sutluj in Upper Kanáwar. The *Tibar-skad*, or "*Tibar* language," is a dialect peculiar to Sungnam, Kánam, Lipe, and other places in Upper Kanáwar. It differs from the *Milchang* chiefly in shades of pronunciation, and in the changes of some initial consonants.

English.	Milchang.	Tibarskad.	Tibetan.
Three ...	súm ...	hum ...	sum.
A horse ...	rang ...	shang ...	tá.
A star ...	skara ...	karma ...	skarma.
Snow ...	pang ...	ang ...	kha.
A house ...	khim ...	khyim ...	khyim.
White ...	thog ...	thungni ...	kar.
Name ...	namang ...	ming ...	ming.
Green ...	rag ...	zangu ...	jangu.

In these examples there is, as might be expected, a greater admixture of Tibetan words in the dialect of Upper Kanáwar, which lies next to Tibet. In that of Lower Kanáwar there is one Hindu word, *namang*, a name.

In the following chapter I have given a copious vocabulary of the Tibetan language, compared with all the surrounding languages: with the *Arniyá*, *Shiná*, and *Khajunah* of the Dards; with the *Pushtu* of the Afghans, and with the *Kashmiri* of the Kasas; with the *Hindi* dialects of the people of Chamba, Kullu, Handur, and Garhwál, as well as with the Indo-Tibetan *Mil-*

chang and *Tibar-skad* of Kanáwar. This comparison will give a much better idea of the language than any thing that I can say.

III.—PRINTING.

Printing has long been known and practised in Tibet, but only by engraved stereotype wooden blocks, and not by moveable types. The printing of a new work is therefore a most expensive and laborious process. The accompanying specimen of a Tibetan horn-book, or primer, is printed from one of these engraved planks.* The letters are most beautifully cut, but the block has been so much used, that the original sharpness is now quite gone.

The first or middle circle is blank.

The second circle contains a mystic formula, which I cannot decipher.

The third circle contains the ejaculation *hih*, eight times repeated.

The fourth circle contains the ejaculation *hún*, ten times repeated.

The fifth circle contains the Tibetan alphabet, arranged according to the Sanscrit order, with all the cerebrals and aspirates complete. These last letters are not used in Tibetan words, but only in the transcription of Sanscrit names; as for instance, the *ṇ* in *Padmapaṇi*. It is remarkable that the *ch*, *chh*, and *j* have all got the mark placed over them, which alters their pronunciation to *ts*, *tsh*, and *ds*. This is, I think, a direct proof that the Tibetans obtained their knowledge of Sanscrit, as well as their alpha-

* See Plate XLIV.

Plate XXVI

THE TIBETAN HORN-BOOK

from a Tibetan Wooden Block

bet, from the Kashmiris, who still pronounce these letters in the above manner, as *Pandsál* for Panjál.

The sixth circle I cannot decipher, but I can trace the repeated ejaculations of hun-hun! hun-hun! hun-hun! hun!

The seventh circle is one of the most interesting, as it contains the famous Indian enunciation of the Buddhist faith, which I found inscribed on a stone which I extracted from the great tope of *Sárnáth*, near Benares. This is the only instance in which I have seen it used in Tibet.

Aum! Muni, Muni, Mahá-Munayé, swáhá!
Yé dharma hetu prabhavá hetun teshán Tathágato
hyavadat teshán cha yá nirodha evam vadi Mahasramanas.

"In the name of the Triad! O, Muni, Muni, great Muni, adoration! Of all things springing from cause, that cause hath the Tathágata explained; the cause of their extinction also hath the great As-cetic declared."

New works are rarely undertaken, but the printing of their standard religious works is still carried on by the Tibetans with the same old blocks that were in use upwards of 100 years ago. The great mass of printing, however, is chiefly confined to the production of the innumerable quantity of prayers and mystical formulæ that are required by the people. I have seen many rolls containing many hundred repetitions of the same sentences. They are printed on sheets of a thin brownish paper called *Grega* (or *Tega*), but the books are printed on a much smoother paper called *Par-shog*, or "printer's paper." The ink is called *Par-snag*, or "printer's ink." The printer himself is named *Par-pa*, and where several are employed the head printer is called *Par-pon*. The printing board, or table, is *Par-shing*, and "copy" is called *Par-bri-pa*. The engraved block is named *Zhi*, and the engraver *Par-ko-pa.* The printing-house is called *Par-khang,* and the book, when completed, is named *Par-ma,* a "printed work."

A book consists of numerous loose leaves, from one to two feet long, and from three to four inches in width. These are numbered, and secured between two planks. The title and number of the volume are sewn upon a piece of silk and inserted at one end.*

IV.—RECKONING OF TIME.

The Ladákis make use of two modes of reckoning time, the cycle of twelve years for common computations, such as a man's age, or the date of any recent event; but both in writing and in accounts they always use the cycle of sixty years, which they borrowed from India.†

In the cycle of twelve years, each year is named after a particular animal, as follows:—

1. Byi-lo ... ... the Mouse year.
2. gLang-lo ... ... the Ox year.
3. Stag-lo ... ... the Tiger year.
4. Yos-lo ... ... the Hare year.
5. hBrug-lo ... ... the Dragon year.
6. sBrul-lo ... ... the Serpent year.
7. rTa-lo ... ... the Horse year.
8. Lug-lo ... ... the Sheep year.
9. Spre-lo ... ... the Ape year.
10. Bya-lo ... ... the Bird year.
11. Khyi-lo ... ... the Dog year.
12. Phog-lo ... ... the Hog year.

My first acquaintance with this cycle was rather startling. I asked a jolly-looking dame, named Thájang,

* A volume in my possession is entitled *Chhos-rGyan*—D—that is, "The Ornament of Religion," 11th vol.

† Csoma's Grammar, pp. 147, 148.

who had three husbands living, and several children,* what her age was. To my great astonishment she replied "twelve." At first I thought that she did not wish to tell her age, but I soon found that she only reckoned by cycles, and that she was not yet two cycles old. I then turned to Csoma de Körös's grammar, and after a little more questioning I discovered that she was twenty years of age. Afterwards, in collecting my tables of longevity, I took some pains to guard against this mode of wholesale reckoning by cycles, and with two exceptions, I was personally successful. But where I was obliged to trust to a munshi for my information, I found that numbers of the old people were sixty, seventy-two, and eighty-four years of age.

The cycle of sixty years is a much more elaborate reckoning. The first cycle is counted from A.D. 1026. The Hindus have a distinct name for each year of the cycle, but the Tibetans have adopted the Chinese nomenclature, which is formed by coupling the names of the twelve animals of the other cycle with the names of the five elements, considered as both male and female alternately. The first element, male and female, is coupled with the first two animals, next with the eleventh and twelfth animals, and so on; by which the change of names is preserved throughout the whole series. The names in English are—

Wood-Mouse	11. Wood-Dog	21. Wood-Ape	31. Wood-Horse	41. Wood-Dragon	51. Wood-Tiger
„ Ox	12. „ Hog	22. „ Bird	32. „ Sheep	42. „ Serpent	52. „ Hare
Fire-Tiger	13. Fire-Mouse	23. Fire-Dog	33. Fire-Ape	43. Fire-Horse	53. Fire-Dragon
„ Hare	14. „ Ox	24. „ Hog	34. „ Bird	44. „ Sheep	54. „ Serpent
Earth-Dragon	15. Earth-Tiger	25. Earth-Mouse	35. Earth-Dog	45. Earth-Ape	55. Earth-Horse
„ Serpent	16. „ Hare	26. „ Ox	36. „ Hog	46. „ Bird	56. „ Sheep
Iron-Horse	17. Iron-Dragon	27. Iron-Tiger	37. Iron-Mouse	47. Iron-Dog	57. Iron-Ape
„ Sheep	18. „ Serpent	28. „ Hare	38. „ Ox	48. „ Hog	58. „ Bird
Water-Ape	19. Water Horse	29. Water-Dragon	39. Water-Tiger	49. Water-Mouse	59. Water-Dog
„ Bird	20. „ Sheep	30. „ Serpent	40. „ Hare	50. „ Ox	60. „ Hog

* See her Portrait, Plate XVIII.

The different cycles began in the following years—

1st	began	1026 A.D.	6th	began	1326 A.D.	11th	began	1626 A.D.
2nd	„	1086 „	7th	„	1386 „	12th	„	1686 „
3rd	„	1146 „	8th	„	1446 „	13th	„	1746 „
4th	„	1206 „	9th	„	1506 „	14th	„	1806 „
5th	„	1266 „	10th	„	1566 „			

The present year, 1851, is therefore the forty-fifth year of the fourteenth cycle.

The months are also named after the twelve animals; but the first month is *hBrug-zLa*, or the "dragon-month," which corresponds with the Hindu *Mágh*, and with our January and February.

XV.

COMPARISON

OF THE

VARIOUS ALPINE DIALECTS,

FROM

THE INDUS TO THE GHÂGRA.

DARDU DIALECTS.	The Arniya dialect is spoken in		Yasan and Chitrál.
	„ Shiná	„	Gilgit, Chalás, Daret, Kohli, and Pálas.
	„ Khajunah	„	Hunza and Nager.
AFGHAN.	„ Pushtu	„	Afghanistan and Eastern Hazára.
KASA.	„ Kashmiri	„	Kashmir.
INDIAN DIALECTS.	„ Panjâbi	„	The Panjáb.
	„ Gádi	„	Chamba, Northern Kangra.
	„ Kulluhi	„	Kullu.
	„ Handuri	„	Handur, Kahlur, and Kyonthal.
	„ Garhwâli	„	Garhwâl and Sarmor.
TIBETAN DIALECTS.	„ Milchang	„	Lower Kanáwar.
	„ Tibarskad	„	Upper Kanáwar.
	„ Tibetan	„	Tibet, Ladák, and Balti.

ENGLISH.	DARDU DIALECTS.			AFGHAN.	KASA.	INDIAN	
	Arniya.	Shiná.	Khajunah.	Pushtu.	Kashmiri.	Sanscrit.	Hindi.
Air	T. hawá	ushé	tishé	bád, wah, wu	hawé, wáho	átmá (ατμη) vayu	hawá
Ant	—	—	—	—	ré	pipilaka	chunta, chinta
Arrow	wishu	kon	hunz	ghasho	tir, kán	tir, ván	tir, bán
Bird	—	bring	balas	marghai	úphátin tsiri	pakshin	pakheru
Blood	le (? lohé)	lohél	multán	vina (αιμα)	ráth	rakta	lohu
Boat	—	nao	nao	berai (βαρος)	nao	nau	nao, khishti, bera
Bone	—	—	—	—	adij	asthi	haddi
Brass	—	rel	rel	ziyar, zyad	sartal	kánsiya	pital
Brick	—	dastak	dán	khikta	sir	ishtaká	inth, ith (πλινθος)
Brother	—	já	achu	rúr, aror	bhoyi, bai	bhrátá (φρατωρ)	bhai
Buffalo	—	S. mahés	S. hés mahés	mekha	mahesh	mahesa	bhains
Camel	S. unth	S. unth	S. unth	ukh, ugh	unth	ushtra	unth
Cat	P. pusha	P. pushi	P. pushi	pishau, pishi	brĕor, bryár, byáür	virál	billi
Cloud	—	ajao	harald	waras	abr	nabhas (νεφος)	bádr, bádal
Copper	—	Tib. záns zangutz	Tib. záns	támba mio	tram	támra	támba
Cotton	—	S. kayás	S. kupás	kupa pamba	kapas	karpása	kapás, rúi
Cow	leshu, lesun	socha-gao	G. buah (βους)	ghúai	gao	gau	gai
Crow	—	—	—	—	kao	kák	kák, kág
Daughter	S. kamera gumod	dhi	ai	lúr	kúr	putri, kanya	beti
Day	chhoi	des	gues (Turki) guns	roz	doh, dah	din	din
Dog	rain	shúng	húk	spai	hún, phú (κυων)	kukkur	kuttá
Ear	S. kar, kád	S. kúnd	iltúmál	wagh ghwaj	kan	karna	kán
Earth	S. bhúm	birdi, saor	birdi	azmuka	bhutrát, meta	bhu, go (γη)	bhumi, prithv
Egg	—	—	—	hagge	thúl	anda	andá
Elephant	—	S. hasto	S. hasto	háthi	húst, hast	hasti	háthi, kunjar
Eye	S. ach; T. ghach	S. achhi	S. ilchin	istargi stirgha	ach, achu	chakshus	ánkh
Father	—	málo	ao	palár	mol, báb	janak, pitta	báp, pitá
Fire	S. ág, ingár	phó, agár	phu	aor, or	nár, agan	agni	ág
Fish	—	chimu	chimu	mahi	ghád	matsya	machhi
Flower	—	S. pusho	askhor	gul	posh	pushpa	phúl
Foot	S. pang	S. pá	goting	akhpe	kor, kúr	pád	pao, pán
Fort	—	S. kot	kan	garhai	kalai	garh, durga	garhi
Fruit	—	S. phalamúl	S. phamúl	bár	méwa	phal	phal
Goat	pai	mugar, ai (αιξ)	haldin	biza	Psáwúl	'Aja (Αιξ) chhág	bakri
Gold	—	S. son	ghenish	sira-zar	son, swan	suvarna swarna	sona

DIALECTS.					TIBETAN.		
Punjábi.	Gádi.	Kuluhi.	Handuri.	Garhwáli.	Milchang.	Tibarskad.	Tibetan.
wáh	bát	bágur	bágar	pon, batás	lang	lang	rLungma
—	makori	chint	chit, makori	kirmila	—	—	Grogma
—	khar	kaneru	kaneru	tir	mo	shim	mDah
tiliyar	chiri	chelu	panchi	chara	bya	bya	Byá (chá)
—	ragat	lohu	lohu	lohu, ragat	pulách	Shuí	Khrag (thak) (ιχωρ)
béri	beri	beri	beri	nao	—	—	Grú
haddi	had	hád	had, hád	hár	hárang	hárang	Rús (οστεον, os)
pital	pítal	pital	pital	pital	pítal	pítal	rághán
itha	ith	ith	ith	ith	—	—	pag
bhai, bhira	bháya	dád	bhai	daji, bhula	acho, bya	acho, bya	spun
—	mahé	mahe	mahes	bhains	—	—	Mahi
unth	unth	unth	unth	unth	—	—	—
billi	billi	bareri	breári	billa	pishi	pishi	Byila, pushi
—	badr	bádal	badali	badal	zú, thing	zú, ding	tin
támbá	trámba	támbá	támbá	támbú	trámang	tramang	zangs
ruwi, gan	kopá	paká	kapá	rui	kapa	kapa	shing-bal
—	goru	gao	gai	gai	lang	balang	Bá, Ba-lang
—	ká	kao	kao, káwá	kág	kák	ká	Khάta
dhi, káki	deyu	beti	dhi, beti	laoni	chimé	Sri-chang	bumo, srasmo
din	dyára	dyára	dyára	din	diár, lai	diár, zangma	Nyin-mo
kuttá	kuttr	kukar	kuttá	kuttu	khuí	khuí	Khyi
kán	kan	kan	kán	kán	kánang	rapang	Sá, Amcho rNa-ba
—	prithvi	jimi, mata	prithi	máta	mátang, sho	mátang	rNa
anda	bat	peni	andi	andá, phul	li, lich	túm	sGonga
háthi	hathi	háthi	háthi	háthi, ganes			gLangchen
akh	akr	ákh	ákh, hákh	ankha	mik	mi	Mig, spyan
peo, bábá	chacha	báb	bápu	bhuva	bábá	apa	Phá, yab
ag	ág	ág	ág	ág	mé	mé	Mé
machhi	machhi	manchi	machhli	mácha	machas	machas	Nya
pushp, phúl	phúl	phúl	phul	phúl	ú	mento	Metog
pao, pai	par	rahar	pair, lát	pair, kuta	bang	bangkhat	rKang-pa zhabs
garh, garhi	garhi	garh	garh	kilah, garh	gorang	gorang	mKhar rDsong
phal	phal	phal	phal	phal	sho	usho	hBrasbu dalbu
bakrá, chhela	bakra	bakra	bakrá	bakra	aj, bakar	lá	Rá
soná	súná	soná	sona	sunu	zang	zang	mSer

ENGLISH.	DARDU DIALECTS.			AFGHAN.	KASA.	INDIAN	
	Araiya.	Shiná.	Khajunah.	Pushtu.	Kashmiri.	Sanscrit.	Hindi.
Grass	—	kats	shikah	wákho purod	gháso	ghás, khar	ghas
Hair	chhámi	bálo	gogeyang	vekhto	mast, wal	kesar	bal
Hand	S. hast, husht	S. hath	gureng ghar (Mog.)	lás	atho, atha	hasta, kai (χειρ)	háth
Head	S. sur	shis	yetis	sar	kalah	sir	sar, mund
Honey	—	macchhé	macché	gabinoh	mánch	madhu	madh, shahad
Horse	astor	P. ashp	bághor	ás	ghor, ghur	aswa	ghora
House	—	got, gosh	hah	kor	gharo, ghacro	nivás, bás	ghar, koti
Husband	—	bareyo	er (Turki) suyér (ανηρ)	mero	mahrás	pati, swámi	kámin, khasam
Iron	—	chimr, kimr	T. temir chimr	uspano ospana	shistar (σιδηρος)	loha	lohá
King	—	Rashra	Tham	pádsháh	pádsháh	rája, despati (δεσποτης)	rája, rais
Lead	nong	náng, nong	náng	siká surp	nág	sisak, sisa	sisá
Leaf	—	S. pattá	thápong	páné	pan	patra	patti, pattá
Light	—	sang	sang-manimi	rokhánah	gásh	prabha, tej	ujálá, roshani
Lightning	—	béchús	—	charak	uzmal	sandamini	bijli
Man	rag; S. moashi	S. musha	hir er (Turki.)	saré, medá	manu, manyu	manushya nara	mánas
Milk	S. chir; B. shid	dudh	mamu	pai, shaodo shide	dod, dwod	dughdam	dúdh
Monkey	—	—	—	bizo	punz	kapi, vánar	bandar, langúr
Moon	—	yún	halans	spog-mai spaj-me	zún, tsandar	chandra	chánd
Mother	—	má	umá	mor	moj, máj, mají	máta	má, amá, mátá
Mountain	an, zúm	chesh	chesh	ghar	pánzál, bál, sangúr, tong, parbat	parvata, giri	parbat, pahár
Mouth	diran	anzi, asi	gokhat	khálo	áso, ás (στομα)	mukh	munh, mukh
Musquito	—	—	—	—	múh	masa	machchar
Name	—	S. noma (ονομα)	goyak	núm	nao	náma	nám
Night	paniyá	S. rát	tipa	ashpá	rát	rátri	rát
Nose	naskár	noto	gomoposh	pozeh, paza	nast	násika	nák
Oil	—	S. teil	dhel	tel	til	tel	tel
Plantain	—	—	—	—	kéla	kadala	kela
Rain	—	azwahi	harilitachil	bárán	rúd	vrishti, varsha	bárish
River	S. sin	S. sin	sindha	sin	kúl, wit	sindhu, ganga	nadi
Road	P. ráh	pon	gand	lár	wat (ὁδος)	vát, márga	gél, rá
Salt	—	lona	beyo	málgá	nún	lavana	lon
Sheep	ashpai	karelo	bashkar	gadúra, maj, mej	kat, gob	bherha, mesh	bhéra
Shoe	kosh (Tib.)	paizár	paizár	paná, kough	kosh (Tib.)	pádukâ	jora, jhuti

DIALECTS.					TIBETAN.		
Punjábi.	**Gádi.**	**Kuluhi.**	**Handuri.**	**Garhwáli.**	**Milchang.**	**Tibarskad.**	**Tibetan.**
ghá	ghá	ghá	ghas, khar	ghás	chi	chi	Sá
bál	khrár	sharár	kes	bál	krá	krá	sKrá, sPú
háth	hath	hath	háth	háth	got, gúd	lá	Lag-pa Phyag
—	múnd	múnd	sir, mund	kapál	bal	pisha	mGo
—	makhír	makhír	makhír	meh, gar	was	pránchi	sBrang-rTsi
ghoda	ghora	ghora	ghora	ghora	rang	shang	rTá
ghar, kota	ghar	ghar	ghar	ghar, jhompra	khim, kyúm	kyúng, kyúm	Khyim, Khang
gharwála	mard	lála	lárá*	dhula	dach	choga	Khyodang
lohá	loha	loha	loha	loha	rang, pron	chák	lChags
raja	rája	rája	raja	raja	—	—	rGyal-po
sikká	sisa	sik	sik	sisa	sik	sik	shání, rilti
pattar	patta	pách	pát, pách	pát	patlang, patrang	patlang	Lomá
—	ujyála	presha	priása	ujyála	—	—	Hod sNang-pa
—	bijli	bijli	bijli	bijli	bijil, bizúng	byzúng	—
—	mánas	mánush	mard, tin	mánus	mi	mi	Mi
dudh	dúdh	dudh	dúdh	dúdh	khirang, bérang	pei	ho, homa
bándar	bandar, langúr	bandar	bandar	bandar, langúr	gonas, bandras	gonas, bandras	sPrebu
chand	chandar	jot	chanda, jun	chandramá	galsang	galsang	rLáva
má, ammá	íji	íji	má, ammá	bhai	amá	amá	Amá, Má, yum
dak, dahak	joth	dahak	dhár, tibba	dhánk, tiba	rang, ranga	yui	Ri, lá
—	mú	jyát	munh	mukh	khágang	á	Khá, zhal
—	máchchar	chach	machchar	máchchar	cháchi	koyang	Stinbu
nao	ná	nám	nám	nám	námang	ming	Ming
rát	rát	nihára	rát	rát	ráting	mundo, múnia	mTshanmo
nak	nák	náka	nák	nák	stágús	nyum	sNa, shanga
tal	tal, tel	tel	tel	tal	telang	máthi	hBrumar marku
kela	kélé	kerá	kalu	kalu	—	—	—.
—	barsárá	bishkál	barshkal	hiyund	rodang, doyang	—	rodang, mukpa
—	nai	khad	nai, khad	nadi	samudrang	tsángpú	gTsang-po
ráh	bat	bát	bát	bátu	om	om, ám	Lám
lun	lon	lon	lun	lún	tshá	tshá	Tshá (αλς)
bhedá, kádu	bhera	bhed	bher, kádu, ruba	bhera	khas	stum	lúg
jhuti	pasla	polra	jora, paoni	jutu	kushera	phoni	kushiri, lham

* In Kashmiri—*lari*, a house; hence, *lárá*, a husband; *lári*, a wife.
Compare Punjábi—*ghar*, " " *gharwala*, " *gharwali*, "

ENGLISH.	DARDU DIALECTS.			AFGHAN.	KASA.	INDIAN	
	Arniya.	Shiná.	Khajunah.	Pushtu.	Kashmiri.	Sanscrit.	Hindi.
Silver	—	S. rúp	búri	spin-zar	rop	rajata	rupa, chándi
Sister	—	S. sas	ayas	khor	binyé, bhenji	bhágini	báhin
Skin	—	—	—	—	tsam	charmma	kál
Sky	ásmán	agáhi	ayesh	ásmán	nab	nabas, swarga	nák
Snake	—	jand	—	már	saruf, sarf	sarpa	sámp
Snow	S. him	S. hin	gyé	vaorah	shin	hima	him
Son	dák (τεκνον)	pucha (παις)	G. aya (υιος)	zoyah	necho	putra, sut	putr, beta
Star	satár (αστηρ)	S. táro	asi	storah	táro, tárak	tárá	tara
Stone	—	bat	dhan	kárnah	káin	prasthara, sila	patthar, sil (πετρα)
Sun	—	S. suri	sa	nawar, imar	aftáb, ayit, suraj	surya (Σειριος)	suraj
Thunder	—	angaigút	—	gharido	gagarai	meghgarjjan, vajranishpesh	garaj, gargaráhat
Tiger	—	dhi	tháb	hamzerah	suh, sih	vyághra	bagh
Tooth	S. dond	S. dhuni	gume	ghakhuna, ghágh	dan, dand	danta	dánt
Town	—	kuí	bushé	khar, ghar	shahar	nagara, pura	nagar, pur
Tree	kan	túm	—	wuna, wanai	kal, kulu	dáru, vriksha	rúkh, per, gáchh
Tribe	—	rúmá	rom	khel, zai	zát	kula, gotra	kul, got, ját
Village	—	thenush-kui	—	kileh, kalai	gám	gráma	gaon, basti, purwa
Water	augr, ugh	wahi	chil	ubo, oba	áb, páni	âpa, uda	jal, pani
Wife	—	hilái	sambal	khiza, ghaza	mahrin	stri	joru, stri
Woman	S. kamri, kumedi	grin	gus	khiza, ghaza	zanánah	stri, nari	rindi, nári
Wood	jin	kátho	gashil	largai, largi	zún (ξυλον)	káshtha, vana	lakri, kath
Wool	postam	pash	(Tib.) bal	warai, wadai (εριον)	yer (ειρος)	urna	un
East	—	*ja*labahi	*jil*manás	narkháto	—	purooa, para	purab
West	—	*bur*abahi	*bur*manás	kibleh	—	pakshina, apara	pachhim
North	—	—	—	kulb	dachin	uttara, váma	úttar
South	—	—	—	shamál	káwar	dakshina	dakhin
Right	—	dachin	dohmo	khi	dachin	dakshina	dahina
Left	—	thail	yáham	khin-gis	káwar	váma	bayan, bám
1	I	ek	hin	yo	ak	eka	ek
2	ju	do	altas	dwá	zih	dwa	do
3	truí	che	usko	dré	trah	tri	tin
4	chod	chhar	walto	salor	tsor	chatur	chhar
5	punj	push	sundo	pinzo	pánz	panchan	pánch
6	chuí	shah	mishando	ashpag	shah	shash	chah, khat
7	sút	sát	talo	awo	sat	saptan	sát
8	ánsht	asht	altambo	ata	ath	ashtan	áth
9	neuhan	no	huncho	nah	noh	navan	nao
10	jash	dahi	tormo	las	dah	das	das
			10+1	1+10			1+10
11	—	akáhi	turmohan	yaolas	kah	ekádas	igárah
			10+2				
12	—	báhi	turmáltas	dolas	bah	dwádas	bárah
20	jishi	bi	altar	shil	wuh	vinsati	bis
			20+10				
30	—	chehi	altartormo	derish	trah	trinsat	tis

DIALECTS.					TIBETAN.		
Panjábi.	Gádi.	Kulluhi.	Handuri.	Garhwáli.	Milchang.	Tibarskad.	Tibetan.
chándi, rupa	rupa	rupa	rupa	rupa	mil, mul	mul	múl
bahen	báhin	báhin	báhin	dhili, bhuli	Apu, Byách	Shing, Bété	achhé
—	kalri	kabri	kalri	chamrá	sha	pakpa	Pags-pa
—	amr	sarg	sarg, ambar	akás	sargang	nam	gNam, Khah
sap	kira	sáp	sáp	sarp	sábás	brul	sBrul (dul)
—	hyún ($\chi\iota\omega\nu$)	hio	hyun	hyún	pam, pang	ang	gangs-khapa
putr, beta	putr	beta	put, beta	nonál	chang	phaali chang	bu, sras
tára	tára	tára	tára	tára	skara	karma	skar-ma
patthar	nar	patthar	patthar	patthar, dhungar	rag, rák	rá	rDo
suraj	dera	suraj	suraj, dyára	suraj	yuné, yunek	nyi	Nyimá
—	gúrkta	gúlkho	grikona, ambargiriya	arjan	gurguri	gurguri	thog, hBrug
sher	brágh	barágh	si, sihi	sher	tar	tar	sTag
dand	dand	dánd	dand	dánt	gár, bang	soa	So, Tshems
nagar, grám	grá	sahar	pur, graon	ghar	—	—	grong-khyer, Gror
rúkh	rúkh	bhút	dár	darkhat	botang	botang	lJonshing, Shing
ját	ját	ját	kul	ját	—	—	—
pind, thatá	grá	graon	graon	ghar	deshang	deshang	Yul-thso, grong
páni	páni	páni	páni, jal	páni	ti	chhú	chhú
gharwáli	zanánah	lári	lári	dhuiin	nar, yas	yolat	chhung-ma
—	betari	chyori	jawánas	janana, istri	chismi	shri	cho-mo
lakr, káth	chiri	chiri	lakri	lakri	shing	shing	Shing
un	uni	un	un	un	cham	chám	Bal
purab	purab	purab	purab	purah	nes	duru, shar	shar
—	pachin	pachan	pacham	pachún	ning	duzur, núk	núb
—	dúr	uttar	uttar	uttar	thoad, ring	zang	cháng (byáng)
—	dakhin	dakhin	dakhan	dakhsin	shúng	zampuling	lho
—	dahina	—	dahina	dahina	zagang	dúré	gYas
kabhi	báwan	—	báwa	báyan	derang	bai	gYon
—	ak	ek	ek	ek	it	ti	gChig
—	do	do	do	do	nish	nishi	g Nyis
—	tré	tin	tin	tin	súm	súm	gSúm
—	chhar	chhar	chhar	chhar	pu, puk	pi	bZhi
—	panj	pánch	panj	pánch	ngá, má	ngai	lNgá
—	cheh	chah	cheh	chah	túk, túg	túki	drúg
—	sát	sát	sat	sát	stish	nashi	bDún
—	áth	áth	ath	áth	rai	gyai	brGyad
—	nao	no	nao	no	sgoí	guí	dGú
—	das	das	das	das	sai	chúí	bChú
—	igárah	igárah	igárah	igárah	sihad	chúti	bChu-gchig
—	bárah	bárah	bárah	bárah	sonish	chúni	bChu-gnyis
—	bi	bi	bi	kori	niza	nisa, niza	nyi-shu
—	tri	dera-bi	tis	tis	deo-niza	deo-niza	gSúm-bChú

ENGLISH.	DARDU DIALECTS.			AFGHAN.	KASA.	INDIAN	
	Arniya.	Shiná.	Khajunah.	Pushtu.	Kashmiri.	Sanscrit.	Hindi.
40	—	dobyo	twice 20 altowaltar	sarvekht	ratheji	chatwarinsat	chhalis
50	—	bobekadáhl	twice 20+10 alto waltar tormo	panzos	pánzáh	panchásat	pachás
100	do shum	shal	tha	sil	hat	sat	sao
1,000	—	S. sás	S. sás	zir	sás	sahasra	hajár
100,000	—	—	—	lakh	lach	laksha	lakh
1st	—	muchono	yarnoma	ahwala, yawaw	godanyuk	prathama	pahla
2nd	—	dogono	makchúm	duyamah, duwam	duyum	dwitiya	dusra
3rd	—	chagono	yilchúm	drémah, dreyam	teyum	tritiya	tisra
4th	—	charyono	waltúm	saloramah, saloram	chorum	chaturtha	chautha
10th	—	dahigono	torúm	lasumah, lasam	doham	dasama	daswa
Red	—	lolo	bardúm	sara, sura	wazul	lohita, rakta	lál
Yellow	—	haliru	shikark	zera, zyad	ledur	pinjar, píta	píla, hhaldiya
Blue	—	nila	shikam	nila, ábi	nyul	nila	níla .
Green	—	cherung	thokrang	shin	sabza	harita	hará
Black	—	kino	matung	tor	krihun	syáma, kála	kala, syám
White	—	sho	brúm	spin	chot	sweta, arjuna	safed, gorá
To-day	—	—	—	man, roz	az	—	áj
To-morrow	—	—	—	sabha roz	pagah, ruta	kalli, swas	kal
Yesterday	—	—	—	parún	yao	gata-kál	kal
Week	—	—	—	—	—	sapta-din	hafta
Month	—	—	—	—	ret	más	mas, mahina
Year	—	—	—	kal	wari	varsha	baras
Above	yang	—	—	porta, boad	—	ŭrddhwa, adhi	upar
Beneath	pást	kari	yárá	akhata	tal	tala, adha	niche
Between	—	—	—	—	—	antar	bich
Before	—	mucho	yar	mukh-ámukh, dodande	bont	para, agra	age
Behind	—	pato	ilji	rústo, dorusto	pat	pakshima	piche
Broad	—	bistino	daldalam	palana	paná	—	chaora
Long	—	jigo	thanung	ugda	zút	lamba	lamba
Crooked	—	kingru	gandér	kaga, koj	hul, haj	vakra	tircha
Straight	—	suntho	san	samah, rást	syúd	—	sidha
Dry	—	sukho	búm	uch, wach	hok	sushka	sukha
Wet	—	azo	hagúm	laondah, nmabd	adúr (υδωρ)	árdra	gila
Far	—	—	—	—	—	dúr	dúr
Near	—	—	—	—	nish, nakha	nikat	neri, pás
Good	jam	mishto	daltas	khá	jwán	su	achha, changa
Bad	dish	phana	wirán	nakhára	yach	dur, manda	bura

DIALECTS.					TIBETAN.		
Panjábi.	Gádi.	Kuluhi.	Handuri.	Garhwáli.	Milchang.	Tibarskad.	Tibetan.
—	cháli	cháli	cháli	chalis	nish-niza	nish-niza	bZhi-bChú
—	panjá	pauchá	panjá	pachás	dai-nizá	dai-niza	lNga-b-Chú
—	kao	sao	sao	sao	rá	gyá	brGya
—	hazár	hajár	das-sao	hazár	hazár	chu-gyá	stong
—	lákh	lakh	lakh	lakh	lákh	lákh	hBúm
—	ak-dera	eyu kadeh	age	pahla	—	dunchi	dang-po
—	do-dera	deju kadeh	dujja	dusra	—	—	gNyis-pa
—	tre-dera	treyu kadeh	tirja	tisra	—	—	gSum-pa
—	char-dera	chaŏn	chautha	chautha	—	—	bZhi-pa
—	das dera	dasou	daswa	daswa	—	—	bChu-pa
—	lál	—	sua	lál	shwig	mángni	dMar-po
—	piola	—	piora	piolo	pik, pikia	Lene	mSer-po
—	nila	—	nila	nilu	rak, rok	tingni	aNgo
—	hara	—	hara	hara	rag	zango	lJang
—	kála	—	kala	kálu	reg, rok	káni	nag-po
—	hachá	—	safed, chita	safed	thog	thaugni, changni	dKar-po
—	—	—	áj	áj	toro, trole,	diring	de-ring
—	—	—	kal	bholo	nasam	airo, yúr	sang, thoré
—	—	—	kal	bholi	me	yangto	mDang
—	—	—	—	—	—	—	bDun-phrag
—	—	—	mah	mahina	gol	la	zla
—	—	—	baras	baras	barsang	barsang	lo
—	uttara	—	upar	uparmáti	thoa, thuk	thárang, chokcho	stangna, gongna, mTho, stod
—	búnú	—	tol, nita	numdi	yua, yug	yogun	hogna,mar-pa dMan, smad
bichkár	bichkár	—	manjh	bichh	manzong, mazang	kilo	mang, bar
—	agé	—	age	agé	úma	donchi	mDúndú
—	pit	—	páché, piche	piché	nyúms	gyab-chi	rGyabtu
—	chaora	—	chaora	chaora	charas, kúnk	zheng-chan	zheng chan
—	bará	—	lambá	lámbú	—	—	ring-pa
—	pheta	—	bhengá	tircha	khungshim, kuta	gúrgúr	kug-pa
—	sidha	—	sidha	sidha	padras	thunia	kyang
—	hukha	—	sukhá	sukhu	charch, chars	phorka	sKam
—	sijji	—	siná, hará	suka	tisre, sping	chiko	gSher-pa, rLan-pa
—	—	—	dúr	dúr	warik, dúr	wár, wárko	thag-ring, ngan-pa
—	—	—	neri	nagich	nérang	nyémo	nyé-pa
changá	cher	—	achha, sobta	acchhu	dam	epo, ebuta	gShinpa, bZang
márá	márá	—	kwaina, bura	khráb	mar, kochang	ko changta	ngan

ENGLISH	DARDU DIALECTS.			AFGHAN.	KASA.	INDIAN	
	Arniya.	Shiná.	Khajunah.	Pushtu.	Kashmiri.	Sanscrit.	Hindi.
Hard	l	koro	dang	sakhta, kak	dor	kathar, kathin	karha
Soft	—	barál	ham	narma	narm	masrin, komal	narm
Heavy	—	angarú	chung	daraná, darúnd	gob	bhári	bhári
Light	—	loko	húmalkúm	spoka	lot	lagha	halka
Hot	—	tatto	garomo	garma	tut	tapta, ushna	tatta
Cold	—	chon	chagarum	yekhnai, sod	tarún	amishna	thanda
Hungry	—	—	—	ghwajai	—	kshudita	bhuka
Thirsty	—	—	—	tajai	—	pipásat	piása
Large	lat	baro	shokum	loyah	bod	vrihat	bara
Small	tsyuk	chuna	jot	warah	lok	kshutora	chhota
New	—	nao	tash	navé (novus)	no, nivi	navya	naya, navin
Old	—	prono	men	zarah	prom, pránu	purána jirna (γερων)	purána
Quick	—	hait	súrdrú	zir, jir	jald	satwar	jald
Slow	—	chot	talámáné	ro-ro	lot-lot	manda	asti, suli
Raw	—	omo	audevanam	kachá, umá, oma	khám	apakwa	kacha
Ripe	—	pakko	degonami	pakká	pop	pakwa	pakka
Rough	—	chacháro	chacharúm	—	—	asamán	
Smooth	—	pichilo	shirishúm	—	—	masrin	sáf, chikna
Round	ult	duduro	bidirim	—	dalom	gola, chakrakar	gola
Square	—	charkuta	walté shutungus	salor kunjah	chokunjah	chaturkona	chaokona, charkuta
Sweet	—	moro	moro	khwaza, khaj	madhur	mishta	mitha
Sour	—	—	—	tarwá	tsuk	amla	khatta
Thick	—	túlo	daganus	ghat	mot	sthula	mota
Thin	bizwa	taluno	beyenus	mahína	tonu, nyúk	saru, kahin	pattala
Within	—	—	—	danana	—	—	bihtar, andar
Without	—	—	—	dabándi	—	—	báhar
Here	ir	—	—	dilta	—	atra	idhar, yahán
There	—	—	—	haita	—	tatra	udhar, wahán
Where	—	—	—	cherta	—	jatra	kahán
Now	—	anu-khen	kutu-khen	os	unikhen	tatkshan, idánis	ab
Then	—	akhen	atikhenu	aga wakt	tamiwakt, adi	tadanis	tab
When	—	koi-khen	amid-khen	kum wakt, kala	kan wakt	—	jab, kab
Who	—	—	—	sok	—	—	kon
What	—	—	—	sáh, as	—	—	kya
Which	—	—	—	—	—	—	kon
This	—	—	—	dáh	—	—	yih
That	—	—	—	agha	—	—	wuh
Why	—	—	—	—	—	—	kyun
How	—	—	—	saranga	—	—	kaisa
Yes	—	—	—	ho	—	—	háh, hán
No	—	—	—	na	—	—	nah, ne
Not	—	—	—	—	zal	—	nahin
And	—	—	—	wo	ta	—	aur
If	—	—	—	ka	—	—	agar, jo
But	—	—	—	wale	lekin, ama	—	lekin
Or	—	—	—	ya	ya	—	ya

DIALECTS.					TIBETAN.		
Panjábi.	Gádi.	Kulinhi.	Handuri.	Garhwáli.	Milchang.	Tibarskad.	Tibetan.
—	karhá	—	kátha, karhá	káthu	tálk	gyongbo	gyong, mKhrang
—	kurhá	—	narm	narm	kolas	bulbo	hJam-pa,sNyi
—	bhára, girka	—	garká	garko	lihig	liko	
—	halká	—	halká	halku	langits	lanko	sLa
—	tattá	—	tattá	garm	záng, zábang	koara	dro-dron, taha
—	thandá, shera	—	thandá	thandu	lisk	khatkeo	grang
—	—	—	bhuka	bhuku	—	—	sBrabs-pa
—	—	—	tihai	piásu, tirka	—	—	skom
badá	bará	—	badá, bará	bara	tek, teg	shangni	chhen, chhé
nikká	chhotá	—	nikká, mattá	chhotú	gato, zaich	taigi, keta	bu, chhung
—	nayá	—	nowá	naya	nyung	nyungni	soma
—	práná	—	purána	puránu	úshk, rúza	nying-pa	gNah,nying-pa
shitábi	taorá	—	jaldi	jaldi	hal, hasil	gyuk-pa	—
—	mattá	—	suli	ásté	mesang	mesang	gulé
—	kachá	—	kachá	káchú	mashos	masho, kachang	—
—	pakká	—	pakka	pákku	shoyo, lungyo	sho, shobang	snimno
	márhá	—	sowa	khurkhura	—	—	rTsing-pa
—	laná	—	kasra	sáf	—	—	hJam-pa
—	golá	—	gol	gala	burbur	burbur	kyir-kyir
—	charkoni	—	charkona	chaokunta	puzrak, puzir	pizúr	gru-bZhi
—	mitha	—	mithá	mithu	thik, — im	nyamko	mNgar-pa
—	—	—	khatta	khatta	súrk	súrko	skyur-pa
—	tula	—	mota	motu	—	—	rGyags pa, sTug-sKa
—	pattala	—	pattala	pattalu	—	—	srab
—	—	—	bihtar	muda	kumo	nangdu	nangna
—	—	—	bahar	báhar	barang	phitála	phyi-rol-na
iti	iti	—	iti, ure	urhi	zua, tua	oya	hDir, hDin
—	gána	—	pure, pare	woká, púni	noa, doa	doa, oua	der, den
—	—	—	keti, kehi	kaká, kahán	ham	goa, go	gar, gan
—	abé	—	ibhu	abi	hun	lisungo	reng
—	tabé	—	tab	tab	—	—	re-zhig
—	jabé	—	kab	jah	terang	eno	nam
—	kon	—	kun	ko	hatto, hal	khaindé, go	su
—	—	—	ká, kyá	kyá	the, ham	gi	chi
—	—	—	kun	ko	—		gang
—	—	—	yih	yih	yo, za	oya, ai, yui	hDi
—	—	—	yih	wuh	no, nu	oza, aru, ádo	dé
—	—	—	kyun	kilé	chara, phu	khairo	—
—	—	—	kisitarah	kaisi, kannu	tera, te	ene, enekta	chi-tsug, chi-ltar
—	—	—	háh	háh	an, a	u, ung, o	—
—	—	—	né	né	mai, máni	máni	—
—	—	—	né, nahin	mat	—	—	—
—	—	—	aur	aur	—	—	—
—	—	—	agar	—	—	—	jiste
—	—	—	lekin	—	—	—	bonte, galté
—	—	—	ya	ya	ki	la	yang-na

ENGLISH.	DARDU DIALECTS.			AFGHAN.	KASA.	INDIAN	
	Arniya.	Shiná.	Khajunah.	Pushtu.	Kashmiri.	Sanscrit.	Hindi.
As	—	—	—	—	—	—	jaisa
So, thus	—	—	—	—	—	—	waise, taise
Also	—	—	—	ham	—	—	bhi
Always	—	—	—	mudám	—	—	hamesha
Although	—	—	—	—	yadanto, agarché	—	—
Until	—	—	—	—	—	—	jab tak, ta
Again	—	—	—	—	—	—	phir
Unless	—	—	—	—	nai	—	—
Except	—	—	—	—	magar, yátu	—	—
Therefore	—	—	—	—	—	—	—
Since	—	—	—	—	—	—	—
Much	—	—	—	—	—	—	—
I	mo	jebá	—	zo	—	aham asmad	main
Of me	anumyo	jyá	—	zamuga	—	mama	mera
To me	mota	jyá dilá	—	mála	—	mahyam	mujh ko
By me	—	—	—	málura	—	mayá	mujh se
From me	—	—	—	málura	—	mat	mujh se
We	—	—	—	munga	—	asmé vayam	ham
Of us	—	—	—	—	—	asmákam	hamárá
To us	—	—	—	—	—	asmabhyam	ham ko
By us	—	—	—	zamungna	—	asmabhis	ham se
From us	—	—	—	zamungna	—	asmat	ham se
Thou	—	—	—	Tah	—	twam yushmad	tu
Of thee	—	—	—	istah, stah	—	tava	tera
To thee	—	—	—	táh lá	—	tubhyam	tujh ko
By thee	—	—	—	talrá	—	twaya	tujh se
From thee	—	—	—	talrá	—	twat	tujh se
Ye	—	—	—	Táhsé	—	yushmé	tum
Of you	—	—	—	istahse	—	yushmákam	tumhara
To you	—	—	—	istáhlá	—	yushmabhyam	tum ko
By you	—	—	—	tásoná	—	yushmábis	tum se
From you	—	—	—	tásoná	—	yushmat	tum se
He	—	—	—	agha	—	sa	wuh
Of him	—	—	—	dagha	—	tasya	us ka
To him	—	—	—	agha ta	—	tasmai	us ko
By him	—	—	—	—	—	tena	us se
From him	—	—	—	—	—	tasmát	us se
They	—	—	—	aghi	—	te	we
Of them	—	—	—	—	—	teshám	un ka
To them	—	—	—	—	—	tebhyas	un ko
By them	—	—	—	—	—	táis	un se
From them	—	—	—	—	—	tebhyas	un se
To ask	—	—	—	—	—	yáchitun	puchhna
To buy	—	—	—	—	—	—	mol-lena
To blow	—	—	—	pukáwal	dolmut	—	phúnkna
To call	—	—	—	jagh kawal	—	—	boiána
To cook	—	—	—	pakháwal	ranun	—	pakhána
To count	—	—	—	—	gonzurun	—	ginna
To cut	—	—	—	parka-wal	garun	—	kátna

DIALECTS.					TIBETAN.		
Panjábi.	Gádi.	Kuluhi.	Handuri.	Garhwáli.	Milchang.	Tibarskad.	Tibetan.
—	—	—	—	jaisi	—	—	—
—	—	—	—	waisi	—	—	chéham
—	—	—	bhi	bhi	—	—	kyang, yang
—	—	—	hameah	hamesh	—	—	—
—	—	—	—	—	—	—	modkyang
—	—	—	tahánte	—	—	—	—
—	—	—	phir	phir	—	—	—
—	—	—	—	—	—	—	—
—	—	—	—	—	—	—	—
—	—	—	—	—	—	—	—
—	—	—	—	—	—	—	—
—	—	—	—	bohat	—	—	mang
—	—	—	Haon	main	gu, ninga ang	gi, gyo	nga
—	—	—	—	main ka	ang-o	—	ngahi, ngayi
—	—	—	—	main ko	ang olo	—	nga-la
—	—	—	—	main se	—	—	ngas, ngayis
—	—	—	—	main sé	—	—	nga-nas, nga-las
—	—	—	asse	ham	—	—	nga-chag
—	—	—	—	—	—	—	nga-chag-gi
—	—	—	—	—	—	—	nga-chag la
—	—	—	—	—	—	—	nga-chag gis
—	—	—	—	—	—	—	nga-chag nas
—	—	—	tu	tu	ki, kas	huni, gnan	khyod
—	—	—	—	—	—	—	khyod kyi
—	—	—	—	—	—	—	khyod la
—	—	—	—	—	—	—	khyod kyis
—	—	—	—	—	—	—	khyod nas
—	—	—	tun	tum	ki, kis kina	gnanishi	khyod-chag
—	—	—	—	—	—	—	khyod-chag gi
—	—	—	—	—	—	—	khyod-chag la
—	—	—	—	—	—	—	khyod-chag gis
—	—	—	—	—	—	—	khyod-chag nas
—	—	—	yih	wuh	no, nos, za	wa, pha, aro	kho
—	—	—	—	—	—	—	kho hi
—	—	—	—	—	—	—	kho la
—	—	—	—	—	—	—	kho yis, khos
—	—	—	—	—	—	—	kho nas
—	—	—	yih	wuh	no, sohugo	artishi	kho-chag
—	—	—	—	—	—	—	kho-chag gi
—	—	—	—	—	—	—	kho-chag la
—	—	—	—	—	—	—	kho-chag gis
—	—	—	—	—	—	—	kho-chag nas
—	—	—	puchhna	puchhnú	unming	thábang, shaopang	gSherpar
—	—	—	mol-lena	mol-lenú	songmig	chongbang	nyobar
—	—	—	phukna	phunknú	phuyamig	—	hBudpar
—	—	—	hák-dena	bolánú	kunig	hotpang	hBodpar
—	—	—	pakkána	pakkánú	lanig	lenmang	gYospar
—	—	—	guma, gauna	ginnu	narmig	shumang	rTsibar bGrangbar
—	—	—	katná	kátnu	malmig	rábang	gChodpar gZhogpar

ENGLISH.	DARDU DIALECTS.			AFGHAN.	KASA.	INDIAN	
	Arniya.	Shiná.	Khajunah.	Pushtu.	Kashmiri.	Sanscrit.	Hindi.
To die	—	mireono	—	mudal	—	—	marna
To do	—	—	—	—	karun	—	karna
To fall	—	—	—	purewatal	pyun	—	girna
To kill	—	—	—	—	—	—	márna
To laugh	—	—	—	khandil	—	—	hasna
To open	—	—	—	khalaswal	—	—	kholna
To raise	—	—	—	porta kawil	—	—	utarna
To read	—	—	—	lawastan	parun	—	parna
To run	—	—	—	zaghastal	dawun, dorun	—	dorna
To sell	—	—	—	—	—	—	bechna
To sew	—	—	—	gandal	súwun	—	siná
To be silent	—	—	—	—	—	—	chup rahna
To sleep	—	—	—	—	shungun	—	sona
To strike	—	—	—	—	layun	—	pitnu
To take	—	—	—	akhistan	hyún	—	lena
To take away	—	—	—	—	—	—	lejána
To tear	—	—	—	sirekawal	—	—	torna
To tell	—	—	—	—	—	—	bolna
To wake	—	—	—	—	—	—	jagna
To weep	—	—	—	jadil	wodun	—	rona
To weigh	—	—	—	tolal	—	—	tolna
To write	—	—	—	—	likhun	—	likhna
To understand	—	—	—	—	zanun	—	samjhna
To be	—	bilo	manimi	khédil	—	—	hona
Be thou	—	bé	húrút	táh sá	—	as	ho
Being	—	bé	—	khéda	—	—	hokar
Been	—	boyé	ni	sawai wu	—	—	ho-gaya
I am	—	mo Hos	já Bá	za Yam	—	asmi	main hun
Thou art	—	tu hao	um bá	tah yé	—	asi	tu hai
He is	—	ah hao	ai bá	azha dai	—	asti	wuh hai
We are	—	bé hás	hurtu báu	mungá yú	—	—	ham hain
Ye are	—	tso háth	má báu	táse yást	—	—	tum ho
They are	—	áh há	menig báu	aghi di	—	santi	we hain
I was	—	mo Asúlús	—	za Wum	—	—	main thá
Thou wast	—	tu asulu	—	tah wé	—	—	tu thá
He was	—	ah asulu	—	agha wú	—	—	wu thá
We were	—	be asilis	—	munga wú	—	—	ham the
Ye were	—	tso asilit	—	tásé wast	—	—	tum the
They were	—	zé asili	—	aghi wu	—	—	we the
I will be	—	mo Ghyem	ja tsujem	za Khéájam	—	—	main honga

DIALECTS.					TIBETAN.		
Panjábi.	Gádi.	Kuluhi.	Handuri.	Garhwáli.	Milchang.	Tibarskad.	Tibetan.
—	—	—	marna	marnu	shimig	shichbang	gShegspar
—	—	—	karna	karnu	langmig	lenmang	byedpar
—	—	—	girna, daina	girnu	gormig	keshbang	nyilbar
—	—	—	márna	márnu	sánmig	sátpang	gSod-par
—	—	—	hasna	hasnu	wannig	wotpang	dGodpar
—	—	—	kholna	kholnu	tongmig	phebang	dByébar
—	—	—	chakna	utánu	thumig	tekpang	gTeg-bar
—	—	—	parna	parnu	parasmig	silbang	kLagpar
—	—	—	dorna	daurnu	dhyamig	gálbang	brGyágpar
—	—	—	bhikhna	—	renig	rangmang	bTsong-bar
—	—	—	seona	sinu	poamig, chemig	púnmang	bTsempar
—	—	—	chup-rahna	chup rahnu	tamtoshmig	—	kha-rog-par
—	—	—	sona, suti-jana	sútnú	yangmig	guchbang	mNalbar
—	—	—	pitna, tilkana	pitnu	—	—	gZhubar brDegpar
—	—	—	lena	lenu	yamig	thábang	bLangbar
—	—	—	lejána	lejánu	tonmig	hánmang	—
—	—	—	chirna	phárnu	chermig	chirabang	dagspar
—	—	—	bolna	bolnu	ringmig	ringbang	bSnyadpar zerbar
—	—	—	jagna	utjánu	toshimig	tekpang	—
—	—	—	rona	ronu	kramig	tobang	ngubar
—	—	—	tolna	tolnu	tolamig	tolabang	dPopgar
—	—	—	likhna	likhnu	chemig	chebang	hBribar
—	—	—	samjhna	samjhnu	—	—	shespar
—	—	—	hona	honu	—	—	hDug par yin-par
—	—	—	—	—	—	—	kyod-gyur-chig
—	—	—	—	—	—	—	yin-pa
—	—	—	—	—	—	—	yod-pa
—	—	—	—	—	—	—	nga-yin
—	—	—	—	—	—	—	khyod-yin
—	—	—	—	—	—	—	kho-yin
—	—	—	—	—	—	—	nga-rNams yin
—	—	—	—	—	—	—	khyod-rNams yin
—	—	—	—	—	—	—	kho-rNams yin
—	—	—	—	—	—	—	nga-hDug-pa
—	—	—	—	—	—	—	khyod hDug-pa
—	—	—	—	—	—	—	kho hDug-pa
—	—	—	—	—	—	—	nga-chag-hDug-pa
—	—	—	—	—	—	—	khyod chag-hDug-pa
—	—	—	—	—	—	—	kho chag-hDug-pa
—	—	—	—	—	—	—	nga-hGyur-ro

ENGLISH.	DARDU DIALECTS.			AFGHAN.	KASA.	INDIAN	
	Arniya.	Shiná.	Khajunah.	Pushtu.	Kashmiri.	Sanscrit.	Hindi.
Thou wilt be	—	tu ghyé	—	tah khéája	—	—	tu honga
He will be	—	ju ghyé	—	agha khéáji	—	—	wuh honga
We will be	—	bu thi	—	munga khéájam	—	—	ham honge
Ye will be	—	tso gayah	—	tásé khéájai	—	—	tum honge
They will be	—	ah lé	—	aghi khéáji	—	—	we honga
To bring	—	areono	tsuh	rávdal, rodal	nyún	—	lána
Bring thou	—	arao	—	raraoda	—	—	lao
Bringing	—	areta	—	raoda	—	—	láta
Brought	—	aro	—	raod	—	—	laya
I bring	—	mos aram	—	za raodam	—	—	main lata
I brought	—	mos aras	—	ma raodal	—	—	main laya
I will bring	—	mos iphem	—	—	—	—	main lawenga
To give	—	deono	—	—	dawun	—	déna
Give thou	—	dé	—	—	—	—	dé
Giving	—	—	—	—	—	—	dekar
Given	—	—	—	—	—	—	degaya
I give	—	mosu das	—	—	—	—	main deta
Thou givest	—	—	—	—	—	—	tu deta
He gives	—	—	—	—	—	—	wuh deta
We give	—	—	—	—	—	—	ham deta
Ye give	—	—	—	—	—	—	tum dete
They give	—	—	—	—	—	—	we dete
I gave	—	mosu dim	—	—	—	—	main duja
Thou gavest	—	—	—	—	—	—	tu duja
He gave	—	—	—	—	—	—	wuh duja
We gave	—	—	—	—	—	—	ham diye
Ye gave	—	—	—	—	—	—	tum diye
They gave	—	—	—	—	—	—	we diye
I will give	—	mosu dásús	—	—	—	—	main dega
Thou wilt give	—	—	—	—	—	—	tu dega
He will give	—	—	—	—	—	—	wuh dega
We will give	—	—	—	—	—	—	ham denge
Ye will give	—	—	—	—	—	—	tum denge
They will give	—	—	—	—	—	—	we denge
To come	hal	ono	dohman	rátalal	—	—	ána
Come thou	—	etá	—	—	—	—	ao
Coming	—	along	—	—	—	—	ákar
Come	—	é	—	—	—	—	ágaya
I come	—	mo alús	ji dayem	—	—	—	áta
I came	—	mo em	ai dayem	—	—	—	áya
I will come	—	mo ghéphúm	ji ghadayah	—	—	—	áwega
To see	poshik	chakyono	—	lidal	déphun	—	dekhna
See thou	—	chakyé	—	—	—	—	dekh

DIALECTS.					TIBETAN.		
Panjábi.	Gádi.	Kuluhi.	Handuri.	Garhwáli.	Milchang.	Tibarskad.	Tibetan.
—	—	—	—	—	—	—	khyod hGyur-ro
—	—	—	—	—	—	—	kho hGyur-ro
—	—	—	—	—	—	—	nga-chag. hGyur-ro
—	—	—	—	—	—	—	khyod hGyur-ro
—	—	—	—	—	—	—	kho hGyur-ro
—	—	—	lána	lána	lyamig kermig	repang	hBraugbar bonpar
—	—	—	—	—	kera, ker	re—repai	—
—	—	—	—	—	kerya, kera	rega	—
—	—	—	—	—	kerkyo	reke	—
—	—	—	—	—	ketúk	reti	—
—	—	—	—	—	kerok	regi	—
—	—	—	—	—	kertok	reti	—
—	—	—	dena	—	kemig	dábang	dBog-par, gTong-bar, bSter-bar
—	—	—	de, do	—	kem	dai	—
—	—	—	—	—	kema	dága	—
—	—	—	—	—	kemkyo	dáke	—
—	—	—	—	—	ké-tuk	Dáni	—
—	—	—	—	—	ké-tún	dánula	—
—	—	—	—	—	ké-ta	dáni, nila	—
—	—	—	—	—	ké-té	dáni	—
—	—	—	—	—	ké-ten	dano, nu, nun	—
—	—	—	—	—	ké-té	dáni	—
—	—	—	—	—	Kemuk	Dági	—
—	—	—	—	—	kemun	datka	—
—	—	—	—	—	kemo	dat	—
—	—	—	—	—	keme	dacho	—
—	—	—	—	—	kemen	dacho	—
—	—	—	—	—	keme	dacho	—
—	—	—	—	—	Kemtok	—	—
—	—	—	—	—	kemton	—	—
—	—	—	—	—	kemtu	—	—
—	—	—	—	—	kemte, tosh	—	—
—	—	—	—	—	kemten, tish	—	—
—	—	—	—	—	kemte, tosh	—	—
—	—	—	ána	—	búnnig	nútpang	sByon-par pheb-par hong-bar
—	—	—	ao	—	bún	nút	—
—	—	—	ákar	—	búnya	nútga	—
—	—	—	—	—	búnkyo	nútke	—
—	—	—	—	—	bútúk	nú-ti	—
—	—	—	—	—	búnuk, búk	nutgi	—
—	—	—	—	—	búntok	núpti	—
—	—	—	—	—	khyamig, tangmig	kanmang, tangmang	mThong-bar
—	—	—	—	—	tang	kan	—

ENGLISH.	DARDU DIALECTS.			AFGHAN.	KASA.	INDIAN	
	Arniya.	Shiná.	Khajunah.	Pushtu.	Kashmiri.	Sanscrit.	Hindi.
Seeing	—	—	—	—	—	—	dekh-kar
Seen	—	—	—	—	—	—	dekh-gaya
I see	—	mos chakyam	—	—	—	—	main dekhta
Thou seest	—	tus chakye	—	—	—	—	tu dekhta
He sees	—	jus chakyé	—	—	—	—	wuh dekhta
We see	—	—	—	—	—	—	ham dekhte
Ye see	—	—	—	—	—	—	tum dekhte
They see	—	—	—	—	—	—	we dekhte
I saw	—	mos chakálús	—	—	—	—	main dekh-liya
Thou sawest	—	tus chakálú	—	—	—	—	tu dekh-liya
He saw	—	jus chakálú	—	—	—	—	wuh dekh-liya
We saw	—	bis chakalis	—	—	—	—	ham dekh-liye
Ye saw	—	tso chakálit	—	—	—	—	tum dekh-liye
They saw	—	asigh chakáli	—	—	—	—	we dek-liye
I will see	—	mos pusham	—	—	desha	—	main dekhega
Thou wilt see	—	tus push	—	—	—	—	tu dekhega
He will see	—	jus pushé	—	—	—	—	wuh dekhega
We will see	—	—	—	—	—	—	ham dekhenge
Ye will see	—	—	—	—	—	—	tum dekhenge
They will see	—	—	—	—	—	—	we dekhenge
To drink	supik	pigono	—	chaghil	chyún	—	pina
Drink thou	—	pi	—	—	—	—	piyo
Drinking	—	piye	—	—	—	—	pi-kar
Drunk	—	piyás	—	—	—	—	piya, pi-gaya
I drink	—	mos pim	—	—	—	—	main pita
I drank	—	mos piyás	—	—	—	—	main piya
I will drink	—	mos piyono kare	—	—	—	—	main piéga
To speak	aurestam	rajono	sen	waiyil	—	—	bolna
Speak thou	—	ras	—	ta wawáya	—	—	bol
Speaking	—	rasi	—	waiya	—	—	bol-kar
Spoken	—	ras	—	wai	—	—	bola, bol-gaya
I speak	—	mos rigas	—	za-waiyam	—	—	main bolta
Thou speakest	—	—	—	tah waiye	—	—	tu bolta
He speaks	—	—	—	agha wai	—	—	wuh bolta
We speak	—	—	—	munga waiyú	—	—	ham bolte
Ye speak	—	—	—	tásé waiyást	—	—	tum bolte
They speak	—	—	—	aghi wai	—	—	we bolte
I spoke	—	mos rajás	—	má waiyal	—	—	main bola
Thou spokest	—	—	—	tah waiyal	—	—	tu bola
He spoke	—	—	—	aghá waiyal	—	—	wuh bola
We spoke	—	—	—	munga waiyal	—	—	ham bole
Ye spoke	—	—	—	tásé waiyal	—	—	tum bole
They spoke	—	—	—	aghi waiyal	—	—	we bole
I will speak	—	mos rasam	—	za Bawo waiyam	—	—	main bolega
Thou wilt speak	—	tús ras	—	tah bawo waiye	—	—	tu bolega
He will speak	—	jus rase	—	agha bawo wai	—	—	wuh bolega
We will speak	—	bis rasilis	—	munga bawo waiyú	—	—	ham bolenge

DIALECTS.					TIBETAN.		
Panjábi.	**Gádi.**	**Kulluhi.**	**Handuri.**	**Garhwáli.**	**Milchang.**	**Tibarskad.**	**Tibetan.**
—	—	—	—	—	tanga	kaná	—
—	—	—	—	—	tangkyo	kangá	—
—	—	—	—	—	ta-túk	kadi	—
—	—	—	—	—	ta-tún	kadula	—
—	—	—	—	—	ta-tá	kadi, kendela	—
—	—	—	—	—	ta-té	kadi	—
—	—	—	—	—	ta-ten	ka-do, du, dun	—
—	—	—	—	—	ta-té	ke-di	—
—	—	—	—	—	Tanguk	Kangi	—
—	—	—	—	—	tangun	kanga	—
—	—	—	—	—	tango	kanga	—
—	—	—	—	—	tangé	kanzo, cho	—
—	—	—	—	—	tangen	kanzo, cho	—
—	—	—	—	—	tangé	kanzo, cho	—
—	—	—	—	—	Tangtok	Kandi	—
—	—	—	—	—	tangton	kandula	—
—	—	—	—	—	tangtu	kandi	—
—	—	—	—	—	tangte, tosh	kandi	—
—	—	—	—	—	tangten, tish	kando	—
—	—	—	—	—	tangte, tosh	kandi	—
—	—	—	—	—	túngmig	túngmang	hThung-bar
—	—	—	—	—	túng	tung	—
—	—	—	—	—	túngá	tungá	—
—	—	—	—	—	tungkyo	tungké	—
—	—	—	—	—	tu-túk	tu-ti	—
—	—	—	—	—	tungúk	túngi	—
—	—	—	—	—	tungtok	tung-ti	—
—	—	—	—	—	lonmig	lopang	gDon par
—	—	—	—	—	lon	lo	—
—	—	—	—	—	lona	loga	—
—	—	—	—	—	lonkyo	loke	—
—	—	—	—	—	latuk, londuk	loni	—
—	—	—	—	—	latun, londun	lonula	—
—	—	—	—	—	lata, londu	loni, nila	—
—	—	—	—	—	laté, londé	loni	—
—	—	—	—	—	laten, londen	lono, nun	—
—	—	—	—	—	late, londe	lono	—
—	—	—	—	—	lorok, lok	Logi	—
—	—	—	—	—	loron, lora	loga	—
—	—	—	—	—	loro, lok	loga	—
—	—	—	—	—	lore, loresh	locho	—
—	—	—	—	—	loren, loresh	locho	—
—	—	—	—	—	loré, loresh	locho	—
—	—	—	—	—	lontok	Loni	—
—	—	—	—	—	lonton	lonula	—
—	—	—	—	—	lontu	loni	—
—	—	—	—	—	lonté, tosh	loni	—

ENGLISH.	DARDU DIALECTS.			AFGHAN.	KASA.	INDIAN	
	Arniya.	Shiná.	Khajunah.	Pushtu.	Kashmiri.	Sanscrit.	Hindi.
Ye will speak	—	tso gasilis	—	tásé bawo waiyást	—	—	tum bolenge
They will speak	—	asigh rasil	—	aghi bawowai	—	—	we bolenge
To go	barai	bajono	nih	talal	—	—	jána
Go thou	—	bobo	nih	—	—	—	jao
Going	—	gyé	niman	—	—	—	já-kar
Gone	—	gyao	niman	—	—	—	gaya
I go	—	mo biyam	ji nicham	—	—	—	main játa
I went	—	mo gás	awiniyam	—	—	—	main gaya
I will go	—	mo kare biyam	je kat hurushan	—	—	—	main jawega
To sit	—	béono	—	kabenastan	bihun	—	baithna
Sit thou	—	betha	—	—	bih	—	baith
Sitting	—	bethus	—	—	—	—	baith-kar
Seated	—	behos	—	—	—	—	baitha baith-gaya
I sit	—	me bethas	—	—	—	—	main baitha
I sat	—	mu behos	—	—	—	—	main baith-gaya
I will sit	—	mo behem	—	—	biha	—	main baithega
To stand	—	—	—	—	wathun	—	khara hona
Stand thou	—	—	—	—	—	—	khara ho
Standing	—	—	—	—	—	—	khara hokar
Stood	—	—	—	—	—	—	khara hogaya
I stand	—	—	—	—	—	—	khara hota
I stood	—	—	—	—	—	—	khara hagaya
I will stand	—	—	—	—	—	—	khara hoéga
To hear	*karaparai*	—	—	—	bazun	—	sunna
Hear thou	—	—	—	—	—	—	sunao
Hearing	—	—	—	—	—	—	sun-kar
Heard	—	—	—	—	—	—	sunna, sungaya
I hear	—	—	—	—	—	—	main sunta
I heard	—	—	—	—	—	—	main suniya
I will hear	—	—	—	—	—	—	main sunega
To eat	juwak	—	—	khudal	khyun	—	khána
Eat thou	—	—	—	—	—	—	khao
Eating	—	—	—	—	—	—	khá-kar
Eaten	—	—	—	—	—	—	kháya, khá-gaya
I eat	—	—	—	—	—	—	main khata
I ate	—	—	—	—	—	—	main khaya
I will eat	—	—	—	—	—	—	main khawega
A king	—	—	—	—	—	rájah	rája
By or with a king	—	—	—	—	—	rájen	rája se
Of a king	—	—	—	—	—	rájasya	rája ka
To a king	—	—	—	—	—	rájaya	rája ko
A king	—	—	—	—	—	rajam	rája
From a king	—	—	—	—	—	ráját	rája se

DIALECTS.				TIBETAN.		
Gádi.	Kulluhi.	Handuri.	Garhwáli.	Milchang.	Tibarskad.	Tibetan.
—	—	—	—	lonten, tish	lono	—
—	—	—	—	lonté	loni	—
—	—	—	—	bimig	debang	hDahbar phyinpar
—	—	—	—	bai	de	—
—	—	—	—	baya	dega	—
—	—	—	—	baikyo	deke	—
—	—	—	—	baituk	deni	—
—	—	—	—	bairuk	degi	—
—	—	—	—	baitok	deni	—
—	—	—	—	toshmig	popang	gZhes-par
—	—	—	—	tosh	po	—
—	—	—	—	tosha	poga	—
—	—	—	—	toshkyo	poke	—
—	—	—	—	to-tuk	poni	..
—	—	—	—	toshak,toshek	pogi	—
—	—	—	—	toshetúk	poni	—
—	—	—	—	—	shotpang	hGreng-ba
—	—	—	—	—	shot	—
—	—	—	—	—	shotga	—
—	—	—	—	—	shotke	—
—	—	—	—	—	shoti	—
—	—	—	—	—	shotgi	—
—	—	—	—	—	shot-ti	—
—	—	—	—	thasmig	rúngpang	mNyanpar TShorbar
—	—	—	—	thas	rung	—
—	—	—	—	thasa	rúnga	—
—	—	—	—	thaskyo	rungke	—
—	—	—	—	tha-túk	rúni	—
—	—	—	—	thasúk	rúngi	—
—	—	—	—	thastúk	rungti	—
—	—	—	—	zámig	zábang	gZanpar za bar
—	—	—	—	zá	zá	—
—	—	—	—	zága	zága	—
—	—	—	—	zágkyo	zágke	—
—	—	—	—	zátuk	záni	—
—	—	—	—	zákúk	zagi	—
—	—	—	—	zakok	záni	—
—	—	—	—	—	—	rGyal-po
—	—	—	—	--	—	rGyal-pos
—	—	—	—	—	—	rGyal-pohi
—	—	—	—	—	—	rGyal-po-la
—	—	—	—	—	—	rGyal-po
—	—	—	—	—	—	rGyal-po-nas

ENGLISH.	DARDU DIALECTS.			AFGHAN.	KASA.	INDI
	Arniya.	Shiná.	Khajunah.	Pushtu.	Kashmiri.	Sanscrit.
Kings	—	—	—	—	—	rájáh
By, with kings	—	—	—	—	—	rajaih
Of kings	—	—	—	—	—	rájánán
To kings	—	—	—	—	—	rájébhya
In kings	—	—	—	—	—	rajan
From kings	—	—	—	—	—	rajebhya
Gold	—	—	—	—	—	—
By, with, gold	—	—	—	—	—	—
Of gold	—	—	—	—	—	—
To gold	—	—	—	—	—	—
Gold	—	—	—	—	—	—
From gold	—	—	—	—	—	—
Gold (pl.)	—	—	—	—	—	—
A hand	—	—	—	—	—	—
By, with a hand	—	—	—	—	—	—
Of a hand	—	—	—	—	—	—
To a hand	—	—	—	—	—	—
A hand	—	—	—	—	—	—
From a hand	—	—	—	—	—	—
Hands	—	—	—	—	—	—

DIALECTS.				TIBETAN.		
Gadi.	Kulluhi.	Handuri.	Garhwâli.	Milchang.	Tibarskad.	Tibetan.
—	—	—	—	—	—	rGyal-po-rNams
—	—	—	—	—	—	rGyal-po-rNams-kyis
—	—	—	—	—	—	rGyal-po-rNams-kyi
—	—	—	—	—	—	rGyal-po-rNams-la
—	—	—	—	—	—	rGyal-po-rNams
—	—	—	—	—	—	rGyal-po-rNams-nas
—	—	—	—	—	—	gSer
—	—	—	—	—	—	gSer-gyis
—	—	—	—	—	—	gSer-gyi
—	—	—	—	—	—	gSer-la
—	—	—	—	—	—	gSer
—	—	—	—	—	—	gSer-nas
—	—	—	—	—	—	gSer-rNams
—	—	—	—	—	—	lag
—	—	—	—	—	—	lag-gis
—	—	—	—	—	—	lag-gi
—	—	—	—	—	—	lag-la
—	—	—	—	—	—	lag
—	—	—	—	—	—	lag-nas
—	—	—	—	—	—	lag-rNams

XVI.

MAGNETICAL OBSERVATIONS.

1.—DECLINOMETER.

2.—DIP CIRCLE.

3.—INTENSITY.

OBSERVATIONS at LÉ in Ladák, on Monday, 4th October, 1847.

Height, 11,712 feet. N. Lat. 34° 09′ 07 ·32.″ E. Long. 77° 59′ 03″.

Mean Time, civil reckoning at station.

A.M.	Scale Reading.	Change per hour.		Remarks.
		Scale.	Arc Value	
1				At 8½ A.M. finally adjusted.
2				Zero of Collimator Magnet ... 7·800
3				„ Weak Brass „ ... 4·900
4				Declination, 2° 46′ 52·02″ East.
5				
6				
7				
8				
9	7·850	+ ·050	1′·1750	
10	7·900	+ ·050	1·1750	
11	7·825	− ·075	1·7625	
Noon	7·650	− ·175	4·1125	
1	7·600	− ·050	1·1750	
2	7·600	± ·000	0·0000	
3	7·750	+ ·150	3·5350	
4	7·800	+ ·050	1·1750	
5	7·800	± ·000	0·0000	
6	7·750	− ·050	1·1750	
7	7·700	− ·050	1·1750	
8	7·650	− ·050	1·1750	
9				
10				
11				
12				
Sums	92·875			
Means	7·739			

		Scale.	Arc Value
Extremes ...	1½ P.M.	7·600	
	10 A.M.	7·900	
Described Arc ...	=	·300	7′·0500

OBSERVATIONS at LÉ, in Ladák, on Tuesday, 5th October, 1847.

Height, 11,712 feet. N. Lat. 34° 09′ 07·32″. E. Long. 77° 59′ 03″.

Mean Time, civil reckoning at station.

A.M.	Scale Reading.	Change per hour. Scale.	Change per hour. Arc Value	Remarks.
1				Mean Scale Reading on 4th ... 7·739
2				" " 5th ... 7·752
3	7·650			Sum of Means ... 15·491
4	7·700	+ ·050	1′·1750	Mean of Means ... 7·7455
5	7·712	+ ·012	0·2937	
6	7·750	+ ·038	0·8813	
7	7·775	+ ·025	0·5875	
8	7·800	+ ·005	0·1175	
9	7·920	+ ·120	2·8200	
10	7·900	− ·020	0·4700	
11	7·800	− ·100	2·3500	
Noon	7·725	− ·075	1·7625	
1	7·650	− ·075	1·7625	
2	7·700	− ·050	1·1750	
3	7·700	± ·000	0·0000	
4	7·750	+ ·050	1·1750	
5				
6				
7				
8				
9				
10				
11				
12				
Sums	108·532			
Means	7·752			

	Scale.	Arc Value
Extremes { 3 A.M. 1 P.M.	7·650	
Extremes { 9 A.M.	7·920	
Described Arc =	·270	6′·3450

	Scale.	Change. Scale.	Change. Arc.
Reading at 4 P.M. ..	7·750		
Torsion Circle moved 90°	8·000	+ ·250	5·8750
" " 90°	8·200	+ ·200	4·7000
" " 90°	8·400	+ ·200	4·7000
" " 90°	8·600	+ ·200	4·7000
" " 90°	8·850	+ ·250	5·8750

OBSERVATIONS at MULBIL, in Ladák, on Wednesday, 20th October, 1847.

Height, 10,480 feet. N. Lat. ° ′ ″. E. Long. ° ′ ″.

Mean Time, civil reckoning at station.

A.M.	Scale Reading.	Change per hour.		Remarks.
		Scale.	Arc Value	
1				At 5 P.M. on 19th finally adjusted.
2				Zero of Collimator Magnet ... 7·800
3				„ Weak Brass „ ... 4·900
4	7·780			Declination, 2° 44′ 29·10″ East.
5	7·825	+ ·025	0′·5812	
6	7·850	+ ·025	0·5812	
7	7·900	+ ·050	1·1625	
8	8·050	+ ·100	2·3250	
9	8·050	+ ·050	1·1625	
10	8·050	± ·000	0·0000	
11	7·900	− ·150	3·4875	
Noon	7·800	− ·100	2·3250	
1	7·775	− ·025	0·5812	
2	7·750	− ·025	0·5812	
3	7·700	− ·055	1·2787	
4	7·675	− ·025	0·5812	
5				
6				
7				At 4 P.M. the wind was too high to allow of any readings being taken by movements of the torsion circle, as the magnet could not rest.
8				
9				
10				
11				
12				
Sums	125·525			
Means	7·845			

		Scale.	Arc Value
Extremes ...	4 P.M.	7·675	
	9½ A.M.	8·050	
Described Arc	=	·375	8′·7187

OBSERVATIONS at KASHMIR City, on Thursday, 4th November, 1847.

Height, 5,350 feet. N. Lat. 34° 05′ 28 ·09″. E. Long. 74° 58′ 00″.

Mean Time, civil reckoning at station.

A.M.	Scale Reading.	Change per hour.		Remarks.
		Scale.	Arc Value	
1				At 5 P.M. on 3rd finally adjusted.
2				Zero of Collimator Magnet (C. 13) 7 ·800
3				" Weak Brass " 4 ·900
4				Declination, 2° 43′ 54 ·90″ East.
5				
6	7 ·700			
7	7 ·750	+ ·050		
8	7 ·775			
9	7 ·800			
10	7 ·750			
11	7 ·725			
Noon	7 ·700			
1	7 ·750			
2	7 ·825			
3	7 ·925			
4	7 ·925			
5				
6				
7	7 ·900			
8				
9				
10				
11				
12				
Sums	93 ·525			
Means	7 ·794			

		Scale.	Arc Value
Extremes ...	6 A.M.	7 ·700	
	4 P.M.	7 ·925	
Described Arc	=	·225	5′ ·2500

OBSERVATIONS at KASHMIR City, on Friday, 5th November, 1847.

Height, 5,350 feet. N. Lat. 34° 05′ 28 ·09″. E. Long. 74° 58′ 00″.

Mean Time, civil reckoning at station.

A.M.	Scale Reading.	Change per hour.		Remarks.
		Scale.	Arc Value	
1				
2				
3				
4				
5				
6				
7	7 ·900			
8	7 ·925	+ ·025		
9	7 ·925	± ·000		
10	7 ·925	± ·000		
11	7 ·900	− ·025		
Noon	7 ·875	− ·025		
1	7 ·860	− ·015		
2	7 ·840	− ·020		
3	7 ·900	+ ·060		
4	7 ·940	+ ·040		
5	7 ·900	− ·040		
6				
7				
8				
9				
10				
11	7 ·900			
12				
Sums	94 ·790			
Means	7 ·899			

Remarks:

		Scale.	Arc Value
Extremes ...	2 P.M.	7 ·840	
	4 P.M.	7 ·940	
Described Arc	=	·100	2′ ·3333

OBSERVATIONS at KASHMIR City, on Saturday, 6th November, 1847.

Height, 5,350 feet. N. Lat. 34° 05′ 28·09″. E. Long. 74° 58′ 00″.

Mean Time, civil reckoning at station.

A.M.	Scale Reading.	Change per hour.		Remarks.
		Scale.	Arc Value	
1				
2				
3				
4				
5				
6	7·760			
7	7·780	+ ·020	0′·4666	
8	7·925	+ ·145	3·3833	
9	8·000	+ ·075	1·7500	
10				
11	7·975	− ·025	0·5833	
Noon				
1	7·850	− ·075	1·7500	
2				
3				
4	7·875	+ ·025	0·5833	
5	7·860	− ·015	0·3500	
6	7·900	+ ·040	0·9333	
7	7·880	− ·020	0·4666	
8				
9				
10				
11				
12				
Sums	78·805			
Means	7·880			

Remarks:

		Scale.	Arc Value
Extremes ...	6 A.M.	7·760	
	9 A.M.	8·000	
Described Arc	=	·240	5′·5998

OBSERVATIONS at KASHMIR City, on Sunday, 7th November, 1847.

Height, 5,350 feet. N. Lat. 34° 05′ 28 ·09″. E. Long. 74° 58′ 00″.

Mean Time, civil reckoning at station.

A.M.	Scale Reading.	Change per hour.		Remarks.
		Scale.	Arc Value	
1				Nov. 4 Mean Scale Reading 7 ·794
2				" 5 " " 7 ·899
3				" 6 " " 7 ·880
4				" 7 " " 7 ·895
5				Sum 31 ·468
6				
7	7 ·900			Mean 7 ·867
8				
9				
10				
11				
Noon				
1				
2	7 ·850			
3				
4				
5	7 ·950			
6				
7				
8				
9	7 ·880			
10				
11				
12				
Sums	31 ·580			
Means	7 ·895			

		Scale.	Arc Value
Extremes	... 2 P.M.	7 ·850	
	5 P.M.	7 ·950	
Described Arc	=	·100	2′ ·3333

OBSERVATIONS at KASHMIR City, on Saturday, 20th November, 1847.
Height, 5,350 feet. N. Lat. 34° 05′ 28·09″. E. Long. 74° 58′ 00″.
Mean Time, civil reckoning at station.

A.M.	Scale Reading.	Change per hour.		Remarks.
		Scale.	Arc Value	
1				At 11 A.M. finally adjusted. Scale.
2				Zero of Collimator Magnet (C.13) 7·800
3				„ Weak Brass „ ... 4·900
4				
5				
6				
7				
8				
9				
10				
11	7·800			
Noon	7·750	+ ·050	1′·1458	
1	7·850	− ·010	0·2291	
2				
3	7·820	− ·030	0·6873	
4				
5	7·860	+ ·040	0·9167	
6	8·000	+ ·140	3·2083	
7	7·825	− ·175	4·0103	
8	7·800	− ·025	0·5729	
9				
10				
11				
12				
Sums	62·705			
Means	7·838			

OBSERVATIONS at KASHMIR City, on Sunday, 21st November, 1847.

Height, 5,350 feet. N. Lat. 34° 05′ 28·09″. E. Long. 74° 58′ 00″.

Mean Time, civil reckoning at station.

A.M.	Scale Reading.	Change per hour.	
		Scale.	Arc Value
1			
2			
3	7·950		
4	7·900	− ·050	1′·1458
5	7·900	± ·000	0·0000
6	7·875	− ·025	0·5729
7	7·800	− ·075	1·7187
8	7·800	± ·000	0·0000
9	7·800	± ·000	0·0000
10	7·820	+ ·020	0·4583
11	7·840	+ ·020	0·4583
Noon	7·820	− ·020	0·4583
1	7·810	− 010	0·2291
2	7·860	+ ·050	1·1458
3	7·850	− ·010	0·2291
4	7·850	± ·000	0·0000
5	7·840	− ·010	0·2291
6	7·825	− ·015	0·3437
7	7·850	+ ·025	0·5729
8	7·825	− ·025	0·5729
9			
10			
11			
12			
Sums	141·215		
Means	7·845		

Remarks.

Nov. 20	Mean Scale Reading	7·838
„ 21	„ „	7·845
	Sum ...	15·683
	Mean	7·8415
Former operations—Mean		7·8670
	Difference	·0255

+ or easterly = 35·06″ of Arc

Former declination −2° 43′ 54·90″ East
+0 0 35·06
Declination =2 44 29·96 East

	Scale.	Change.	
		Scale.	Arc.
Reading at 7 A.M. 22nd	8·050		
Torsion Circle moved 90°	7·850	·200	4·5832
„ „ 90°	7·650	·200	4·5832
„ „ 90°	7·450	·200	4·5832
„ „ 90°	7·250	·200	4·5832
„ „ 90°	7·075	·175	4·0103

REMARKS upon OBSERVATIONS taken in KASHMIR during November, 1847.

1847. Month.	Day.	Described Arc.		Remarks.
Nov.	4th	5′·2500		By an examination of these arcs of daily vibration, it will be seen that the increase and decrease takes place on alternate days; and farther, that the mean smaller arc is, as nearly as possible, one-half of the larger arc, the difference being only ·06′, equal to 3·6″. This coincidence may, however, be accidental.
„	5th		2′·3333	
„	6th	5·5998		
„	7th		2·3333	
„	20th	5·7292		
„	21st		3·4374	
	Sums	16·5790	8·1040	
	Means	5·5263	2·7013	During these six days' observations, from 9 A.M. to 6 P.M., the magnet was in constant oscillation, or in *tremulous* vibration, through an arc of from ·4 to ·8, equal to from 10′ 25″ to 20′ 50″, the air being perfectly still, excepting at sunrise, when there were occasional light puffs. At night the magnet was at rest. This phenomenon was remarked only in Kashmir.

OBSERVATIONS at SHAMSÁBÁD, in Panjáb, on Wednesday, 22 Dec. 1847.

Height, 1,000 feet. N. Lat. 33° 52′ 00·88″. E. Long. 72° 30′ 00″.

Mean Time, civil reckoning at station.

A.M.	Scale Reading.	Change per hour. Scale.	Change per hour. Arc Value	Remarks.
1				At 11 A.M. on 22nd finally adjusted.
2				Zero of Collimator Magnet (C. 13) 7·800
3				„ Weak Brass „ 4·900
4				
5				
6				
7				
8				
9				
10				
11	7·800			
Noon	7·772	− ·028	0′·6440	
1	7·770	− ·002	0·0460	
2	7·761	− ·009	0·2070	Extremes … 2 P.M. 7·761; 3 P.M. 7·840
3	7·840	+ ·079	1·8170	Described Arc = Scale ·079, Arc Value 1′·8170
4	7·775	− ·065	1·4950	
5	7·825	+ ·050	1·1500	
6				
7				
8	7·830	+ ·005	0·1150	
9	7·800	− ·030	0·6900	
10				
11				
12				
Sums	70·173			
Means	7·797			

		Scale.	Arc Value
Extremes …	2 P.M.	7·761	
	3 P.M.	7·840	
Described Arc	=	·079	1′·8170

OBSERVATIONS at SHAMSÁBÁD, in Panjáb, on Thursday, Dec. 23, 1847.

Height, 1,000 feet. N. Lat. 33° 52′ 00·88″. E. Long. 72° 30′ 00″.

Mean Time, civil reckoning at station.

A.M.	Scale Reading.	Change per hour.	
		Scale.	Arc Value
1			
2			
3			
4			
5	7·910		
6	7·840	− ·070	1′·6100
7	7·775	− ·065	0·8950
8	7·780	+ ·005	0·1150
9	7·860	+ ·080	1·8400
10	7·890	+ ·030	0·690
11			
Noon			
1			
2			
3			
4			
5			
6			
7			
8			
9			
10			
11			
12			
Sums	47·055		
Means	7·842		

Remarks.

Dec. 22	Mean Scale Reading	7·797
„ 23	„ „	7·842
	Sum	15·639
	Mean of Means ...	7·8195

		Scale.	Arc Value
Extremes ...	5 A.M.	7·910	
	7 A.M.	7·775	
Described Arc	=	·135	3′·1050

	Scale.	Change.	
		Scale.	Arc.
Reading at 10 A.M. ..	7·890		
Torsion Circle moved 90°	7·690	·200	4·6000
„ „ 90°	7·480	·210	4·8300
„ „ 90°	7·370	·110	2·5300
„ „ 90°	7·175	·195	4·5885

OBSERVATIONS taken at LE, in Ladák, on Wednesday, 6th October, 1847.

Time, 3 P.M. Temperature, 60°.

Face.	Reading.	Needle A.—I.T.B. Poles. E.	Needle A.—I.T.B. Limb. W.	Needle B.—I.T.B. Poles. E.	Needle B.—I.T.B. Limb. W.
with limb	upper	45° 50′ ″	46° 20′ ″	47° 15′ ″	48° 05′ ″
	upper	46 35	45 25	46 00	46 36
	lower	46 00	46 15	47 35	47 55
	lower	46 40	45 20	46 00	46 40
from limb	upper	46 30	46 57 30	48 30	46 00
	upper	47 10	47 45 00	44 25	47 40
	lower	46 40	47 00	48 30	46 05
	lower	47 22 30	47 45	44 40	47 30
Sums		372 47 30	372 47 30	372 55 00	376 31 00
Means		46 35 56	46 35 56	46 36 52	47 03 52
Sum of Means A. ...			93 11 52	Sum of Means B. ...	93 40 44
Mean of Means A. ...			46 35 56	Mean of Means B. ...	46 50 22
A + B =			93 26 18	½ (A + B) = Dip =	46 43 09

OBSERVATIONS taken at MULBIL, in Ladák, on Wednesday, 20th October, 1847.

Time, 4½ P.M. Temperature, 49°.

Needle A.—I.T.B.				Needle B.—I.T.B.			
Face.	Reading.	Poles. E. (Limb)	Poles. W. (Limb)	Face.	Reading.	Poles. E. (Limb)	Poles. W. (Limb)
with limb	upper	46° 20′ ″	47° 20′ ″	with limb	upper	46° 25′ ″	48° 00′ ″
		47 00	47 10			47 50	46 25
	lower	46 25	47 20		lower	46 35	47 55
		47 05	47 05			48 00	46 25
from limb	upper	46 50	47 05	from limb	upper	47 10	46 45
		46 05	46 40			46 05	47 35
	lower	47 00	47 00		lower	47 10	46 45
		46 10	46 40			46 15	47 30
Sums		372 55 00	376 20 00	Sums		375 30 00	377 20 00
Means		46 36 52	47 02 30	Means		46 56 15	47 10 00
Sum of Means A. ...			93 39 22	Sum of Means B. ...			94 06 15
Mean of Means A. ...			46 49 41	Mean of Means B. ...			47 03 07
A + B =			93 52 48	½ (A + B) = Dip =			46 56 24

OBSERVATIONS taken in KASHMIR City, on Saturday, 6th November, 1847.

Time, 4 P.M. Temperature, 56°.

Needle A.—I.T.B.				Needle B.—I.T.B.			
Face.	Reading.	Poles. E.	Limb. W.	Face.	Reading.	Poles. E.	Limb. W.
with limb	upper	46° 10′ ″	46° 45′ ″	with limb	upper	46° 00′ ″	45° 05′ ″
		46 08	46 50			48 02	46 20
	lower	46 10	46 50		lower	46 12	45 00
		46 10	46 45			47 55	46 20
from limb	upper	47 10	46 30	from limb	upper	47 30	46 40
		46 22	46 35			46 42	47 50
	lower	47 08	46 35		lower	47 38	46 45
		46 30	46 32			46 45	47 15
Sums		371 48 00	373 22 00	Sums		376 44 00	371 15 00
Means		46 28 30	46 40 15	Means		47 05 30	46 24 22
Sum of Means A. ...			93 08 45	Sum of Means B. ...			93 29 52
Mean of Means A. ...			46 34 22	Mean of Means B. ...			46 44 56
A + B =			93 19 18	½ (A + B) = Dip =			46 39 39

OBSERVATIONS taken in KASHMIR City, on Sunday, 21st November, 1847.

Time, 1½ P.M. Temperature, 53°.

Needle A.—I.T.B.				Needle B.—I.T.B.			
Face.	Reading.	Poles. E. Limb.	Poles. Limb. W.	Face.	Reading.	Poles. E. Limb.	Poles. Limb. W.
with limb	upper	48° 30′ ″	46° 50′ ″	with limb	upper	45° 20′ ″	48° 40′ ″
		45 50	47 05			46 30	45 10
	lower	46 40	46 48		lower	45 30	48 35
		46 05	47 02			46 30	45 10
from limb	upper	47 20	45 40	from limb	upper	47 20	45 30
		45 55	46 20			44 45	47 05
	lower	47 25	45 45		lower	47 20	45 30
		46 05	46 15			44 55	46 55
Sums		373 50 00	371 45 00	Sums		370 10 00	372 35 00
Means		46 43 45	46 28 07	Means		46 16 15	46 34 22
Sum of Means A. ...			93 11 52	Sum of Means B. ...			92 50 37
Mean of Means A. ...			46 35 56	Mean of Means B. ...			46 25 18
A + B =			93 01 14	½ (A + B) = Dip =			46 30 37

OBSERVATIONS taken at SHAMSÁBÁD, in Chach, on Wednesday, 22nd December, 1847.

Time, 3 P.M. Temperature, 64¼°.

Needle A.—I.T.B.					Needle B.—I.T.B.				
Face.	Reading.	Poles. E. ° ′ ″	Limb.	Poles. W. ° ′ ″	Face.	Reading.	Poles. E. ° ′ ″	Limb.	Poles. W. ° ′ ″
with limb	upper	46 30		46 05	with limb	upper	42 05		45 05
		44 45		44 05			45 15		47 20
	lower	46 25		46 05		lower	42 00		45 05
		44 20		44 10			45 30		47 10
from limb	upper	46 20		47 15	from limb	upper	44 15		42 50
		46 50		46 15			46 50		46 15
	lower	46 30		47 12		lower	44 25		42 40
		46 45		46 15			47 00		46 15
Sums		368 25 00		367 22 00	Sums		357 20 00		362 40 00
Means		46 03 07		45 55 15	Means		44 40 00		45 20 00
Sum of Means A. ...				91 58 22	Sum of Means B. ...				90 00 00
Mean of Means A. ...				45 59 11	Mean of Means B. ...				45 00 00
A + B =				90 59 11	½ (A + B) = Dip =				45 29 35

GENERAL SUMMARY of OBSERVATIONS.

Date.	Time.	Temp.	Places.	N. Latitude.			Dip.		
Sept. 3	11 A.M.	65°	Lara, in Spiti	32°	09′	45″	43°	36′	52″
„ 15	10½ A.M.	63	Hánlé, in Rukchu ...	32	44	20	44	23	22
„ 20	3 P.M.	61½	Raldang, in Rukchu	33	13	50	44	52	00
Sept. 21	3 P.M.	60	Puga, in Rukchu......	33	12	30	45	03	30
„ —	6 P.M.	45	Ditto ditto		—		45	05	30
„ 22	7½ A.M.	21	Ditto ditto		—		45	21	30
„ —	10½ A.M.	49	Ditto ditto		—		45	21	15
„ —	3 P.M.	59¾	Ditto ditto		—		45	00	15
			Puga Mean ...	33	12	30	45	10	24
Oct. 6	3 P.M.	60	Lé, in Ladák	34	09	07	46	43	09
„ 20	4½ P.M.	49	Mulbil, in Ladák......	34	21	09	46	56	24
Nov. 6	4 P.M.	56	Kashmir City	34	05	28	46	39	39
„ 21	1½ P.M.	53	Ditto ditto	34	05	28	46	30	37
			Kashmir Mean	34	05	28	46	35	08
Dec. 22	3 P.M.	64¼	Shamsábád, in Chach	33	52	00	45	29	35

OBSERVATIONS of MAGNETIC INTENSITY taken at LÉ,

On Wednesday, 6th October, 1847, by Major A. Cunningham.

No. 1 Magnet.

Mean Time by Watch.	Differences.	No. of Vibrations.	Time of One Vibration	Temp. of Magnet.	Arc described.	Remarks.
H. M. S.						
1 17 1				92°	146°	
1 19 24½	143″·5	30	4″·783		106	
1 21 42	138·5	30	4·617		82	
1 23 56½	134·5	30	4·483		58	
1 26 9	133·5	30	4·450		42	
1 28 21½	132·5	30	4·417		28	
1 30 32	131·5	30	4·383		20	
	814·0	180	4·522			

OBSERVATIONS of MAGNETIC INTENSITY taken at KASHMIR,

On Wednesday, 22nd November, 1847, by Major A. Cunningham.

No. 1 Magnet.

Mean Time by Watch.	Differences.	No. of Vibrations.	Time of One Vibration	Temp. of Magnet.	Arc described.	Remarks.
H. M. S.						
2 0 17				52°	131°	
2 2 30	133″	30	4″·433		117	Compared with the observations taken at other places, the magnetic intensity is much less in the volcanic country of KASHMIR.
2 4 40	130	30	4·333		91	
2 6 47	127	30	4·233		79	
2 9 4	127	30	4·233		69	
2 11 19	125	30	4·166		59	
2 13 34	125	30	4·166		49	
	770	180	4·261			

OBSERVATIONS of MAGNETIC INTENSITY at SHAMSÁBÁD,

On Thursday, 23rd December, 1847, taken by Major A. Cunningham

No. 1 Magnet.

Mean Time by Watch.	Differences.	No. of Vibrations.	Time of One Vibration	Temp. of Magnet.	Arc described.	Remarks.
H. M. S. 2 12 25				80°	167°	
2 15 0	155"	30	5"·166		121	
2 17 20	140	30	4·666		87	
2 19 35	135	30	4·500		69	
2 21 49	134	30	4·466		57	
2 24 1	132	30	4·400		43	
2 26 13	132	30	4·400		31	
	828	180	4·600			

OBSERVATIONS of MAGNETIC INTENSITY at SIMLA,

On Saturday, 9th June, 1849, taken by Major A. Cunningham.

No. 1 Magnet.

Mean Time by Watch.	Differences.	No. of Vibrations.	Time of One Vibration	Temp. of Magnet.	Arc described.	Remarks.
H. M. S. 8 58 22				76°	149°	
9 0 45	143"	30	4"·766		117	
9 3 0	135	30	4·500		97	
9 5 15	135	30	4·500		81	
9 7 28	133	30	4·433		67½	
9 9 40	132	30	4·400		57½	
9 11 50	130	30	4·333		47½	
	808	180	4·489			

XVII.—METEOROLOGICAL OBSERVATIONS.

ACTINOMETER.

OBSERVATIONS at LÁRA, in Spiti, on Friday, 3rd September, 1847.

Height, 13,118 feet. N. Lat. 32° 09′ 45″. E. Long. 78° 03′ 35″.

Mean Time, civil reckoning at station.

	Time.		Sun or Shade.	Readings.		Change per Minute.	Radiation in parts of Scale.	Remarks.
	Initial.	Terminal.		Initial.	Termi.			
H. M. S.	H. M. S.	H. M. S.		A	B			
2 50 00	2 48 00	2 49 00	⊙	3	34	+31		
	49 00	50 00	×	34	22	−12		
	50 00	51 00	⊙	22	54	+32		
	51 00	52 00	×	54	39	−15		
	52 00	53 00	⊙	39	71	+32		

OBSERVATIONS at RANGRIG, in Spiti, on Saturday, 4th September, 1847.

Height, 12,954 feet. N. Lat. 32° 15′ 00″. E. Long. 77° 57′ 25″.

Mean Time, civil reckoning at station.

	Time. Initial.	Time. Terminal.	Sun or Shade.	Readings. Initial.	Readings. Termi.	Change per Minute.	Radiation in parts of Scale.	Remarks.
	H. M. S.	H. M. S.						
H. M. 12 58	12 55 00	12 56 00	⊙	6	47	+41		Very light wind Sky, clear
	56 30	57 30	×	50	43	− 7		
	58 00	59 00	⊙	40	85	+45		
	59 30	1 00 30	×	82	78	− 4		
	1 01 00	1 02 00	⊙	7	54	+47		
1 53	1 50 00	1 51 00	⊙	9	49·5	+40·5		Do. do.
	51 30	52 30	×	52	46	− 6		
	53 00	54 00	⊙	7	51	+44		
	54 30	55 30	×	47	42	− 5		
	56 00	57 00	⊙	3	52	+49		
2 53	2 50 00	2 51 00	⊙	14	56·5	+42·5		Wind, gusty Sky, clear
	51 30	52 30	×	57	45	−12		
	53 00	54 00	⊙	6	40	+34		
	54 30	55 30	×	36·5	22	−14·5		
	56 00	57 00	⊙	4	40	+36		
3 53	3 50 0	3 51 00	⊙	9	59	+50		Wind, steady Sky, clear
	51 30	52 30	×	65	70	+ 5		
	53 00	54 00	⊙	3	51	+48		
	54 30	55 30	×	55	58¼	+ 3¼		
	56 00	57 00	⊙	3½	49½	+46		

OBSERVATIONS at GYIHBAR, in Spiti, on Sunday, 5th September, 1847

Height, 14,513 feet. N. Lat. 32° 19′ 05″. E. Long. 77° 58′ 00″.

Mean Time, civil reckoning at station.

	Time.		Sun or Shade.	Readings.		Change per Minute.	Radiation in parts of Scale.	Remarks.
	Initial.	Terminal.		Initial.	Termi.			
	H. M. S.	H. M. S.						
	12 55 00	12 56 00	⊙	11	42	+31		Wind, lig Sky, clear
	56 30	57 30	×	40·5	32·5	− 8		
	58 00	59 00	⊙	26·5	56·5	+30		
	59 30	1 00 30	×	56	47	− 9		
	1 01 00	02 00	⊙	43	72·5	+29·5		
	1 52 00	1 53 00	⊙	25·5	57·5	+32		Do. do.
	53 30	54 30	×	59·5	53	− 6		
	55 00	56 00	⊙	49	81·5	+32·5		
	56 30	57 30	×	80·5	64·5	−16		
	58 00	59 00	⊙	5·5	38·5	+33		
	2 55 00	2 56 00	⊙	29	66	+37		Do. do.
	56 30	57 30	×	63½	49·5	−14		
	58 00	59 00	⊙	10·5	47·5	+37		
	59 30	3 00 30	×	45·5	36·5	− 9		
	3 01 00	3 02 00	⊙	31	62·5	+31·5		
	3 55 00	3 56 00	⊙	10	55·5	+45·5		Do. do.
	56 30	57 30	×	57·5	56·5	− 1		
	58 00	59 00	⊙	10	55·5	+45·5		
	59 30	4 00 30	×	57·5	54	− 3·5		
	4 01 00	4 02 00	⊙	14·5	61	+46·5		

METEOROLOGICAL OBSERVATIONS in KASHMIR.

May and June by Colonel Bates. November by Major Cunningham.

Time.	Place.	Height.	Radiation.		Moisture.			Temperature.		
			Sol.	Terr.	Dry.	Wet.	Dep.	Min.	Max.	Mean.
May 2								54	70	
6								54	64	
7	Basant Bágh ..	5,300						56	63	
8	Kashmir City ..							57	60	
9								48	61	
10								53	62	
11								50	70	
								53·14	64·3	57·4
June 3	Gulmarg	8,225						52	—	
4	,, ...	—						54	63	
5	,, ...	—						54	78	
6	Pathan........	5,300						68	—	
7	Baráhmula	—						—	82	
8	,, ...	—						64	—	
—	Mudigám......	—						—	80	
9	,, ...	—						58	—	
—	Handiwán	—						—	74	
10	,, ...	—						59	—	
—	Níchihámа	—						—	74	
12	Jagapur	—						64	79	
13	,, ...	—						64	—	
—	Lolar	—						—	72	
14	,, ...	—						63	77	
15	,, ...	—						60	—	
								60	75·44	65·9
Nov. 4	Dilawar Bágh	5,300	78·5	28	52	45·75	6·25	39	52·5	
5	in	—	83·0	33	53	46	7	36·5	53	
19	Kashmir	—	82·0	—	49	43·25	5·75	35	49	
20	City	—	82·0	38	55	47·5	7·5	35	55	
21	,,	—	84·0	—	56·5	46	10·5	36·25	56·5	
22	Márttand......	6.000	86·0	28	60·75	48·25	12·5	31	60·75	
	Means		82·6	31·75	54·37	46·12	8·2	35·46	54·46	42·69

The observations of terrestrial radiation are to be compared with the minima temperatures.

NOTE.—If we compare the climate of Kashmir with that of Kanáwar, we may obtain the mean annual temperature, approximately, in the following manner :—

Mean temperature of May	57·4	− $\frac{1}{8}$	=	50·225
Mean temperature of June	65·9	− $\frac{1}{5}$	=	52·720
Mean temperature of November	42·69	+ $\frac{1}{5}$	=	51·230
Mean annual temperature				51·392

METEOROLOGICAL OBSERVATIONS in ASTOR and RONGDO,

Taken by Colonel Bates.

Time.	ASTOR.	Height.	Radiation.		Moisture.			Temperature.		
			Sol.	Terr.	Dry.	Wet.	Dep.	Min.	Max.	Mean.
Aug. 9	Near Gures	11,437						58	68	
10	Gures	6,950						49	57	
11	„	6,950						66	72	
12	Zian	7,468						56	—	
13	„	7,468						52	55	
14	„	7,468						50	71	
15	Mapanon	8,667						41	76	
17	Suli Syu	12,068						40	60	
18	„	12,068						—	76	
19	Kurim	9,715						38	76	
20	„	9,715						55	77	
21	Pukhora	—						61	64	
23	Tink..........	9,220						56	72	
24	Near Tink	9,811						39	65	
	Means	9,154						50·8	68·4	59·6
	RONGDO.									
Aug. 26	Torche	11,386						37	74	
27	Harpo	9,879						56	88	
28	Rongdo	5,978						70	82	
29	Zingphu	8,703						68	69	
30	Bashu	6,468						64	81	
	Means	8,483						59	78·8	68·9

NOTE.—The mean annual temperature of Astor may be found by comparing the mean temp rature of August with that of Kanáwar—from which $\frac{9}{40}$ths are to be deducted, thus—

$$59\cdot6 \quad - \quad \frac{9}{40} \quad = \quad 46\cdot19^\circ \text{ mean annual temperature.}$$

The mean annual temperature of Rongdo may be found in the same manner, thus—

$$68\cdot9 \quad - \quad \frac{9}{40} \quad = \quad 53\cdot40^\circ \text{ mean annual temperature.}$$

METEOROLOGICAL OBSERVATIONS in BALTI, KHAPOLOR, and CHHORBAD, taken by Colonel Bates.

Time.	Place.	Height.	Radiation.		Moisture.			Temperature.		
			Sol.	Terr.	Dry.	Wet.	Dep.	Min.	Max.	Mean.
Sept. 1	Katsora	7,000						58	—	
—	Skardo	7,157						—	84	
2	„	7,157						—	91	
3	„	7,157						71	—	
—	Nur	7,400						—	85	
4	„	7,400						68	—	
—	Gon	7,700						—	81	
5	„	7,700						63	—	
—	Kunes	7,654						—	80	
6	Dugni	—						56	—	
—	Khapolor	8,143						—	76	
7	„	8,143						61	—	
—	„ *	8,143						55	85	
22	„ *	8,143						—	74	
7	Lanka	8,200						—	81	
8	Kubas	8,300						64	—	
—	Chhorbad	8,400						—	77	
9	Dora..	12,587						42	—	
10	Hanu	9,860						54	—	
	Means	8,124						59·2	81·4	69·9

* These two days' observations are taken from Vigne's Travels in Kashmir, Ladák, &c., Vol. II. p. 266—probably in A.D. 1838.

NOTE.—If we compare the climate of Balti with that of Kanáwar, we may obtain the mean annual temperature by deducting one-fifth from the mean temperature of September, thus—

$$69·9 \; - \; \tfrac{1}{5} \; = \; 55·92^{\circ} \text{ mean annual temperature.}$$

METEOROLOGICAL OBSERVATIONS in LAHUL and SPITI,

Taken by Major A. Cunningham.

1846.	LAHUL.	Height.	Radiation.		Moisture.			Temperature.		
			Sol.	Terr.	Dry.	Wet.	Dep.	Min.	Max.	Mean.
Aug. 24	Koksar........	10,675			74	54	20	43	74	
30	Gundla.........	10,387			79	55·5	23·5	46	79	
31	Kárdang	10,813			80	57	23	48	80	
Sept. 2	Dárcha.........	11,400			84	56	28	50	84	
4	Kitpobrang	13,397			63	50	13	40	63	
29	Patseo	12,451			66	44	22	32	66	
	Means	11,520			74·28	52·93	21·35	43·16	74·33	58·47
1847.	SPITI.									
Aug. 31	Lári	11,894	98	78	78·25	53·25	25	43	79·5	
Sept. 1	Pog	12,095	102	76	84·5	54·5	30	42	84·5	
2	Dangkhar	13,598	101	64·5	73	48	25	41·5	72·5	
3	Lára	13,118	89	65·5	71·5	45·5	26	44	72	
4	Rangrig	12,954	100·5	62·0	72	46	26	36·5	72	
5	Gyihbar	14,513	87	49·5	61·5	38·5	23	22	65·5	
6	Jukta	15,058	84	49	64·5	39·5	25	26	64·5	
7	Bongrochan...	17,435	69	38·5	55	35·75	19·25	18·5	55	
	Means	13,833	91·31	60·37	70	45	25	34·25	70·25	51·86

The observations of terrestrial radiation are to be compared with the maxima temperatures.

NOTE.—The mean annual temperature of Lahul may be found by a comparison with that of Kanáwar, which gives

47·30° for the mean annual temperature.

The mean annual temperature of Spiti has been determined by a whole year's observations, taken chiefly by my brother. It is 38·89°.

METEOROLOGICAL OBSERVATIONS in RUKCHU,

Taken by Major A. Cunningham.

1846.	Place.	Height.	Radiation.		Moisture.			Temperature.		
			Sol.	Terr.	Dry.	Wet.	Dep.	Min.	Max.	Mean.
Sept. 7	Cherpa River ..	14,268			75	44	31	18	75	
12	More Tsho ...	15,864			69	39	30	19	73	
14	Rukchin	16,058			60	39	21	20	61	
15	Tsho-kar	15,762			—	—	—	9	62·5	
16	Polokonka	16,200			66	40	26	11	66	
17	Nakpo Gonding	16,800						23	54	
19	Tshomo Riri ..	15,000						32	62	
	Means	15,707			67·5	40·5	27	18·86	64·8	40·98
1847.										
Sept. 8	Trátang	16,916	74·5		56·5	36	20·5	20·5	56·5	
9	Phálang	16,383	87		62·75	40	22·75	29	62·75	
10	Norbu	15,946	80		69	45·75	23·25	32	69	
11	Dunyar	15,617	94		64·25	43	21·25	32	67·5	
12	Dongan	16,016	93·5		70	46·5	23·5	36	70	
15	Hánlé	15,117	94		72	47	25	35·5	71·5	
17	Mángkang	15,020	93		69·75	45·75	24	42	70	
19	Rának	14,586	—					31	67	
22	Puga	15,264	78	9	61·75	39·25	22·5	13	61·75	
23	Angkhang	16,100						20	56	
24	Tsho-kar	15.762						26	53	
25	Larsa	16,349						20	50	
	Means	15,756			65·75	42·90	22·85	28·08	62·75	45·18
Mean of 1846 and 1847 ..		15,731			66·62	41·7	24·92	23·47	63·77	43·08

By comparing the climate of Rukchu with that of Spiti we obtain 28·72° for the mean annual temperature.

METEOROLOGICAL OBSERVATIONS in LADÁK Proper,

Taken by Colonel Bates and Major A. Cunningham.

Time.	Place.	Height.	Radiation.		Moisture.			Temperature.		
			Sol.	Terr.	Dry.	Wet.	Dep.	Min.	Max.	Mean.
Sept. 11	Skerpechan	9,900						64		
12	Nurla	10,065						—	80	
13	Sáspol	10,460						55		
—	Bazgo	10,573						—	74	
14	Nyimo	10,500						52		
15	Lé............	11,712						54	82	
16	„	11,712						42	82	
17	„	11,712						49	—	
18	„	11,712						46	—	
19	„	11,712						42	76	
20	„	11,712						46	64	
21	Chachot	11,345						46	—	
—	Marchalang	11,522						—	75	
22	Ukshi	11,654						48	—	
—	Gya	13,587						—	61	
23	„	13,587						31		
27	„	13,587	76		47	31·5	15·5	24	47	
29	Ukshi	11,654	82		59	40·5	19·5	30	59	
	Means	11,594						44·93	70·0	57·01
Oct. 3	Lé............	11,712	86·5	27	60·5	38·5	22	28	60·5	
4	„	11,712						24	60·5	
5	„	11,712						22		
6	„	11,712						20		
7	„	11,712						32		
8	„	11,712						23	59	
9	„	11,712	92·5		53	39·5	13·5	17	53	
13	„	10,145	85·5		66	40·5	25·5	28	66·5	
15	„	10,024	92		65·75	43·5	22·25	26	65·75	
	Means	11,350	89·1		61·21	40·5	20·71	22·2	60·87	38·95

NOTE.—By comparing the climate of Ladák with that of Spiti, both for September an October, we obtain

37·00° as the mean annual temperature.

ABSTRACT of the METEOROLOGICAL OBSERVATIONS in KASHMIR, BALTI, and LADÁK.

Months.	Districts.	Temperature.			Extremes.		Probable Mean Annual Temp.
		Min.	Max.	Mean.	Min.	Max.	
May	KASHMIR ...	53 ·14	64 ·3	57 ·4	48	70	
June... ...	Ditto ...	60	75 ·4	65 ·9	52	82	51 ·39
November ...	Ditto ...	35 ·46	54 ·46	42 ·69	31	60 ·75	
August ...	ASTOR ...	50 ·8	68 ·4	59 ·6	38	77	46 ·19
Ditto ...	RONGDO ...	59	78 ·8	68 ·9	37	88	53 ·40
September ...	BALTI ...	59 ·2	81 ·4	69 ·9	42	91	55 ·92
August, Sept.	LAHUL ...	43 ·16	74 ·33	58 ·47	32	84	47 ·30
September ...	SPITI ...	34 ·25	70 ·25	51 ·86	18 ·5	84 ·5	38 ·89
Ditto ...	RUKCHU ...	23 ·47	63 ·77	43 ·08	9	75	28 ·72
Ditto ...	LADAK ...	44 ·93	70 ·0	57 ·01	24	82	37 ·00
October ...	Ditto ...	22 ·20	60 ·87	38 ·95	17	66 ·5	

METEOROLOGICAL OBSERVATIONS at LÁRI, in Spiti,

On Tuesday, 31st August, 1847.

Height, 11,894 feet. N. Lat. 32° 04′ 00″. E. Long. 78° 22′ 40″.

Mean time, civil reckoning at station.

A.M.	Barom.	Therm.		Bulb.		Depression.	Registers.		Radiation.		Wind.		Weather.
		Att.	Det.	Dry.	Wet.		+ Max.	— Min.	Solar.	Terr.	Direction.	Press	
1													
2													
3													
4													
5								43					
6													
7													
8													
9													
10													
11													
Noon													
1				77¾	53½	24¼			98	78½	cloudy		
2	20·083	79	79½	79½	55	24½	79·5		98	78			
3	20·068	85½	78¼	78¼	53¼	25			96	79			
4													
5													
6													
7													
8													
9													
10													
11													
12													
Totals				235½	161¾	73¾	248¼	237	292	235½			
Means				78½	53¾	24½	82	79	97⅓	78½			

METEOROLOGICAL OBSERVATIONS at POG, in Spiti,
On Wednesday, 1st September, 1847.

Height, 12,095 feet. N. Lat. 32° 02′ 00″. E. Long. 78° 16′ 05″.

Mean time, civil reckoning at station.

A.M.	Barom.	Therm.		Bulb.		Depression.	Registers.		Radiation.		Wind.		Weather.
		Att.	Det.	Dry.	Wet.		+ Max.	− Min.	Solar.	Terr.	Direction.	Press	
1													
2													
3													
4													
5								42					
6													
7													
8													
9													
10													
11													
Noon													
1	19·857	80	81½	81½	55½	26			102	76			
2	19·832	86	84½	84½	54½	30	84·5		99½	81½			cloudy.
3	19·822	87	84	84	55	29			95	78½			do.
4													
5													
6													
7													
8													
9													
10													
11													
12													
Totals													
Means													

METEOROLOGICAL OBSERVATIONS at DANGKHAR,

On Thursday, 2nd September, 1847.

Height, 13,598 feet. N. Lat. 32° 04′ 40″. E. Long. 78° 09′ 00″.

Mean time, civil reckoning at station.

A.M.	Barom.	Therm.		Bulb.		Depression.	Registers.		Radiation.		Wind.		Weather.
		Att.	Det.	Dry.	Wet.		+ Max.	— Min.	Solar.	Terr.	Direction.	Press	
1													
2													
3													
4													
5								41½					
6													
7													
8													
9													
10													
11													
Noon													
1				69	46½	22½			101	64½			
2				72½	47½	25			95	67			
3				73	48	25	73		87½	66			
4													
5													
6													
7													
8													
9													
10													
11													
12													
Totals													
Means													

METEOROLOGICAL OBSERVATIONS at LÁRA, in Spiti,

On Friday, 3rd September, 1847.

Height, 13,118 feet. N. Lat. 32° 09′ 45″. E. Long. 78° 03′ 35″.

Mean time, civil reckoning at station.

A.M.	Barom.	Therm.		Bulb.		Depression.	Registers.		Radiation.		Wind.		Weather.
		Att.	Det.	Dry.	Wet.		+ Max.	− Min.	Solar.	Terr.	Direction.	Press	
1													
2													
3													
4													
5								44					
6													
7													
8													
9													
10													
11													
Noon													
1	19·392	81½	71¼	71½	45½	26			88	65½			
2	19·380	81½	72	72	47	25	72		89	67			
3	19·301	80½	71	71	48½	22½			85	66½			
4													
5													
6													
7													
8													
9													
10													
11													
12													
Totals													
Means													

METEOROLOGICAL OBSERVATIONS at RANGRIG, in Spiti,
On Saturday, 4th September, 1847.

Height, 12,954 feet. N. Lat. 32° 15′ 00″. E. Long. 77° 57′ 25″.

Mean time, civil reckoning at station.

A.M.	Barom.	Therm.		Bulb.		Depression.	Registers.		Radiation.		Wind.		Weather.
		Att.	Det.	Dry.	Wet.		+ Max.	— Min.	Solar.	Terr.	Direction.	Press	
1													
2													
3													
4													
5								36½					
6													
7													
8													
9													
10													
11													
Noon													
1	19·292	77½	72	72	46½	25½			100½	63½			
2	19·277	75	72	72	46	26	72		99½	67			
3	19·264	73½	70	70	45½	24½			92	66			
4	19·264	68½	69½	69½	46½	23			84½	62			
5													
6													
7													
8													
9													
10													
11													
12													
Totals													
Means													

METEOROLOGICAL OBSERVATIONS at GYIHBAR, in Spiti,

On Sunday, 5th September, 1847.

Height, 14,513 feet. N. Lat. 32° 19′ 05″. E. Long. 77° 56′ 35″.

Mean time, civil reckoning at station.

A.M.	Barom.	Therm.		Bulb.		Depression.	Registers.		Radiation.		Wind.		Weather.
		Att.	Det.	Dry.	Wet.		+ Max.	− Min.	Solar.	Terr.	Direction.	Press.	
1													
2													
3													
4													
5								22					
6													
7													
8													
9													
10													
11													
Noon													
1	18·190	70	64¾	64¾	43½	21¼			87	54½			
2	18·166	67	65½	65½	42¾	22¾	65½		87	57			
3	18·160	62½	61½	61½	38½	23			72	55			
4	18·158	60	59¼	59¼	38¼	21			69½	50½			
5				57½	37½	20			67	49½			
6													
7													
8													
9													
10													
11													
12													
Totals													
Means													

METEOROLOGICAL OBSERVATIONS at JUKTA, in Spiti,

On Monday, 6th September, 1847.

Height, 15,058 feet. N. Lat. 32° 22′ 00″. E. Long. 77° 58′ 00″.

Mean time, civil reckoning at station.

A.M.	Barom.	Therm.		Bulb.		Depression.	Registers.		Radiation.		Wind.		Weather.
		Att.	Det.	Dry.	Wet.		+ Max.	− Min.	Solar.	Terr.	Direction.	Press	
1													
2													
3													
4													
5								26°					
6													
7													
8													
9													
10													
11													
Noon													
1	17·674	66	64½	64½	42½	22			78	55½			
2	17·652	65	64½	64½	39½	25	64·5		84	57½			
3	17·636	55	56½	56½	36	20½			*	49			
4													
5													
6													
7													
8													
9													
10													
11													
12													
Totals													
Means													

* Sun-set behind hill.

METEOROLOGICAL OBSERVATIONS at BONGROCHAN, in Spiti, On Tuesday, 7th September, 1847.

Height, 17,435 feet. N. Lat. 32° 23′ 00″. E. Long. 77° 58′ 00″.

Mean time, civil reckoning at station.

A.M.	Barom.	Therm.		Bulb.		Depression.	Registers.		Radiation.		Wind.		Weather.
		Att.	Det.	Dry	Wet.		+ Max.	− Min.	Solar.	Terr.	Direction.	Press	
1													
2													
3													
4													
5								18½					
6													
7													
8													
9													
10													
11	16·240	50	47¾	47¾	34½	13¼			69	36½			
Noon													
1	16·238	57	52½	52½	35½	17			68½	38½			
2	16·230	56	55	55	35¾	19¼	55		67	44			
3	16·222	55	54	54	35	19			64½	46			
4													
5													
6													
7													
8													
9													
10													
11													
12													
Totals													
Means													

METEOROLOGICAL OBSERVATIONS at TRATANG, in Rukchu,

On Wednesday, 8th September, 1847.

Height, 16,916 feet. N. Lat. 32° 31′ 40″. E. Long. 78° 04′ 10″.

Mean time, civil reckoning at station.

A.M.	Barom.	Therm.		Bulb.		Depression.	Registers.		Radiation.		Wind.		Weather.
		Att.	Det.	Dry.	Wet.		+ Max.	— Min.	Solar.	Terr.	Direction.	Press	
1													
2													
3													
4													
5								20½					
6													
7													
8													
9													
10													
11													
Noon													
1													
2	16·548	60	56½	56½	36	20½	56½		74½	47½	Occasionally in strong gusts down the Párang river.		Fine and clear.
3	16·532	57	53½	53½	35½	18			69	47			
4													
5													
6													
7													
8													
9													
10													
11													
12													
Totals													
Means													

METEOROLOGICAL OBSERVATIONS at PHÁLANG, in Rukchu,

On Thursday, 9th September, 1847.

Height, 16,383 feet. N. Lat. 32° 34′ 15″. E. Long. 78° 11′ 20″.

Mean time, civil reckoning at station.

A.M.	Barom.	Therm.		Bulb.		Depression.	Registers.		Radiation.		Wind.		Weather.
		Att.	Det.	Dry.	Wet.		+ Max.	− Min.	Solar.	Terr.	Direction.	Press	
1													
2													
3													
4													
5								29					
6													
7													
8													
9													
10													
11													
Noon													
1	17·054	65	62¾	62¾	40	22¾	67½	62¾	84	56	Occasionally in strong gusts down the Párang river.		
2	17·046	70	62¾	62¾	40¼	22½	62¾	63	87	58			
3	17·028	68½	60¾	60¾	40	20¾	64¾	60½	73	53½			
4													
5													
6													
7													
8													
9													
10													
11													
12													
Totals													
Means													

METEOROLOGICAL OBSERVATIONS at NORBU, in Rukchu,

On Friday, 10th September, 1847.

Height, 15,946 feet. N Lat. 32° 39′ 50″. E. Long. 78° 19′ 00″.

Mean time, civil reckoning at station.

A.M.	Barom.	Therm.		Bulb.		Depression.	Registers.		Radiation.		Wind.		Weather.
		Att.	Det.	Dry.	Wet.		+ Max.	— Min.	Solar.	Terr.	Direction.	Press	
1													
2													
3													
4													
5								32					
6													
7													
8													
9													
10													
11													
Noon													
1	17·334	71	69	69	46	23	73	66½	80	57			
2	17·306	69½	69	69	45¾	23¼	69	67¼	81	58	Down the Párang river.		
3													
4	17·274	68½	65½	65½	43	22½	69½	64	75	55			
5													
6													
7													
8													
9													
10													
11													
12													
Totals													
Means													

METEOROLOGICAL OBSERVATIONS at DUNYAR, in Rukchu,

On Saturday, 11th September, 1847.

Height, 15,617 feet. N. Lat. 32° 39′ 20″. E. Long. 78° 24′ 30″.

Mean time, civil reckoning at station.

A.M.	Barom.	Therm.		Bulb.		Depression.	Registers.		Radiation.		Wind.		Weather.
		Att.	Det.	Dry.	Wet.		+ Max.	− Min.	Solar.	Terr.	Direction.	Press	
1													
2													
3													
4													
5								32					
6													
7													
8													
9													
10													
11													
Noon													
1	17·502	81½	67½	67½	47	20½	67½	68	94	55			
2	17·477	65	64¼	64¼	43	21¼	68	64½	96½	60			
3	17·446	66	64¼	64¼	45	19¼	68½	64½	79	60			
4													
5													
6													
7													
8													
9													
10													
11													
12													
Totals													
Means													

METEOROLOGICAL OBSERVATIONS at DONGAN, in Rukchu,

On Sunday, 12th September, 1847.

Height, 16,016 feet. N. Lat. 32° 43′ 45″. E. Long. 78° 30′ 30″.

Mean time, civil reckoning at station.

A.M.	Barom.	Therm.		Bulb.		Depression.	Registers.		Radiation.		Wind.		Weather.
		Att.	Det.	Dry.	Wet		+ Max.	− Min.	Solar.	Terr.	Direction.	Press	
1													
2													
3													
4													
5								36					Cloudy.
6													
7													
8													
9													
10													
11													
Noon													
1				70	46½	23½	70	68	93½	60	Blowing up towards the Lanak pass.		Cloudy.
2				68½	45½	23	78	70	73	63½			do.
3				69	46½	22½	74	70	84	63			do.
4													
5													
6													
7													
8													
9													
10													
11													
12													
Totals													
Means													

METEOROLOGICAL OBSERVATIONS at HÁNLÉ, in Rukchu,

On Wednesday, 15th September, 1847.

Height, 15,117 feet. N. Lat. 32° 44′ 20″. E. Long. 78° 53′ 00″.

Mean time, civil reckoning at station.

.M.	Barom.	Therm.		Bulb.		Depression.	Registers.		Radiation.		Wind.		Weather.
		Att.	Det.	Dry.	Wet.		+ Max.	— Min.	Solar.	Terr.	Direction.	Press	
1													
2													
3													
4													
5								37					
6													
7													
8													
9													
10				63	45¾	17¼	67	65½	75	52½			Cloudy.
11				63	45¾	17¼	67	62½	69½	54			Cloudy.
oon				68	46¾	21¼	73¼	70	94	62½			Cloudy.
1				72	47	25	72	73	89	68			Cloudy.
2				68½	45½	23	73	69¼	89	62½	South.		Cloudy.
3				66½	44¾	21¾	71	67	76	61	South.		Cloudy.
4				66	44½	21½	70	66	72	60	South.		
5													
6													
7													
8													
9													
10													
11													
12													
otals													
eans													

METEOROLOGICAL OBSERVATIONS at MÁNGKANG, in Rukchu,

On Friday, 17th September, 1847.

Height, 15,020 feet. N. Lat. 32° 53′ 30″. E. Long. 78° 47′ 40″.

Mean time, civil reckoning at station.

A.M.	Barom.	Therm.		Bulb.		Depression.	Registers.		Radiation.		Wind.		Weather.
		Att.	Det.	Dry.	Wet.		+ Max.	— Min.	Solar.	Terr.	Direction.	Press	
1													
2													
3													
4													
5								42					very cloudy
6													
7													
8													
9													
10													
11													
Noon													
1				70	48	22	70	70	92	64½	South.		cloudy.
2				69¾	45¾	24	68½	64½	93	59			
3				65	45¼	19¾	68	64	93½	60½			
4													
5													
6													
7													
8													
9													
10													
11													
12													
Totals													
Means													

METEOROLOGICAL OBSERVATIONS at PUGA, in Rukchu,
On Wednesday, 22nd September, 1847.

Height, 15,264 feet. N. Lat. 30° 12′ 30″. E. Long. 78° 18′ 20″.

Mean time, civil reckoning at station.

.M.	Barom.	Therm.		Bulb.		Depression.	Registers.		Radiation.		Wind.		Weather.
		Att.	Det.	Dry.	Wet.		+ Max.	— Min.	Solar.	Terr.	Direction.	Press	
1													
2													
3													
4													
5				13				13					
6				15¼			17½	15½					
7				18			20½	18		9			
8				25			27½	25	48	18	still		
9				38½			45	36	59	27½			
10				45¾	33	12¾	49½	44½	65	35			clear.
11				54	37½	16½	59	54½	68	43	faint,		
oon				56	37¾	18¼	59½	55½	70½	45			
1				58	38½	19½	62	58	74	49			
2				61¾	39¼	22½	66½	62	78	55			
3				59¾	37¾	22	63½	59	73	52½	steady.		cloudy.
4				56	35	21	60	56	66½	48			
5				50½	33	17½	55	50½	56	44			
6													
7													
8													
9													
10													
11													
12													
otals													
eans													

METEOROLOGICAL OBSERVATIONS at GIYA, in Ladák,

On Monday, 27th September, 1847.

Height, 13,587 feet. N. Lat. 33° 38′ 55″. E. Long. 77° 43′ 00″.

Mean time, civil reckoning at station.

A.M.	Barom.	Therm.		Bulb.		Depression.	Registers.		Radiation.		Wind.		Weather.
		Att.	Det.	Dry.	Wet.		+ Max.	− Min.	Solar.	Terr.	Direction.	Press	
1													
2													
3													
4													
5													
6								24					
7													
8													
9				39	29	10	43½	39	71	—			
10				40	29	11	44½	40½	75	31	blowing down the Giya rivulet.		clear.
11				40¾	28	12¾	45½	41½	75	32			
Noon				45½	34	11½	49½	45½	76	36		• .	do.
1				45¾	31	14¾	45¾	46	76	36½	gusty.		
2				45	32¾	12¼	49½	45½	76	36½			do.
3				47	31¼	15½	51	47	64½	38			cloudy.
4													
5													
6													
7													
8													
9													
10													
11													
12													
Totals													
Means													

METEOROLOGICAL OBSERVATIONS at UGSHI, in Ladák,

On Wednesday, 29th September, 1847.

Height, 11,654 feet. N. Lat. 33° 48′ 25″. E. Long. ° ′ ″.

Mean time, civil reckoning at station.

A.M.	Barom.	Therm.		Bulb.		Depression.	Registers.		Radiation.		Wind.		Weather.
		Att.	Det.	Dry.	Wet.		+ Max.	− Min.	Solar.	Terr.	Direction.	Press	
1													
2													
3													
4													
5				30									
6													
7													
8													
9													
10													
11													
Noon				56	40	16	59	54½	82	49			
1				58½	40½	18	62½	58½	79½	50½			
2				59	40½	19½	62½	58½	78	54			
3				58	40	18	62½	58	69	51			
4													
5													
6													
7													
8													
9													
10													
11													
12													
Totals													
Means													

METEOROLOGICAL OBSERVATIONS at LE, in Ladák,

On Sunday, 3rd October, 1847.

Height, 11,712 feet. N. Lat. 34° 09′ 07″ ·32. E. Long. ° ′ ″.

Mean time, civil reckoning at station.

A.M.	Barom.	Therm.		Bulb.		Depression.	Registers.		Radiation.		Wind.		Weather.
		Att.	Det.	Dry.	Wet.		+ Max.	− Min.	Solar.	Terr.	Direction.	Press	
1													
2													
3													
4													
5				28	—			28					
6				32	—								
7				37	—		41	37		31			
8				38	—		43	38	60	33			
9				46	33½	12½	51	46	70	37			
10				48½	35	13½	54	50	75	42			
11				55	36	19	60½	56½	82	48			
Noon				56½	38	18½	60½	56½	84	49			
1				58½	38	20½	63	59	84	49			
2													
3				60½	38½	22	60½	61½	86½	55			
4				57	37¼	19¾	61	57	85	51			
5				53	35	18	57	53	66	47			
6													
7													
8													
9													
10													
11													
12													
Totals													
Means													

METEOROLOGICAL OBSERVATIONS at LE, in Ladák,
On Saturday, 9th October, 1847.

Height, 11,712 feet. N. Lat. 34° 09′ 07″·32. E. Long. ° ′ ″.

Mean time, civil reckoning at station.

A.M.	Barom.	Therm.		Bulb.		Depression.	Registers.		Radiation.		Wind.		Weather.
		Att.	Det.	Dry.	Wet.		+ Max.	— Min.	Solar.	Terr.	Direction.	Press	
1													
2													
3													
4													
5				17				17					
6				22									
7				27									
8				36			40½	35½	40½	31			
9				39			43	33	48½	32			
10				41½	34½	7	46	36	60	36			
11				45½	35¼	10¼	49½	40	79½	40			
Noon				53	39½	13½	57½	48	92½	47			
1				52¼	38½	13¾	55½	45½	71	47½			
2				47½	34½	13	51½	42	51½	40½			Solar eclipse.
3				48½	34¼	14¼	53	43½	69¾	44			
4				47	34½	12½	51	41	53½	40			
5													
6													
7													
8													
9													
10													
11													
12													
Totals													
Means													

METEOROLOGICAL OBSERVATIONS at HEMIS, in Ladák,

On Wednesday, 13th October, 1847.

Height, 10,145 feet. N. Lat. 34° 16′ 14″ ·02. E. Long. ° ′ ″.

Mean time, civil reckoning at station.

A.M.	Barom.	Therm.		Bulb.		Depression.	Registers.		Radiation.		Wind.		Weather.
		Att.	Det.	Dry.	Wet.		+ Max.	− Min.	Solar.	Terr.	Direction.	Press	
1													
2													
3													
4													
5								28					
6													
7													
8													
9													
10													
11													
Noon				63¾	40½	23¼	68	59	82½	58			
1				64½	40¼	24¼	68½	59½	84	59½			
2				66	40½	25½	69½	61	85	60			
3				66½	40¼	25¼	70	61	85½	61			
4													
5													
6													
7													
8													
9													
10													
11													
12													
Totals													
Means													

METEOROLOGICAL OBSERVATIONS at KHALLACH, in Ladák,
On Friday, 15th October, 1847.

Height, 10,024 feet. N. Lat. 34° 20′ 15″·97. E. Long. ° ′ ″.

Mean time, civil reckoning at station.

A.M.	Barom.	Therm.		Bulb.		Depression.	Registers.		Radiation.		Wind.		Weather.
		Att.	Det.	Dry.	Wet.		+ Max.	— Min.	Solar.	Terr.	Direction.	Press	
1													
2													
3													
4													
5								26°					
6													
7													
8													
9													
10													
11													
Noon													
1				65	43	22			88	54			
2				65¾	43½	22¼	65¾		92	55½			
3				62¾	40½	22¼			70	58			
4													
5													
6													
7													
8													
9													
10													
11													
12													
Totals													
Means													

METEOROLOGICAL OBSERVATIONS at HESKU, in Purig,

On Sunday, 17th October, 1847.

Height, 12,270 feet. N. Lat. 34° 18′ 13″·22. E. Long. ° ′ ″.

Mean time, civil reckoning at station.

A.M.	Barom.	Therm.		Bulb.		Depression.	Registers.		Radiation.		Wind.		Weather.
		Att.	Det.	Dry.	Wet.		+ Max.	− Min.	Solar.	Terr.	Direction.	Press	
1													
2													
3													
4													
5								20					
6													
7													
8													
9													
10													
11													
Noon				57¾	40	17¾	61¾	51½	71	46			
1				58½	39½	19	62	52½	73	46½			
2				59½	39¾	19¾	59½	54	73	48			
3				58¼	39	19¼	62½	53	69	47½			
4													
5													
6													
7													
8													
9													
10													
11													
12													
Totals													
Means													

METEOROLOGICAL OBSERVATIONS at MULBIL, in Purig,
On Wednesday, 20th October, 1847.

Height, 10,480 feet. N. Lat. 34° 21′ 09″·53. E. Long. ° ′ ″.

Mean time, civil reckoning at station.

A.M.	Barom.	Therm.		Bulb.		Depression.	Registers.		Radiation.		Wind.		Weather.
		Att.	Det.	Dry.	Wet.		+ Max.	− Min.	Solar.	Terr.	Direction.	Press	
1													
2													
3													
4													
5				29				29					
6				30									
7				32									
8				36¾			41	37	47	30			
9				40½			44½	41	44	36			
10				44¼			48	44	47½	40			
11				45½	36	9½	50	46	50½	42			
Noon				47½	36	11½	52	48½	65	44			hazy.
1				49½	36½	13	53½	50	55½	46			
2				52	33¾	18¼	52	52	56½	48			
3				51¼	37½	13¾	55	52	54½	46½			
4				50	36½	13½	54	51	52	46			
5													
6													
7													
8													
9													
10													
11													
12													
Totals													
Means													

METEOROLOGICAL OBSERVATIONS at DRÁS,

On Monday, 25th October, 1847.

Height, 10,253 feet. N. Lat. 34° 23′ 49″·31. E. Long. 34° 23′ 49″·31.

Mean time, civil reckoning at station.

A.M.	Barom.	Therm.		Bulb.		Depression.	Registers.		Radiation.		Wind.		Weather.
		Att.	Det.	Dry.	Wet.		+ Max.	— Min.	Solar.	Terr.	Direction.	Press	
1													
2													
3													
4													
5								25					
6													
7													
8													
9													
10													
11													
Noon				52½	40	12½	56	54	81½	40			
1				46¾	34½	12¼	51	48	53	37			Sun completely clouded.
2				56	41¼	14¾	56	56½	83	47½			
3				56	38	18	60	57	75½	49			
4													
5													
6													
7													
8													
9													
10													
11													
12													
Totals													
Means													

METEOROLOGICAL OBSERVATIONS at KASHMIR, City,

On Thursday, 4th November, 1847.

Height, 5,350 feet. N. Lat. 34° 05′ 28″ ·69. E. Long. 74° 58′ 00″.

Mean time, civil reckoning at station.

A.M.	Barom.	Therm.		Bulb.		Depression.	Registers.		Radiation.		Wind.		Weather.
		Att.	Det.	Dry.	Wet.		+ Max.	— Min.	Solar.	Terr.	Direction.	Press	
1													
2													
3													
4													
5													
6				39				39					
7				39									
8				42	39½	2½	46	42½	59½	28			
9				43½	40½	3	48½	44	66½	31			
10				47¾	43¾	4	52	48	72	33½			
11				50	45	5	53½	50	73	40			
Noon				50½	45¼	5¼	54½	51	73½	44			
1				50¾	45½	5¼	55	51½	78½	45½			
2				52	45¾	6¼	56	52	79	47½			
3				52½	46½	6	52½	53	76	49			
4				52¼	46	6¼	55½	53	72½	48			
5													
6													
7													
8													
9													
10													
11													
12													
Totals													
Means													

METEOROLOGICAL OBSERVATIONS at KASHMIR, City,

On Friday, 5th November, 1847.

Height, 5,350 feet. N. Lat. 34° 05′ 28″·69. E. Long. 74° 58′ 00″.

Mean time, civil reckoning at station.

A.M.	Barom.	Therm.		Bulb.		Depression.	Registers.		Radiation.		Wind.		Weather.
		Att.	Det.	Dry.	Wet.		+ Max.	− Min.	Solar.	Terr.	Direction.	Press	
1													
2													
3													
4													
5				38	34	4	41	38					
6				39½	34½	3	42	39					
7				36½	34½	2	40¼	36½					
8				40	37¾	2¼	44	40					
9				45¾	42¼	3½	50	46	67	33			
10				48½	44	4½	53	49	69	36			
11				49¾	45	4¾	53½	50	70½	37			
Noon				50½	45	5½	54½	51	78	39			
1				51¾	45¼	6½	55½	52	83	48			
2				52½	45¾	6¾		53	77½	51½			
3				53	46	7	53	53	79½	51½			
4				53	46¼	6¾	57	53	69	51			
5				53	46½	6½	56½	53	53	50½			
6													
7													
8													
9													
10													
11													
12													
Totals													
Means													

METEOROLOGICAL OBSERVATIONS at MÁRTTAND, in Kashmir,

On Friday, 13th November, 1847.

Height, 6,000? feet. N. Lat. 33° 44′ 28″·76. E. Long. ° ′ ″.

Mean time, civil reckoning at station.

A.M.	Barom.	Therm.		Bulb.		Depression.	Registers.		Radiation.		Wind.		Weather.
		Att.	Det.	Dry.	Wet.		+ Max.	− Min.	Solar.	Terr.	Direction.	Press	
1													
2													
3													
4													
5				31				31					
6				31									
7				32									
8				36			40	36	40	28			
9				48½	43	5½	53	49	57	36			
10				51	44	7	56¼	52½	62½	38			
11				54	45¼	8¾	60	56½	79	41			
Noon				59½	48½	11	65	61½	84½	46½			
1				60½	48½	12	66	62	86	48			
2				60¾	48¼	12½	60¾	61	76½	50			
3				60	47¾	12¼	62½	59½	58½	49½			
4													
5													
6													
7													
8													
9													
10													
11													
12													
Totals													
Means													

METEOROLOGICAL OBSERVATIONS at KASHMIR, City,
On Friday, 19th November, 1847.

Height, 5,350 feet. N. Lat. 34° 05′ 28″ ·69. E. Long. 74° 58′ 00″.

Mean time, civil reckoning at station.

A.M.	Barom.	Therm.		Bulb.		Depression.	Registers.		Radiation.		Wind.		Weather.
		Att.	Det.	Dry.	Wet.		+ Max.	− Min.	Solar.	Terr.	Direction.	Press	
1													
2													
3													
4													
5													
6								35					
7													
8													
9													
10				45			49	45					
11				46			50	46					
Noon				48	43½	4½	52	48½	80	45			
1				49	43¼	5¾		49½	82	47			
2													
3													
4													
5													
6													
7													
8													
9													
10													
11													
12													
Totals													
Means													

METEOROLOGICAL OBSERVATIONS at KASHMIR, City,

On Saturday, 20th November, 1847.

Height, 5,350 feet. N. Lat. 34° 05′ 28″·69. E. Long. 74° 58′ 00″.

Mean time, civil reckoning at station.

A.M.	Barom.	Therm.		Bulb.		Depression.	Registers.		Radiation.		Wind.		Weather.
		Att.	Det.	Dry.	Wet.		+ Max.	− Min.	Solar.	Terr.	Direction.	Press	
1													
2													
3													
4													
5													
6													
7				37½	35½	2	42	37½					
8				40	37¾	2¼	44½	40½					
9				43¼	40¾	2½	47¼	43¾					
10				47¼	43¾	3½	51¼	47½	70½	38			
11				49	44¼	4¾	58	49¾	67	43			
Noon				50½	45½	5	54¾	51¼	75	48½			
1				51¾	46¼	5½	56	52½	82	52			
2													
3				53¼	47¾	5½	57½	54¼	78½	56			
4													
5				55	47½	7½	59	55¾	54	52			
6				53	47	6	58½	54½					
7													
8													
9													
10													
11													
12													
Totals													
Means													

METEOROLOGICAL OBSERVATIONS at KASHMIR, City, On Sunday, 21st November, 1847.

Height, 5,350 feet. N. Lat. 34° 05′ 28″·69. E. Long. 74° 58′ 00″.

Mean time, civil reckoning at station.

A.M.	Barom.	Therm.		Bulb.		Depression.	Registers.		Radiation.		Wind.		Weather.
		Att.	Det.	Dry.	Wet.		+ Max.	− Min.	Solar.	Terr.	Direction.	Press	
1													
2													
3				38¼	37½	¾					very faint air.		fleecy clouds
4				37	34¾	2¼					do.		”
5				37½	34½	3					light puffs.		”
6				36¼	34	2¼		36¼			still.		”
7				37¾	35	2¾							”
8				37¾	34¾	3							”
9				46	41½	4½							”
10				49	43¼	5¾			71	40			”
11				51	44	7			73	45			”
Noon				52¼	45	7¼			80	48			”
1				52¼	45	7¼			84	51½			”
2				53½	45¼	8¼			77½	53			”
3				54½	45½	9			82	54½			”
4				56½	46	10½	56½		75	51½			”
5				56	45½	10½				45			”
6													
7													
8													
9													
10													
11													
12													
Totals													
Means													

METEOROLOGICAL OBSERVATIONS at MOZAFARÁBÁD,

On Thursday, 9th December, 1847.

Height, 2,166 feet. N. Lat. 34° 21′ 45″·51. E. Long. ° ′ ″.

Mean time, civil reckoning at station.

A.M.	Barom.	Therm.		Bulb.		Depression.	Registers.		Radiation.		Wind.		Weather.
		Att.	Det.	Dry.	Wet.		+ Max.	— Min.	Solar.	Terr.	Direction.	Press	
1													
2													
3													
4													
5													
6													
7													
8													
9				53	45¼	7¾	57½	54					
10				54¾	46¼	8½	59	56	65	49			
11				56¾	48	8¾	61	57½	76½	53			
Noon				57¼	47¾	9½	57¼	58	64½	54½			
1													
2													
3													
4													
5													
6													
7													
8													
9													
10													
11													
12													
Totals													
Means													

METEOROLOGICAL OBSERVATIONS at SHAMSÁBÁD,

On Tuesday, 21st December, 1847.

Height, 1,000 feet. N. Lat. ° ′ ″. E. Long. ° ′ ″.

Mean time, civil reckoning at station.

A.M.	Barom.	Therm.		Bulb.		Depression.	Registers.		Radiation.		Wind.		Weather.
		Att.	Det.	Dry.	Wet.		+ Max.	— Min.	Solar.	Terr.	Direction.	Press	
1													
2													
3													
4													
5													
6													
7													
8													
9													
10				57	54	3	58	58	75	40			
11				56½	52¼	4¼	62	62	76½	47			
Noon				60½	52	7½	60½	65	72	53			
1													
2													
3													
4													
5													
6													
7													
8													
9													
10													
11													
12													
Totals													
Means													

METEOROLOGICAL OBSERVATIONS at SHAMSÁBÁD,

On Wednesday, 22nd December, 1847.

Height, 1,000 feet. N. Lat. ° ′ ″. E. Long. ° ′ ″.

Mean time, civil reckoning at station.

A.M.	Barom.	Therm.		Bulb.		Depression.	Registers.		Radiation.		Wind.		Weather.
		Att.	Det.	Dry.	Wet.		+ Max.	− Min.	Solar.	Terr.	Direction.	Press	
1													
2													
3													
4													
5													
6													
7													
8													
9													
10													
11				56¼	48¾	7½	59½	59½	79	51			
Noon				60½	48	12½	64	64	78	57			
1				62¾	49¼	13½	66½	66½	75	60			
2				63¾	49¾	14	67½	67½	74	60			
3				64¼	50	14¼	64¼	68½	70	61			
4				63½	51	12½	67½	67½	67	58			
5				57½	48½	9	62	62					
6													
7													
8													
9													
10													
11													
12													
Totals													
Means													